DETENTION AND ARREST

ESSENTIALS OF
CANADIAN LAW

DETENTION
AND
ARREST

STEVE COUGHLAN
Professor, Schulich School of Law, Dalhousie University

GLEN LUTHER
Associate Professor, College of Law, Saskatchewan

IRWIN
LAW

Published in 2010 by

Irwin Law Inc.
14 Duncan Street
Suite 206
Toronto, ON
M5H 3G8

www.irwinlaw.com

ISBN: 978-1-55221-193-9

Cataloguing in Publication data available from Library and Archives Canada

The publisher acknowledges the financial support of the Government of Canada
through the Book Publishing Industry Development Program (BPIDP) for its publishing activities.

We acknowledge the assistance of the OMDC Book Fund, an initiative of
Ontario Media Development Corporation.

Printed and bound in Canada.

1 2 3 4 5   14 13 12 11 10

SUMMARY
TABLE OF CONTENTS

DETAILED
TABLE OF CONTENTS

FOREWORD

The publication of this book is opportune for the Canadian legal system. Arrest and detention are important police powers that tell us much about the relationship between citizens and police in a democratic society. Exploring the balance between legitimate law enforcement and the freedom of citizens to be left alone has led to some controversy about when a detention or arrest is justified. Interactions between the police and citizens are increasingly under scrutiny for a number of reasons: there is uncertainty about the police force's power to assert authority in certain situations; there have been allegations of police using excessive force; and there is the constant question of whether racial profiling has factored into the decision to detain — and sometimes all of these issues surface at once.

Contributing to the legal uncertainty, the Supreme Court of Canada recognized a common law investigative detention power in *R. v. Mann* (2004), 21 C.R. (6th) 1. Unfortunately, that decision made it even less clear when a detention for *Charter* purposes had occurred. In *R. v. Grant* (2009), 66 C.R. (6th) 1, the Supreme Court of Canada has just recently refined the test for when a detention for *Charter* purposes has occurred and, for the first time, defined when such a detention is arbitrary contrary to section 9 of the *Charter*. Thus, the time is ripe for a comprehensive work on detention and arrest.

Steve Coughlan and Glen Luther have met that need with this book. Although the book does not analyze every situation in which an individual might be detained or arrested, it does address the major powers of arrest and detention, whether at common law or by statute. The authors have consciously focused on street level encounters between police and the citizenry, although they have expanded the coverage to include the arrest and compelling appearance processes. They have wisely decided not to attempt to deal with all of the myriad provincial powers of detention or arrest or with specialized contexts such as at border crossings. Even with ignoring those topics, the book is a comprehensive guide to this area of criminal procedure and criminal law. Practitioners, judges, and academic lawyers will all benefit from its exposition of this varied and complex terrain.

After an introductory chapter, the bulk of the book is presented in four chapters. Chapter Two provides a clear and lucid explanation of the various powers to detain and arrest, and some important but incidental powers and issues. A key section carefully sets out the differences between reasonable grounds to believe — the typical standard for an arrest — and reasonable grounds to suspect, the standard for *Mann* investigative detentions and the use of sniffer dogs. A very useful adjunct to this discussion lies in the appendices which summarize cases in which a reasonable belief or reasonable suspicion was or was not shown on the evidence.

Chapters Three and Four then focus more closely on detention and arrest, respectively. Detention powers tend to arise by means of the common law, although the authors are careful to point out that the drinking and driving provisions in place in the *Criminal Code* and by legislation in most provinces constitute statutory detention powers. The interplay between provincial and federal laws and constitutional requirements are fully explored by the authors. Chapter Four does more than simply deal with arrest powers (which are statutory in nature) but includes a helpful discussion of the various means, other than by an arrest, of compelling an accused person to attend court. Chapter Five then discusses the effect of the *Charter* on this area of the law. Throughout this discussion, the authors clearly explain the current legal position, and they do not refrain from offering criticism where they think it is appropriate. As a result, the book is not only a comprehensive review of the law, but it also offers critical analysis that is (or should be) food for thought for others to digest. This book will be a welcome addition to any legal collection.

Tim Quigley
Professor of Law
University of Saskatchewan

ACKNOWLEDGMENTS

This book began, a bit surprisingly, because of a trip to China. In 2006 Steve Coughlan of the Schulich School of Law at Dalhousie University was invited to organize a group of Canadian criminal law scholars to attend an international seminar on the theory of criminal law at Shandong University in Jinan, China. In the wake of that conference, the chief organizer, Professor He Bingsong, expressed an interest in learning more about the law in Canada. In the course of putting together a bibliography and collection of books, it occurred to Steve that although there were many good books covering criminal law and procedure generally, and specialist volumes in some areas such as search and seizure, bail, or sentencing, no book devoted exclusively to the topics of detention and arrest existed.

With an initial idea, Steve enlisted the help of Glen Luther of the Faculty of Law, University of Saskatchewan. Glen contributed important ideas on the structure and coverage of the book, resulting in its reframing to the form it has now. The authors each undertook half of the initial writing, but, with first drafts in hand, they consulted closely, discussing and offering suggestions on one another's work. This book is the result of their joint effort.

Like any other book, however, it is not the result solely of their efforts. Steve is grateful to the Foundation for Legal Research for their material support of this research project. He would also like to thank in particular Alex McNabb and Matt Kelly, both of whom undertook the role of research assistant with great industry and imagination, and contributed greatly to the final form of the book. Glen would like to thank Nathan Forrester for his industry and research assistance. His insight into the many issues presented helped form the book in many ways. He also thanks Zeke Ziminock and Troy Baril for their editing assistance. In addition, both authors are indebted to many of their colleagues for their suggestions, feedback, and other assistance during the course of writing. Foremost among these is Tim Quigley, Glen's colleague at the University of Saskatchewan, who not only consulted with each of us at various times but also agreed to undertake writing the Foreword to the book. Our appreciation goes as well to Don Stuart and David Tanovich. Glen would also like to thank M. Ian Savage for his timely assistance in preparing the book's section on right to counsel. In addition, we would like to express our gratitude to Jeff Miller at Irwin Law, not only for agreeing to publish the book but also for his support throughout, and to Curtis Fahey and Alisa Posesorski for their diligent work in the preparation of the book.

Finally, we wish to thank our partners, Sherry Luther and Dale Darling, not merely for their sufferance but for their moral support during the course of writing this book.

Steve Coughlan   Glen Luther

CHAPTER 1

INTRODUCTION

The central goal of a proper criminal justice system must be to maintain a balance between the individual interest of private citizens to carry on their lives free from state interference, and the communal interest in maintaining a safe society. One of the most visible ways in which those two goals come into conflict with each other is when agents of the state physically take control of private citizens: that is, when they exercise their powers to detain or to arrest.

Powers to detain and arrest arise at a number of points in the criminal justice system, and indeed outside it. Travellers arriving in the country are detained at customs. Motorists can be detained for a variety of purposes, ranging from checking the mechanical fitness of the vehicle to determining the blood-alcohol level of the driver. Someone accused of an offence might be detained pending trial or to be assessed to determine fitness to stand trial, or he might be detained afterward, whether pursuant to a sentence, following a finding of not being criminally responsible, or for having been found to be a dangerous offender. Statutory schemes authorize detention for immigration, deportation, or security-related reasons. The police might arrest a person in order to charge her with an offence, might arrest her at a later stage if a surety for the accused's bail withdraws, or might arrest her on a bench warrant if she fails to appear for trial. An absconding witness is subject to being arrested.

This book does not attempt to deal with all situations in which detention and arrest occurs. Its focus is on "street-level" encounters, detentions and arrests that occur in the course of investigating crime and

1

laying charges. Our focus is on the initial interaction between agents of the state or others authorized to detain and arrest and the private citizens whose liberty is interfered with. It is at that point that the balance between societal safety and individual liberty is most keenly in play.

This book is also not focused on the issue of remedies for non-compliance with the law. Particularly in the detention context, the questions of what powers exist and whether there has been a violation of the *Charter of Rights and Freedoms*[1] are quite closely linked: many, though by no means all, powers of detention arise out of discussions of whether the police were violating an accused's rights when they stopped him. Nonetheless, our concern is with the powers of detention and arrest themselves, including, of course, those *Charter* rights that arise in these circumstances. The more well-defined and understood these powers are, the less likely it is that there will be *Charter* violations, and the easier it will be to conduct the section 24 analysis. Whether an improperly arrested or detained accused might be able to obtain a remedy under section 24 of the *Charter*, or for that matter to bring a civil action, will sometimes be relevant but will not be a central focus.[2]

The law in this area comes from a variety of sources. Some investigative powers to detain have been created by statute: for example, the provisions in various provincial statutes to stop motor vehicles, or the companion provisions in the *Criminal Code*[3] allowing further detentions in order to obtain breath samples. Although we do not attempt to delve into all the intricacies of the law relating to breathalyzers, we do pursue the detention aspects of those powers. Powers of arrest are almost entirely statutory, and are found primarily in sections 494 and 495 of the *Code*, which will be the focus of discussion.[4] In addition, the *Criminal Code* contains a number of statutory supporting powers, dealing with issues such as the use of force.

---

1   *Canadian Charter of Rights and Freedoms*, Part 1 of the *Constitution Act, 1982*, being Schedule B to the *Canada Act 1982* (U.K.), 1982, c. 11 [*Charter*].

2   The approach to analyzing s. 24(2) claims for exclusion of evidence has been reconfigured by the Court in *R. v. Grant*, 2009 SCC 32 [*Grant*]. On this decision, see Tim Quigley, "Was It Worth the Wait? The Supreme Court's New Approaches to Detention and Exclusion of Evidence" (2009) 66 C.R. (6th) 88. For a recent discussion of the relationship between damages in tort and under s. 24(1), see *Vancouver (City) v. Ward*, 2010 SCC 27.

3   *Criminal* Code, R.S.C. 1985, c. C-46 [*Criminal Code*].

4   Even beyond "later stage" arrests such as bench warrants, there are other "initial contact" arrest powers. For example, s. 199(2) permits a peace officer who finds a common gaming house to take into custody the person keeping it or anyone found in it. Section 83.3(4) permits an arrest to prevent suspected terrorist activity. The discussion in this book will focus on the powers in ss. 494 & 495, which are in more general use.

On the other hand, the common law is also important. Some powers to detain were created entirely at common law: the ability of police to stop vehicles randomly, for example, or the relatively recent power of police to conduct investigative detentions. Indeed, to the extent that the Supreme Court has recently become much more willing to create common law powers, this is a phenomenon almost peculiar to the detention context. In addition, the common law remains relevant to arrest: the definition of what constitutes an arrest comes solely from the common law.

Of course, the *Charter* is significant as well. Section 9 of the *Charter* guarantees everyone the right to be free from arbitrary detention, and section 10 guarantees various rights to people who have been arrested or detained. Section 8, guaranteeing the freedom from unreasonable search and seizure, is also often relevant. Searches, like arrests, must generally be justified on reasonable grounds: the phrase does not necessarily have the same meaning in both contexts, but caselaw can be at least cautiously transferred from one context to another. Further, in many cases, the purpose of a detention is to carry out some investigative technique. In that event, a *Charter* claim might plausibly be made under either section 8 or section 9, and it is not uncommon for a court to decide that the issues can be adequately dealt with simply by considering the section 8 claim.[5]

Note, too, that whether a power to arrest or detain exists can be relevant in more than one way. Most obviously, the existence or non-existence of the power settles whether a peace officer or other person can compel an individual to remain in a particular location or take part in a particular activity. However, even those are potentially different questions. In the case of a breathalyzer, the power to detain is also a power to compel the person to provide a breath sample. An investigative detention, on the other hand, allows the police to stop an individual to ask questions but imposes no obligation on that individual to provide any answers. Even so, the questioning inherent in any detention might raise questions of whether the person has been searched, or whether the privilege against self-incrimination has been called into play. A power to arrest allows the police to, if necessary, compel a person physically to attend in court. Beyond that, however, whether the police officer had a power to arrest or detain can be important in determining whether an officer is acting "in the execution of duty." This matters in assessing whether an uncooperative individual will have committed the offence of resisting or obstructing. Whether the police officer or other person acted with legal authority will also be relevant in the private law context, if an individual brings an action for false arrest or false imprisonment.

---

5   See, for example, *R. v. Shepherd*, 2009 SCC 35.

The material in this book is arranged in four chapters following this one. Chapter 2 focuses on a number of the underlying and background issues relating to arrest and detention. It begins with a discussion of the sources of powers in criminal law and then looks in detail at the supporting powers that are given to people exercising authority: for example, rules around the use of force, entry to carry out an arrest, or searches that accompany arrest or detention. It also considers the extent to which caselaw has (or has not) placed an emphasis on the purpose that is in a peace officer's mind as she performs her duty, and discusses who may be considered an agent of the police for the purpose of exercising those powers. Finally, the chapter undertakes an extensive discussion of the "reasonable ground" standard which underlies the vast majority of powers to detain or arrest. This discussion gives greater emphasis to the "reasonable grounds to believe" standard but also considers the issue of "reasonable grounds to suspect."

Chapter 3 turns to a discussion of powers of detention. It looks at these powers in both the motor vehicle and other contexts, and considers both statutory and common law powers. A particular focus of discussion is the recent tendency of the Supreme Court to create new common law powers allowing the police to detain individuals.

Chapter 4 is entitled "Arrest" but in fact its focus is broader than that. There are a number of ways in which the initial contact between an individual and the state can occur, including not just arrests with and without a warrant but also the use of appearance notices and summonses. A good part of the chapter, therefore, deals in some depth with those other methods, and in particular with the interplay between police and justices of the peace, who are meant to act as a guardian of individual interests. In addition, the chapter examines the definition of arrest and considers the powers given to both private citizens and peace officers to make arrests.

Finally, Chapter 5 studies the *Charter* issues involved in questions of detention and arrest. In the section 9 context, *Charter* claims have ironically led to the creation of new state powers to detain. Further, section 9 jurisprudence has tended to be underdeveloped: it is only with *R. v. Grant* in 2009 that a real analytical framework for that section has arisen.[6] Those issues, as well as other questions around the meaning of the phrase "arbitrary detention," are pursued. In addition, we discuss section 10 of the *Charter*, and the way in which the various rights listed there — to be informed of the reason for the arrest and to be informed of the right to counsel — have changed policing practice.

---

6   *Grant*, above note 2.

CHAPTER 2

NATURE OF THE INTERACTION BETWEEN POLICE AND INDIVIDUALS

A. SOURCES OF POLICE POWERS

1) Introduction

Police powers in Canada have long involved a lack of clarity and have engendered sharp divisions among the members of the Supreme Court of Canada. In this section we will review the sources of police power, which involve a combination of statutory rules and common law practices. We shall see that the Supreme Court of Canada has played a large role in the field as it has interpreted the various statutory police powers, all the while leaving a very large role for the common law in the delineation and exposition of such powers.

Prior to enactment of the *Charter* in 1981, the existence of police powers was not something in the forefront of the Supreme Court of Canada's agenda. This was because unlawfully obtained evidence was generally admissible in criminal trials so that it was usually not necessary for a court to decide whether a particular police action was lawful or not.[1] Occasionally, an accused faced a charge of resisting arrest or obstruction of a police officer in the lawful execution of duty.[2] In such cases the Court had to determine the lawfulness of police action, and it seemed to the majority of the Court then that the question was an either/or proposition. Either the police or the resisting individual acted

---

1   *R. v. Wray*, [1971] S.C.R. 272.
2   *R. v. Biron*, [1976] 2 S.C.R. 56 [*Biron*].

unlawfully. Indeed, in 1975 in *Biron*,[3] a case to be discussed in detail elsewhere,[4] the division of the Court was precisely on this point. In dissent Chief Justice Bora Laskin, supported by Justice (as he then was) Brian Dickson and by Justice Wishart Spence, attempted to separate the question of an officer's civil liability for false arrest from that of whether the arrested individual could be said to have had the right to resist in the circumstances and thus be entitled to an acquittal on the criminal charge of resisting arrest. To Laskin C.J.C., the question of civil liability was to be determined by application of section 25 of the *Criminal Code*, which he held presented a shield, but not a sword, to the officer when the officer acted upon reasonable grounds. In Laskin C.J.C.'s view, then, an officer could be said to be not acting in the lawful execution of duty (on the facts, because the officer did not "find the accused committing"[5] the summary conviction offence there in question) even though he may have been protected from civil liability by the shield of section 25 (because the officer acted on reasonable grounds). Accordingly, to Laskin C.J.C., the question of lawful police action was multi-layered and multi-faceted.

The majority of five in *Biron*, on the other hand, saw the question more simply. To them, the crucial question was whether the police had the power to do what they did. Justice Ronald Martland, who wrote the majority judgment,[6] held that the focus needed to be on the time the police acted and not at some later time when the courts had had a chance to decide whether the officer's belief that he had found the accused committing an offence was correct or not.[7] In other words, to the majority it made no sense to bifurcate the analysis. Either the officer was acting lawfully or he was not and the majority therefore felt compelled to read in to the statute in question the word "apparently" to make clear that an officer acted lawfully if he or she found the eventual accused "apparently committing" an offence. The majority in *Biron*, then, rejected the shield/sword analysis of the Chief Justice and refused to see an officer's actions as lawful for one purpose and unlawful for another. If nothing else, this approach presented a brightline, simple question for courts when analyzing the lawfulness question. It did, though, have the effect of increasing the police power in question.

---

3   *Ibid.*

4   See Chapter 4, Section C(2)(b)(iii).

5   *Biron*, above note 2 at 67–68.

6   Martland J. wrote for four judges. De Grandprè J. concurred with Martland J. but wrote a short judgment of his own.

7   *Biron*, above note 2 at 76.

Once the *Charter* came into effect, many wondered how Martland J.'s approach would apply to section 9 of the *Charter*, which says that "[e]veryone has the right not to be arbitrarily detained or imprisoned." At least initially, the question became muddied as the courts struggled with the concept of arbitrary detention. The early decisions under the *Charter* introduced the concept of unlawful police action which was not arbitrary. Such unlawful but constitutional police action allowed the police to act unlawfully without breaching the arrested person's *Charter* rights, where the police action did not depart from lawfulness by an unacceptable degree. The leading case soon became the decision of the Ontario Court of Appeal in *Duguay*.[8] There the court recognized that, while unlawful, a police action in arresting individuals became arbitrary only if that action departed from the police's lawful powers in such a way that it could be considered capricious and thus arbitrary. The court said:

> It cannot be that every unlawful arrest necessarily falls within the words "arbitrarily detained." The grounds upon which an arrest was made may fall "just short" of constituting reasonable and probable cause. The person making the arrest may honestly, though mistakenly, believe that reasonable and probable grounds for the arrest exist and there may be some basis for that belief. In those circumstances the arrest, though subsequently found to be unlawful, could not be said to be capricious or arbitrary. On the other hand, the entire absence of reasonable and probable grounds for the arrest could support an inference that no reasonable person could have genuinely believed that such grounds existed. In such cases, the conclusion would be that the person arrested was arbitrarily detained. Between these two ends of the spectrum, shading from white to grey to black, the issue of whether an accused was arbitrarily detained will depend, basically, on two considerations: first, the particular facts of the case, and secondly, the view taken by the court with respect to the extent of the departure from the standard of reasonable and probable grounds, and the honesty of the belief and basis for the belief in the existence of reasonable and probable grounds on the part of the person making the arrest.[9]

---

8   *R. v. Duguay* (1985), 50 O.R. (2d) 375 (Ont. C.A.) [*Duguay*]. The decision was upheld on the facts in *R. v. Duguay*, [1989] 1 S.C.R. 93, where the majority of the Supreme Court, in three short paragraphs, dismissed the appeal, saying, *inter alia*: "The majority in the Court of Appeal for Ontario did not enunciate any principle or rule of law with which we disagree" (at para. 2).

9   *Duguay*, *ibid.* at para. 25. It is interesting to note that a similar debate occurred early in the decisions on s. 8 of the *Charter* where early court of appeal deci-

The idea that a police action might be unlawful but not arbitrary seemed to come down strongly on the part of the police and to remove the old line between lawfulness and unlawfulness. It should be noted that the law around section 9 of the *Charter* has taken a long time to develop, owing to the fact that in a typical case section 8 and/or section 10 of the *Charter* have also been in play and those sections have tended to receive the most attention from the courts.

Recently the Supreme Court of Canada has shown it has come to disagree with *Duguay* and has started to clarify the limits on police powers to arrest or detain individuals under section 9 of the *Charter*. In *Mann* the Court said:

> As stated earlier, the issues in this case require the Court to balance individual liberty rights and privacy interests with a societal interest in effective policing. Absent a law to the contrary, individuals are free to do as they please. By contrast, the police (and more broadly, the state) may act only to the extent that they are empowered to do so by law. The vibrancy of a democracy is apparent by how wisely it navigates through those critical junctures where state action intersects with, and threatens to impinge upon, individual liberties.[10]

The principle stated here is that the police are allowed to do what they are authorized to do by law. After *Mann* the Court has made clear that an unlawful detention is also arbitrary. In *Clayton*, for example, Justice Rosalie Abella said:

> If the police conduct in detaining and searching Clayton and Farmer amounted to a lawful exercise of their common law powers, there was no violation of their *Charter* rights. If, on the other hand, the conduct fell outside the scope of these powers, it represented an infringement of the right under the *Charter* not to be arbitrarily detained or subjected to an unreasonable search or seizure.[11]

Likewise, in the subsequent decision in *Grant*, the majority said:

---

sions suggested that a search could be unlawful but might not as a result thereof be unreasonable. See most clearly the Alberta Court of Appeal decision in *R. v. Heisler* (1984), 57 A.R. 230 (C.A.). This position was rejected by the Supreme Court of Canada in its judgment in *R. v. Collins*, [1987] 1 S.C.R. 265 [*Collins*], and has given rise to the clear principle that a search might be unconstitutional for one of three reasons: the search was unlawful, the law was unreasonable, or the manner of search was unreasonable.

10   *R. v. Mann*, 2004 SCC 52 at para. 15 [*Mann*].
11   *R. v. Clayton*, 2007 SCC 32 at para. 19.

The s. 9 guarantee against arbitrary detention is a manifestation of the general principle, enunciated in s. 7, that a person's liberty is not to be curtailed except in accordance with the principles of fundamental justice. As this Court has stated: "This guarantee expresses one of the most fundamental norms of the rule of law. The state may not detain arbitrarily, but only in accordance with the law" (*Charkaoui v. Canada (Citizenship and Immigration)*, 2007 SCC 9, [2007] 1 S.C.R. 350, at para. 88). Section 9 serves to protect individual liberty against unlawful state interference. A lawful detention is not arbitrary within the meaning of s. 9 (*Mann*, at para. 20), unless the law authorizing the detention is itself arbitrary. Conversely, a detention not authorized by law is arbitrary and violates s. 9.[12]

Nevertheless, it is clear that, following the enactment of the *Charter*, the issues have become (and will remain) much more focused and commonplace than they were before. That is because, prior to the enactment of the *Charter*, and owing to the absence of a meaningful exclusionary rule, the lawfulness of police arrests was an issue only in those cases in which the accused or the police officer was charged with an offence arising out of an altercation which gave rise to the question of whether the officer was acting in the "lawful execution of his or her duties." Only in those relatively rare situations was the issue central to the litigation. Today, even without an "altercation," the lawfulness of police action can give rise to arguments about the actions of the police. Post-*Charter*, that is, courts are regularly faced with deciding whether the police action in question might be considered lawful or not.

Further, part of the reason for this result has been the Supreme Court's determination in a number of cases that police action is, in the absence of clear notice to the individual that she need not comply, by its very nature, coercive.[13] A citizen faced with a demand or even a request according to this line of authority needs to be seen as acting under the effects of coercive state power. Therefore, an apparently "voluntary" response to a police demand or request needs to be seen as coerced and therefore not truly voluntary. Any police action, accordingly, needs to be scrutinized for lawfulness, and whether the citizen acted voluntarily or not is overborne by the coercive nature of police action.

Throughout the following discussion we will discuss how it is determined that a police action is "authorized" by law.

---

12   *R. v. Grant*, 2009 SCC 32 at para. 54 [*Grant*].
13   See *R. v. Borden*, [1994] 3 S.C.R. 145; *Dedman v. The Queen*, [1985] 2 S.C.R. 2 [*Dedman*]; *R. v. Woods*, 2005 SCC 42.

2) Statute

Clearly, the most authoritative way in which police actions to arrest or detain are created is by statute. Statutory powers tend to be of two kinds, general powers and specific powers. The *Criminal Code* sets out general powers of arrest by police and citizens that apply to most any offence while other statutes will tend to set out particular powers for particular kind offences or investigations. Further, both the provinces and the federal government specify powers of arrest.[14]

Later we will discuss particular statutory powers; here we wish to discuss how statutory powers are interpreted and applied by the courts. There is not a lot of guidance on how statutory powers to arrest or detain should be interpreted and there remain several outstanding issues on this front. Initially, the issue becomes how expansively the courts should interpret particular statutory powers. Of course, as elsewhere in the criminal law, the issue is whether such powers should be read restrictively in accord with the purported principle of "strict construction" or whether the primary issue is one of legislative purpose. Further, there are increasing signs that the courts need to interpret statutory provisions in accord with "*Charter* values," which in itself can be seen as a sort of strict construction result.

Likewise, as we will see, our statutory law is replete with powers of "regulation," especially at the provincial level. It often is said that the provinces have the power to regulate dangerous activities in the interests of public safety. What should the courts do when a state action, which is authorized for public safety purposes, is used, not primarily for the purpose of ensuring public safety, but rather for the purpose of detecting and prosecuting criminal offences? It needs to be recognized that all police action can be seen as fitting somewhere along a spectrum from ensuring compliance with regulatory rules to the investigation of serious crime. On the other hand, state action may, even in the most mundane regulatory inspection, be seen as marginally done for the purpose of protecting the public. For example, highway traffic laws require all drivers to carry with them, and to produce, a driver's licence on demand to a police officer. Clearly, driver licensing regulation is done in an overall sense to protect the public by ensuring that

---

14   For arrest procedures in the case of provincial offences, some provinces have adopted a general statute which incorporates the *Criminal Code* arrest provisions into provincial law. See, for example: *Provincial Offences Procedure Act*, R.S.A. 2000, c. P-34. s. 3. In others there is a general provincial statute which sets out arrest and other powers available in the case of a provincial offence. See, for example: *Provincial Offences Act*, R.S.O. 1990, c. P.33.

only qualified drivers are operating motor vehicles. However, where a properly authorized and qualified driver forgets her paper licence at home and is fined for not producing it, citizens will often feel that the resulting ticket is not particularly aimed at ensuring safety but at punishing the individual for forgetfulness. Nonetheless, such police actions are largely non-controversial and usually lawful. Indeed, traffic safety laws largely allow the police to stop drivers at random for the purpose of checking licences and for sobriety, and even if such actions can be seen as arbitrary, as standardless, the courts have had little difficulty upholding such actions as reasonable limits justified in a democratic society under section 1 of the *Charter*.[15]

On the other hand, where the police use traffic safety or other regulatory powers not for the predominant purpose of enforcing those laws but rather as a way to justify the stopping, detention, search, or interrogation of those they suspect of criminal offending, this practice becomes much more controversial and problematic. Generally, the courts have resisted authorizing overreaching or "misuse" of such powers created for one purpose for another purpose, particularly where the police purpose can be seen as unrelated to the purpose of the regulatory power's existence.[16] For example, while no one doubts that laws against impaired driving, even though criminal in nature, are primarily aimed at protecting highway safety, the same cannot be said of drug laws — at least when such laws are aimed at possessory and trafficking activities as opposed to driving under the influence. In circumstances where the police put up a roadblock for the purpose of catching a bank robber leaving a certain locale, it soon becomes clear that the stopping of such a getaway driver is primarily about catching the offender post-offence and not at prevention or ensuring public safety on the roads. As we will see, then, the courts have been struggling to draw a line in the sand by purposive interpretation of police statutory powers so as to attempt to keep them in check and within their "proper" spheres.[17] In such cases the focus has tended to be on whether the police have used the power for its particular purpose or whether their "predominant purpose" was actually to investigate criminal offending.

Before the enactment of the *Charter*, the common law had started to recognize a power in the courts to create police powers, which later became known as the ancillary powers doctrine. Currently, this power

---

15   See *R. v. Ladouceur*, [1990] 1 S.C.R. 1257 [*Ladouceur*]; *R. v. Hufsky*, [1988] 1 S.C.R. 621 [*Hufsky*].

16   See *Dedman*, above note 13, particularly the Court's discussion on subterfuge or pretext. See also *R. v. Mellenthin*, [1992] 3 S.C.R. 615 [*Mellenthin*].

17   See Section B(2), below in this chapter.

is better known as the *Waterfield* test,[18] of which we will have much more to say below. The Crown has often noted that the various Police Acts generally require the police to keep the peace and to investigate criminal offending.[19] The courts have struggled with when they should read in powers to a statute that are not there specifically set out. The Supreme Court has been faced with questions, for example, as to whether a wiretap order could authorize the entry into a home to place a listening device,[20] and even earlier — in the cases of *Eccles v. Bourque,*[21] *Landry*[22] and *Macooh*[23]— it had to decide whether a power to arrest included the right to enter a home for the purposes of arrest. The ancillary powers doctrine appeared at times to be simply a recognition of a power that was "necessarily implied" into a statutory power and that was seen by the Court as consistent with police general duties. And yet such a power remained controversial and engendered strong dissents from several leading jurists, including former chief justices Laskin and Dickson.[24]

The high-water mark for accused persons is likely the 1981 pre-*Charter* judgment of the Supreme Court in *Colet* where the Court was asked to decide whether a warrant to seize weapons included the power to enter a home to search for those weapons. The Court declined to so hold, stating that:

> . . . I am of the opinion that any statutory provision authorizing police officers to invade the property of others without invitation or permission would be an encroachment on the common law rights of the property owner and in case of any ambiguity would be subject to a strict construction in favour of the common law rights of the owner. This is made plain from the following excerpt from *Maxwell on Interpretation of Statutes*, 12th ed., at p. 251 where it is said:
>
>> Statutes which encroach on the rights of the subject, whether as regards person or property, are subject to a strict construction in the same way as penal Acts. It is a recognised rule that they should be interpreted, if possible, so as to respect such

---

18   Arising from *R. v. Waterfield*, [1963] 3 All E.R. 659 (C.C.A.) [*Waterfield*].
19   See, for example, the *Royal Canadian Mounted Police Act*, R.S.C. 1985, c. R-10, s. 18; *Police Services Act*, R.S.O. 1990, c. P.15, s. 42.
20   See *Lyons v. R.*, [1984] 2 S.C.R. 633 [*Lyons*]; *Reference re: Judicature Act (Alberta), s. 27(1)*, [1984] 2 S.C.R. 697.
21   *Eccles v. Bourque*, [1975] 2 S.C.R. 739 [*Eccles*].
22   *R. v. Landry*, [1986] 1 S.C.R. 145 [*Landry*].
23   *R. v. Macooh*, [1993] 2 S.C.R. 802 [*Macooh*].
24   See *Dedman*, above note 13; *Lyons*, above note 20.

rights, and if there is any ambiguity the construction which is in favour of the freedom of the individual should be adopted.

It appears to me to follow that any provision authorizing police officers to search and enter private property must be phrased in express terms and the provisions of the *Interpretation Act* are not to be considered as clothing police officers by implication with authority to search when s. 105(1) and the warrant issued pursuant thereto are limited to seizure.[25]

Today the Supreme Court seems to continue to view *Colet* as authoritative since it has often cited the decision.[26] As noted above, however, the Court has not been consistent in its approach. In *Lyons,* for example, the majority contented itself with citing *Colet* for the purpose of noting that, where Parliament has regulated search and seizure, it has been express in doing so.[27] As the question before the Court in *Lyons* was whether Part VI of the *Criminal Code* allowed entry to put in place a listening device, and since such an entry was not a search, *Colet* had no application. According to the majority, then, the legislation impliedly authorized the entry to place the device. Indeed, as one reviews *Colet's* treatment by the Court, it seems clear that the intent is to limit it to circumstances involving trespass on real property and that it may now not be correct to describe the case as involving any general statutory interpretation advice involving police powers. For example, in *Grant* in 1993, the majority cited *Colet* only for the proposition that there was a "strong common law rule against warrantless intrusions onto private property."[28] While significant, such treatment seems to downplay the principle of strict construction there espoused. In some ways, when one thinks of the Supreme Court's treatment of statutory interpretation, one needs to ask what has the Court done, as opposed to what it says it should do. It is unfortunately clear that the Court has been very willing to let the common law fill gaps in legislation and to interpret legislation expansively so as to authorize police actions.

---

25   *R. v. Colet*, [1981] 1 S.C.R. 2 at 10.

26   See, for example, *R. v. Asante-Mensah*, 2003 SCC 38 at para. 41 [*Asante-Mensah*], where Binnie J. says: "I accept, of course, that statutes which encroach on the liberty of the subject should be construed, where ambiguous, in favour of upholding such liberty: *Colet v. The Queen*, [1981] 1 S.C.R. 2, at p. 10." However, Binnie J. then proceeds to find that the word "arrest" is clear and unambiguous, leaving no room for the doctrine of strict construction to operate (*ibid.*). See also *R. v. Kokesch*, [1990] 3 S.C.R. 3 [*Kokesch*].

27   *Lyons*, above note 20 at 692–93.

28   *R. v. Grant*, [1993] 3 S.C.R. 223 at 239.

The more relevant question now might be to look to the *Charter* for guidance. For our present purposes, it is useful to see what the Supreme Court of Canada has said about the interpretation of section 9 of the *Charter*. Most recently, in 2009's *Grant*, the majority of the Court said:

> [15] As for any constitutional provision, the starting point must be the language of the section. Where questions of interpretation arise, a generous, purposive and contextual approach should be applied.
>
> [16] Constitutional guarantees such as ss. 9 and 10 should be interpreted in a "generous rather than . . . legalistic [way], aimed at fulfilling the purpose of the guarantee and securing for individuals the full benefit of the *Charter*'s protection" (*R. v. Big M Drug Mart Ltd.*, [1985] 1 S.C.R. 295, at p. 344). Unduly narrow, technical approaches to *Charter* interpretation must be avoided, given their potential to "subvert the goal of ensuring that right holders enjoy the full benefit and protection of the *Charter*" (*Doucet-Boudreau v. Nova Scotia (Minister of Education)*, 2003 SCC 62, [2003] 3 S.C.R. 3, at para. 23).
>
> [17] While the twin principles of purposive and generous interpretation are related and sometimes conflated, they are not the same. The purpose of a right must always be the dominant concern in its interpretation; generosity of interpretation is subordinate to and constrained by that purpose (P.W. Hogg, *Constitutional Law of Canada* (5th ed. Supp.), vol. 2, at pp. 36-30 and 36-31). While a narrow approach risks impoverishing a *Charter* right, an overly generous approach risks expanding its protection beyond its intended purposes. In brief, we must construe the language of ss. 9 and 10 in a generous way that furthers, without overshooting, its purpose: *Big M Drug Mart*, at p. 344.[29]

It therefore behooves a court to attempt to identify the purpose of a right and then to attempt to interpret statutory language in such a way that the purpose of the *Charter* right is respected. It is evident, of course, that the purpose of the *Charter* right and the purpose of the statute granting a particular power to the police may be in conflict.[30] In such circumstances, one assumes that the legislation will be struck down if it cannot be interpreted in such a way so as to respect the *Charter* right in question.

---

29   *Grant*, above note 12 at paras. 15–17.
30   An early post-*Charter* example would be search pursuant to writs of assistance which were struck down in *R. v. Noble* (1984), 48 O.R. (2d) 643 (C.A.).

A large challenge for a book such as this, then, is to identify the purpose of the right in question, and the latest Supreme Court cases bring us closer to being able to do so. In *Grant* the majority analyzed the purpose of section 9 in conjunction with the correlative rights under section 7 and section 10 of the *Charter.* The latter section delineates the right to be informed of the reasons for the arrest or detention and the right to retain and instruct counsel — rights that, like those in section 9, arise at the point of arrest or detention. Thus, the majority, in noting that these rights are interconnected, suggests that section 9 is intended to protect individuals from "unjustified" detentions.[31] Further, the Court has held that section 8's protection against unreasonable search and seizure encompasses personal privacy[32] and amounts to the right, in the absence of express powers to invade privacy, to "be let alone."[33] This obviously has some relevance in the context of section 9 as well. Unfortunately, the reasoning remains circular in that it seems to suggest that, in order to respect the right to privacy, all the state needs do is to specify a power while doing little in the way of protecting Canadians' freedom (other than being explicit about it). We will see, though, that the concept of "justified" police powers has played a large role in the creation of police powers in Canada. Whether the concept is up to the task remains to be seen.

3) Common Law

As discussed above, through the ancillary powers doctrine, the Supreme Court has decided when a court should read in to a statute a power not there expressly provided and when to create a police power at common law. After the *Charter,* this issue came to the fore as attention was directed to the lack of specificity in police powers to arrest and detain and, for that matter, to search and seize. As noted, the ancillary powers doctrine soon became known as the *Waterfield* test, because the Court relied upon the English decision in R. v. *Waterfield*[34] as providing useful guidance to a court regarding when a police officer could be said to be acting lawfully. Interestingly, the first citing of *Waterfield* by the Supreme Court appears to be *Stenning,* where in 1970 Martland J. said:

---

31   *Grant*, above note 12 at para. 20.
32   See *Canada (Combines Investigation Act Director of Investigation & Research) v. Southam Inc*, [1984] 2 S.C.R. 145 [*Hunter*].
33   See *R. v. Stillman*, [1997] 1 S.C.R. 607 [*Stillman*]; See also Sopinka J's discussion in *Kokesch*, above note 26.
34   *Waterfield*, above note 18.

Assuming that Wilkinson did, technically, trespass on the premises, the fact remains that he was there to investigate an occurrence which had happened earlier in the evening, which involved the firing of a rifle. He had been sent out for that purpose. He was charged, under s. 47 of *The Police Act*, R.S.O. 1960, c. 298, with the duty of preserving the peace, preventing robberies and other crimes, and apprehending offenders. He was in the course of making an investigation, in the carrying out of that duty, when he was assaulted by the respondent.

We were referred to a number of English authorities and some Canadian cases, all of which turned upon facts which differed from the facts found in this case. Their effect is stated in the judgment of the Court of Criminal Appeal in *R. v. Waterfield* [[1964] 1 Q.B. 164 at 170, [1963] 3 All E.R. 659, 48 Cr. App. R. 42.]:

> In the judgment of this court it would be difficult, and in the present case it is unnecessary, to reduce within specific limits the general terms in which the duties of police constables have been expressed. In most cases it is probably more convenient to consider what the police constable was actually doing and in particular whether such conduct was prima facie an unlawful interference with a person's liberty or property. If so, it is then relevant to consider whether (*a*) such conduct falls within the general scope of any duty imposed by statute or recognised at common law and (*b*) whether such conduct, albeit within the general scope of such a duty, involved an unjustifiable use of powers associated with the duty.

On the facts of this case, as found by the trial judge, whether Wilkinson was, technically, a trespasser, or not, he was engaged in the execution of his duties at the time when he was assaulted by the respondent, and at that time there had been no unlawful interference with either the liberty or the property of the respondent.[35]

As one can see, the English court expressly held that it is better to look at specific facts rather than to try to identify the police power being employed.[36] This point was soon forgotten, as the Supreme Court

---

35   *R. v. Stenning*, [1970] S.C.R. 631 at 636-37 [*Stenning*].

36   *Waterfield* was also relied upon by the Supreme Court in *R. v. Knowlton*, [1974] S.C.R. 443, where the Court held that the police were acting lawfully and were justified in controlling access to a public place when the Russian premier was visiting the city of Edmonton. Likewise, in *Poupart v. Lafortune*, [1974] S.C.R. 175 [*Poupart*], a case involving a civil suit against a police officer by an innocent bystander who was shot by the police officer, the Court noted that the officer was

of Canada began to use the *Waterfield* formulation to declare general police powers.

Post-*Charter*, the Court started in *Dedman* to employ *Waterfield* as "a test for whether the officer had common law authority for what he did,"[37] Justice Gerald LeDain, writing for the majority (and over the strong dissent of Dickson C.J.C.), stated that in his opinion the test required a court to determine which police powers are "reasonably necessary" in the execution of police duties.[38] While many authors have criticized the Court for a willingness to create police powers at common law, it is clear that the Court has done so on several occasions.[39] In almost all occasions where the Court has taken this step, it has rued the fact that the issue had not been dealt with by statute. Yet, in the face of a perceived failure of such parliamentary action, the Court has, for the most part, seen it as its obligation to clarify what police power exists and what police powers the courts are prepared to create and recognize. In *Dedman*, for example, the Court created the power to conduct checkstops to combat impaired driving. There, Dickson C.J.C. complained that this was not the Court's job but rather was a job that should be left to Parliament and quoted himself in dissent in the *Wiretap Reference* as saying: "Any such principle would be nothing short of a fiat for illegality on the part of the police whenever the benefit of police action appeared to outweigh the infringement of an individual's rights."[40]

. . . engaged in the hazardous performance of a grave duty imposed on him by law. In carrying out such a duty a peace officer must undoubtedly refrain from making any unjustifiable use of the powers relating to it. This principle was recognized in *Regina v. Waterfield and Another* [L.R. [1964] 1 K.B. 164.], at p. 170 et seq., and recently recalled in this Court in the as yet unpublished decision of *Knowlton v. The Queen*. However . . . the actions of Lafortune cannot, in a case like that before the Court, be evaluated as they would be if it were a case in which the precautions to be taken in accordance with the duty not to injure others were not conditioned by the requirements of a public duty. In short, the police officer incurs no liability for damage caused to another when without negligence he does precisely what the legislature requires him to do . . . ."

(*ibid.* at 183-84).

37   *Dedman*, above note 13 at para. 67.
38   *Ibid.* at para. 69.
39   See Glen Luther, "Police Power and the *Charter of Rights and Freedoms*: Creation or Control?" (1986–87) 51 Sask. L. Rev. 217; James Stribopoulos, "The Forgotten Right: Section 9 of the *Charter*, Its Purpose and Meaning" (2008) 40 Sup. Ct. L. Rev. (2d) 211; Stephen Coughlan, *Criminal Procedure* (Toronto: Irwin Law, 2008) at 11–23, 59–125, 126–46 [Coughlan, *Criminal Procedure*].
40   *Dedman*, above note 13 at para. 24.

The Supreme Court's actions seem a bit blinkered in that it is clear that the area of arrest is largely statutory and one wonders why the Court has never suggested that the failure to legislate should be seen as an intentional omission on the part of the legislators. Further, where the Court has found gaps but has not created powers at common law, especially in the area of search, Parliament has often responded by enacting statutory powers.[41] As well, given the now broad power given to courts to grant so-called general warrants, there is expressly a power in an issuing court to authorize the police in a given situation to "do any thing" specified in the warrant.[42] To suggest, therefore, that there is no legislative action in areas of search and seizure and in arrest and detention seems somewhat unreal.

There is no question that there is a substantial body of legislation in force that authorizes arrests and detentions. Yet the Supreme Court of Canada has continued to create powers almost at will. Recently it appears that some members of the Court have recognized that more caution is required in this regard. For example, in *Kang-Brown*, Justice Louis LeBel, who spoke for four of the justices, had this to say about the creation at common law of a police power to search with a sniffer-dog on less than reasonable grounds and without a warrant:

> The common law has long been viewed as a law of liberty. Should we move away from that tradition, which is still part of the ethos of our legal system and of our democracy? This case is about the freedom of individuals and the proper function of the courts as guardians of the Constitution. I doubt that it should lead us to depart from the common law tradition of freedom by changing the common law itself to restrict the freedoms protected by the Constitution under s. 8 of the *Charter*.[43]

Alas, the majority seemed prepared to create such a power. They were led by Justice Ian Binnie, who rejected the position taken by Justice LeBel, saying the Court had "crossed the Rubicon," by which he apparently meant that the Court should now feel its responsibility to further declare and refine police powers when it thinks it appropriate to do

---

41   See Michal Fairburn, "Twenty-five Years in Search of a Reasonable Approach" (2008) 40 Sup. Ct. L. Rev. (2d) 56. In that article, Fairburn traces how ss. 184.2, 487.01, 492.2, 492.1, 487.05, and 487.092 were all enacted in response to court decisions in which police were found not to have had the power to do what they had done.

42   See Steve Coughlan, "General Warrants at the Crossroads: Limit or Licence?" (2003) 10 C.R. (6th) 269.

43   *R. v. Kang-Brown*, [2008] 1 S.C.R. 456 at para. 12 [*Kang-Brown*].

so.[44] Interestingly, Binnie J. based his position largely on a belief that the litigants were entitled to know that a court was prepared to make law when necessary. This is quite ironic as a justification. The argument seemingly rests on the notion that there ought to be more certainty in the law, and that it should be knowable in advance. By their very nature, however, new common law powers are known to exist only after the fact, and it is the possibility of their creation that renders the law uncertain.

4) *Charter*

As noted above, since the enactment of the *Charter*, police powers have expanded greatly. At least this is true in terms of the actual declaration of such powers by courts and by Parliament. This is indeed ironic in that, in its first major *Charter* decision, the Supreme Court declared the *Charter* to represent a check on state power and not a source thereof:

> I begin with the obvious. The *Canadian Charter of Rights and Freedoms* is a purposive document. Its purpose is to guarantee and to protect, within the limits of reason, the enjoyment of the rights and freedoms it enshrines. It is intended to constrain governmental action inconsistent with those rights and freedoms; it is not in itself an authorization for governmental action. In the present case this means, as Prowse J.A. pointed out, that in guaranteeing the right to be secure from unreasonable searches and seizures, s. 8 acts as a limitation on whatever powers of search and seizure the federal or provincial governments already and otherwise possess. It does not in itself confer any powers, even of "reasonable" search and seizure, on these governments. This leads, in my view, to the further conclusion that an assessment of the constitutionality of a search and seizure, or of a statute authorizing a search or seizure, must focus on its "reasonable" or "unreasonable" impact or the subject of the search or the seizure, and not simply on its rationality in furthering some valid government objective.[45]

Instead, the Supreme Court's own approach to *Charter* interpretation has resulted in a seemingly increased willingness to employ the *Waterfield* test to create or declare new powers almost willy-nilly. In cases

---

44   *Ibid.* at para. 22.
45   *Hunter*, above note 32 at 156–57.

such as *Godoy*,[46] *Mann*, *Clayton*, and *Kang-Brown*, the Supreme Court itself has done so.

It does appear that some of the justices may have changed their position on these matters. For example, in *Clayton*, Justice Louise Charron concurred with Justice Abella, who was decidedly for approving the police action at issue, while in *Kang-Brown* Charron J. concurs with LeBel J., who strongly argues for more caution. Conversely, Binnie J. in *Clayton* insisted that common-law-created powers should be subject to a full *Charter* analysis including that required by section 1 of the *Charter*, and yet in *Kang-Brown* he was decidedly in favour of employing the *Waterfield* test to authorize the dog-sniffer power in appropriate circumstances. Indeed, it remains a bit of a mystery as to how a court should decide whether to apply the *Waterfield* test to a given situation. As we have attempted to show, initially the test was designed only to assess a particular action by a particular officer. Now that the same formulation has been employed regularly to create general police powers, it appears that we have lost sight of what the Court was attempting to do in devising the *Waterfield* test. The current attitude seems to conflate the two branches of *Waterfield* into a single question that asks, "Do the police need this power to carry out their general duties?" If so, the answer seems to be that "they shall have it." This is the point made by LeBel J. in his dissent in *Orbanski*, a decision discussed in detail below, when he said:

> The adoption of a rule limiting *Charter* rights on the basis of what amounts to a utilitarian argument in favour of meeting the needs of police investigations through the development of common law police powers would tend to give a potentially uncontrollable scope to the doctrine developed in the *Waterfield-Dedman* line of cases, which - and we sometimes forget such details - the court that created it took care not to apply on the facts before it (*R. v. Waterfield* ...). The doctrine would now be encapsulated in the principle that what the police need, the police get, by judicial fiat if all else fails or if the legislature finds the adoption of legislation to be unnecessary or unwarranted. The courts would limit *Charter* rights to the full extent necessary to achieve the purpose of meeting the needs of the police. The creation of and justification for the limit would arise out of an initiative of the courts. In the context of cases such as those we are considering here, this kind of judicial intervention would pre-empt any serious *Charter*

---

46   *R. v. Godoy*, [1999] 1 S.C.R. 311 [*Godoy*].

review of the limits, as the limits would arise out of initiatives of the courts themselves.[47]

It seems that such a formulation is not a "test" at all, but simply a method by which police powers will forever be extended and declared with little attention being paid to the inherent value of statutory construction and parliamentary responsibility and equally for the fundamental freedoms at stake. It is the latter that the *Charter* was surely designed to espouse, and yet the Court's continued willingness to expand police powers seems the most distinctive feature of this *Charter* era.

5) "Default" Powers

Given that the police in Canada enjoy immense respect and, of course, possess considerable power, they have what might be called practical or default powers over any given situation. The law is intended to guide the police in their everyday actions. But, where the law is unclear or unstated, the police in practice control most situations in which they interact with the public. In fact, the police typically have control to decide what should occur. At common law, as discussed above, litigation often centred on whether an officer was acting in the execution of duty. In each case the police acted as they decided at the time to act. The nature of our law, at least when undeveloped, is that generally only in an *ex post facto* sense do the courts control what the police actually do or did, as opposed to controlling their actions at the time. In the area of search and seizure, of course, the requirement for prior authorization in the form of a search warrant, or other court order where feasible, means that the law actually authorizes the actions of the police (or not) before they act.[48] Generally, though, such is not the case and it certainly is not in the area of arrest and detention. While there are arrest warrants, the courts have not made them a precondition in any meaningful sense in advance of arrest or detention and in advance of the exercise of powers that arise incidental thereto.

Accordingly, the police carry an immense responsibility to exercise their powers responsibly and with restraint. *Mann*'s focus on the need for lawfulness of police actions (supported now by *Grant*) is welcome, in that the Court stresses what the common law had always said, that a citizen is not required to do anything not expressly required under the law. Nonetheless, the Supreme Court has consistently allowed the police considerable latitude to pursue their crime-fighting activities and

47   *R. v. Orbanski; R. v. Elias*, [2005] 2 S.C.R. 3 at para. 81 [*Orbanski*].
48   See, generally, *Hunter*, above note 32.

has not often seen the case before it as presenting a challenge because the law did not expressly authorize the police action in question.

In some situations, especially in the context of section 8, where the Court has held that there is no reasonable expectation of privacy, the Court's decisions have seemingly allowed the police carte blanche to investigate the crime in which they are interested. In *Tessling*,[49] for example, where the Court held that the FLIR technology as currently used by the police does not invade a homeowner's reasonable expectation of privacy, the police are apparently free to fly over Canadian's houses and take heat-emanation readings, even though no law authorizes such an investigative step. Likewise, after *Patrick*,[50] the police are seemingly free to snoop through people's garbage since there is no reasonable expectation of privacy once the individual has put the garbage "out" for collection. It is to be noted that these police actions do not involve the arrest or detention of an individual. On the other hand, no power authorizes such activity. It can be argued, of course, that since each police officer, too, is an individual rights holder, police officers are free to do what they wish in the absence of a law constraining them from so acting.

Likewise, when the courts admit evidence in the face of finding a breach of rights, it often seems the courts have *de facto* authorized the police to act in accord with the result of the case. It can be argued that to take away such an understanding from the cases is wrong, and indeed at times the Court has been express in saying to the police that particular police conduct, in the future, will result in exclusion even though on this occasion the Court has not so decided. In *Silveira,* for example, Justice Peter Cory explicitly said:

> Yet, the question remains, how should the police act in a situation where they have a serious and valid concern pertaining to the preservation of evidence while awaiting a search warrant. As a result of this case, police officers will be aware that to enter a dwelling-house without a warrant, even in exigent circumstances, constitutes such a serious breach of *Charter* rights that it will likely lead to a ruling that the evidence seized is inadmissible.[51]

On the other hand, where a court finds any given breach of rights to be not serious, one imagines the police seeing such a decision as in fact authorizing them to act similarly in the future. Indeed, one can sometimes read between the lines of the court decisions to see that some

---

49   *R. v. Tessling*, 2004 SCC 67.
50   *R. v. Patrick*, 2009 SCC 17 [*Patrick*].
51   *R. v. Silveira*, [1995] 2 S.C.R. 297 at para. 152.

courts actually are not at all happy with the result the law has led them to in finding rights breaches. Indeed, on occasion such disappointment by a court is even express.[52]

As well, in cases where the law is unclear, it seems that the police are often seen as acting appropriately when they push the limits of their powers. Generally, when deciding cases, the courts have intentionally not been clear in specifying what it is they expect the police to do in the future. If the police know that a given action *may* be illegal, are they encouraged to so act nonetheless in the absence of an express prohibition? Or rather, is such conduct by the police to be seen as reckless in regard to the rights of the accused and therefore, in itself, to be held to represent a serious breach of rights? While this book is decidedly not about section 24(2), that being an evidentiary matter beyond its scope, the majority in *Grant* took a positive step when they held that where a police officer is disbelieved, the police actions breaching an accused's rights will be seen as more serious.[53] If the police honestly believed that they are authorized to do what they did, let them say so and the court will assess their actions based thereon. Where the police attempt to gloss over or rationalize their actions in ways that are not believed by the court, it is to be welcomed that the court will not look favourably upon their actions for that very reason.

The existence, then, of *de facto* or default police power in Canada is a reality and generally the courts have been unable or unwilling to control police everyday actions. It was only once the Supreme Court came to the realization that the police were consistently using an (as of yet undeclared) power to detain people for investigative purposes that

---

52 Consider, for example, the position of the British Columbia Court of Appeal in *R. v. Martin* (1995), 97 C.C.C. (3d) 241 where the majority said this:

>   It follows from all of the above that the police constables denied the appellant's s. 8 *Charter* rights when they walked through the house. That is the unfortunate result of the inexorable operation of the Law of Unintended Consequences on the principles pronounced in *Hunter v. Southam, Collins, Kokesch*, and other cases which apply those principles. Unfortunate because it forces police officers to become law breakers whenever they trespass while engaging in the performance of what might be called "good Samaritan" functions. (para. 15)

 The decision was upheld by the Supreme Court in *R. v. Martin*, [1996] 1 S.C.R. 463 which contented itself by saying: "We are all of the view that the appeal should be dismissed. Assuming without deciding that there was a breach of s. 8 of the *Canadian Charter of Rights and Freedoms*, we agree with the majority of the Court of Appeal that admission of the evidence would not bring the administration of justice into disrepute." (*ibid.*).

53 *Grant*, above note 12 at paras. 72–75.

it finally decided to recognize such a power in *Mann*.[54] As noted, courts have generally been reluctant to expressly direct police action in the future and thus the common law has not often been effective in providing such direction to the police.

It is submitted that every criminal accused that brings a *Charter* challenge to police conduct in her case *de facto* represents other persons who may have been subjected to a similar police exercise of power. Therefore, it seems that the widespread use of the impugned technique by the police may become a matter of relevance at least at the remedies stage in a *Charter* proceeding. The Supreme Court recently acknowledged that the accused litigant is in fact often representative of others when arguing such points in the court. In *Grant,* the majority expressly acknowledged this when it said:

> It should also be kept in mind that for every *Charter* breach that comes before the courts, many others may go unidentified and unredressed because they did not turn up relevant evidence leading to a criminal charge. In recognition of the need for courts to distance themselves from this behaviour, therefore, evidence that the *Charter*-infringing conduct was part of a pattern of abuse tends to support exclusion.[55]

B. PRELIMINARY ISSUES

1) Incidental and Supporting Powers and Provisions

The *Criminal Code* contains, under the heading "Protection of Persons Administering and Enforcing the Law," a number of supporting provisions relevant to the exercise of powers under the *Code*.[56] Strictly

---

54   *Mann*, above note 10. Several academic articles had discussed the phenomenon of investigative detention prior to the Supreme Court's decision in *Mann*. See, for example, Alan Young, "All Along the Watchtower: Arbitrary Detention and the Police Function" (1991) 29 Osgoode Hall L.J. 329; Steve Coughlan, "Search Based on Articulable Cause: Proceed with Caution or Full Stop?" (2002) 2 C.R. (6th) 49; and James Stribopoulos, "A Failed Experiment? Investigative Detention: Ten Years Later" (2003) 41 Alta. L. Rev. 335.

55   *Grant*, above note 12 at para. 75.

56   We shall here discuss ss. 25 to 31, with one exception: s. 25.1, which allows certain police officers to break the law in some cases, is not included in the discussion. It is quite unlike the other provisions, involving as it does the designation of particular officers and the submission of an annual report to Parliament. See the discussion of those provisions in Coughlan, *Criminal Procedure*, above note 39 at 126.

speaking, the sections are, for the most part, phrased as "justifications" rather than powers, and litigation over their meaning frequently occurs in the context of civil litigation.[57] They are therefore framed as though they are conceptually similar to, for example, the self-defence provisions in the *Code*. Nonetheless, their greater significance is the extent to which they authorize police and others to act in ways which would not otherwise be permitted, and so it is reasonable to think of them as a sort of police power.

That said, not all the provisions are limited to police: section 25, for instance, justifying the use of force, applies as well to private persons who are required or authorized by law to do anything in the administration or enforcement of the law. And, although the provisions are relevant to the powers of arrest and detention which are the subject of this book, they are not limited to that context. The rules about warrants apply equally to search warrants, and whether the amount of force that was used in executing a search was reasonable can also be questioned.[58]

The supporting provisions will be discussed under three headings: use of force, rules regarding warrants, and breaches of the peace.

a) Use of Force

The use of force is governed by a combination of several provisions: sections 25, 26, and 27.[59]

Sections 25 and 26 have to do with the use of force in the execution of legal authority, and must be read in conjunction with one another.[60] Section 25 states that anyone who is required or authorized by law to do anything in the administration or enforcement of the law (whether a private person, a peace officer, or a public officer, someone aiding one of those officers, or a person acting by virtue of some other office) "is, if he acts on reasonable grounds, justified in doing what he is required

---

57 See, for example, *R. v. Garcia-Guiterrez* (1991), 5 C.R. (4th) 1 at para. 37 (B.C.C.A.) [*Garcia-Guiterrez*], speaking of s. 25: ". . . [I]n the narrow sense, it provides no authority for the use of force, it merely provides a defence that may be raised when the force used is challenged as unlawful."

58 *Ibid.*; see also *R. v. Al-Fartossy*, 2007 ABCA 427 [*Al-Fartossy*].

59 These provisions govern the use of force in enforcing the provisions of the *Criminal Code*. A peace officer can also have the authority to use force in enforcing other statutes, such as a provincial Highway Traffic Act: *R. v. Tricker* (1995), 21 O.R. (3d) 575 (C.A.). In addition, the common law recognized a power to use force in making an arrest, an authority that attaches to the power, not to the person: accordingly, a private citizen can also have the authority to use force in making an arrest: see generally *Asante-Mensah*, above note 26.

60 *R. v. Hebert*, [1996] 2 S.C.R. 272 [*Hebert*].

or authorized to do and in using as much force as is necessary for that purpose."[61] This must be seen in light of section 26, which states that "[e]very one who is authorized by law to use force is criminally responsible for any excess thereof according to the nature and quality of the act that constitutes the excess."[62] Note that the statutory justification attaches to anyone authorized to act, not merely to the police. This is consistent with the position at common law, which was that "the right to use reasonable force attaches at common law to the institution of an arrest, not to the status of the individual making the arrest."[63] Accordingly, private citizens might also be justified in using force.

The more significant question is what is actually authorized under section 25. The first thing to note is that the section has not been read to be nearly as broad as it might seem to be at first glance. It is *not* a broad-based grant of power for a person to do "what he is required or authorized to do": that is, it is not a grant of ancillary powers beyond those explicitly enumerated elsewhere. As noted above, police only have the powers they are explicitly given by statute or common law: section 25 is not a source of further powers. The section does not provide a defence to a police officer who generally acts reasonably and in good faith.[64] Rather, it applies to govern the use of force when the person involved has already been authorized to act in some other way. As the British Columbia Court of Appeal has observed, "section 25 does not confer extra powers on the police, but serves as a shield from criminal or civil liability."[65]

Even more specifically, the section has been read as limited to the use of force in the specific context of conducting an arrest. The Supreme Court of Canada is often taken to have concluded in *Cluett*[66] that the section means that "police officers are not entitled to use force

---

61 *Criminal Code*, R.S.C. 1985, c. C-46 [*Criminal Code*], s. 25(1).

62 *Ibid.*, s. 26.

63 *Asante-Mensah*, above note 26 at para. 52.

64 *Hudson v. Brantford Police Services Board* (2001), 204 D.L.R. (4th) 645 at para. 32 (Ont. C.A.) [*Hudson*]. See also the judgment of Dickson J. (as he then was) in *Eccles*, above note 21; *R. v. Peters* (1990), 84 Sask. R. 231 (C.A.) [*Peters*]; *Swansburg v. Canada (Royal Canadian Mounted Police)* (1996), 141 D.L.R. (4th) 94 (B.C.C.A.) [*Swansburg*]. Note, of course, that there is much less significance to s. 25 not being a source of ancillary powers since courts began much more freely using the *Waterfield* decision as a basis for granting police ancillary powers: see the discussion above.

65 *Richardson v. Vancouver (City)*, 2006 BCCA 36 at para. 26, quoting *Crampton v. Walton*, 2005 ABCA 81 [*Crampton*], quoting *R. v. Asante-Mensah* (2001), 204 D.L.R. (4th) 51 at para. 51 (Ont. C.A.), aff'd 2003 SCC 38.

66 *Cluett v. R.*, [1985] 2 S.C.R. 216.

unless an arrest is warranted and properly made."[67] The decision in *Cluett* is not entirely clear on that point, however, and might also be read as rejecting the use of force only because the officer in that case was acting without any legal authority: without legal authority because there was no power to detain short of an arrest. The Court's decision in *Mann* has since created a limited power of investigative detention.[68] Whether the justification in section 25 would apply to a police officer using that power, rather than the power to arrest, remains unsettled and indeed largely unaddressed.[69] The likeliest result is that the section would apply.

Lower courts, for example, have laid down rules regarding the use of section 25 which presume a broader application than merely using force to effect an arrest. The Alberta Court of Appeal has held :

> Section 25(1) contains three branches. In order to access the protection of the section, a police officer must prove that he or she:
> (i)   was required or authorized by law to perform an action in the administration or enforcement of the law;
> (ii) acted on reasonable grounds in performing that action; and
> (iii) did not use unnecessary force.[70]

Other guidelines have also been laid down. It has been held that actions taken under section 25 should not be assessed through hindsight, but rather must be judged based on the situation as it appeared to the officer at the time. As with self-defence, police officers are not expected

---

67   See *Swansburg*, above note 64 at para. 31, describing the result in *Cluett*, ibid. See also *Peters*, above note 64; and *R. v. Sheridan*, [1993] B.C.J. No. 2784 at para. 10 (S.C.):

> 10   The learned Trial Judge seemed to be of the view that a peace officer, as long as he is in the execution of his or her duty, may apply force to a citizen even though that force would otherwise amount to an assault. With the greatest respect such is not the law as I read the case of *Cluett v. The Queen* (1985), 21 C.C.C. (3d) 318, a decision of the Supreme Court of Canada. In that case it was held that, notwithstanding the provisions of s. 25 of the *Criminal Code* which empower a peace officer to use reasonable force in the execution of his or her duties, such officer has no power to forcibly detain a citizen short of exercising a power of arrest.

68   See Chapter 3.

69   The decision in *Webster v. Edmonton (City) Police Service*, 2007 ABCA 23 [*Webster*], considers s. 25 in discussing an investigative detention, without considering the prior question of whether it applies in that context. In its pre-*Mann* decision *R. v. Yum*, 2001 ABCA 80, that same court approved the use of force in a detention short of arrest, without actually discussing s. 25.

70   *Crampton*, above note 65 at para. 6.

to measure the precise amount of force the situation requires and will not fall outside the protection of section 25(1) for failing to use the least amount of force actually necessary: in this regard, it is sometimes said that the officer is not required to weigh to nicety the force required, which is the same standard used in section 34(1) self-defence claims.[71] Rather, allowance must be made for an officer misjudging the degree of force required, given the exigencies of the moment.[72] Depending on the facts of the case, quite considerable force can be found to be justified.[73] On the other hand, the section is intended only to protect reasonable decisions: negligence precludes the application of section 25.[74]

There are further aspects to section 25, beyond the general authorization of reasonable force in subsection (1). Section 25(2) provides that a person executing process or carrying out a sentence in good faith is justified in doing so even if it later transpires that the process or sentence was defective or in excess of jurisdiction. The thrust of this section was explained by the Supreme Court in *Finta*:

> The purpose of s. 25(2) is to provide legal protection to a police officer, who, acting in good faith and on a reasonable belief that his or her actions are justified by law, later finds out that those actions were not authorized because the law was found to be defective.
>
> Section 25 is akin to the defence of mistake of fact. Unless, the law is manifestly illegal, the police officer must obey and implement that law. Police officers cannot be expected to undertake a comprehensive legal analysis of every order or law that they are charged with enforcing before taking action. Therefore, if it turns out that they have followed an illegal order they may plead the peace officer defence just as the military officer may properly put forward the defence of obedience to superior orders under certain limited conditions. The qualification is that the military officer must act in good faith and must have reasonable grounds for believing that the actions taken were justified. An officer acting pursuant to a manifestly unlawful

---

71   R. v. Canada (Royal Canadian Mounted Police) (1981), 60 C.C.C. (2d) 211 (B.C.C.A.) [R. v. Canada].

72   Crampton, above note 65 at para. 45.

73   Webster, above note 69, justifies the use of a police tactical team under the section. Other cases have accepted that the use of a battering ram to break down a door or the use of a chokehold in apprehending a suspect could be justified: see, for example, R. v. DeWolfe, 2007 NSCA 79; R. v. Al-Fartossy, above note 58 (re: battering rams); and Collins, above note 9, or Garcia-Guiterrez, above note 57 (re: chokeholds).

74   Poupart, above note 36; Green v. Lawrence (1998), 163 D.L.R. (4th) 115 (Man. C.A.); Chartier v. Greaves, [2001] 103 A.C.W.S. (3d) 1054 (Ont. S.C.J.).

order or law would not be able to defend his or her actions on the grounds they were justified under s. 25 of the *Criminal Code*.[75]

Section 25(2) is not meant to provide a defence in the case of a mistake of law. If a peace officer is simply mistaken about what powers she has, section 25(2) is of no assistance. Thus, for example, a police officer who forces entry into a dwelling to effect an arrest in circumstances where no power to do so existed cannot rely on section 25(2).[76] The distinction between a mistake of fact and one of law can be unclear, of course, in this context as in others.[77]

Three subsections deal with the use of potentially deadly force, attaching restrictions to when it is available. Section 25(3) limits the circumstances in which section 25(1) could authorize deadly force, and so is available to anyone who falls within that former section. Section 25(4) is a modern version of the "fleeing felon" rule, available to peace officers who are attempting to arrest a person who flees, and section 25(5) deals with the use of deadly force by peace officers in the case of a penitentiary escape.

There are some common features to the subsections. All three, it should be noted, refer to force "that is intended *or is likely to cause* death *or grievous bodily harm*": to refer to them as the "deadly force" provisions is a convenient shorthand, but in fact they apply whether death has actually occurred or not. It has been held, for example, that section 25(3) is applicable in assessing whether the use of a chokehold was acceptable.[78] Note conversely that whether an injury has actually been suffered does not settle whether the limits in these subsections apply. A peace officer might use a level of force in making an arrest which in fact results in injury: if that was neither intended nor likely, then the limits in sec-

---

75   *R. v. Finta*, [1994] 1 S.C.R. 701 at 842 [*Finta*].

76   See, generally, *Hudson*, above note 64.

77   See, for example, *R. v. Devereaux* (1996), 147 Nfld. & P.E.I.R. 108 (Nfld. C.A.), in which a correctional officer placed a person back in a cell when he refused to sign a form. The Court of Appeal agreed that s. 19 of the *Code* would be applicable, in that the accused (the correctional officer) had made a mistake of law which would not excuse him. It then went on to conclude that his honest belief that he was acting legally entitled him to the defence in s. 25, which seems inconsistent with *Finta*, above note 75. The court held that "[t]o be denied the 'peace officer defence' the conduct or act would have to be so patently illegal that a plea of acting in good faith would have absolutely no plausibility whatsoever, making no sense at all": (*ibid.* at para. 54). It does not seem to consider whether the officer in the case could have been described as executing a process or carrying out a sentence, which is also a requirement of the section.

78   *Garcia-Guiterrez*, above note 57.

tion 25(3) would not be relevant.[79] In addition, note that, if the officer is justified in using deadly force under one of these provisions, then that justification applies against the world, not simply against the person the force was intended to be directed toward: that is, if an officer is justified in firing a weapon at a fleeing suspect, that justification protects her even if the person in fact shot is an innocent bystander.[80] Of course, the force used by the officer must still meet the reasonableness requirement: "if an escaping criminal ran into a crowd of people and was obscured from the view of a pursuing police officer, it could not be suggested that it would be permissible for the latter to fire through the crowd in the hope of stopping the fleeing criminal."[81]

There are features worth discussing separately in each section. Section 25(3) is the most limited of the sections, which is partly a reflection of the fact that it potentially authorizes deadly force on the part of private citizens, not only by peace officers.[82] It sets further requirements, beyond those in section 25(1), which must also be met for deadly force to be justified. In particular, it requires a belief on reasonable grounds that the force is necessary for the self-preservation of the person or the preservation of any one under that person's protection from death or grievous bodily harm.

Section 25(4) sets out a number of requirements for the use of deadly force against a fleeing felon:

(a) the arrest is lawful;
(b) the offence is one for which that person may be arrested without warrant;
(c) the person to be arrested takes flight to avoid arrest;

---

79   See, for example, *Mohamed v. Vancouver (City) Police Department*, 2001 BCCA 290, where a police officer set his dog to chase one suspect, Mohamed, while he apprehended two others. Mohamed attempted to climb a wall to escape the dog, in the result falling and breaking his leg. The British Columbia Court of Appeal held that s. 25(3) did not arise since there was no evidence the officer intended the result or knew it was likely to ensue. See also *R. v. Canada*, above note 71.

80   See *Priestman v. Colangelo*, [1959] S.C.R. 615 [*Priestman*]. The facts of *Priestman* are somewhat more complex than the example suggested. The officer, Priestman, was attempting to shoot out a tire on a fleeing car. Because his own vehicle hit a bump he actually fired through the back window of the vehicle, and the bullet ricocheted, knocking out the driver. That vehicle then struck and killed two pedestrians. Because the decision to try to shoot out the tire met the requirements of s. 25(4) (as it stood at the time), the officer was justified and so was not liable to the estates of the deceased pedestrians. See also *Poupart*, above note 36.

81   *Priestman, ibid.* at 624.

82   *Roberge v. R.*, [1983] 1 S.C.R. 312 [*Roberge*].

(d) the peace officer or other person using the force believes on reasonable grounds that the force is necessary for the purpose of protecting the peace officer, the person lawfully assisting the peace officer or any other person from imminent or future death or grievous bodily harm; and

(e) the flight cannot be prevented by reasonable means in a less violent manner.

Those requirements are cumulative, and so all must be met to fall within the justification. As with section 25(1), the use of force must have been intentional for the justification to apply.[83]

In its original form, the section was more or less a codification of the common law "fleeing felon" rule, which allowed the use of deadly force to prevent those who had committed felonies from escaping. Until 1994 the predecessor section did not contain any equivalent to the requirement in subsection (d) of a risk of death or grievous bodily harm if the felon escaped.[84] When the common law developed this was understandable, since anyone guilty of a felony was subject to the death penalty. However, the disproportionality of the rule in its codified form was often noted,[85] and the further limitation was eventually introduced. The rule is now much more proportionate, in that deadly force is permitted only to prevent an escape when an equivalent risk would be created by the escape.

Finally, there is section 25(5), also added in 1994. Like section 25(4), it is limited to peace officers and permits the use of deadly force against an inmate attempting to escape a penitentiary. Parallel to section 25(4), the officer must believe on reasonable grounds that any of the inmates pose a threat of death or grievous bodily harm to the officer or any other person, and that the escape cannot reasonably be prevented in a less violent manner.

The Supreme Court has also pronounced on the meaning of section 27, which permits the use of force to prevent the commission of

---

83   *R. v. Levert* (1994), 76 O.A.C. 307 (C.A.).

84   At which point it was amended under *An Act to Amend the Criminal Code and the Coastal Fisheries Protection Act*, S.C. 1994, c. 12. The previous section read:

> 25 (4) When protected-exception — A peace officer who is proceeding lawfully to arrest, with or without warrant, any person for an offence for which that person may be arrested without warrant, and every one lawfully assisting the peace officer, is justified, if the person to be arrested takes flight to avoid arrest, in using as much force as is necessary to prevent the escape by flight, unless the escape can be prevented by reasonable means in a less violent manner.

85   *Roberge*, above note 82.

an offence. The section applies only if the offence committed is one for which the person who committed it could be arrested without warrant and which would be likely to cause immediate and serious injury to the person or property of anyone. If these conditions are met (or under section 27(b) the person using force reasonably believes them to be met), then that person is permitted to use as much force as is reasonably necessary to prevent it. The Court has noted that this section potentially permits the use even of deadly force, provided that that was reasonably necessary, holding :

> In determining whether the force used was reasonable the court will take into account all the circumstances of the case, including the nature and degree of force used, the seriousness of the evil to be prevented and the possibility of preventing it by other means. This provision is of general application and is not limited to arrestable or any other class of offences, but it would not be reasonable to use even slight force to prevent very trivial offences. The circumstances in which it can be considered reasonable to kill another in the prevention of crime must be of an extreme kind; they could probably arise only in the case of an attack against the person which is likely to cause death or serious bodily injury and where killing the attacker is the only practicable means of preventing the harm. It cannot be reasonable to kill another merely to prevent a crime which is directed only against property.[86]

In determining whether the force used was reasonably necessary, many factors can be relevant but none are determinative. Whether the commission of an assault is imminent can be relevant, though it is not necessarily a requirement. Any injuries suffered by the person prevented from committing an offence could shed light on the force which was used, though a judge should not simply reason back from the existence of injuries to the conclusion that the force must have been excessive. Ultimately, the decision is one best made by the trier of fact and considerable deference should be given by courts of appeal.[87]

The relationship between section 27 and the self-defence provisions is also worth noting. That is to say, section 27 is intended to permit a bystander who witnesses an offence being or about to be committed to use force to prevent that offence. It cannot be used by an accused who was preventing an assault against herself: as the Court has noted,

---

86   *R. v. Gee*, [1982] 2 S.C.R. 286 at 302 [*Gee*], quoting Lord Hailsham of St. Marylebone, ed., *Halsbury's Laws of England*, 4th ed., vol. 11 (London: Butterworths, 1974) at 630.

87   *R. v. Guay*, 2008 NBCA 72.

that interpretation would render sections 34 to 37 redundant.[88] Note as well that, if a person's actions are justified under section 27, then that person will not be committing an unlawful assault: in other words, the self-defence provisions in section 34 will not be available to the person against whom force is used, if he uses force in return.[89]

The Court has also determined that no qualified partial defence of excessive use of force in preventing an offence, reducing murder to manslaughter, exists in Canada: either section 27 is met and an accused was justified, or it is not met and the accused is guilty of whatever offence can be proven on the facts.[90]

Finally, on the use of force, note the relatively recent section 27.1 of the *Code*, which justifies every person on an aircraft in flight in using as much force as is reasonably necessary to prevent the commission of an offence that would be likely to cause immediate and serious injury to the aircraft or to any person or property on it.

b) Rules regarding Warrants

Two supporting provisions relate to warrants: sections 28 and 29. The former provides protection to peace officers, while the latter imposes obligations on them.

Section 28(1) of the *Criminal Code* protects a person from criminal liability for arresting the wrong person under a warrant, provided the arrest was made in good faith and on reasonable grounds. Section 28(2) extends that protection beyond peace officers making an arrest to anyone assisting in the arrest or to any keeper of a prison to which the person is taken.

The noteworthy thing about section 28 is the way in which it differs from the use-of-force provisions. That is, it is not phrased as a justification generally: it is merely a protection from *criminal* liability. Arresting the wrong person under a warrant could amount to the tort of wrongful imprisonment, depending on the facts of the case, and if that were so then section 28 would provide no protection.[91]

Section 29 sets out rules, some of which apply to warrants generally and some to arrests specifically. Under section 29(1), everyone executing a warrant has a duty to have the warrant with him and produce it on request: this rule applies to search warrants as well as to arrest war-

---

88   *R. v. Hebert*, above note 60.
89   *R. v. Taylor* (2004), 189 O.A.C. 388 (C.A.).
90   *Gee*, above note 86.
91   See, for example, *Fletcher v. Collins*, [1968] 2 O.R. 618 (H.C.J.). Also: *Romilly v. Weatherhead* (1975), 55 D.L.R. (3d) 607 (B.C.S.C.).

rants.[92] A failure to comply with this requirement will render an arrest unlawful.[93]

Section 29(2) is specific to arrests, and in fact to arrests whether made with a warrant or not. It creates a duty for the arresting person to give notice of "(a) the process or warrant under which he makes the arrest; or (b) the reason for the arrest."[94] Finally, subsection 29(3) provides that a failure to comply with subsections (1) or (2) does not by itself deprive a person of protection from criminal responsibility.

The leading case on section 29(2) is *Gamracy*.[95] In that case, an accused was arrested by a police officer who knew that an arrest warrant existed but did not know the nature of the charge. When arresting the accused, the officer simply informed him that there was a warrant for his arrest.[96] At common law an accused would have been entitled to know "on what charge or on suspicion of what crime he is seized,"[97] and so the officer's actions would not have been sufficient. However, the Supreme Court held that the rule in Canada was that set out in section 29(2), and that subsections (a) and (b) were to be read disjunctively: an officer could comply with one or the other. In *Gamracy*, therefore, "[t]he duty was fully discharged by telling the accused that the outstanding warrant was the reason for his arrest."[98]

It is not clear that *Gamracy* still reflects the current state of the law: there is a strong argument that it does not. Specifically, it is a pre-*Charter* case, and so now anyone arrested would have the right under section 10(a) to be informed of the reason for the arrest. Section 10(a) is discussed more fully below (see Chapter 5). In brief, it has been interpreted to entitle an accused to know the nature of her jeopardy, so that she can decide whether to submit to the arrest and will be in a position

---

92   See, for example, *R. v. Cornell*, 2009 ABCA 147 aff'd 2010 SCC 31. The Supreme Court held that this rule is complied with as long as at least one member of the team conducting the search has a copy of the warrant; and *R. v. Bohn*, 2000 BCCA 239 [*Bohn*], which notes that the rule is imperative. That case concerned a search warrant, and the British Columbia Court of Appeal concluded that "[f]ailure to produce the warrant on request, without good reason, is in my view, a significant breach of s. 8." (*Bohn, ibid.* at para. 34). On the other hand, the Alberta Court of Appeal specifically rejected this conclusion in *R. v. Patrick*, 2007 ABCA 308 at para. 49. This issue was not before the Supreme Court of Canada when it affirmed the result in *Patrick*, above note 50.

93   *Bohn, ibid.*

94   *Criminal Code*, above note 61, s. 29(2).

95   *R. v. Gamracy*, [1974] S.C.R. 640 [*Gamracy*].

96   Section 495(1)(c) of the *Criminal Code* creates a power to arrest without a warrant based on the reasonable belief that a warrant exists.

97   *Christie v. Leachinsky*, [1947] 1 All E.R. 567 at 567 (H.L.).

98   *Gamracy*, above note 95 at 644.

to exercise the right to consult with counsel. Whatever section 29(2) might mean, being told "you are under arrest because there is a warrant for your arrest" seems clearly not to comply with the standard under section 10(a). Indeed, it has specifically been held that section 10(a) enshrines the common law rule in *Christie v. Leachinsky*.[99] The Court in *Gamracy* had held that section 29(2) set out a narrower rule than that common law one.

Further, *Gamracy* has been held only to have settled the question of whether, for purposes of resisting arrest, an officer will have been acting in the execution of duty. Simply saying "there is a warrant" might not be sufficient to protect an officer from civil liability in an action for personal trespass.[100]

Section 29(2) has been read narrowly in other ways. For example, it has been held that it is sufficient for an arrested person to be told in general terms the behaviour which grounds the arrest, rather than the particular charge. On that basis it has been held that a person who was told that he was arrested for driving while under suspension could not complain that section 29(2) was not complied with, even though he did not know whether it was a *Criminal Code* or provincial statute he was alleged to have violated.[101] On the other hand, it has also been suggested that that approach might not comply with section 10(a).[102]

c) Breaches of the Peace

Sections 30 and 31 of the *Code* create two further justifications. Section 30 justifies anyone who witnesses a breach of the peace in interfering to prevent it. In addition, that person may detain the person committing the breach of the peace for the purpose of handing him over to a peace officer. A person acting under this section is entitled to use force, but it must be no more than is reasonably necessary, and also must be "reasonably proportioned to the danger to be apprehended from the continuance or renewal of the breach of the peace."[103]

Accompanying this is section 31(1) of the *Code*, which justifies a peace officer who witnesses a breach of the peace to arrest anyone she finds committing it, or whom she reasonably believes is about to join in

---

99 *R. v. Nguyen*, 2008 ONCA 49 at para. 16.

100 See *Campbell v. Edmonton (City) Police Service* (1985), 66 A.R. 222 (C.A.); *Schuck v. Stewart* (1978), 87 D.L.R. (3d) 720 (B.C.S.C.).

101 *R. v. Fielding*, [1967] 3 C.C.C. 258 (B.C.C.A.) [*Fielding*].

102 See *R. v. Smith* (1990), 53 C.C.C. (3d) 97 at 104–7 (N.S.S.C.A.D.), commenting on *Fielding*, *ibid.*: "While that may express too narrow a view for the purposes of the *Charter* it was the practice followed under the *Code*."

103 *Criminal Code*, above note 61, s. 30.

or renew it. In addition, a peace officer is justified under section 31(2) in receiving any person delivered in accordance with section 30.

A breach of the peace "does not include any and all conduct which right thinking members of the community would regard as offensive, disturbing, or even vaguely threatening. A breach of the peace contemplates an act or actions which result in actual or threatened harm to someone."[104]

Although (like the use-of-force provisions) these are phrased as justifications, the sections can equally be seen as powers: this is clear from the result in *Biron*. The accused there was arrested outside a bar by one peace officer, Maissoneuve, who gave him to a second officer, Gauthier, who in turn handed him over to Dorion, a third officer. The accused ended up in a scuffle with Dorion, the third of the officers, and was charged with resisting a peace officer in the execution of his duty.[105] The dissenting judges argued that the accused was not guilty, on the basis that the officer was not in execution of his duty:

> Section 31 is not an arrest power, but a protection for the person or persons making an arrest, just as is s. 25. Moreover, it is limited to protection in respect of an arrest for breach of the peace, and in that respect has a connection with s. 30, which does speak expressly of detention of a person committing a breach of the peace. By no stretch of the imagination can either s. 30 or s. 31 be turned into a general power of either arrest or justification in respect of any criminal offence on the theory that all offences under the *Criminal Code* constitute breaches of the peace.[106]

The majority, however, concluded:

> Section 31(2) of the *Code* provides that Dorion was justified in receiving Biron into custody. The arrest made by Maisonneuve was because he considered Biron to be committing a disturbance, in a public place, which would be a breach of the peace. It is evident that Dorion, who was a part of the police force conducting the raid, reasonably believed that Gauthier, who turned Biron over to him, had witnessed a breach of the peace.

---

104 *Brown v. Durham (Regional Municipality) Police Force* (1998), 43 O.R. (3d) 223 at para. 73 (C.A.) [*Durham*].

105 *Biron*, above note 2 at 58–59. This case is best known for its interpretation of the "finds committing" warrantless arrest power, which is discussed in Chapter 4. A different issue is raised here.

106 *Ibid.* at 65–66.

> I interpret the word "justified" in s. 31(2) as meaning that Dorion had lawful sanction to receive Biron into his custody. He received him into his custody in the course of performance of his duties as a peace officer at the scene of the raid. Biron offered resistance to him in the execution of that duty. In my opinion that is sufficient to make Biron guilty of the offence with which he was charged under s. 118(a).[107]

On this reasoning, the fact that Dorion was "justified" results in him being in the execution of his duty, which is essentially to say that he had the power to act as he did.

It is worth noting that the justifications in sections 30 and 31 are both predicated on a breach of the peace being witnessed: although the justifications extend to preventing others from joining in, there must actually be a breach of the peace. That is, those sections do not justify action with regard to participants in a breach of the peace which has concluded, nor do they justify preventing a breach of the peace from occurring in the first place. However, it has been held that, independently of these *Code* sections, the police have the power at common law to prevent an apprehended breach of the peace.[108] Although this decision was controversial when made,[109] courts have since become much more willing to create common law police powers.

Some limitations have been attached to this common law power to arrest for an apprehended breach of the peace. The apprehended breach, it has been held, must be imminent, and the police officer must have reasonable grounds for believing that breach of the peace will likely occur if the person is not detained. The power has been said to be analogous to the power to arrest in anticipation of an indictable offence, to be discussed in Chapter 4: however, not all indictable offences would be breaches of the peace, and an apprehended breach of the peace need not involve committing any offence.[110]

d) Entry into a Dwelling House to Effect an Arrest

As has been repeatedly observed in this book, peace officers only have the authority specifically given to them. Much of this book will deal with their power to compel a person's appearance in court, in particu-

---

107 *Ibid.* at 76–77.
108 *Hayes v. Canada (Royal Canadian Mounted Police)* (1985), 17 D.L.R. (4th) 751 (B.C.C.A.) [*Hayes*].
109 Bruce P. Archibald, "*Hayes v. Thompson and Bell*: Annotation" (1985) 44 C.R. (3d) 316.
110 *Hayes*, above note 108 at para. 24.

lar through an arrest. In some cases, however, more than the power to arrest is needed. If peace officers are to enter a private dwelling, they need some authority to do so: like anyone else, peace officers can be found to be trespassers. If peace officers are trespassing, this can have several effects. First, it renders the arrest illegal.[111] Second, it can mean that the officer was not acting in the execution of duty, which can be important if that is an element of the offence with which the accused was charged.[112] Accordingly, there must be some source of authority for peace officers to enter dwelling houses in addition to the power to arrest itself, or no one who fled into a home could be arrested.[113]

The power to enter a dwelling house to carry out an arrest is, today, largely governed by statute, and in particular by sections 529 to 529.5 of the *Criminal Code*. It is not exclusively governed by those provisions, since there remains a common law exception to those rules. To properly understand the statutory scheme and the current state of the law, it is necessary to take something of an historical perspective on the issue: the current statutory scheme was sparked by the ways in which the former common law rules violated the *Charter*.

Pre-*Charter*, the rules for forcible entry into a dwelling house to make an arrest under a warrant were set out in *Eccles v. Bourque*. That case held that

> Entry can be made against the will of the householder only if (a) there are reasonable and probable grounds for the belief that the person sought is within the premises and (b) proper announcement is made prior to entry.[114]

The later decision in *Landry* extended that power to warrantless arrests as well: that is, if the requirements of section 495(1) were made out, then a reasonable belief that the person was in the premises and proper prior announcement were sufficient to authorize the police to enter a private dwelling.[115]

In *Feeney*,[116] the Supreme Court considered these requirements and concluded that they did not comply with the minimum standards that

---

111 See, generally, *Hudson*, above note 64; See also *R. v. Delong* (1989), 47 C.C.C. (3d) 402 (Ont. C.A.).

112 See *Godoy*, above note 46; *Stenning*, above note 35.

113 See *Macooh*, above note 23 at 815: "It would be unacceptable for police officers who were about to make a completely lawful arrest to be prevented from doing so merely because the offender had taken refuge in his home or that of a third party."

114 *Eccles*, above note 21 at 744.

115 *Landry*, above note 22.

116 *R. v. Feeney*, [1997] 2 S.C.R. 13, 146 D.L.R. (4th) 609 [*Feeney*].

had subsequently come to be developed under the *Charter*. In particular, they relied upon the interplay with the law around unreasonable searches, where it had been established that a warrantless search was *prima facie* an unreasonable one.[117] The purpose of a warrant requirement, of course, is to obtain judicial authorization for the police action before it takes place: the major rationale for that was the desire to prevent *Charter* violations from occurring in the first place, rather than simply remedying them after the fact.

Given that, the Court held, it would be anomalous if a peace officer required a warrant to be able to enter a dwelling house to conduct a search but could enter to carry out an arrest based only on her own judgment of reasonable grounds and prior announcement. Indeed, given that the police might well be able to search the house incident to the arrest, there was a direct contradiction in setting a lower standard for arrest powers and search powers. Accordingly, the Court concluded that, before entering a dwelling house to effect an arrest, the police would require a warrant authorizing them to do so:

> 49   In my view, then, warrantless arrests in dwelling houses are in general prohibited. Prior to such an arrest, it is incumbent on the police officer to obtain judicial authorization for the arrest by obtaining a warrant to enter the dwelling house for the purpose of arrest. Such a warrant will only be authorized if there are reasonable grounds for the arrest, and reasonable grounds to believe that the person will be found at the address named, thus providing individuals' privacy interests in an arrest situation with the protection *Hunter* required with respect to searches and seizures. Requiring a warrant prior to arrest avoids the *ex post facto* analysis of the reasonableness of an intrusion that *Hunter* held should be avoided under the *Charter*; invasive arrests without a basis of reasonable and probable grounds are prevented, rather than remedied after the fact . . .

> 50   I would add that the protection of privacy does not end with a warrant; the other requirements in *Landry* for an arrest in a dwelling house must be met along with the warrant requirement. Specifically, before forcibly entering a dwelling house to make an arrest with a warrant for an indictable offence, proper announcement must be made. As Dickson C.J. stated in *Landry*, at p. 161, these additional requirements "minimize the invasiveness of arrest in a dwelling and

---

117   *Hunter*, above note 32.

permit the offender to maintain his dignity and privacy by walking to the doorway and surrendering himself."[118]

The Court did acknowledge that there were other interests which competed with the privacy interest of the homeowner. In cases of hot pursuit, for example, it would be unrealistic and unnecessary to require a warrant (see the further discussion of hot pursuit, below). The Court also raised the issue of whether exigent circumstances other than hot pursuit might override the requirement for a warrant, but did not decide the point. Ultimately, the Court concluded that the minimum *Charter* requirements for forcible entry into a dwelling house to carry out an arrest were as follows:

> 51 To summarize, in general, the following requirements must be met before an arrest for an indictable offence in a private dwelling is legal: a warrant must be obtained on the basis of reasonable and probable grounds to arrest and to believe the person sought is within the premises in question; and proper announcement must be made before entering. An exception to this rule occurs where there is a case of hot pursuit. Whether or not there is an exception for exigent circumstances generally has not been fully addressed by this Court, nor does it need to be decided in the present case given my view that exigent circumstances did not exist when the arrest was made.[119]

With its decision in *Feeney*, the Court created a need for a type of warrant which did not, at the time, exist.[120] Parliament therefore enacted sections 295 to 295.1 in order to authorize entries into dwelling houses. Primarily, the statutory scheme calls for a warrant to be obtained before the police enter a dwelling house to arrest a person. Under section 529, when an arrest warrant is initially issued, the judge or justice issuing it can authorize the officer to enter a dwelling house to execute it. In this event, there are two further requirements that must be met. First, the justice must be satisfied on reasonable grounds that

---

118 *Feeney*, above note 116 at paras. 49–50.

119 *Ibid.* at para. 51.

120 See *Feeney*, *ibid.* at para. 48, where the Court held: "If the *Code* currently fails to provide specifically for a warrant containing such prior authorization, such a provision should be read in." This was quite a remarkable position to have taken, particularly given that the Court had quite explicitly concluded in *Hunter*, above note 32 at 156 (the case prompting the change), that the *Charter* "does not in itself confer any powers." However, the Court shortly thereafter granted a re-hearing and stayed the operation of the requirement for a warrant for six months (*R. v. Feeney*, [1997] 3 S.C.R. 1008) by which time the warrant provisions had been put into the *Criminal Code*.

the person to be arrested is or will be in the dwelling house. Second, even if the warrant does authorize entry:

> the peace officer may not enter the dwelling-house unless the peace officer has, immediately before entering the dwelling-house, reasonable grounds to believe that the person to be arrested or apprehended is present in the dwelling-house.[121]

Section 529.1 deals with entry warrants obtained other than at the same time as the arrest warrant itself, namely where: 1) there is an arrest warrant but it does not already authorize entry; 2) there are grounds to arrest the person without warrant under paragraph 495(1) (a) or (b);[122] or 3) there are grounds under some Act other than the *Criminal Code* to arrest the person without a warrant. In such cases, a judge or justice may issue a warrant authorizing a peace officer to enter a dwelling house to effect the arrest. Once again, the judge or justice must be satisfied that there are reasonable grounds to believe that the person is or will be present in the dwelling house, and additional conditions can be attached to the warrant "to ensure that the entry into the dwelling-house is reasonable in the circumstances."[123]

Whether the authorization to enter is obtained at the same time as the arrest warrant or later, a peace officer may apply by telewarrant if it is impracticable to appear in person.[124] In addition, the *Code* provides for the possibility of a forcible entry to be made without a warrant in certain circumstances. First, the *Code* makes clear that it is not limiting any other authorization a peace officer might have to enter: at a minimum, this preserves the "hot pursuit" exception to the warrant requirement which was recognized in *Feeney*. In addition, the *Code* goes on to do what the Court had left unsettled in *Feeney*, that is, create an "exigent circumstances" exception. If all the other requirements are met, and it would be impracticable to obtain a warrant because of exigent circumstances, the officer can enter without a warrant. "Exigent circumstances" are then defined:

> . . . [E]xigent circumstances include circumstances in which the peace officer

---

121 *Criminal Code*, above note 61, s. 529(2).
122 Also see *ibid.*, s. 672.91, which deals with warrants relating to assessment orders or dispositions under the Mental Disorder provisions.
123 *Ibid.*, s. 529.2.
124 *Ibid.*, s. 529.5.

(a) has reasonable grounds to suspect that entry into the dwelling-house is necessary to prevent imminent bodily harm or death to any person; or

(b) has reasonable grounds to believe that evidence relating to the commission of an indictable offence is present in the dwelling-house and that entry into the dwelling-house is necessary to prevent the imminent loss or imminent destruction of the evidence.[125]

Note that the above is a non-exhaustive definition of the term; this is likely a reflection of the fact that hot pursuit is another exigent circumstance, and the statutory scheme does not affect the common law rules surrounding it. In addition, although reasonable grounds to *believe* are required in the case of the potential loss of evidence, entry to prevent imminent bodily harm or death requires only reasonable grounds to *suspect*.[126]

In the ordinary course, the warrant provisions (and the exigent circumstances exception) do not override the common law requirement for entry that the officer is required first to make prior announcement. However, section 529.4 permits the judge or justice to authorize the officer *not* to make prior announcement if at least one of two criteria is met, often referred to as a "no-knock entry." That is, the warrant can authorize omitting prior announcement if:

[T]here are reasonable grounds to believe that prior announcement of the entry would

(a) expose the peace officer or any other person to imminent bodily harm or death; or

(b) result in the imminent loss or imminent destruction of evidence relating to the commission of an indictable offence.[127]

The judge or justice must be satisfied of one of these criteria. In addition, the officer executing the warrant must also have reasonable grounds immediately before executing the warrant.[128] However, although the "reasonable grounds to believe" standard applies to both criteria when the judge is authorizing the no-knock entry, the same is not true of the officer's required belief. The officer, at the time of the entry, must have

---

125 *Ibid.*, s. 529.3(2).

126 See Heather Pringle, "Kicking in the Castle Doors: The Evolution of Exigent Circumstances" (2000) 43 Crim. L.Q. 86, for criticism of Parliament's approach to exigent circumstances in this provision.

127 *Criminal Code*, above note 61, s. 529.4(1).

128 *Ibid.*, s. 529.4(2).

reasonable grounds *to believe* in the case of the loss of evidence, but only reasonable grounds *to suspect* in the case of bodily harm or death. Exactly these same criteria apply to the officer when she is making a no-knock entry without a warrant under the exigent circumstances exception.[129] In both these cases, the standards applied to the peace officer correspond to those used in the exigent circumstances exception itself.

To summarize, the basic rule is that an officer must: 1) have authority to arrest; 2) have a warrant to enter the dwelling house; and 3) make prior announcement. However, the requirement for the warrant to enter and the obligation to make prior announcement, or even both, can be dispensed with in certain cases. The statutory scheme creates exceptions in the case of exigent circumstances, and the common law creates exceptions in the case of hot pursuit.

Various aspects of the application of these provisions have been developed by courts of appeal. It has been settled, for example, that the need for a warrant is not limited to cases where an accused is arrested in his *own* dwelling house: the issue is simply whether he is in *some* dwelling house. An accused cannot assert a *Charter* right where only a third party's right was violated: where an unreasonable search takes place in a location in which the accused has no reasonable expectation of privacy, for example.[130] However, when an accused is arrested (and in the usual course searched incident to that arrest) in a third party's house, it is the accused's own rights that have been violated.[131]

Some elaboration of the exigent circumstances exception has also taken place. First, note that this exception removes only the need for a warrant to enter: it does not eliminate the other requirements. In *Guiboche*,[132] for example, the police were investigating a murder which had occurred only hours earlier, and were searching for the accused, who had been reported as the perpetrator. The murder had been committed with a bat, and so the accused was likely to have blood stains on him. The trial judge concluded that the police fell within the exigent circumstances exception on these facts when they entered the accused's father's home. However, the Court of Appeal found that to be an error. The accused's whereabouts had been unknown and officers were look-

---

129 *Ibid.*, s. 529.4(3).
130 See *R. v. Edwards*, [1996] 1 S.C.R. 128. See also *R. v. Belnavis*, [1997] 3 S.C.R. 341 [*Belnavis*].
131 See *R. v. Adams* (2001), 203 D.L.R. (4th) 290 (Ont. C.A.). See also *R. v. Couturier*, 2004 NBCA 91 [*Couturier*], and *R. v. Guiboche*, 2004 MBCA 16 [*Guiboche*], in both of which the accused was arrested at another person's house.
132 *Guiboche, ibid.*

ing for him in various places: some had gone to his father's house as one possible location. It was not until after they had entered and been told by the accused's father that the accused was upstairs that they knew he was there. On those facts, they did not have reasonable grounds to believe that he was in the dwelling house before entering: without that precondition for entry being met, the exigent circumstances exception to obtaining a warrant was not available.

The exigent circumstances exception talks of the risk of bodily harm to "any person."[133] This phrase includes the accused himself, and so where the police have reason to think a person is suicidal, exigent circumstances could be made out.[134] Further, it is not necessary that *all* evidence might be destroyed if the police wait to obtain a warrant. In *Duong* the police entered a marijuana grow operation that they had discovered by chance and arrested the accused. The accused argued that the exigent circumstances exception did not apply, since "a commercial marihuana grow operation could not be dismantled and destroyed in the hour it would have taken" to obtain a warrant.[135] The Court of Appeal rejected this argument, noting that documents and fingerprints were found in the house linking the accused to the offence, and that this evidence could have been destroyed had the officers not entered immediately. The court characterized this evidence as "important," suggesting that the mere existence of *some* evidence in danger of destruction might not be sufficient.

It is also necessary to consider the hot pursuit exception, which is preserved by the statutory scheme. The Supreme Court noted in *Macooh* that the existence of a hot pursuit exception to the sanctity of the home was well settled at common law. It quoted *Halsbury's Laws of England*[136] to the effect that:

> [i]f a felony has been committed and the felon is followed to a house, and there is no other means of entering, any person may, it seems, break open the door of the house, to arrest the offender. This may also be done if a felony will probably be committed unless some person interferes to prevent it.
>
> If an affray occurs in the presence of a constable, and the offenders run away and are immediately pursued by the constable and they

---

133 *Criminal Code*, above note 61, s. 529.3(2)(a).
134 *R. v. Phillips*, 2006 NSCA 135.
135 *R. v. Duong*, 2002 BCCA 43 at para. 29 [*Duong*].
136 Lord Simonds, ed., *Halsbury's Laws of England*, 3d ed., vol. 10 (London: Butterworths, 1954).

enter a house, then the doors may be broken open by the constable to apprehend them in the course of the immediate pursuit.[137]

The Court also defined what is meant by "hot pursuit":

Generally, the essence of fresh pursuit is that it must be continuous pursuit conducted with reasonable diligence, so that pursuit and capture along with the commission of the offence may be considered as forming part of a single transaction.[138]

The rationale for the hot pursuit exception was neatly summarized by the Ontario Court of Appeal in *Van Puyenbroek*:

20 The court also discussed the justifications for this exception to the important principle that protects the sanctity of a private home. First, where an offender is a fugitive who has gone to his home while fleeing for the sole purpose of escaping arrest, when the police come, they are not unexpected or intruding on the person's "domestic tranquility." Second, from a practical point of view, offenders should not be encouraged to run or drive for home to seek refuge from the police, creating dangerous situations for members of the public . . . Third, the police officer may have personal knowledge of the commission of an offence justifying arrest, thereby greatly reducing the risk of error. Fourth, flight usually indicates awareness of guilt. Fifth, in some circumstances it may be difficult to identify the offender without arresting him on the spot. Sixth, evidence of the offence may be lost, such as evidence of impairment. Seventh, the offender may again flee or continue the offence while the police are waiting for him to emerge.[139]

These factors are not a checklist that must be satisfied in order for the hot pursuit exception to apply. For example, if a peace officer personally witnessed the offence, it is that much more likely that "pursuit and capture along with the commission of the offence may be considered as forming part of a single transaction."[140] It is not an absolute rule that the officer must have witnessed the offence, however.[141] An officer might arrive at the scene just after the offence has taken place, or

---

137 *Macooh*, above note 23 at para.13, quoting *Halsbury's Laws of England*, *ibid.* at 354.

138 *Macooh*, *ibid.* at para. 24, quoting Roger E. Salhany, *Canadian Criminal Procedure*, 5th ed. (Aurora, ON: Canada Law Book, 1989) at 44 [Salhany].

139 *R. v. Van Puyenbroek*, 2007 ONCA 824 at para. 20 [*Van Puyenbroek*].

140 *Macooh*, above note 23 at 817, quoting Salhany, above note 138 at 44.

141 *R. v. Haglof*, 2000 BCCA 604 [*Haglof*].

might take over a pursuit begun by someone else.[142] Nonetheless, "[i]t is a necessarily narrow exception."[143] In *Van Puyenbroek*, for example, a police officer received a report of a traffic accident and drove fifty-five kilometres to the scene; after conducting an investigation, he formed a suspicion about the accused and went to his house, did a further investigation by examining the accused's truck and speaking with the accused's wife, and only then entered the house. The trial judge found that the hot pursuit exception applied on these facts, in part by discounting the officer's travel time. The Court of Appeal overturned this conclusion, holding that, if the officer had reasonable grounds to arrest the accused before entering his house, there was no reason he could not have obtained a warrant to do so. The hot pursuit exception should not be read so broadly but rather should be limited to situations "in which the officer is literally at the heels of a suspect at the moment the suspect enters a dwelling-house."[144] It remains unsettled as to whether an officer is required to give prior notice before entering in hot pursuit, in part because they seem generally to do so, and so the issue does not arise.[145]

As a final point regarding police entry into premises, observe the limit on the relevance of the *Feeney* decision and the statutory scheme for entry warrants: it is not the only source of authority for police to enter a dwelling house. The Supreme Court observed in *Godoy* that "*Feeney* was concerned solely with when the police can enter a dwelling without a warrant to make an arrest."[146] In *Godoy* itself, the police received a 911 call that had been disconnected, and so they went to the address to investigate. The Court relied on *Waterfield* to find that the police had the authority, at common law, to force entry into the apartment to verify that there was no emergency. Similarly, in other cases peace officers have entered a home without an entry warrant and have arrested a person therein. If they did not enter with the intention of arresting, then a precondition for the entry warrant provisions will not be made out and those sections cannot be a source of authority for the entry.[147] It does not follow that the entry was unauthorized, however. In essence, the statutory scheme deals with forced entries, but not all entries are forced: the police might have been given permission to enter

---

142 *Macooh*, above note 23.
143 *Van Puyenbroek*, above note 139 at para. 32.
144 *Ibid.*
145 *Macooh*, above note 23; *Haglof*, above note 141.
146 *Godoy*, above note 46 at para. 26.
147 See *R. v. Custer*, [1984] 4 W.W.R. 133 (Sask. C.A.); *R. v. Thomas* (1991), 67 C.C.C. (3d) 81 (Nfld. C.A.).

by someone with authority to do so.[148] Some other power to enter might also exist, and might have been the reason for the entry, rather than an intention to arrest. The fact that the situation subsequently develops in a way that leads to the arrest of the accused does not mean that the scheme in sections 529–529.5 governed the entry.[149] Alternatively, it might be that the statutory scheme does not apply and no other basis for entry exists, in which case the arrest will be illegal.[150]

e) Search Incident to Arrest

The power to search incident to arrest was long recognized at common law. With its decision in *Cloutier v. Langlois*,[151] the Supreme Court affirmed its continued vitality under the *Charter*. Accordingly, it is well established that a common law power to search incident to arrest exists. That said, the Court has also recognized that the "search incident to arrest power has been framed by nebulous parameters."[152] Over a period of roughly a decade, the Court defined some features of the power, and a number of rules can be articulated with some confidence. On the other hand, there remain unanswered questions, and indeed two separate lines of authority which have never been entirely reconciled. It appears that the Court has created two slightly different "search incident to arrest" powers, one governing arrests that take place in vehicles, the other governing arrests in other circumstances. These two powers differ in only a minor way, and the Court has never explicitly said that there are two sets of rules; nonetheless, that description accurately characterizes its decisions.

We shall begin with a discussion of those aspects of the power that are settled, and leave to the end the ambiguities that remain. In *Cloutier*, the Court set out three basic rules concerning search incident to arrest:

> 1. This power does not impose a duty. The police have some discretion in conducting the search. Where they are satisfied that the law can be effectively and safely applied without a search, the police may see fit not to conduct a search. They must be in a position to assess the circumstances of each case so as to determine whether a search meets the underlying objectives.
>
> 2. The search must be for a valid objective in pursuit of the ends of criminal justice, such as the discovery of an object that may be a threat

---

148 See, for example, *Couturier*, above note 131. See also *Guiboche*, above note 131.
149 See, for example, *R. v. Laliberte*, 2007 SKCA 7.
150 See *Van Puyenbroek*, above note 139.
151 *Cloutier v. Langlois*, [1990] 1 S.C.R. 158 [*Cloutier*].
152 *R. v. Golden*, 2001 SCC 83 at para. 23 [*Golden*].

to the safety of the police, the accused or the public, or that may facilitate escape or act as evidence against the accused. The purpose of the search must not be unrelated to the objectives of the proper administration of justice, which would be the case for example if the purpose of the search was to intimidate, ridicule or pressure the accused in order to obtain admissions.

3. The search must not be conducted in an abusive fashion and in particular, the use of physical or psychological constraint should be proportionate to the objectives sought and the other circumstances of the situation. A search which does not meet these objectives could be characterized as unreasonable and unjustified at common law.[153]

More succinctly, the Court said in *Stillman*:

Three conditions must be satisfied in order for a search to be validly undertaken pursuant to the common law power of search incident to a lawful arrest. First, the arrest must be lawful . . . Second, the search must have been conducted as an "incident" to the lawful arrest. To these almost self-evident conditions must be added a third, which applies to all searches undertaken by police: the manner in which the search is carried out must be reasonable.[154]

Other aspects of the power have been settled. For example, the authority to search flows directly from the arrest itself: no separate reasonable grounds for the search are required. Indeed, this is what is meant by saying that the search is "incident to" the arrest: its legality stands or falls with the arrest. If the arrest is valid, that justifies a search: if the arrest is invalid, then so too is the search. As the Court has said:

No search, no matter how reasonable, may be upheld under this common law power where the arrest which gave rise to it was arbitrary or otherwise unlawful.[155]

Because the accused has been arrested, she is, of course, entitled to be informed of the right to counsel. However, the obligation to hold off from obtaining evidence until an accused has had a chance to exercise

---

153   *Cloutier*, above note 151 at 186.
154   *Stillman*, above note 33 at para. 27.
155   *Ibid*. See also *R. v. Caslake*, [1998] 1 S.C.R. 51 at para. 13 [*Caslake*]: "[S]ince the legality of the search is derived from the legality of arrest, if the arrest is later found to be invalid, the search will be also."

that right does not mean that police are unable to search incident to arrest: they can do so immediately in any case.[156]

Like the power to arrest itself, search incident to arrest has both a subjective and an objective requirement. Although the search does not require reasonable grounds, it must be, as the Court said in *Cloutier*, "for a valid objective in pursuit of the ends of criminal justice."[157] We shall discuss at greater length below exactly what those objectives are, but for the moment it is sufficient to note that the subjective requirement means that the officer must personally think that his search is aimed at one of those objectives. This requirement is related to the first criterion in *Cloutier*, that each search is a discretionary one, based on an assessment of the circumstances of the case.

This is a fine line the Court is drawing, though that does not mean it isn't worth the effort. On the one hand, the power to search flows directly from the arrest; but on the other hand, the search should not be conducted automatically. In effect, police might well be able to decide, each time, "I will now conduct a search": what they *cannot* do is decide in advance "every time I arrest someone I will conduct a search." A search that is simply conducted in accordance with a general policy to search will not satisfy the subjective criterion: "the police must be able to explain . . . why they searched."[158]

In *Caslake*,[159] for example, the police officer searched the vehicle but testified that he had done so in order to inventory its contents. In that event, the Court held, even though a search incident to arrest was objectively justifiable, that was not subjectively what the officer was doing, and so the search was unlawful. Similarly, in *Rutten* the police would have been able to conduct a search incident to the accused's arrest for having open liquor in his vehicle; however, their actual purpose in searching was to look for drugs, and so the search did not qualify as a search incident to the arrest.[160]

In addition, any search incident to arrest must be objectively justified: it must be the case that a reasonable person would agree that a search involving one of the goals of search incident to arrest was justified.

A broad range of searches is allowed under this power. Frisk searches and fingerprinting are permitted,[161] and the power has been

---

156 R. v. *Debot*, [1989] 2 S.C.R. 1140 [*Debot*]. See also R. v. *Lewis*, 2007 NSCA 2.

157 *Cloutier*, above note 151 at 186.

158 *Caslake*, above note 155 at para. 25.

159 *Caslake*, above note 155.

160 R. v. *Rutten*, 2006 SKCA 17 [*Rutten*].

161 R. v. *Beare*, [1988] 2 S.C.R. 387, 55 D.L.R. (4th) 481; *Cloutier*, above note 151.

held to include the ability to perform a gunshot residue test on an accused by "dabbing" his hands with two-sided tape to get samples.[162] As well, vehicle searches are often permissible and can be quite extensive. Searches of vehicles in which police removed loose door panels, or in which they took interior and exterior measurements of a truck and then partly disassembled the inside to find a false compartment, have been found to fall within the scope of the power.[163]

On the other hand, there are limits to the power. It does not entitle police officers to conduct invasive searches of the person. In *Stillman*, for example, the police took hair samples from the accused (including pubic hair samples), obtained buccal swabs, and undertook a procedure to make dental impressions, all without the accused's consent. The Supreme Court held that these procedures were not permissible under the search incident to arrest power.[164] In addition, although in principle strip searches incident to arrest are permissible in some circumstances, the Court has imposed additional requirements around them: see the discussion below.

There are no strict temporal limits on when a search incident to arrest can take place. Obviously, it must be relatively close in time to the actual arrest, though the Court held in *Caslake* that a search of a vehicle six hours later could still have been incident to the arrest, given the limited number of officers available. It has been suggested that a search incident to arrest can even precede the arrest itself, provided that grounds for arrest already existed. This point has not been settled by the Supreme Court of Canada, however.[165]

There are also no strict spatial limits to a search incident to arrest, though there are some guidelines. The search might well include an accused's vehicle: where a search of the accused turns up both drugs and money and he has been stopped in an area known for drug trafficking, searching the car for more drugs is permissible.[166] Searches of items in a vehicle, such as reading through documents in a briefcase, might

---

162 R. v. *Backhouse* (2005), 194 C.C.C. (3d) 1 (Ont. C.A.) [*Backhouse*].

163 See R. v. *Smellie* (1994), 95 C.C.C. (3d) 9 (B.C.C.A.) [*Smellie*]. See also R. v. *Nolet*, 2010 SCC 24 [*Nolet*].

164 *Stillman*, above note 33.

165 The Ontario Court of Appeal reached this conclusion in R. v. *Debot* (1987), 30 C.C.C. (3d) 207 (Ont. C.A.). The Supreme Court of Canada affirmed the decision in *Debot*, above note 156, but Wilson J. (writing the majority decision on this point) found the search in question lawful based on the *Food and Drugs Act* and concluded that it was unnecessary to decide whether the search could also be justified as incidental to a valid arrest.

166 R. v. *Polashek* (1999), 45 O.R. (3d) 434 (C.A.) [*Polashek*].

also fall within a permissible search.[167] Indeed, there is some authority (though the point seems not to have reached any Court of Appeal) suggesting that police can search the electronic contents of a BlackBerry or a computer incident to an arrest if the physical object is seized.[168] On the other hand, a contrived arrest at a particular location as a pretext for searching that location is not allowed.[169]

However, searches of the home are, generally speaking, not permissible incident to an arrest. Consistent with the finding in *Feeney* that the home is entitled to a high degree of privacy protection in the arrest context, the Ontario Court of Appeal held in *Golub* that

> searches of a home as an incident of an arrest, like entries of a home to effect an arrest, are now generally prohibited subject to exceptional circumstances where the law enforcement interest is so compelling that it overrides the individual's right to privacy within the home.[170]

In *Golub* itself, the accused was arrested four and a half metres from his apartment door. However, the police had reasonable grounds to believe that there was a submachine gun in his apartment, and reason to suspect that another person might be there, either an accomplice or someone hurt. In those circumstances, the court held that there was an exception to the general rule and entry into the apartment to search incident to the arrest was permissible. More frequently, when an accused is actually arrested in a house or apartment, the police should conduct a minimal search for safety purposes, but, even if they discover evidence of an offence (such as a grow operation), they should seek a warrant to conduct any further search.[171]

Yet, just as there are no strict spatial limits, there are equally no spatial entitlements. For example, although vehicle searches are often permissible, it is quite explicitly *not* the rule that the police can always search a vehicle incident to an arrest. In *Caslake* the Supreme Court specifically rejected the notion that there was a "vehicle inventory search" exception to the rule that warrantless searches violate section

---

167 *R. v. Mohamad* (2004), 69 O.R. (3d) 481 (C.A.).
168 See *R. v. Giles*, 2007 BCSC 1147, in which the BlackBerry was seized in Kelowna but analyzed in Ottawa two months later, but the trial judge found that these facts did not interfere with the status of the search as one incident to the arrest. See also *R. v. Lefave*, [2003] O.T.C. 872 (S.C.J.).
169 See *Smellie*, above note 163, citing *R. v. Lim (No. 2)* (1990), 1 C.R.R. (2d) 136 (Ont. Ct. J.) [*Lim*]. See also *R. v. Chubak*, 2009 ABCA 8 at para. 22 [*Chubak*]: "[P]retextual searches will meet neither the subjective not [*sic*] the objective elements of the *Caslake* test."
170 *R. v. Golub* (1997), 117 C.C.C. (3d) 193 at para. 41 (Ont. C.A.) [*Golub*].
171 See, for example, *R. v. Wu*, 2008 BCCA 7.

8.[172] In *Bulmer*, for example, the accused was arrested in his car when a Canadian Police Information Centre check determined that there was a warrant for his arrest based on an unpaid seatbelt ticket. The officer then searched the vehicle, claiming that he did so to see whether he could find a receipt for the ticket, which the accused said he thought he had paid. The officer also suggested that he was searching for safety purposes, though the accused was at the time locked in the back of the police vehicle and other officers were on hand.[173]

What really settles both the spatial and temporal limits is the question of whether the search is truly "incidental" to the arrest. That is, although no reasonable grounds for the search are required, it must be both subjectively and objectively related to one of the legitimate purposes of search incident to arrest. Broadly speaking, there are two such purposes: safety and evidence relating to the offence for which the accused was arrested. Hence, a search that cannot plausibly be said to serve one of those two goals is not legitimately a search incident to arrest. As the Court noted in *Caslake*, it is not permissible to search the trunk of a car if the arrest is for a traffic violation: nothing could be found there which would be relevant to proving the offence.[174] Similarly, if a known drug offender is arrested for some non-drug-related offence, it is not permissible to search that accused for narcotics.[175]

That is not to say that evidence of other offences would not be admissible: it would be. If an accused is validly searched incident to arrest and evidence of some other crime is discovered — possession of a narcotic, for example — the accused can also be arrested for and charged with that offence.[176] That is quite distinct, however, from searching for evidence of some other crime.[177]

The potential confusion, and the area in which ambiguity still exists, is that the Court has not been entirely consistent in its statements about what qualifies as the "legitimate purposes" of a search incident to arrest. There is no question that it is legitimate to search

---

172   *Caslake*, above note 155 at para. 30. The Court reaffirmed this point in *Nolet*, above note 163 at para. 30.

173   *R. v. Bulmer*, 2005 SKCA 90 at para. 16 [*Bulmer*]: "[T]here is no automatic right to search a vehicle incident to arrest." See also *R. v. Luc*, 2004 SKCA 117, where the police claimed to have searched a rubber tub in the trunk of the car in order to be certain of the accused's identity.

174   This is in fact exactly the scenario in *Bulmer*, *ibid.*, which arose well after *Caslake*, above note 155.

175   See *Golden*, above note 152.

176   See, for example, *Polashek*, above note 166. See also *R. v. Alkins*, 2007 ONCA 264; and *Chubak*, above note 169.

177   *Rutten*, above note 160.

for safety purposes. There is also no question that a search for evidence which is in danger of going out of existence is also a legitimate objective. The question is whether a broader search, for evidence that is in no danger of going out of existence but that could be used at trial, is also a legitimate objective of search incident to arrest.

In *Stillman*, the Court noted this precise issue and acknowledged that many lower courts had adopted the view that search incident to arrest was not limited to obtaining evidence which was in danger of going out of existence. It then made clear that it did not, on the facts of that case, accept such an expansion of the power:

> Searches made incidentally to an arrest are justified so that the ar-
> resting officer can be assured that the person arrested is not armed
> or dangerous and seizures are justified to preserve evidence that may
> go out of existence or be otherwise lost . . . the power to search and
> seize does not extend beyond those purposes.[178]

However, one year later in *Caslake*, the Court said:

> [T]he three main purposes of search incident to arrest are ensuring
> the safety of the police and public, the protection of evidence from
> destruction at the hands of the arrestee or others, and the discovery
> of evidence which can be used at the arrestee's trial.[179]

This is, of course, the opposite of the position that the Court had taken in *Stillman*, though that point was not acknowledged.[180]

Three years afterwards, in *Golden*, the Court appeared to return to the position it had set out in *Stillman*:

> The reasonableness of a search for evidence is governed by the need
> to preserve the evidence and to prevent its disposal by the arrest-
> ee.[181]

Once again, the Court did not acknowledge the ambiguity created.

---

178 *Stillman*, above note 33 at para. 41, quoting from *R. v. Paul* (1994), 155 N.B.R.
     (2d) 195 at 203 (C.A.).
179 *Caslake*, above note 155 at para. 19.
180 See *Stillman*, above note 33 at para. 39, in which the Court distinguished
     between a search of the person and a search of a vehicle, saying of the latter:
     "This type of search is not in issue in this case and I need not express any
     opinion with regard to them." See also *Caslake*, above note 155, which concerns
     a vehicle search, and so referring back to this proviso would have made sense.
181 *Golden*, above note 152 at para. 93.

What seems to be the solution here is the different contexts of the searches in each case. *Stillman* and *Golden*, the two cases adopting the narrower view, concerned searches of the person; *Caslake* involved a search of the accused's vehicle. Indeed, the Court noted in *Stillman* that the lower court decisions expanding the search incident to arrest power all concerned vehicles. The explanation that best fits the cases, then, is that there are two slightly different sets of rules for search incident to arrest. If a person is being searched, then only a search for evidence that is in danger of going out of existence is permissible; if a vehicle is being searched, then the broader purpose of obtaining evidence for use at trial also arises. The Court has not clearly stated that this is the rule, but it is an accurate characterization of the Court's practice.[182] It is also how courts of appeal have tended to behave. In *Tontarelli*, for example, the New Brunswick Court of Appeal concluded that there was no need for exigent circumstances before a vehicle could be searched incident to arrest.[183] On the other hand, in *Backhouse* the Ontario Court of Appeal stressed the need for a gunshot residue test to be done quickly, while the residue potentially still remained on an accused's hands, in author-izing that form of testing as a search incident to arrest.[184]

It would be helpful if this ambiguity were clarified, so that it would be more apparent that there are in fact two sets of rules, or at least two different sets of considerations. An explicit discussion would also help clarify the boundary between the two sets of rules. As *Stillman* and *Golden* make plain, there is a higher than normal expectation of privacy in one's person. On the other hand, the Supreme Court has made clear that there is a *lower* expectation of privacy than normal in a vehicle.[185] That said, the justification for a search incident to arrest is the enhanced state interest, not any diminution in the accused's pri-vacy interest, so perhaps that consideration is not relevant.[186] Even so, there are many searches that fall "in between" a search of the person and a vehicle search, so it would be helpful to know where the dividing line falls. Are searches of the person the "special case," or is it vehicle searches that are the exception? There are authorities that would allow one to argue either way.

---

182   See *Stillman*, above note 33 at para. 39, in which the Court said, while dis-tinguishing its facts from the vehicle search cases, that "completely different concerns arise where the search and seizure infringes upon a person's bodily integrity, which may constitute the ultimate affront to human dignity."

183   *R. v. Tontarelli*, 2009 NBCA 52 at paras. 7 and 35–51.

184   *Backhouse*, above note 162 at para. 154.

185   See *Belnavis*, above note 130.

186   See *Caslake*, above note 155 at para. 17.

Explicitly having a stricter rule in the case of all searches of the person would be consistent with the approach the Supreme Court took in *Golden* to strip searches. In that case the Court concluded that strip searches could, in certain circumstances, be conducted incident to an arrest. However, it also stressed that strip searches "represent a significant invasion of privacy and are often a humiliating, degrading and traumatic experience for individuals subject to them,"[187] Accordingly, it attached additional restrictions beyond those that apply to other searches incident to arrest. First, it held that a strip search incident to arrest, unlike other searches incident to arrest, required reasonable grounds justifying the search itself, not just the arrest. Further, it held that strip searches must in most cases be conducted at the police station, not in the field. Only if there were exigent circumstances (in addition to reasonable grounds) could a strip search take place before going to the police station. This amounts to saying that, of the legitimate purposes of safety and gathering evidence, only the former could lead to a strip search in the field:

> Strip searches conducted in the field could only be justified where there is a demonstrated necessity and urgency to search for weapons or objects that could be used to threaten the safety of the accused, the arresting officers or other individuals.[188]

f) Search during an Investigative Detention

The Supreme Court of Canada created a common law power of investigative detention with its decision in *Mann*: see the discussion of this case, and this power, in Chapter 3. At the same time, it also relied on the *Waterfield* test[189] to create a common law search power associated with such detentions. It referred to this power as "search *incident to* an investigative detention"[190] but, for reasons that will shortly become apparent, that is not really an accurate name.

It is easiest to define the investigative detention search power by the ways in which it differs from search incident to arrest. As noted above, there is some lingering uncertainty over whether searching for any evidence or only for evidence in danger of going out of existence is a legitimate objective of a search incident to arrest. That confusion does not arise in this context: during an investigate detention, the only permissible basis for conducting a search relates to safety concerns, not

---

187 *Golden*, above note 152 at para. 83.
188 *Ibid.* at para. 102.
189 See Section B(1)(c), above in this chapter, for more on this topic.
190 *Mann*, above note 10 at paras. 37 and 40.

the gathering of evidence. In *Mann*, the Court relied on the *Waterfield* test, which meant that any interference had to "involve a justified use of a police power associated with a general duty to search in relation to the protection of life and property."[191] A power to search would not automatically exist, it stressed, but sometimes police would be entitled to search a detained person for reasons of safety:

> The general duty of officers to protect life may, in some circumstances, give rise to the power to conduct a pat-down search incident to an investigative detention. Such a search power does not exist as a matter of course; the officer must believe on reasonable grounds that his or her own safety, or the safety of others, is at risk.[192]

Note that the search power is initially limited to a pat-down search, and no more than that. The facts of *Mann* itself make that point particularly clear. The accused was stopped near the scene of a suspected break-in and the police patted him down. Having detected something soft in a pocket, they searched further to find what it was: it transpired that it was marijuana, and so he was charged with possession. The Court found that the evidence had been unlawfully obtained. Although the initial pat-down search was legal, feeling something soft did not give rise to any concerns about safety. In that event there was no justification for searching further, and so the police acted without authority in reaching into the accused's pocket.

The second way in which these types of searches differ from search incident to arrest is with regard to the standard required to justify one. As was noted above, search incident to arrest is available automatically upon arrest. It is a discretionary decision and the officer searching must be able to point to the way in which the search is related to one of the legitimate objectives, but no separate reasonable grounds are required for the search. If an officer wants to search incident to an arrest for safety reasons, it is not necessary for her to show reasonable grounds to believe that such a search is necessary: the reasonable grounds for the arrest justify the search.

In the case of an investigative detention, that is not the case. Rather, the Court concluded that reasonable grounds to believe that the search is necessary must be shown. It is tempting to say that "separate" reasonable grounds for the search must be shown, but of course part of the point here is that the detention itself did not require reasonable grounds, only reasonable suspicion.

---

191 *Ibid.* at para. 39.
192 *Ibid.* at para. 40.

Three observations should be made. First, one can argue that this approach is perfectly in line with the Court's approach to section 8 and unreasonable searches generally: reasonable grounds to believe should exist somewhere if the search is to be justified, and so, if they do not arise in the context of the detention, then they must arise independently.

Second, though, one can equally argue that this is a contradictory approach for the Court to have taken. As James Stribopoulos points out, the standard that has been set for this search is equivalent to that set for an arrest, which as a practical matter is hard to reconcile with the fact that the detention was based only on reasonable suspicion:

> [t]he judgment in *Mann* indicates that a protective pat-down search is only permitted where a police officer has "reasonable grounds to believe" that his or her safety or that of others is at risk. This language seems to import the standard for conventional arrests, which makes little sense. If the police have such grounds, they could arrest a suspect on a charge of weapons dangerous and then conduct a far more probing search.[193]

In practice, the application of the reasonable grounds standard can seem to be a bit problematic. In *Mann*, for example, the Court found that there were reasonable grounds on the basis that

> [T]here was a logical possibility that the appellant, suspected on reasonable grounds of having recently committed a break-and-enter, was in possession of break-and-enter tools, which could be used as weapons. The encounter also occurred just after midnight and there were no other people in the area.[194]

A "logical possibility" would not normally be seen as sufficient to meet the reasonable grounds standard. In addition, the logical possibility of the accused having break-and-enter tools itself hinges on him being the person who had committed the break and enter: by definition the police did *not* have reasonable grounds to believe that.[195]

Finally, note that it is because reasonable grounds are required that this power ought not really to be referred to as "search incident to in-

---

193 James Stribopoulos, "The Limits of Judicially Created Police Powers: Investigative Detention after *Mann*" (2007) 52 Crim. L.Q. 299 at 311 [footnotes omitted].
194 *Mann*, above note 10 at para. 48.
195 See, in contrast, *Duong*, above note 135, where a search incident to investigative detention was found to be justified because the accused was found with an apparently stolen stereo with its wires cut. The court there held that since the wires had been cut, it was reasonable to believe that the accused had a knife.

vestigative detention." The point of a search being "incident to" an arrest is the fact that it stands or falls with the arrest and requires no independent reasonable grounds. That is not true of searches during an investigative detention.

2) The Importance of Police Purpose

An issue that arises in a variety of contexts around police powers is police purpose. That is, police are given a variety of powers, both by statute and at common law. In either case courts interpret those powers as having been given to police for a particular reason, and they try to interpret those powers in a way that will balance the state's needs against individual liberty. However, police do not necessarily have that same goal in mind: rather, they can be inclined simply to use the powers they have been given to achieve their goals, without necessarily having regard to the underlying purpose of those powers.[196] Accordingly, courts do, at least in some cases, find themselves obliged to put particular stress on the purpose that is in an officer's mind at the time she acts. As the Supreme Court noted in *Mellenthin*:

> Check stop programs result in the arbitrary detention of motorists. The programs are justified as a means aimed at reducing the terrible toll of death and injury so often occasioned by impaired drivers or by dangerous vehicles. The primary aim of the program is thus to check for sobriety, licences, ownership, insurance and the mechanical fitness of cars. The police use of check stops should not be extended beyond these aims. Random stop programs must not be turned into a means of conducting either an unfounded general inquisition or an unreasonable search.[197]

In part, this is reflected in the simple requirement that many powers — for example, to arrest, to detain, to search — have both subjective and objective components. Typically, it is the objective components that are in dispute (see the discussion of reasonable grounds, below) but that does not mean that the subjective component is unimportant.

---

196 See, for example, *R. v. Wynter*, 2005 ONCJ 516 at para. 29:

> In my view, a review of Halman's evidence gives rise to a conclusion that he really had no articulable cause. And he basically concedes this. He says that he would have stopped and investigated even if Mr. Wynter had not fled. He said that his real concerns were drugs, not the *Highway Traffic Act*. The *Highway Traffic Act*, to him, seems to be some kind of a tool in his tool kit that permits him to stop people.

197 *Mellenthin*, above note 16 at 624.

In *Feeney*, for example, police were found not to have made a legal arrest in part because the officer acknowledged in his testimony that he did not subjectively think he had grounds to arrest: that alone made the arrest illegal, whatever the conclusion on the objective test.[198] Similarly in *Caslake*, the Court found that a search incident to arrest of the accused's vehicle would have been objectively reasonable. The officer who had searched the car, however, testified that he was performing an inventory search, not a search incident to arrest: in that event, the search was not legal.[199]

Purpose can matter in other ways. For example, the power to search can arise in connection with both arrests and detentions. In the case of arrests, police are entitled to search either for the purpose of discovering evidence or to protect officer safety. A search incident to an investigative detention, on the other hand, can be based only on safety concerns. The result is that the officer's purpose can determine the legality or not of the search: a search conducted for the purpose of discovering evidence will violate the *Charter* in the case of an investigative detention, where the same search would be permitted if it were for the purpose of officer safety.[200]

Purpose can play other roles relevant to arrest or detention, including helping to determine whether a detention has occurred at all. As the Supreme Court noted in *Grant*:

> [G]eneral inquiries by a patrolling officer present no threat to freedom of choice. On the other hand, such inquiries can escalate into

---

198 *Feeney*, above note 116.

199 See generally *Caslake*, above note 155. But see *R. v. Latimer*, [1997] 1 S.C.R. 217 [*Latimer*], in which the police had decided not to arrest the accused but merely to take him in for questioning: that is, they appear to have decided to do something they had no power to do. The accused claimed a violation of his s. 9 right to be free from arbitrary detention. The Court rejected this claim on the basis that there had been a "*de facto* arrest." It held that "notwithstanding what the *intention* of the officers may have been, their conduct had the *effect* of putting Mr. Latimer under arrest" (*Latimer*, *ibid.* at para. 24 [emphasis in original]). Since that arrest was also found to be legal, it is a little hard to reconcile this result with the normal emphasis the Court places on intention. Possibly the answer lies somewhere in the fact that the police did subjectively believe they had reasonable grounds for arrest, even though they did not subjectively intend to arrest: however, it is not entirely apparent that this would distinguish the case from *Caslake*. See the further discussion of this case below in Chapter 4, Section C(1)(b).

200 *Mann*, above note 10 at paras. 37 and 43. An officer cannot merely assert "it was for safety," of course, and there must be reasonable grounds supporting that claim.

situations where the focus shifts from general community-oriented concern to suspicion of a particular individual. Focussed suspicion, in and of itself, does not turn the encounter in [sic] a detention. What matters is how the police, based on that suspicion, interacted with the subject . . . The police must be mindful that, depending on how they act and what they say, the point may be reached where a reasonable person, in the position of that individual, would conclude he or she is not free to choose to walk away or decline to answer questions.[201]

On the other hand, the majority in *Grant* did not let police purpose be the controlling factor settling whether an accused was detained; rather, that question was to be settled by looking at whether "the reasonable person in the individual's circumstances would conclude that he or she had been deprived by the state of the liberty of choice."[202]

Various courts have also noted that an improper purpose can vitiate what would otherwise be legitimate police action. The Supreme Court has observed that an arrest that would otherwise be lawful might be rendered invalid if it were "made because a police officer was biased towards a person of a different race, nationality or colour, or that there was a personal enmity between a police officer directed towards the person arrested."[203] Similarly, stopping a vehicle might be found to violate the *Charter*, even if the power to do so existed, if the circumstances supported the conclusion that the stop power was misused and was merely a pretext.[204] It has also been held that, even though a search incident to arrest can include the vehicle in which the accused was arrested, that power could not be used if the time and place of the arrest were contrived in order to justify the vehicle search.[205]

---

201 *Grant*, above note 12 at para. 41.
202 *Ibid.* at para. 44. Also, the Court noted that "the subjective intentions of the police are not determinative" (*ibid.* at para. 32).
203 *R. v. Storrey*, [1990] 1 S.C.R. 241 at 251 [*Storrey*]. See also *R. v. Byfield* (2005), 74 O.R. (3d) 206 at para. 21 (C.A.) [*Byfield*], referring to a detention not being "undermined by improper purposes."
204 See *R. v. Calderon* (2004), 188 C.C.C. (3d) 481 at para. 67 (Ont. C.A.) [*Calderon*].
205 See *Lim*, above note 169 at paras. 49–50. But see *Stillman*, above note 33 at paras. 9 and 29, where it appears that the police arrested the accused on a second occasion for the same offence primarily in order to search him incident to that arrest. The Supreme Court does not comment one way or the other on this aspect of the police's behaviour or whether it was acceptable, but this could be because it found *Charter* violations on other grounds in relation to all the evidence gathered. Not permitting warrantless arrests for the purpose of obtaining evidence would be consistent with the way in which the ability of a justice to issue a summons has been interpreted. If the primary purpose of compelling the accused to attend court has already been satisfied in some other

However, the effect of this emphasis on purpose is muted by several other rules. First, although the justification for a search might rest on having the proper purpose, that does not mean that the ultimate scope of the search is limited by that purpose. For example, a police officer can search incident to an investigative detention only in order to try to discover a weapon; but, if an officer is searching for that purpose and in fact finds narcotics, that discovery will justify laying a possession charge against the accused and the narcotics will be admissible. More generally, so long as an officer is legally searching for some purpose, whatever evidence is found will normally be admissible, whether it related to that purpose or not.[206] Further, even if the search is unconstitutional, that does not necessarily mean the evidence will be excluded. In *Caslake*, for example, although the search violated the accused's section 8 rights because the subjective test was not met, the evidence was not excluded. One factor leading to the admission of the evidence was precisely that the objective test had been met, whatever the officer's subjective state of mind.

Finally, "police purpose" in the detention context is not as central as it might be. This can most easily be seen by contrasting the rule in this context to that in the search context.

When it comes to searches, the Supreme Court has held that different rules should govern different contexts. For example, in the criminal law context, *Canada (Combines Investigation Act Director of Investigation & Research) v. Southam Inc.* establishes that a search conducted without a warrant is *prima facie* unreasonable. However, there are many other circumstances in which individuals are required to provide information. Many of these are simple regulatory contexts, such as providing audit information with regard to income taxes. In those contexts, the panoply of procedural protections that are appropriate to criminal law are not required: there is no warrant requirement in the case of a tax audit, for example. In essence, the greater the potential consequences to the individual from the information being made available to the state, the greater the procedural protections provided.

One obvious danger of this situation, of course, is that the state could use powers created for one purpose in order to gather information to be used for another: investigators might use tax-audit powers to help produce evidence for a criminal fraud investigation, for example.

---

way, a justice cannot issue a summons for the purpose of requiring the accused to attend for purposes of the *Identification of Criminals Act*, R.S.C 1985, c. I-1: see *Re Michelsen* (1983), 4 C.C.C. (3d) 371, 33 C.R. (3d) 285 (Man. Q.B.).

206 See, for example, *R. v. Ferris* (1998), 162 D.L.R. (4th) 87 (B.C.C.A.) [*Ferris*]; *R. v. Favorite* (2008), 57 C.R. (6th) 183 (Ont. S.C.J.); or *R. v. Asp*, 2008 BCSC 794.

In that event the individual would not be receiving the appropriate level of protection. To guard against that possibility, in the search context the Supreme Court has created the "predominant purpose" test: where the predominant purpose of a particular inquiry is the determination of penal liability, investigators are no longer allowed to use regulatory powers.[207]

The Supreme Court seems to have concluded that the same rule does *not* apply in the detention context. The issue is what should happen when a stop power created for one purpose is used in pursuit of another purpose. More specifically, when police have two purposes for the stop, one proper and one improper, does the proper purpose save the search or does the improper one render it a *Charter* violation?

Courts of appeal had disagreed over this question. A Saskatchewan Court of Appeal decision, *Ladouceur*, had held that combining two purposes in this way would result in an unlawful detention:

> 66   Why cannot the two aims co-exist? The notion that in conducting a check-stop a police officer can neatly compartmentalize the lawful aim separately from the unlawful one and not be influenced or affected by the latter is, in my respectful view, stretching reality to a breaking point. (This case amply illustrates this point.) Furthermore it is important not to encourage the establishment of check-stops where a nominally lawful aim is but a plausible facade for an unlawful aim.[208]

In contrast, the Ontario Court of Appeal had held in *Brown v. Durham Regional Police Force* that, as long as the police had *a* legitimate reason for making a stop, the fact that they also had other purposes for which they would not have been permitted to make the stop did not matter:

> 30   The trial judge rejected the submission that other purposes in addition to highway traffic concerns rendered the stops unlawful. . . .
>
> 31   I agree with this conclusion as long as the other purposes motivating the stop are not themselves improper. For example, the police are entitled on a s. 216(1) stop to require drivers to produce their licences. That requirement is consistent with the highway safety concerns which underlie the power granted by the section. In addition to ensuring that the driver is properly licensed, the police may wish to identify the driver for other purposes. It may be, as in this case, that

---

207 See *R. v. Jarvis*, 2002 SCC 73 [*Jarvis*].
208 *R. v. Ladouceur*, 2002 SKCA 73 at para. 66 [*Ladouceur* (2002)].

the police are interested in knowing the identity of all those who are connected with what they believe to be organized criminal activity. The gathering of police intelligence is well within the ongoing police duty to investigate criminal activity. As long as the additional police purpose is not improper and does not entail an infringement on the liberty or security of the detained person beyond that contemplated by the purpose animating s. 216(1) of the *HTA* [Highway Traffic Act], I see no reason for declaring that a legitimate police interest beyond highway safety concerns should taint the lawfulness of the stop and detention.[209]

In *Nolet*, the Supreme Court turned to consider this question, though their discussion is framed around the legality of the search conducted pursuant to a highway traffic act stop, rather than the legality of the stop itself.[210]

In that case an RCMP officer had stopped a tractor trailer and after some questioning of the occupants had searched it. The trial judge acknowledged that there were reasons for the officer to search connected to the improper registration offences, but held that that had not in fact been his motivating factor: instead, the trial judge held, the officer's primary purpose had been to search for evidence of a criminal offence. The trial judge had therefore held that the search violated section 8 of the *Charter*. The Supreme Court disagreed, upholding the order for a new trial issued by the Saskatchewan Court of Appeal.

One the one hand the Court recognised the legitimacy of the concern raised in *Ladouceur*.[211] They agreed that highway traffic powers could not be used as a pretext, accepting that "it is important not to encourage the establishment of checkstops where a nominally lawful aim is but a plausible facade for an unlawful aim".[212] On the facts, however, they distinguished *Nolet*, holding that the highway traffic stop powers were not merely used as a ruse: those concerns were among the ones genuinely in the officer's mind.

They went on, then, to reject the "predominant purpose" approach to the use of those powers. They held that police officers were likely to be interested in both criminal and provincial infractions most of the time, and so the existence of some purpose outside the regulatory one

---

209 *Durham*, above note 104 at paras. 30 and 31.
210 *Nolet*, above note 163. In the interests of disclosure, note that Glen Luther, one of the authors of this book, was also one of the counsel for Nolet in front of the Supreme Court.
211 *Ladouceur* (2002), above note 208.
212 *Nolet*, above note 163 at para. 36, quoting *Ladouceur* (2002), above note 208 at para. 66.

did not invalidate the search. Rather, the issue was whether there was still some authority for the search. They held:

> I agree with Wilkinson J.A. that the question is not "determining which purpose is predominate or subordinate" (para. 85). As long as there is a continuing regulatory purpose on which to ground the exercise of the regulatory power, the issue is whether the officer's search of the duffle bag infringed the reasonable expectations of privacy of the appellants.[213]

The Court also rejected the argument that the approach in *Jarvis*, where a question of income tax audit powers being used for a criminal investigation arose, was analogous. In *Jarvis* the Court had spoken about "crossing the Rubicon" in moving from an audit to a criminal investigation, noting that a higher level of *Charter* protection applied in the latter situation. In this case, they held, "the context was always penal" since the initial stop concerned a provincial offence.[214]

3) Racial Profiling

One particular aspect of police purpose worth singling out for separate discussion is the issue of racial profiling. In various contexts the phrase might be taken to mean different things,[215] but in the context of powers of arrest, and particularly detention, the essence of it has been explained by the Ontario Court of Appeal:

> 7 There is no dispute about what racial profiling means. In its factum, the appellant defined it compendiously: "Racial profiling involves the targeting of individual members of a particular racial group, on the basis of the supposed criminal propensity of the entire group" and then quoted a longer definition offered by the African Canadian Legal Clinic in an earlier case, *R. v. Richards* (1999), 26 C.R. (5th) 286 (Ont. C.A.), as set forth in the reasons of Rosenberg J.A. at p. 295:
>
> > Racial profiling is criminal profiling based on race. Racial or colour profiling refers to that phenomenon whereby certain criminal activity is attributed to an identified group in society on the basis of race or colour resulting in the targeting of individual members of that group. In this context, race is illegitimately used as a proxy for the

---

213 *Nolet, ibid.* at para. 41.
214 *Ibid.* at para. 45.
215 Further discussion of profiling is found below in this section.

criminality or general criminal propensity of an entire racial group.

8   The attitude underlying racial profiling is one that may be consciously or unconsciously held. That is, the police officer need not be an overt racist. His or her conduct may be based on subconscious racial stereotyping.[216]

Racial profiling is a frustratingly illusive phenomenon in criminal law. There is no dispute that it is an objectionable process. The Supreme Court has observed in both the arrest and the detention contexts that a racial motive will override the fact that a legitimate power might otherwise have existed if used for the proper reason. In *Storrey*, for example, the Court held:

> [T]here is no indication that the arrest was made because a police officer was biased towards a person of a different race, nationality or colour, or that there was a personal enmity between a police officer directed towards the person arrested. These factors, if established, might have the effect of rendering invalid an otherwise lawful arrest.[217]

Equally, there is no dispute that racial profiling does occur in practice. The Ontario Court of Appeal noted in *Brown* (2003):

> 9   In the opening part of his submission before this court, counsel for the appellant said that he did not challenge the fact that the phenomenon of racial profiling by the police existed. This was a responsible position to take because, as counsel said, this conclusion is supported by significant social science research. I quote from the *Report of The Commission on Systemic Racism in the Ontario Criminal Justice System* (Toronto: Queen's Printer for Ontario, 1995) (Co-chairs: M. Gittens and D. Cole) at 358:
>
>> The Commission's findings suggest that racialized characteristics, especially those of black people, in combination with other factors, provoke police suspicion, at least in Metro Toronto. Other factors that may attract police attention include sex (male), youth, make and condition of car (if any), location, dress, and perceived lifestyle. Black persons perceived to have many of these attributes are at high risk of being stopped on foot or in cars. This

---

216 *R. v. Brown* (2003), 64 O.R. (3d) 161 at paras. 7–8 (C.A.) [*Brown* (2003)].

217 *Storrey*, above note 203 at 251–52. See also *Ladouceur*, above note 15, noting that vehicle stops based on factors such as the race of the accused would be objectionable.

explanation is consistent with our findings that, overall, black people are more likely than others to experience the unwelcome intrusion of being stopped by the police, but black people are not equally vulnerable to such stops.[218]

If there is clear recognition that the practice occurs, and it is unambiguously objectionable, one would expect to find violations of section 9 of the *Charter*, the right to be free from arbitrary detention, based on this ground. In fact, however, successful racial profiling claims are extremely rare.[219]

The problem, in practice, is getting from "the phenomenon occurs sometimes" to "this is one of the times it occurred." A police officer is unlikely to admit that he or she has acted on the basis of racial stereotypes, and so any individual case must be decided based on inference.[220] The difficulty is that it can be hard to persuade a court to make the inference. A variety of situations can arise.

Often, objectively there was some basis which could authorize the detention or arrest: an accused might be speeding, for example, or a court might be persuaded that there was sufficient reasonable suspicion for an investigative detention. Indeed, something like this is the scenario imagined by the Court in *Storrey* – an "otherwise lawful" arrest or detention. However, when there objectively is a basis for the stop, it is difficult to persuade a court to infer that that objective basis was not the real reason for the stop. It has been recognized that racial profiling can occur unconsciously and need not be deliberate. Unconscious racial profiling would mean that an officer was more likely to stop a person of colour who was driving slightly over the speed limit where she would have allowed someone else to drive on. Nonetheless, it would remain

---

218 *Brown* (2003), above note 216 at para. 9.
219 See David M. Tanovich, *The Colour of Justice: Policing Race in Canada* (Toronto: Irwin Law, 2006), for a discussion of racial profiling in general.
220 See, for example, *Brown* (2003), above note 216 at para. 45, in which the Ontario Court of Appeal held:

> The respondent submits that where the evidence shows that the circumstances relating to a detention correspond to the phenomenon of racial profiling and provide a basis for the court to infer that the police officer is lying about why he or she singled out the accused person for attention, the record is then capable of supporting a finding that the stop was based on racial profiling. I accept that this is a way in which racial profiling could be proven. I do not think that it sets the hurdle either too low (which could be unfair to honest police officers performing their duties in a professional and unbiased manner) or too high (which would make it virtually impossible for victims of racial profiling to receive the protection of their rights under section 9 of the *Charter*).

the case that there *was* a power to stop, even if it would not have been exercised against another person.

And, of course, the detention or arrest power might in fact have been used properly. Even if the particular accused has been frequently stopped by the police, even if his feeling that he is stopped more frequently than others who are not visible minorities is correct, it does not automatically follow that this particular stop was an improper one. Some people of colour, like anyone else, do commit crimes. By definition, evidence of some crime will have been found on the particular occasion in question, or the case would not be in court. The accused will have the onus of proof to show that racial profiling was the motive, and will often not be able to discharge that burden.

Further, in many cases it will be difficult even to pursue the question. Vehicle stops, for example, can be made randomly by any officer in any place. They do not require a reason at all, and so it is difficult for an accused to pursue the issue of whether the reason was an improper one. As the dissent in *Ladouceur* pointed out:

> . . . the roving random stop would permit any individual officer to stop any vehicle, at any time, at any place. The decision may be based on any whim. Individual officers will have different reasons. Some may tend to stop younger drivers, others older cars, and so on. Indeed, as pointed out by Tarnopolsky J.A., racial considerations may be a factor too. My colleague states that in such circumstances, a *Charter* violation may be made out. If, however, no reason need be given nor is necessary, how will we ever know? The officer need only say, "I stopped the vehicle because I have the right to stop it for no reason. I am seeking unlicensed drivers."[221]

Finally, in some cases it might ultimately be found that there was no authority for the detention or arrest. Even then, it does not follow from the illegality of the stop that it was motivated by the improper purpose of racial profiling. In any case, since the Court's decision in *Grant*, an unlawful detention will be an arbitrary one, and so a further finding of racial profiling would be unnecessary.[222]

It cannot be said that racial profiling can never be proven. Some accused have succeeded in persuading courts that the inference to be drawn on the particular facts of the case — particularly when police

221 *Ladouceur*, above note 15 at 1297.
222 *Grant*, above note 12.

have been found not to be credible in their own testimony — was that the police had been motivated to act by the race of the accused.[223]

However, courts do not seem to be making it easier for accused to prove the allegation. If an accused is to show that her own facts do fall into the racial-profiling category, it is necessary for her to demonstrate that the officer was motivated not by the facts of the situation but by race. To do that, one would think that evidence of other stops by the same officer, to show a pattern, would assist. Yet there is little support in the caselaw for adopting such an approach. In *Ngo*, for example, the accused sought the records relating to 212 highway seizures that the arresting officer referred to on his *curriculum vitae*, in order to pursue a claim of racial profiling based on a pattern of stopping Asian drivers. The application was refused on the basis that the accused had not shown the relevance of the records: specifically because "[t]here was no evidence that in any way raised the issue of racism as a factor in any of the stops."[224] The court was unpersuaded by the defence claim that, if it already had such evidence, it would not need the disclosure in the first place.

4) Agents of the Police

Not all powers of arrest and detention rest with the police: a wide variety of powers is given to a wide variety of people. Further, there can be ambiguity in some circumstances as to exactly who has some particular powers.

Many powers are given to "peace officers." It is natural to think of that category as synonymous with "police officers," and certainly they are included in the definition and as a matter of fact are the group who exercise those powers most frequently. However, the definition of "peace officer" in section 2 of the *Code* is broader than that. It includes some other people with enforcement responsibilities: fisheries officers, immigration officer, customs officers, correctional workers, and military police, for instance. It also includes the captain of an airplane while it is in flight. In addition, various elected or appointed officials — mayor, warden, reeve, sheriff, deputy sheriff, sheriff's officer, and justice of the peace — fall into the definition. Further, other officials may have some or all of these powers by way of the operation of other

---

223 See, for example, *R. v. Ahmed*, [2009] O.J. No. 5092 (S.C.J.); *R. v. Khan* (2004), 244 D.L.R. (4th) 443 (Ont. S.C.J.); *R. v. Peck*, [2001] O.J. No. 4581 (S.C.J.).

224 *R. v. Ngo*, 2006 MBQB 143 at para. 59. See also *R. v. Fitch*, 2006 SKCA 80, leave to appeal to S.C.C. refused, [2006] S.C.C.A. No. 345.

acts.[225] See the more in-depth discussion of this issue in Chapter 4, as well as the discussion of the applicability of the *Charter* to non-state actors in Chapter 5.

Private citizens also have some powers: in particular (as will be discussed at greater length below, in Chapter 4), private citizens have the power to arrest in some circumstances. Indeed, the Supreme Court has noted that the concept of arrest predates the existence of police forces, and that "it is the peace officer's powers which are in a sense derivative from that of the citizen, not the other way around."[226] The most obvious instance of citizen's arrest powers occurs in section 494, and these powers will be discussed at greater length below. The point to note here is that powers can be assigned to private citizens based on particular roles they play: some arrest powers are given to all private citizens, others to property owners.[227] Yet another arrest power is given to sureties: people who have acted as guarantors that a person released on bail will appear in court. A surety can apply to be released from that obligation, and if the application is granted then either the surety or a peace officer can arrest the accused.[228]

In contrast, powers of detention — at least those powers of detention that are relevant to this book, aimed primarily at "street level" encounters — are almost exclusively in the hands of the police. The reason for this is their source: for the most part, powers of detention in Canada are not statutory but rather have been created at common law through use of the *Waterfield* test.[229] That test is specific in its application, and asks, first, whether the conduct falls within the general scope of any duty imposed by statute or recognized at common law; and second, whether the conduct, albeit within the general scope of

---

225 See, for example, *R. v. Decorte*, 2005 SCC 9 [*Decorte*], noting that First Nations constables in Ontario have the powers of peace officers, by virtue of the *Police Services Act*, R.S.O. 1990, c. P.15, and that they can exercise these powers off-reserve so long as they are doing so in relation to the community they serve.

226 *Asante-Mensah*, above note 26 at para. 40.

227 See *Criminal Code*, above note 61, ss. 494(1)–(2).

228 *Ibid.*, s. 766(2).

229 This is a good generalization, but it is not without exceptions. For example, the power to demand a breath sample to determine whether a person has committed the offence of driving while impaired involves both a search and a detention, and the power is created by s. 254 of the *Code*. Similarly, although the power to conduct random stops to check for impaired drivers exists at common law (see *Dedman*, above note 13), it can also be authorized under provincial highway traffic legislation: see, for example, *Hufsky*, above note 15; *Decorte*, above note 225.

such a duty, involves an unjustifiable use of powers associated with the duty.[230]

The clear result of this test is that common law powers, if created, can at least under the existing test rest only in the hands of police officers. This does not mean that the common law can never be relevant to private citizens: for example, the common law historically allowed private citizens to use force in effecting an arrest, and that remains the case.[231] However, to the extent that *Waterfield* has provided an "ancillary powers" doctrine allowing for the creation of new abilities to detain, search, or otherwise interfere with liberty, it is limited to creating such powers for police officers, not for others.[232]

As with anything in criminal law, however, things become murky once one delves a little below the surface. Two particular sources of ambiguity should be noted: implied statutory powers, and the absence of a brightline indicating when *Charter* rights do and do not arise. It makes sense to discuss the latter of these two first.

By virtue of section 32, the *Charter* applies to Parliament and the legislatures or, put another way, applies only when there is state action. In practical terms, this can make a great difference. For example, according to section 10(b), everyone has the right to counsel on arrest or detention. However, this is true only where there is state action. It therefore definitely applies when a police officer — who is an agent of the state — uses the power in section 495 of the *Code* to arrest a person. Somewhat surprisingly, however, the question of whether the section 10(b) right arises in the case of a citizen's arrest under section 494 has yet to be settled. Some courts of appeal have held that the common law origin of the power of arrest as a means of keeping "the King's peace" shows that even a private citizen is performing a government function when arresting.[233] Others have concluded that section 494 neither delegates the state function to private citizens nor abandons it, in which

---

230 *Godoy*, above note 46 at para. 12.
231 See generally *Asante-Mensah*, above note 26.
232 This point does not always appear to have been noticed by courts. See, for example, *R. v. Dell*, 2005 ABCA 246, in which the Alberta Court of Appeal held that the *Charter* does not apply to investigative detentions conducted by private citizens. The more important point, one would have thought, and it is not noted at all, is that the power of investigative detention arises at common law from the application of the *Waterfield* test in *Mann*, above note 10, and is given only to police officers: in other words there is no such thing as a "citizen's investigative detention."
233 See, for example, *R. v. Lerke* (1986), 24 C.C.C. (3d) 129 (Alta. C.A.). Note that the Alberta Court of Appeal's later decision in *Dell* does not immediately seem consistent with this earlier conclusion.

case citizens' arrests do not count as state action and so do not trigger the *Charter*.[234] The Supreme Court of Canada has so far expressly declined to settle the issue.[235]

The Supreme Court has, however, given some general guidance on how to tell when the actions of a private citizen will attract *Charter* scrutiny. In *Broyles*, dealing with a police informer, the Court set out a test for when a private citizen will be considered to be a state agent. It held there that

> Only if the relationship between the informer and the state is such that the exchange between the informer and the accused is materially different from what it would have been had there been no such relationship should the informer be considered a state agent for the purposes of the exchange . . . . [W]ould the exchange between the accused and the informer have taken place, in the form and manner in which it did take place, but for the intervention of the state or its agents?[236]

Broyles was decided in the particular context of an informer, but the test has been applied more broadly. It has been used, for example, to determine in *M.(M.R.)*[237] that a school vice-principal who searched a student for drugs in accordance with a school rule was not thereby a state agent, and in *Buhay*[238] that private security guards at a bus station who searched a locker rented by the accused were not bound by the *Charter*. In *Buhay* the Court held that "the mere fact that an entity performs what may loosely be termed a 'public function,' or the fact that a particular activity may be described as 'public' in nature, will not be sufficient to bring it within the purview of 'government' for the purposes of s. 32 of the *Charter*."[239] It also said that "[v]olunteer participation in the detection of crime by private actors, or general encouragements by the police authorities to citizens to participate in the detection of crime, will not usually be sufficient direction by the police to trigger the application of the *Charter*."[240] Yet the Court carried on to state that "[i]t may be that if the state were to abandon in whole or in part an essential public function to the private sector, even without an express

---

234 See, for example, *R. v. Skeir*, 2005 NSCA 86.
235 *Asante-Mensah*, above note 26 at para. 77.
236 *R. v. Broyles*, [1991] 3 S.C.R. 595 at 608.
237 *R. v. M.(M.R.)*, [1998] 3 S.C.R. 393 [*M.(M.R.)*].
238 *R. v. Buhay*, 2003 SCC 30 [*Buhay*].
239 *Ibid.* at para. 28, quoting *Eldridge v. British Columbia (A.G.)*, [1997] 3 S.C.R. 624 at para. 43.
240 *Ibid.* at para. 30.

delegation, the private activity could be assimilated to that of a state actor for *Charter* purposes."[241]

M.(M.R.) is also worth considering for another aspect of *Charter* applicability. As noted, the Court concluded that the vice-principal was not, on the facts of the case, acting as an agent of the police when he searched one of his students, even though a police officer was present at the time. Nonetheless, the Court found the *Charter* was applicable to the vice-principal's actions: school boards, schools, and their employees are part of government. That the *Charter* applied for this latter reason but not the former was of some significance, because *Charter* rights have different meanings in different contexts.[242]

In the search context, the Court has long held that a search without a warrant will *prima facie* violate section 8 of the *Charter*, if it is conducted for criminal law purposes. On the other hand, a more relaxed standard applies to searches in administrative contexts.[243] In *M.(M.R.)*, therefore, a different set of rules would have applied to the search depending on *why* the *Charter* applied: if the vice-principal had been an agent of the police, then a stricter standard for justifying the search would have been applied.

The Court has not yet adopted any exact analog to those differing search standards in the detention context. However, a similar point arose in *M.(M.R.)* in considering whether the accused was entitled to the right to counsel under section 10(b). Had the vice-principal been acting as an agent of the police when he took the student to the police officer on the scene, then there likely would have been a *Charter* violation, since the accused was not told of his right to counsel at that point. However, the Court found that there was no section 10(b) violation because there was no "detention" within the meaning of that term in the vice-principal's actions. It was true that the accused had felt compelled to obey the vice-principal's directions, but such compulsion in the school environment, the Court held, did not constitute detention within the meaning of section 10(b).[244]

The result, then, is that it will not always be clear whether a given private citizen is acting as a state agent or not, and so, to a certain extent, whether the *Charter* applies remains to be settled on a case-by-case basis. Beyond that, even if the *Charter* does apply, it will matter why the *Charter* applies. Different sets of rules might apply, depending

---

241 *Ibid.* at para. 31.
242 *M.(M.R.)*, above note 237 at paras. 26–30.
243 See *Jarvis*, above note 207. See also Coughlan, *Criminal Procedure*, above note 39, c. 4.
244 *M.(M.R.)*, above note 237 at paras. 65–68.

on whether the private citizen is generally an agent of the state or is more specifically an agent of the police.

This point leads fairly naturally into the other ambiguity arising in the *Charter* context, that of implied statutory powers. The legality of actions is often closely tied to the question of whether there has been a *Charter* violation. In most cases, a relatively straightforward statutory interpretation should determine whether a power to arrest or detain exists or not. However, that is not necessarily the case. *M.(M.R.)* illustrates this point as well.

The central issue in *M.(M.R.)* related to the search, but in that case, as in many others, the power to search also entailed a power to detain.[245] Under the analytical approach laid out by the Court for dealing with section 8, a search must have been prescribed by law.[246] In this case, no explicit search power was created by statute for the vice-principal, and, since he was not a peace officer, no common law power could be created. However, the Court noted that the *Education Act* called for teachers and school officials to maintain proper order and discipline in the school and to attend to the health and comfort of students: this responsibility, the Court held, "by necessary implication authorizes searches of students."[247]

Similarly, in *Orbanski*[248] the police had stopped a motorist and required him to perform various roadside sobriety tests before allowing him to contact counsel. There was no dispute that this violated the right to counsel in section 10(b), and the issue was whether that violation was justified under section 1. Within the section 1 analysis, there was only one real point of contention: whether the violation was prescribed by law. On the surface, it was quite obvious that the relevant statute did not explicitly state that "police may delay informing a person of the right to counsel in order to perform roadside sobriety tests." Indeed, the statute did not even explicitly say that police could conduct roadside sobriety tests. However, the majority of the Court held that that power was "necessarily implicit under the general statutory vehicle stop provision."[249] They then concluded that the operational requirements of exercising that power amounted to an implied limit in the statute to the right to counsel: in that event, the section 1 requirement was met.

---

245 See, for example, *Mann*, above note 10; *R. v. Greaves*, 2004 BCCA 484 [*Greaves*]; *Ferris*, above note 206.

246 *Collins*, above note 9.

247 *M.(M.R)*, above note 237 at para. 51.

248 *Orbanski*, above note 47.

249 *Orbanski*, *ibid.* at para. 43.

Obviously, finding implied powers in statutes is something of a slippery slope. As the dissenting judges in *Orbanski* note:

> The adoption of a rule limiting *Charter* rights on the basis of what amounts to a utilitarian argument in favour of meeting the needs of police investigations through the development of common law police powers would tend to give a potentially uncontrollable scope to the doctrine developed in the *Waterfield-Dedman* line of cases, which — and we sometimes forget such details — the court that created it took care not to apply on the facts before it (*R. v. Waterfield*, [1963] 3 All E.R. 659 [C.C.A.]). The doctrine would now be encapsulated in the principle that what the police need, the police get, by judicial fiat if all else fails or if the legislature finds the adoption of legislation to be unnecessary or unwarranted. The courts would limit *Charter* rights to the full extent necessary to achieve the purpose of meeting the needs of the police. The creation of and justification for the limit would arise out of an initiative of the courts. In the context of cases such as those we are considering here, this kind of judicial intervention would pre-empt any serious *Charter* review of the limits, as the limits would arise out of initiatives of the courts themselves.[250]

C. GROUNDS TO ARREST AND DETAIN

1) Introduction: Belief versus Suspicion

There are two relevant standards to be considered in discussing the basis upon which individuals can be arrested or detained: reasonable grounds to *believe*, and reasonable grounds to *suspect*. The two standards share some common features, which is unsurprising since in each case "reasonableness" is in issue. The central difference between the two is the degree of certainty required, which is, of course, the difference between believing a thing and merely suspecting that thing. "Reasonable grounds to believe" is often referred to simply as "reasonable belief,"[251] while "reasonable grounds to suspect" is often referred to simply as "reasonable suspicion."[252]

These standards are used beyond the contexts of arrest and detention. Before issuing a search warrant, for example, a justice must be satisfied there are reasonable grounds to believe that an offence has been committed. Number-recorder warrants and warrants to plant

---

250 *Ibid.* at para. 81.
251 See *Debot*, above note 156; *R. v. Wiley*, [1993] 3 S.C.R. 263 [*Wiley*].
252 See, for example, *Kang-Brown*, above note 43; *R. v. A.M.*, 2008 SCC 19 [*A.M.*].

tracking devices, on the other hand, can be issued based on reasonable grounds to suspect: this difference is justified on the basis that the latter warrants are less intrusive on privacy, and therefore can be more easily justified.[253] Similarly, a police officer may make a demand for breath samples for an approved screening device to determine whether a person has any alcohol in their system based on reasonable suspicion. However, a breathalyzer demand, to determine the actual concentration of alcohol in the person's system, requires that the officer have a reasonable belief. Once again, the lower standard is justified in less intrusive circumstances: that is, failing the former test does not by itself provide evidence that the accused is guilty of an offence, whereas failing the breathalyzer does prove such guilt.

One would expect this same pattern to be maintained in the use of the standards in the arrest and detention context, and for the most part this is correct. Generally speaking, arrests are more intrusive than investigative detentions, and arrests depend upon reasonable grounds while investigative detentions only require reasonable suspicion.[254] However, the division is not a perfect one. There is, for example, a specific arrest power relating to apprehended terrorist activity which depends in part only on reasonable suspicion.[255] More important (as will be discussed below in Chapter 3), courts are not always careful to ensure that the investigative detention power *remains* unintrusive, given the low standard upon which it is based.

Although the two standards share many common features, it is worth discussing them separately. In addition, see Appendices I and II, summarizing the kinds of facts that have been taken to establish either reasonable belief or reasonable suspicion in various cases.

2) Reasonable Grounds to Believe

a) What Constitutes Reasonable Grounds to Believe?
Discussion of this subject in the caselaw can frequently end up reduced to the relatively mechanical question of whether particular facts do or do not justify reasonable belief. It is worth starting a discussion, there-

---

253 *R. v. Wise*, [1992] 1 S.C.R. 527.

254 See *Criminal Code*, above note 61, s. 495(1); *Mann*, above note 10.

255 See *Criminal Code*, ibid., s. 83.3(4), which permits an arrest without warrant where a peace officer:

    (a) believes on reasonable grounds that a terrorist activity will be carried out; and

    (b) suspects on reasonable grounds that the imposition of a recognizance with conditions on a person, or the arrest of a person, is necessary to prevent the carrying out of the terrorist activity.

fore, by observing the importance of the role that this requirement plays, as a protection of individual liberty interests against the state. As the Supreme Court has observed:

> Without such an important protection, even the most democratic society could all too easily fall prey to the abuses and excesses of a police state. In order to safeguard the liberty of citizens, the *Criminal Code* requires the police, when attempting to obtain a warrant for an arrest, to demonstrate to a judicial officer that they have reasonable and probable grounds to believe that the person to be arrested has committed the offence.[256]

There are some general observations that can be made about the "reasonable belief" standard.

First, note that the Court has said that "reasonable and probable grounds" can mean different things in different contexts.[257] Even in the arrest context, the standard applies both to arrests with a warrant and to those without, but it does not necessarily operate in exactly the same way in each case.

The Court has said that

> In the case of an arrest made without a warrant, it is even more important for the police to demonstrate that they have those same reasonable and probable grounds upon which they base the arrest.[258]

In the arrest context, the standard does not require so high a standard as a *prima facie* case.[259] However, it does require that the thing believed be more likely than not, that it be probable. At one point, the arrest section in the *Code* was specifically phrased to say that an officer must have

---

256 *Storrey*, above note 203 at 249.

257 *R. v. Jacques*, [1996] 3 S.C.R. 312 at para. 20 [*Jacques*], quoting *R. v. Bernshaw*, [1995] 1 S.C.R. 254 at 304–6.

258 *Storrey*, above note 203 at 249. See also *Golub*, above note 170 at para. 18, in which the Ontario Court of Appeal adopts roughly the opposite reasoning, arguing that "The law does not expect the same kind of inquiry of a police officer deciding whether to make an arrest that it demands of a justice faced with an application for a search warrant." That is, the Supreme Court holds that a police officer acting without judicial scrutiny must be *more* careful, while the Court of Appeal is willing to let such an officer be less careful. The Court of Appeal's reasoning seems to place a greater emphasis on the needs of the police, while the Supreme Court in *Storrey* seems more concerned to safeguard individual liberty. See also *R. v. Janvier*, 2007 SKCA 147 at para. 28 [*Janvier*], concluding that the "finds committing" standard for arrest without a warrant in s. 495(1)(b) is more strict than the "reasonable grounds" standard for arrest in s. 495(1)(a).

259 See *Storrey*, above note 203.

reasonable "and probable" grounds, though that wording has since been simplified to "reasonable grounds." It has been settled that this change in wording was not meant to cause a change in meaning. Many courts, the Supreme Court among them, have continued to use the phrase "reasonable and probable" when speaking of the required grounds for arrest.[260] The Supreme Court has noted in the search context that the removal of the word "probable" does not actually change the standard, because reasonableness by itself incorporates a probability requirement.[261] It has also held, again in the search context, that synonyms for "reasonable grounds to believe" include "reasonable probability" and "credibly-based probability."[262] Various other courts have applied these findings to conclude that the removal of the words "and probable" from the arrest provisions is of no consequence, and therefore that the "more likely than not" standard must still be met.[263] In *Janvier*, for example, the Saskatchewan Court of Appeal noted that the change was made as the *Criminal Code* was amended with the Revised Statutes, and observed:

> "[A]nd probable" was dropped in the revision, but s. 4 of the *Revised Statutes of Canada*, 1985 makes it clear that no change in the law was effected:
>
>> The Revised Statutes shall not be held to operate as new law, but shall be construed and have effect as a consolidation of the law as contained in the Acts and portions of Acts repealed by section 3 and for which the Revised Statutes are substituted.[264]

260 See, for example, *Storrey*, *ibid.*, See also *R. v. Shepherd*, 2009 SCC 35 [*Shepherd*], in which the Court refers to the need for "reasonable and probable grounds" in discussing the breathalyzer provisions, though in fact s. 254(3) refers only to "reasonable grounds." See also *R. v. Grotheim*, 2001 SKCA 116 at para. 30, referring to "the requirement for 'reasonable grounds' (or 'reasonable and probable grounds' as this requirement may be more fully referred to)." See also *R. v. Crocker*, 2009 BCCA 388.

261 *Baron v. Canada*, [1993] 1 S.C.R. 416 [*Baron*].

262 See *Debot*, above note 156 at para. 47 and *Hunter*, above note 32 at 167, respectively.

263 See *Janvier*, above note 258 at paras. 15–16. See also *Smellie*, above note 163 at para. 15; and, for example, *Goodine v. R.*, 2006 NBCA 109 at para. 21 [*Goodine*]:

> It is settled law that, for a warrantless arrest to be lawful, it must be based upon reasonable and probable grounds: *R. v. Storrey*, [1990] 1 S.C.R. 241, [1990] S.C.J. No. 12 (QL). The standard is "credibly based probability" (*Baron v. Canada*, [1993] 1 S.C.R. 416, [1993] S.C.J. No. 6 (QL)), not proof beyond a reasonable doubt or even a *prima facie* case of guilt (*R. v. Storrey*, at pp. 250-51).

264 *Janvier*, above note 258 at para. 15.

It has occasionally been suggested that "reasonable grounds" in the arrest context can be satisfied based on something less than probability,[265] but this interpretation arises from a failure to pay attention to context. The source of the confusion is a statement by the Supreme Court in *Mugesera v. Canada (Minister of Citizenship & Immigration)*[266] in which the Court said that reasonable grounds to believe required less than the civil standard of proof on the balance of probabilities. To apply this in the arrest context is to ignore that it is a statement about the standard in the *Immigration Act* for refusing entry to suspected war criminals, not a standard in the *Criminal Code*. Specifically, it is a statutory standard based on a treaty in which "the international community was willing to *lower the usual standard of proof* in order to ensure that war criminals were denied safe havens".[267] There is no basis for thinking that it overrides the statements in *Storrey*, *Debot*,[268] *Baron v. Canada*,[269] or other cases, which maintain the probability requirement.

Further, note that, in some sense, making any comparison between "balance of probabilities" for arrest and "proof beyond a reasonable doubt" for conviction is a little misleading. The information that can enter into forming a basis for reasonable and probable grounds need not be evidence that would be admissible in court as proof that the accused was guilty. Hearsay evidence can be used as a basis for forming reasonable grounds, for example.[270] Similarly, an accused's past history of involvement in violent crimes can help inform a peace officer's reasonable belief that the accused has committed an offence,[271] though for a trier of fact to rely on that same information to make the same inference at trial would be propensity reasoning, which is improper. An accused's reputation can also contribute to forming reasonable grounds, though it could not alone be enough to create them.[272] Similarly, police are entitled to rely on eyewitness identifications without cautioning

---

265 See, for example, *R. v. Whitaker*, 2008 BCCA 174, though the point was not crucial to the reasoning in that case.

266 *Mugesera v. Canada (M.C.I.)*, 2005 SCC 40 [*Mugesera*].

267 *Sivakumar v. Canada (M.E.I.)*, [1994] 1 F.C. 433 at para. 18 (C.A.) [emphasis added]. Note that *Sivakumar* is the case relied on by the Court in making the statement it does in *Mugesera*, *ibid*.

268 *Debot*, above note 156.

269 *Baron*, above note 261.

270 See, for example, *Eccles*, above note 21; *Collins*, above note 9; *Debot*, above note 156.

271 See *Storrey*, above note 203.

272 *Debot*, above note 156.

themselves against the frailty of such evidence in the way that a jury would be instructed.[273]

It can also be observed that reasonable grounds are "transferable" between officers. This is more than saying that an officer can rely on hearsay: rather, the point is that more than one officer can act, provided that one officer has reasonable grounds. In *Debot*, for example, a search was conducted by one officer, after he was directed to conduct it by a prior officer. The issue, the Court held, was not whether the second officer could somehow rely on that direction as hearsay, creating reasonable grounds for him personally to search. Rather, the second officer was entitled to presume that the person who ordered the search had reasonable grounds to do so: the only legal issue was whether the first officer actually did have such grounds.[274] This approach is consistent with that taken to the "finds committing" arrest power (discussed in Chapter 4), where an officer who receives an accused from another officer is entitled to assume that the first officer genuinely did witness the accused commit an offence.

Note as well that the reasonable grounds must relate directly to the offence for which an arrest is to be made. In *Janvier*, for example, the Saskatchewan Court of Appeal considered whether the smell of burned marijuana in a truck gave reasonable grounds to believe that more marijuana would be found. It noted the difference between a smell of raw marijuana and burned marijuana; the former would be an observation that might justify a belief in marijuana's presence, while the latter would simply be evidence that there *had been* marijuana. To constitute reasonable grounds to believe that the person currently possessed marijuana, a smell of burned marijuana would need to be coupled with some basis for believing that other marijuana would still be present.[275]

In deciding whether she has reasonable probability, a peace officer must take into account all the information available to her, and is entitled to disregard only that which there is good reason to believe is not reliable.[276] More specifically, police are not entitled simply to rely on the incriminating evidence they discover and to ignore the exculpatory evidence: reasonable grounds must be judged against all known information.[277] Further, an officer will not necessarily have reasonable grounds simply because there is some information she can point to: for

---

273 *R. v. M.A.L.* (2003), 173 C.C.C. (3d) 439 (Ont. C.A.) [*M.A.L.*].
274 See also *Eccles*, above note 21.
275 *Janvier*, above note 258 at paras. 42–44.
276 See *Storrey*, above note 203; *Chartier v. Quebec (A.G.)*, [1979] 2 S.C.R. 474 [*Chartier*].
277 *Chartier*, ibid. at 499.

example, an arrest based on a tipster's uncorroborated report of criminal conduct might not be lawful.[278] The Supreme Court has also found that "reasonable grounds" is both a subjective and an objective standard: that is, "an arresting officer must subjectively have reasonable and probable grounds on which to base the arrest. Those grounds must, in addition, be justifiable from an objective point of view."[279]

The subjective standard is important: the Court has noted that "it would be inconsistent with the spirit of the *Charter* to permit a police officer to make an arrest without a warrant even though he or she does not believe reasonable grounds for the arrest exist."[280] Nonetheless, as a general rule the difficult issue is whether the objective standard is made out: a peace officer will seldom say, "I did not subjectively feel that I had grounds to arrest." One cannot claim that that never happens, of course, but it is rare.[281] Nonetheless, more commonly on the facts, a peace officer has testified that he felt he did have reasonable grounds, and the issue for a judge is whether that belief was objectively justified.

There is an issue that has not actually been addressed by the Supreme Court, relating to the nature of the objective standard. In the area of substantive criminal law, a debate raged for some years over whether the objective standard was a uniform one or whether it should be modified to take account of the knowledge and experience of the particular accused.[282] The Court's eventual conclusion was that, when it came to assessing objective fault crimes, the uniform objective standard should be used. In that event, the objective standard would take into account the relevant circumstances (anyone might drive oddly if a bee flew in the car window) but not the personal characteristics or other experience of the accused (a young person would be held to the same driving standard as

---

278 *Goodine*, above note 263. See also Section C(2)(b), below in this chapter, for a separate discussion on the contribution of tips to reasonable grounds.

279 *Storrey*, above note 203.

280 *Feeney*, above note 116 at para. 29.

281 See Section B(2), above. See also *Feeney*, above note 116, where in fact the officer did testify that he did not subjectively feel that he had grounds to arrest, and the Court held that that alone was sufficient to render the arrest illegal, without even considering whether the objective test was met. The Court also noted that the two tests are related: "Any finding that the subjective test is not met will generally imply that the objective test is not met, unless the officer is to be considered to have an unreasonably high standard." (*ibid.* at para. 34).

282 See, for example, *R. v. Tutton*, [1989] 1 S.C.R. 1392; *R. v. Hundal*, [1993] 1 S.C.R. 867; *R. v. Creighton*, [1993] 3 S.C.R. 3 [*Creighton*].

an adult).[283] On the other hand, the modified objective standard would be used when dealing with defences.[284]

The Supreme Court has never directly considered the question of whether the objective standard used in assessing reasonable and probable grounds is a uniform objective standard or a modified one. Some lower courts, however, have adopted the view that a modified objective standard is to be used, though their basis for doing so rests on an ambiguity. The Court did hold in *Storrey* that the objective requirement meant that a reasonable person "standing in the shoes of the police officer" would have believed that there were reasonable and probable grounds.[285] One could perfectly plausibly interpret that as a direction for all the circumstances to be taken into account, which would still simply be a uniform objective standard. It has been taken by some courts, however, to create a modified objective standard, and therefore to allow the past training and experience of the officer to be taken into account in deciding the objective reasonableness of her belief. This can result in some oddities, and is a questionable approach. It appears to allow police officers to, in effect, testify as their own experts, without actually being qualified as such.

The issue is demonstrated quite clearly in the Court of Appeal decision in *Nolet*.[286] The accused had been stopped for a random vehicle-safety check, and an officer found $115,000 in cash in a duffle bag. In support of having reasonable grounds for a detention, the officer had wanted to testify that the way in which the money was bundled indicated that it was drug proceeds, a fact he claimed to know based on his own experience. The accused objected to this evidence being admitted, on the basis that the officer had not been qualified as an expert and therefore was not entitled to express that opinion. The trial judge upheld the objection, but the Court of Appeal held that this was an error. In its view, the evidence was simply a part of the officer's experience and therefore a person "in the shoes of the police officer" would also know this. In that event, this evidence was admissible not only to show that the officer subjectively had reasonable grounds but also to show that those grounds were objectively reasonable. The court held:

> The officer stated he had had past experience with seizures of cash, and his testimony regarding the small denominations and distinct bundling of the cash should have been admitted and considered by

---

283 See *Creighton, ibid.*; *R. v. Gosset*, [1993] 3 S.C.R. 76; *R. v. Naglik*, [1993] 3 S.C.R. 122.

284 *R. v. Hibbert*, [1995] 2 S.C.R. 973.

285 *Storrey*, above note 203 at para. 16.

286 *R. v. Nolet*, 2009 SKCA 8.

the trial judge in relation to the question whether of [sic] the officer's belief that a crime had probably been committed was objectively reasonable.[287]

Other courts have adopted the same approach to allow police officers to testify to their own experience that hydroponic drug operations use lamps which generate a great deal of heat and therefore that condensation on windows is suspicious;[288] that the smell of Bounce fabric softener sheets in luggage is an indication that the owner is transporting narcotics;[289] that a particular area is known for drug trafficking and indeed that a particular person had a history of drug use;[290] that "undesirables" are more likely to be active at night;[291] that seeing balls of tinfoil is an indication of raw cocaine;[292] that it is "unique" in parts of Vancouver for black and white people to be together,[293] that a particular travel agency was used by drug traffickers booking flights;[294] that particular cities are either source points or consumption points for drugs;[295] and so on.[296] Some of these suggestions might seem like common sense (in which case it is not actually necessary to rely on the officer's particular experience, of course), while others seem much more esoteric. Even the most unlikely such facts, however, are on the modified objective approach admissible without any proof other than the officer's testimony that her experience showed it to be true. That testimony will not prove the ultimate fact at trial (i.e., in *Nolet* the officer's testimony about the way drug money is bundled could not be used to prove that the cash found was in fact the proceeds of drug sales), but it will help to satisfy the objective test. Given this approach, much of the value of *having* an objective requirement at all would disappear.

One danger of this approach is the lack of consistency it can produce. A wide variety of factors have been offered by police officers as contributing to their reasonable grounds, and indeed contradictory factors have been offered. For example, peace officers have testified that they have been suspicious of drivers because the vehicle was exceeding

---

287 *Nolet, ibid.* at para. 141.
288 See *R. v. Jacobsen* (2006), 207 C.C.C. (3d) 270 (Ont. C.A.).
289 *R. v. Rajaratnam*, 2006 ABCA 333 [*Rajaratnam*].
290 *R. v. Johnson* (2006), 213 O.A.C. 395 (C.A.).
291 *R. v. Houben*, 2006 SKCA 129 [*Houben*].
292 *R. v. Sinclair*, 2005 MBCA 41.
293 *Greaves*, above note 245 at paras. 9 and 42.
294 *R. v. Bui*, 2005 BCCA 482 [*Bui*].
295 *R. v. Bramley*, 2009 SKCA 49 at para.11 [*Bramley*]. See also *R. v. Geroux*, 2008 ABPC 49 [*Geroux*].
296 See also *R. v. Sekhon*, 2009 BCCA 187; *R. v. Juan*, 2007 BCCA 351; *Geroux, ibid.*

the speed limit,[297] was going under the speed limit,[298] or was observing the speed limit.[299] Quite commonly, officers will testify that their experience, or their training, has taught them that whichever of these facts they are reporting is a cause for suspicion. Similarly, officers have testified that they have become suspicious — and indeed that their training and experience have taught them to be suspicious — both of individuals who avoid eye contact[300] and of those who prolong it.[301] Indeed, individual officers have testified in the same case that they would have their suspicions aroused by a person making eye contact or by not making it.[302] Some courts have been critical of reliance on this factor in particular, describing it as "neutral" and "equivocal at best."[303] However, in the absence of a requirement for expert evidence proving that particular factors really should be seen as giving rise to suspicion, the problems inherent in this approach remain.

---

297 See, for example, *R. v. Bracchi*, 2005 BCCA 461; *R. v. Yaran*, 2009 ABPC 31. Note that these are not cases where an officer relied on exceeding the speed limit to justify a belief that the accused was impaired, or about something related specifically to his driving. In *Bracchi*, for example, the British Columbia Court of Appeal accepted that the accused's exceeding the speed limit contributed to reasonable grounds to believe that he was trying to avoid surveillance, and so was acting suspiciously.

298 See *Houben*, above note 291, in which the officers offered this as a reason to be suspicious about the accused in a general way — that he might be intending to break in somewhere or otherwise be up to no good — rather than for a reason related to operation of the motor vehicle. See also *Geroux*, above note 295, where a peace officer testified that he became suspicious of a driver because he was going below the posted speed limit.

299 See, for example, *R. v. Mouland*, 2006 SKQB 100 at para. 20, in which a police officer testified that "(c) Driver's [sic] of vehicles containing contraband do not usually break the law, that is, they follow speed limits and drive appropriately." See also *R. v. White*, 2007 QCCQ 992 or *R. v. Harrison*, 2009 SCC 34 at para. 6 [*Harrison*], for the same suggestion.

300 See *R. v. Jones*, [1992] B.C.J. No. 231 (S.C.): "He had been trained in the ways of detecting persons who might be carrying drugs and to be on the lookout for certain 'indicators' such as: 1) behavioural factors such as unusual speech patterns and a tendency to avoid eye contact . . . . " See also *R. v. Schuhknecht*, 2005 BCPC 161.

301 See *Kang-Brown*, above note 43 at para. 29: "RCMP Sergeant MacPhee testified that his training in the Jetway program taught him to watch for what he referred to as an 'elongated stare,' a locked eye contact for a period of a few seconds." See also *Bui*, above note 294.

302 See *Kang-Brown*, ibid. at para. 83, referring to *R. v. Dinh*, 2001 ABPC 48.

303 See *Geroux*, above note 295 at paras. 132–33. See also Binnie J. in *Kang-Brown*, ibid. at para. 83: "If 'eye contact' or 'no eye contact' are both of concern to the RCMP, this seems an ambiguous basis for particularized suspicion. Everyone getting off the bus will either be making eye contact or not making eye contact."

Consider, as an example, two factors relied on in *Monney*, where the accused was stopped at an airport as he was re-entering the country because it was thought he might be smuggling narcotics. The officer who stopped him noted that the accused was Ghanaian and was returning from Switzerland: this made him suspicious because of his "informal knowledge of Switzerland as a "transit routing" country for narcotics and Ghana as a source country."[304] Obviously, those assertions about these two countries are either correct or not. Equally obviously, they are not matters of common knowledge nor, for example, something about which a judge might take judicial notice. If they are incorrect but the officer believed them to be correct, then the officer would subjectively have had grounds to search but those grounds would not meet the objective test. On the other hand, if the assertions actually are correct, then the objective test would be met. In that event, one would like to have some evidence to show whether the officer's belief was or was not correct. Unfortunately, adopting a modified objective approach apparently means that the only proof required of whether the officer's belief is correct becomes that the officer says he believes it — or, as in this case, has "informal knowledge" of it.[305] As noted, that threatens to collapse the objective requirement into the subjective one.

Similarly, the result of this approach would be that the very same arrest would be *objectively* justified if conducted by officer A but not if conducted by officer B. That seems entirely counterintuitive: on the objective part of the test, either the smell of Bounce fabric softener sheets justifies a belief or it doesn't. The officer's knowledge of that fact or lack thereof should go only to the subjective part of the test.

Some courts have expressed caution over the modified objective approach to establishing reasonable grounds. It has been held, for example, that

> [t]he appellant made much of the fact that officer Paradis was an experienced police officer who, because of his experience, was justified in being suspicious. With respect, that is an *ad hominem* and circular argument, since by definition and because of their training, good police officers must be suspicious in order to be effective. That is why Parliament has established guidelines in the public interest by

---

304 *R. v. Monney*, [1999] 1 S.C.R. 652 at para. 3 [*Monney*]. Note that this case concerned a statutory search under s. 98 of the *Customs Act*, based on reasonable suspicion.

305 *Ibid.* at paras. 49–52. It is not entirely clear in *Monney* that the Court considered this aspect of its reasoning, since it does not separately discuss objective and subjective aspects of the officer's reasonable belief.

requiring that officers have reasonable grounds for their suspicions and that their suspicions must be objectively assessed. An officer's experience is clearly an important element which must be considered in the assessment of reasonable grounds for suspicion, but it cannot alone provide the objectivity required to exercise authority such as this.[306]

Similarly, the holding that "[a]n officer cannot exercise the power to detain on a hunch, even a hunch born of intuition gained by experience" casts some doubt on the legitimacy of using a modified objective standard.[307]

Equally, of course, it is quite possible for courts to receive evidence about a police officer's experience but nonetheless reject the notion that her conclusions were objectively reasonable.[308] The Supreme Court has yet to explicitly consider this issue, though there is some reason to think that it would not interpret the passage from *Storrey* as lower courts have. In *Golden* the police conducted a strip search of the accused, on the basis that he might have drugs hidden in his private areas. In assessing whether there was an objective basis for conducting that search, the Court noted that "[o]ther than Constable Ryan's personal experience, the arresting officers had no reasonable and probable basis for conducting the strip search in the restaurant." It went on to find the search not objectively justified, since it was "premised largely on a single officer's hunch, arising from a handful of personal experiences."[309]

Related to but apart from the question of whether an officer's personal experience can be used in assessing the objective component,

---

306 *Hamel v. Canada*, [1999] 3 F.C. 335 at para. 8 (C.A.).

307 *Calderon*, above note 204 at para. 69.

308 See *R. v. N.O.*, 2009 ABCA 75; *R. v. Cox* (1999), 210 N.B.R. (2d) 90 (C.A.) [*Cox*].

309 *Golden*, above note 152 at para. 110. See also the Supreme Court's decision in *Nolet*, above note 163, which is ambiguous on the point. The Court notes that the arresting officer had testified that he thought the way in which the money he had found was bundled indicated that it was the proceeds of crime. The Court does not explicitly say whether the "modified objective" approach was generally acceptable, though they do find that based on all of the evidence (improper licensing, an empty truck travelling late at night in the wrong location, inconsistent explanations in this case, and so on) the arrest was lawful:

> While the Crown did not attempt to qualify the officer as an expert on drug monies, the officer's experience and training supported the probative value of his evidence on this point. The *cumulative* effect of the factual elements previously described provides objective support for the officer's subjective belief that he had reasonable and probable grounds to make the arrests. (para 48).

many other facts have been offered and often accepted as contributing to creating reasonable grounds. These include the fact that an airline or bus ticket was purchased at the last minute,[310] the payment method for such tickets,[311] the use of rental cars (in particular those rented by third parties),[312] the presence of fast-food wrappers or maps,[313] energy drinks,[314] multiple cellphones,[315] long hair,[316] the type of vehicle,[317] a strong scent of cologne or air freshener,[318] nervousness,[319] driving long distances in a short time span,[320] driving from British Columbia eastward to Regina,[321] flying from Toronto to Vancouver,[322] place of residence,[323] rubbernecking,[324] and others.

Many of these facts could be seen as quite innocuous on their own, and quite neutral. That does not necessarily prevent them from contributing to reasonable grounds: it has been observed that "[f]actors which are benign in·and of themselves take on some (perhaps limited) significance when ranged together with other circumstances."[325] However, this can be problematic, and indeed courts have also recognized

---

310 See *Kang-Brown*, above note 43 at paras. 88, 118, and 187, as well as *R. v. MacEachern*, 2007 NSCA 69 at para. 9 [*MacEachern*]. See also *R. v. Ambrose*, 2008 NBPC 32 at para. 3 [*Ambrose*].

311 See *Kang-Brown*, above note 43 at para. 88; *MacEachern*, ibid. at para. 3. See also *Bramley*, above note 295 at paras. 7 and 53; *Bui*, above note 294 at para. 22.

312 See *Bramley*, above note 295 at paras. 7, 11, and 47. See also *R. v. Burgis*, 2009 BCPC 74 at para. 4 [*Burgis*]; *Ambrose*, above note 310 at para. 3.

313 See generally *Calderon*, above note 204.

314 See *Ambrose*, above note 310 at para. 3.

315 See *Ambrose*, ibid.; *Burgis*, above note 312 at paras. 11 and 14.

316 See *Bramley*, above note 295 at paras. 6, 9, 11, 42, 47, and 53.

317 See *R. v. Cormier* (1995), 166 N.B.R. (2d) 5 at para. 2 (C.A) [*Cormier*]; *Cox*, above note 308 at para. 2.

318 See *Cox*, ibid. at para. 3; *Burgis*, above note 312 at para. 11; *Ambrose*, above note 310 at para. 3. See also *R. v. Nguyen*, 2008 SKCA 160 at para. 20 [*Nguyen*].

319 See *Kang-Brown*, above note 43 at paras. 31 and 187; *Bui*, above note 294 at paras. 9 and 22–23; *R. v. Grant* (2006), 81 O.R. (3d) 1 at paras. 19 and 29; *R. v. Duong*, 2006 BCCA 325 at paras. 25 and 48; *Bramley*, above note 295 at para. 8.

320 See *Cox*, above note 308 at para. 11. See also generally *Nguyen*, above note 318.

321 See *Bramley*, above note 295; See also *Nguyen*, ibid.

322 See *Bui*, above note 294 at paras. 22–23.

323 See *Cormier*, above note 317 at para. 3; *Bramley*, above note 295 at paras. 7 and 11.

324 See *Kang-Brown*, above note 43 at paras. 30, 114, and 218.

325 *R. v. Drury*, 2000 MBCA 100 at para. 90. See also *M.A.L.*, above note 273.

that fact.[326] For example, in *Calderon*[327] the police testified that they suspected a vehicle was being used to transport narcotics because of training they had received as to certain "indicators," which included fast food, duffel bags, a road map, cellphones, and a pager. Between the two officers concerned, they had stopped between 60 and 120 cars based on those indicators and had never before found drug couriers. The Ontario Court of Appeal concluded that, given the "neutrality and apparent unreliability of these indicators," they could not amount to reasonable grounds.[328]

Lurking in the background here is the question of profiling — not the narrower and particularly controversial issue of racial profiling, but profiling more generally. The reason why so many factors that are potentially innocuous on their own are offered as justifications is that police forces have put together "profiles" of the characteristics which they feel are likely to be associated with drug couriers in particular, and then consciously target those individuals. The most well-known such program is "Operation Jetway," described by Justice Binnie in *Kang-Brown*:

> "Operation Jetway" is an RCMP program designed to curtail drug trafficking. It monitors the travelling public in transportation hubs such as airports and bus depots. It appears to be modelled on drug "courier" profiles developed since 1974 by the United States Drug Enforcement Administration. Police officers contend that certain types of behaviour, demeanour, dress and other visible personal character-

---

326 See *Rajaratnam*, above note 289, where the Court of Appeal allowed the smell of Bounce fabric softener to contribute to reasonable grounds, but acknowledged the danger of allowing ordinary household items to have this effect, and stressing the other facts that were relevant in that case as well.

327 *Calderon*, above note 204.

328 *Ibid.* at para.72. Note that in *Calderon* the issue was whether this evidence met the lower standard of reasonable suspicion. See also *Cox*, above note 308, where the police officer testified that his reasons for thinking a particular car was that of a drug courier was that it was an older vehicle with clothes hanging up in it, and that it was observing the speed limit. The court commented:

> Furthermore, the evidence of the smuggler's profile upon which the officer says he relied, does not meet the standard of articulable cause: (1) an older vehicle, a 1987 LTD with a large trunk area; how unusual is this in the Atlantic Provinces? (2) clothing hanging off the clothes hook in the car; the man was passing through New Brunswick and travelling hundreds of kilometres to his residence in Cape Breton in a car with Nova Scotia licence plates; and (3) he was travelling within the speed limit, a requirement of the law.

(*Cox, ibid.* at para. 11.)

istics of travellers may be indicative of criminal activity. The RCMP target these individuals as they pass through a terminal and attempt to engage them in "voluntary conversation." The aim is to have suspicious individuals consent to a search to determine whether they are carrying drugs on their person or in their luggage. In circumstances where consent is withheld or equivocal, the RCMP may decide to use a sniffer dog to try to detect any odour of narcotics around the suspect's person or belongings.[329]

The types of factors that enter into a profile can concern behaviour (eye contact or rubbernecking), personal traits (sex or age), and other circumstances (luggage with no tags, country from which returning).[330]

Profiling in this sense is theoretically distinct from "racial profiling," at least given one caveat, which is that there is really no agreed-upon definition of exactly what "racial profiling" means. This has the result that denials from some agencies that they engage in racial profiling might mean a variety of different things.[331] Popularly, the term has largely come to mean "singling out an individual based solely on his race" and in that sense is definitionally objectionable. Nonetheless, it seems that, as a practical matter, race does enter into some profiles. In *Monney*, for example, that the accused was Ghanaian was seen as a legitimate consideration; similarly, "returning from a source country for drugs" in large measure amounts to "returning from the Caribbean."[332] In this event, apparently neutral profiles will in fact target members of particular races to a greater degree.

David Tanovich argues that the *Kang-Brown* decision severely limits the ability of the police to rely on drug-courier profiles. It is not really clear, however, that any court has ever come to grips with the practice of profiling itself, as opposed to the accuracy of particular profiles. *Monney* does not explicitly accept the "profile" relied upon by the customs officer, but it does accept that the officer in fact had reasonable

---

329 *Kang-Brown*, above note 43 at para. 47. Operation Jetway focuses on airports as well as train and bus stations. Its counterpart, Operation Pipeline, is aimed at couriers travelling in motor vehicles and uses "pretext traffic stops": David M. Tanovich, "A Powerful Blow against Police Use of Drug Courier Profiles" (2008) 55 C.R. (6th) 379 [Tanovich, "A Powerful Blow Against Police Use of Drug Courier Profiles"].

330 See Tanovich, "A Powerful Blow against Police Use of Drug Courier Profiles," *ibid.* at 379–80.

331 See, generally, *ibid.* See also Anna Pratt & Sara K. Thompson, "Chivalry, 'Race' and Discretion at the Canadian Border" (2008) 48 Brit. J. Crim. 620.

332 Tanovich, "A Powerful Blow against Police Use of Drug Courier Profiles," above note 329 at 389.

suspicion based on the factors listed. Other cases have taken the same approach. For example, in *Bramley* the Saskatchewan Court of Appeal held:

> The point, as indicated earlier, is not that everyone who drives a third party rental vehicle, or travels from British Columbia to Saskatchewan, or hides his long hair, or has a history of drug offences, or who apparently lives in a different province than his wife, is a drug courier. The point is that, taken together, these kinds of considerations sometimes constitute a "constellation" of facts which justifies a reasonable suspicion an individual is involved in illegal drug activity.[333]

On the other hand, *Kang-Brown*, *Calderon*, and *Cox* reject the reliability of the particular facts that entered into the profiles relied on in those cases, holding that those officers did not have reasonable suspicion. None of these cases, however, can really be said to have pronounced on the underlying practice. This is an issue that would benefit from sustained judicial scrutiny.

Finally, note that, on appeal, the question of whether a police officer had reasonable grounds is a question of law. The question is based on factual findings by the trial judge, but the issue of whether the facts as found by the trial judge constitute reasonable and probable grounds is a question of law.[334]

b) The Role of "Tips" in Reasonable Grounds to Believe

A factor that frequently enters into the analysis of whether a police officer has had reasonable grounds to arrest (or, for that matter, reasonable suspicion) relates to "tips" received from informers. Some tips come from anonymous informers not previously known to the police, others from sources that have been used in the past and have proved either reliable or unreliable. The Supreme Court, in *Garofoli*,[335] laid down guidelines surrounding the use of such information in seeking wiretaps, though it relied on caselaw surrounding search warrants to do so. Those guidelines have since been frequently applied to assess whether reasonable grounds exist in the arrest context too.[336] The Court held:

---

333 *Bramley*, above note 295 at para. 47.
334 *Shepherd*, above note 260 at para. 20.
335 *R. v. Garofoli*, [1990] 2 S.C.R. 1421 [*Garofoli*].
336 See, for example, *Goodine*, note 263 at para. 23: "There is every reason to apply those guidelines in determining whether a peace officer had the requisite reasonable and probable grounds when he or she relied upon the hearsay statements of an informer to effect a warrantless arrest." See also *R. v. Campbell*, 2003 MBCA 76 [*Campbell* 2003].

(i) Hearsay statements of an informant can provide reasonable and probable grounds to justify a search. However, evidence of a tip from an informer, by itself, is insufficient to establish reasonable and probable grounds.

(ii) The reliability of the tip is to be assessed by recourse to "the totality of the circumstances." There is no formulaic test as to what this entails. Rather, the court must look to a variety of factors including:

(a) the degree of detail of the "tip";
(b) the informer's source of knowledge;
(c) indicia of the informer's reliability such as past performance or confirmation from other investigative sources.

(iii) The results of the search cannot, *ex post facto*, provide evidence of reliability of the information.[337]

More simply, the criteria, from *Debot*, are "three 'C's,"[338] namely: 1) is the tip compelling?; 2) is the source credible? and 3) is the tip corroborated? These three criteria are to be considered in the "totality of circumstances." That is, all three enter into the analysis, and so a weakness in one area can be compensated for by strengths in the other two.[339] For example, an anonymous tip has very little credibility, since there is nothing giving it any, but there is no rule that a tip from a previously untested source cannot be relied upon. If the anonymous tip were quite detailed (compelling) and the police were able to confirm much of it (corroborated), then it might well create reasonable grounds.[340]

It is important to recall that the test does speak of the three factors compensating for one another. That is, one can find in the caselaw tips with little to make them compelling being accepted, and tips that are accepted despite the absence of very much corroboration. One must not see those cases as setting a "minimum bar" in each category; rather, the point is that an inadequacy in one area can be made up for by a strength in another area which exceeds the norm.

i)   Is the Tip Compelling?

To ask whether a tip is compelling is to ask about the quality of the information. Is the information so particular, precise, unique, or detailed

---

337 *Garofoli*, above note 335 at para. 68.
338 *R. v. Woodworth*, 2006 NSSC 22 at para. 53 [*Woodworth*].
339 *Debot*, above note 156.
340 *Goodine*, above note 263.

as to compel belief?[341] Conclusory statements from a tipster will not be sufficient, nor will a tip that lacks detail: it must be clear that the tipster is reporting more than mere rumour or gossip, and the possibility of coincidence must be excluded.[342] The standard is whether the tip has sufficient detail as to exclude the possibility that it was based upon rumour, gossip, or coincidence.

Generally speaking, the more detail a tip includes the more compelling it will be, and this is particularly so if the tip includes information not publicly known. In *Wiley*, for example, an informer gave a detailed description of the residence of the accused and reported having personally seen sixty marijuana plants growing in a lab in a concrete bunker below a hot tub attached to the house.[343] This reflects that the more intimate and personal the details in the tip, the more likely it is that the information has come from a person well placed to have reliable knowledge. So, for example, reporting that a house is heated by a wood stove is not compelling evidence when there is a large woodpile visible: reporting that the wood stove is on the main floor, and that the furnace was removed from the basement in order to have more room to grow marijuana plants, is compelling. It is specific, unique, and detailed, and it is not information that a member of the public would be likely to know.[344]

That the information is detailed and compelling is not, of course, sufficient alone to make a tip constitute reasonable grounds, if the other two areas are weak. In *Lewis*,[345] for example, the police received a detailed tip identifying the accused by name, describing him and his companion accurately, stating when he would be at the airport, which airline he would be flying on, his destination, and indicating that he would be carrying cocaine. The Ontario Court of Appeal noted that the level of detail excluded the possibility that the tipster was relying on rumour or gossip, and characterized the tip as compelling. Nonetheless, they found that it could not constitute reasonable grounds. The tip had been an anonymous one, and so there was no basis for assessing credibility. The only corroboration had been of entirely innocent details, such as that the accused had arrived at the airport when predicted. Although the court specifically held that a tip's information about illegal

---

341 *Woodworth*, above note 338 at para. 55.
342 *Ibid.*; *Campbell* 2003, above note 336 at para. 19.
343 *Wiley*, above note 251.
344 *Woodworth*, above note 338 at paras. 58–59.
345 *R. v. Lewis* (1998), 38 O.R. (3d) 540 (C.A.) [*Lewis*].

conduct did not always require corroboration,[346] it held that in this case there were no reasonable grounds:

> Although the details provided in the tip and the confirmation of many of those details go some way to providing the requisite reasonable grounds, the danger in holding that they go the entire way is clear. Literally thousands of people go to the Pearson International Airport every day to fly to various destinations. No doubt, there are thousands more who are sufficiently familiar with a traveller's plan to know the traveller's flight, destination and who, if anyone, will accompany that traveller. Any one of those thousands could supply the police with exactly the same kind of information about any one of the thousands of travellers that this tipster provided about the respondent. It takes little imagination to conceive of situations in which a person familiar enough with another person to know his or her travel plans would also have a motive to falsely accuse that person of a serious crime.[347]

ii) Is the Tip Credible?

Whether a tip is credible is really a question about the informer personally, and whether she is trustworthy and the disclosure reliable. It requires consideration of the informer, the informer's history of giving information, and the informer's motive for giving information.[348] If the informer is known to the police, for example, and has given information in the past which has proven reliable, then the source will likely be seen as credible.[349] A prior relationship between the officer receiving the information and the informer will be relevant.[350] Other factors, such as whether the informer was being paid or whether an officer has seen the informer with the person he reports to be receiving information from, can matter.[351] The fact that the informer is already known to the police, however, is not sufficient to make the tip constitute reasonable grounds if the actual information received remains too general to distinguish it from mere rumour, and where there is no indication of the informer's means of knowledge.[352]

---

346 See Section C(2)(b)(iii), below in this chapter.
347 *Lewis*, above note 345 at para. 18.
348 *R. v. Zammit* (1993), 13 O.R. (3d) 76 at 83–84 (C.A.) [*Zammit*].
349 *Wiley*, above note 251.
350 *R. v. Deol*, 2006 MBCA 39 at para. 16.
351 *Debot*, above note 156.
352 See *Zammit*, above note 348 at 83–84.

At the other end of the spectrum would be an anonymous informer providing an anonymous tip on a single occasion. In such a case, the tip could constitute reasonable grounds only where the information provided by the informer is detailed enough and there is enough corroborative evidence to adequately compensate for the inability to assess credibility and reliability. Further, if that is the case, the police ought to seek corroborative evidence which confirms the credibility of the informer as well as of the tip itself.[353]

On this reasoning, the questions of credibility and corroboration become intermingled to some extent. To corroborate the reliability of the informer, the information confirmed should be something that suggests the informer was privy to special knowledge about the situation. For example, in *Zammit* the informer had described the accused and his vehicle and had given his home address and the name and address of his workplace. The Ontario Court of Appeal held that these facts did not confirm the reliability of the informer because "[t]hey would be known to anyone familiar with the appellant and would not in any way substantiate the allegation that the appellant was involved in drugs."[354]

iii) Is the Tip Corroborated?
Whether the tip has been corroborated is the most complex question, because it is hard to lay down any very precise rules. The police need not confirm every detail in an informer's tip, but there must be enough corroborative evidence "to remove the possibility of innocent coincidence."[355] A greater amount of corroborative evidence is required where the tip does not provide enough details to preclude the possibility of innocent coincidence, or where the informer's credibility cannot be assessed.[356]

The most difficult situation is when there is no corroboration of criminal aspects of the tip. There is no general rule that a tip must, to form reasonable grounds, be confirmed in portions of it relating to illegal behaviour. For example, in *Warford*, the police received a quite specific tip concerning trafficking in cocaine by the accused, giving the date the drugs had been received, prices, method of delivery, locations of sale, and a description of the accused's vehicle including the information that he always had some cocaine in it. The informer, a proven and reliable source, also indicated that the accused would be selling cocaine at a particular nightclub, giving the date and time. The police intercepted the accused in the vehicle described at the date and time in question on a route con-

---

353 See *Debot*, above note 156; *Campbell* 2003, above note 336 at paras. 22 & 23.
354 *Zammit*, above note 348 at para. 84.
355 See *Debot*, above note 156 at 1144.
356 See *Debot*, above note 156; *Campbell* 2003, above note 336 at para. 20.

sistent with travelling to the named nightclub. The Newfoundland Court of Appeal held that this provided confirmation of the informer's tip and indeed was "as much confirmation as the police could be expected to obtain from their surveillance."[357]

That case was made easier because the informer there had provided reliable information on six previous occasions. The situation is trickier when the information comes from an anonymous source. It has been held that, where an anonymous informer is used, there should be corroboration of some criminal aspect of the tip.[358] In *Lewis*, for example, the Ontario Court of Appeal considered an anonymous tip that the accused would be carrying drugs, and the only confirmation of the tip was that the accused met the description given, including travelling with a two-year-old child, and was in fact booked on the flight the informer had indicated. The Court of Appeal held that this was not sufficient, given the anonymous nature of the tip:

> The Crown's position comes down to this. If a person shows up at the airport and acts exactly as one would expect a normal traveller to act, that person is subject to arrest if an anonymous, unproven tipster has predicted that the person would attend at the airport in possession of cocaine and act like a normal traveller. I cannot accept that contention. Absent confirmation of details other than details which describe innocent and commonplace conduct, information supplied by an untested, anonymous informant cannot, standing alone, provide reasonable grounds for an arrest or search.[359]

On the other hand, it has also been held that the "totality of circumstances" test precludes a rule that an anonymous tip must be corroborated in some criminal aspects. In *Goodine* the New Brunswick Court of Appeal held:

---

357 R. v. *Warford*, 2001 NFCA 64 at para. 27 [*Warford*].

358 See *Campbell* 2003, above note 336. The case is somewhat ambiguous. In para. 26 the court says there is no strict requirement for confirmation: "This does not mean that there must be confirmation of the accused's criminality in every case involving an anonymous informant. But where, as in this case, it is not clear whether the information provided is 'firsthand' the lack of corroborative evidence connecting the accused to the crime will be most relevant when considering the totality of the circumstances." However in para. 27, the very next paragraph, the court says: "Where an anonymous informer is used, it is my opinion that information which corroborates the 'criminal' aspect of the informer's tip in some material respect should be present."

359 *Lewis*, above note 345 at para. 19.

[L]ack of corroboration of the "criminal" aspect of a tip by an untested anonymous source does not preclude a finding that an arrest based on that tip was lawful, at least where the following circumstances are in play: (1) there is no evidence that an improper motive underlies the tipster's report; (2) the corroborated "neutral" data would lead a reasonable and dispassionate observer to infer that the tipster is both closely acquainted with the target and privy to the criminal activity being reported; and (3) that observer would be at a loss to point to any fact-based, as opposed to speculative, justification for the conclusion that the allegation of criminal conduct is unreliable.[360]

More generally, there is also room for dispute over whether the confirmation of particular facts actually amounts to corroboration or not. In *Plant*,[361] for example, the informer had described the accused's house without giving its address: the Supreme Court held that this was corroboration, because the description had allowed the police to find the house in question. Lower courts have questioned whether that reasoning is sound. *Zammit* holds that confirmation of "only what would probably have been known by anyone familiar with the appellant" is not corroboration.[362]

3) Reasonable Grounds to Suspect

a) The Relationship between Reasonable Suspicion and Reasonable Belief

The standard of reasonable grounds to suspect, or reasonable suspicion, shares many characteristics with reasonable grounds to believe. Indeed, it has been referred to as "a lesser but included standard in the threshold of reasonable and probable grounds to believe."[363] It, too, requires that the police have more than a hunch, but its threshold is "somewhat lower than the reasonable and probable grounds required for lawful arrest."[364] In that event, much of what has been said about reasonable

---

360 *Goodine*, above note 263 at para. 20.

361 R. v. *Plant*, [1993] 3 S.C.R. 281 [*Plant*].

362 *Zammit*, above note 348 at para. 27. See also *Woodworth*, above note 338 at para. 56, noting on facts similar to *Plant*, *ibid.*, that "this Court is concerned that any member of the public who knew the Woodworths or their Residence, could acquire and pass on this kind of information. While it is good information as to the location of the alleged illegal activity, it is not compelling evidence of an alleged crime."

363 *Monney*, above note 304 at para. 49.

364 *Mann*, above note 10 at para. 27. See also Binnie J.'s judgment in *Kang-Brown*, above note 43 at para. 75.

grounds — for example, the subjective and objective components,[365] the problematic nature of police acting as their own experts, or the extent to which tips from informers constitute sufficient grounds — applies equally here. In essence, the same *type* of evidence is still needed, but reasonable suspicion can be justified based on less of it.

A simple example can be found in *Baddock*, where the police telephoned a person they had been told would sell narcotics and arranged a meeting. When a car arrived at the designated place, waited a few minutes, then left again, the police officer was said to have reasonable suspicion and so was justified in stopping the car as it drove away. While walking to the vehicle, the police officer again dialled the number he had originally called, and observed the cellphone in the vehicle driver's hand vibrate. This additional fact, the court held, gave the officer reasonable grounds to arrest, although he had not had such grounds when he stopped the vehicle.[366]

As with reasonable grounds, the standard of reasonable suspicion applies in a number of different contexts. Investigative detention will be the most important to this work, but the standard is also used for some searches under the *Customs Act*,[367] in issuing tracking warrants or dial number recorder warrants, in assessing whether the test for entrapment has been made out, to justify a demand for the use of an approved screening device, and in other contexts.[368] Some members of the Supreme Court were in favour of using the standard for searches involving the use of tracking dogs.[369]

There is also caselaw, predating the Court's decision in *Mann*, which refers to the standard of "articulable cause" in dealing with investigative detention. This terminology, in Canada, originated with the

---

365 *Mann, ibid.*

366 *R. v. Baddock*, 2008 BCCA 48.

367 R.S.C. 1985 (2d Supp.), c. 1.

368 See the judgment of Binnie J. in *A.M.*, above note 252 at para.77. Note that the list included there claims that *M.(M.R.)*, above note 237, provided that searches of a student by a school official can be based on reasonable suspicion. This seems to be an error. The Court in *M.(M.R.)* discussed caselaw from the United States concerning reasonable-suspicion searches in the school context. However, the test the Court actually articulates in *M.(M.R.)* is that "(2) The school authority must have *reasonable grounds to believe* that there has been a breach of school regulations or discipline and that a search of a student would reveal evidence of that breach" (*M.(M.R.)*, *ibid.* at para. 50 [emphasis added]). The Court did relax the *Hunter v. Southam* standards by dispensing with the need for judicial pre-authorization and eliminating the need to believe that an offence had been committed, but it did not change from the "reasonable grounds" to the "reasonable suspicion" standard.

369 See *A.M.*, above note 252; *Kang-Brown*, above note 43.

Ontario Court of Appeal decision in *Simpson*.[370] The Court in *Mann* replaced this with the terminology of "reasonable suspicion" but notes that it intended by it the same standard which had previously been referred to as "articulable cause." This means that that prior caselaw is still applicable on that specific issue.[371] However, it is important to note that the *Mann* decision did not simply affirm *Simpson*: it created a different test. Investigative detention in *Simpson* required more than "articulable cause" and investigative detention in *Mann* requires more than "reasonable grounds to suspect."

In dealing with reasonable grounds, the Court, as noted, has been clear that the standard varies in different contexts. With reasonable suspicion, on the other hand, there have been suggestions that the standard means the same thing in all different contexts, whether investigative detention, a customs search, or other situation. In *Mann*, for example, the Court noted that the standard of reasonable suspicion for customs searches, in *Jacques*,[372] was the same as the standard for investigative detention.[373] Similarly, in *Kang-Brown*, when discussing searches involving the use of sniffer dogs, Justices Deschamps and Rothstein noted:

---

370 *R. v. Simpson* (1993), 12 O.R. (3d) 182 (Ont. C.A.) [*Simpson*].

371 Strictly, the majority adopted the language of "reasonable grounds to detain" instead of articulable cause, a decision that the dissent objected would lead to confusion with the standard of "reasonable grounds to believe." In fact "reasonable suspicion" has tended to be the terminology used to deal with investigative detention, which avoids the confusion the dissent feared. See the comments of Justices Deschamps and Rothstein, dissenting in *Kang-Brown*, above note 43 at para. 164:

> Some clarification is required regarding what the reasonable suspicion standard entails. The grounds required to justify an investigative detention were defined by the majority of this Court in *Mann*. Iacobucci J. referred, citing the relevant cases, to a number of different formulations of the applicable standard, including "reasonable grounds to suspect," "reasonable suspicion," "articulable cause" and "sufficient reasonable articulable suspicion": paras. 31-32 and 45. He expressed a preference for a new term: "reasonable grounds to detain" (para. 33). But in summarizing the standard being applied in that case, Iacobucci J. then used the expression "reasonable grounds to suspect": para. 45. In my view, "reasonable grounds to suspect" is substantively equivalent to "reasonable suspicion."

372 *Jacques*, above note 257.

373 *Mann*, above note 10 at para. 30.

[T]the "reasonable suspicion" standard is readily applicable in practice, is meaningful to the police and trial judges, and is likely to be used in cases other than those involving detention.[374]

They carry on to discuss the use of that same standard with regard to approved screening devices and in customs searches, with no suggestion that the standard has different meanings in different contexts. Similarly, Justice Binnie in *Kang-Brown* notes that "[t]he 'reasonable suspicion' standard is not a new juridical standard called into existence for the purposes of this case" and discusses its use in entrapment cases.[375]

This leads to the observation that one has to separate the questions "are there reasonable grounds to suspect" and "to suspect what?" In the former question, the standard will be the same, but suspicion with regard to what differs from context to context. In the case of approved screening devices, it is that the suspect has alcohol in his system; in the case of a customs search, it is that the person is concealing contraband; and so on. The point is that a reasonable suspicion "in the air" is never sufficient, and indeed would quickly become indistinguishable from acting on a mere hunch.

b)   What Constitutes Reasonable Grounds to Suspect?

In the investigative detention context, police must rely on "a constellation of objectively discernible facts" to meet the requisite standard of reasonable suspicion.[376] No single factor can on its own ground reasonable suspicion, and so a number of factors taken together may cause the police to entertain a reasonable suspicion.[377] A mere "hunch based on intuition gained by experience" will not meet the reasonable suspicion standard.[378] As the Supreme Court has noted, "[w]hile an officer's

---

374 *Kang-Brown*, above note 43 at para. 164. Justices Deschamps and Rothstein were dissenting in the result, but it is quite difficult to say exactly what the majority *rule* from *Kang-Brown* is, and nothing in this passage is central to their disagreement with the majority.

375 *Ibid.* at para. 75. Justice Binnie was not dissenting in the result, though only Chief Justice McLachlin actually concurred with his reasons. Four justices believed that sniffer-dog searches should not be allowed based only on reasonable suspicion: Justice Binnie felt that that was an acceptable standard but that reasonable suspicion was not made out on the facts of the case.

376 *Simpson*, above note 370 at 202.

377 See, for example, *Monney*, above note 304 at para. 49, where reasonable suspicion referred to "the cumulative effect of several factors, and that no one factor can be assessed in isolation."

378 *Mann*, above note 10 at para. 30.

'hunch' is a valuable investigative tool . . . it is no substitute for proper *Charter* standards when interfering with a suspect's liberty."[379]

The type of evidence needed to justify reasonable suspicion, as noted, does not differ from that needed for reasonable grounds: all that differs is the amount. It is worth nonetheless noting some things which have been taken either to show or to fail to show that reasonable suspicions justifying an investigative detention existed. In *Mann*, for example, the officers were taken to be justified in stopping the accused because he closely matched the description they had been given of a person who had just committed an offence, and he was found very shortly afterward only a few blocks from the scene of that crime. The Court stressed that what mattered about the accused's location was that he was in the vicinity of the actual reported offence. It stressed that

> [t]he presence of an individual in a so-called high crime area is relevant only so far as it reflects his or her proximity to a particular crime. The high crime nature of a neighbourhood is not by itself a basis for detaining individuals.[380]

Lying to the police or presenting false identification has also been taken to be grounds for suspicion,[381] as has changing one's story, or offering an inherently implausible story. For example, in *Monney* the accused initially denied having visited Ghana while out of the country, but then later changed his story and said that he had. In *Schrenk* the accused explained that he had flown from Vancouver to Calgary and then rented a car to drive to Toronto because he could not afford to fly the whole way, though in fact the car rental was more expensive than a flight would have been.[382]

There is some authority suggesting that fleeing from the police can enter into creating reasonable suspicion.[383] This is a problematic con-

---

379 *Harrison*, above note 299 at para. 20.
380 *Mann*, above note 10 at para. 47.
381 *Kang-Brown*, above note 43 at para. 87.
382 *R. v. Schrenk*, 2007 MBQB 93.
383 See *Kang-Brown*, above note 43 at para. 87, in which Binnie J. notes that there is US authority for this position. In *Byfield*, above note 203, the Ontario Court of Appeal appears to accept the trial judge's reliance on this consideration. See also *R. v. Nesbeth*, 2008 ONCA 579, where the fact that the accused bolted upon seeing the police was a factor entering into reasonable suspicion. In *R. v. Jackson*, [2002] O.J. No. 4005 (S.C.J.), it is held that fleeing from the police does give rise to reasonable suspicion and is unlike simply refusing to answer questions. Further, *R. v. McKay* (2006), 200 Man. R. (2d) 259 (P.C.), suggests that an accused's *failure* to flee was relevant to deciding that reasonable grounds did not exist.

sideration, however. There is, of course, an intuitive attraction to the idea that if a person flees it is because she has something to hide. However, a person who is already lawfully detained is not entitled to flee: therefore, if flight is to enter into the reasonable grounds, then it must have occurred before the person was detained. In that event, the person was entitled to leave, and it could seem problematic to allow their decision to do so to constitute reasonable grounds. Justice Binnie in *Kang-Brown* held that this type of reasoning ought not to be permitted. In that case he refused to allow the fact that the accused declined to allow his bag to be searched to justify reasonable suspicion, precisely because the accused had the right to refuse.[384] Allowing flight to enter into reasonable suspicion would also create a kind of double-bind, effectively expanding police powers too broadly: anyone who does not flee might be taken to have remained by consent, but anyone who leaves could justifiably be detained.

Other factors are contextual and depend on the circumstances. That a person has bought a plane ticket at the last moment and with cash might be suspicious, for example, while no similar inference should be drawn about a bus ticket.[385] The mere fact that a person is nervous when confronted by the police should not create reasonable suspicion.[386]

---

384 See *Kang-Brown*, above note 43 at para. 92. Because four different judgments were handed down, it is difficult to know exactly what *Kang-Brown* stands for. The Saskatchewan Court of Appeal in *Bramley*, above note 295 at para. 54, observed that "of the five judges in *Kang-Brown* who considered the issue, three found that the dog search was grounded on a reasonable suspicion Mr. Kang-Brown was in possession of drugs." That suggests a 3:2 vote in favour of reasonable suspicion. On the other hand, Tanovich, "A Powerful Blow against Police Use of Drug Courier Profiles," above note 329, points out that the other four judges found that the facts did not rise above "generalized suspicion," which suggests a 6:3 majority against the existence of reasonable suspicion.

385 See *Kang-Brown*, above note 43 at para. 88:

> . . . Sergeant MacPhee considered significant the appellant's acknowledgement that he had bought his bus ticket at the "last minute . . . for cash" (R.R., at p. 53). This is a factor developed in the original Jetway program at airports where ordinary travellers usually book air transportation in advance and do not pay for an expensive ticket in cash (see, e.g., *Monney*). I think we can take judicial notice of the fact that people travelling by bus frequently buy their tickets not long before boarding. There is no evidence that cash payments are unusual.

386 See *Kang-Brown*, above note 43 at para. 95. See also *Geroux*, above note 295.

CHAPTER 3

POWERS OF DETENTION

A. INTRODUCTION

As has been noted above, powers of arrest and detention in Canada are created by statute and by the common law. In this chapter we address powers of detention. Initially, it is worth noting that detention can be seen as a broad concept that might include arrest and subsequent detentions surrounding issues of pre-trial detention and incarceration as well as indefinite detentions under dangerous-offender legislation. Here, though, we will focus on "on-the-street" encounters where police powers short of arrest remain controversial.[1] In this area, the law is fast developing owing, it seems, to the need in our law for greater specificity in police powers since the enactment of the *Charter of Rights and Freedoms.*[2]

Generally in Canada, powers of arrest, as discussed in Chapter 4, arise where the police or the citizen either find the person committing an offence or, in the case of the police, they have reasonable grounds to believe the person has committed certain criminal offences. These powers to arrest are discussed below; for now we wish to address those other powers that enable police to detain an individual on

---

1   In *R. v. Thomsen*, [1988] 1 S.C.R. 640 [*Thomsen*] and in *R. v. Therens*, [1985] 1 S.C.R. 613 [*Therens*], LeDain J. speaks of detention as a "restraint of liberty other than arrest" (*Thomsen, ibid.* at para. 8).

2   *Canadian Charter of Rights and Freedoms*, Part 1 of the *Constitution Act, 1982*, being Schedule B to the *Canada Act 1982* (U.K.), 1982, c. 11 [*Charter*].

less than a reasonable belief of criminal offending. Since the enactment of the *Charter*, the Supreme Court has been active in addressing this area of the law, particularly in its recognition of powers of detention in *Dedman*,[3] *Hufsky*,[4] *Mellinthin*,[5] *Ladouceur*,[6] *Mann*,[7] and *Clayton*.[8] The scope and requirements of such powers are of central concern to this discussion. Initially, however, we will discuss statutory powers of detention before moving to discuss the common law. As we do so, we emphasize that our discussion is intended to focus on the detention aspect of the issues and not on related issues that arise, particularly in the context of search and seizure.

B. STATUTORY POWERS OF DETENTION

The most obvious statutory power to detain arises in the impaired-driving context, where, not atypically as a feature of powers of detention, it is based on something less than reasonable belief.

As we have noted above, this area is plagued by inconsistency and by varying opinions on many issues; statutory context, both federal and provincial, has been important and the Supreme Court has allowed the common law a large role in expanding powers given by statute. Because provincial statutes are significant and because provinces have not acted in unison, each statute will need, at times, to be consulted to determine the particular powers available to enforcement officers in a given jurisdiction.

It is also worth noting that a "detention" is not necessarily a detention power. As we will note, the definition of the word "detention," which appears in sections 9 and 10 of the *Charter* and which plays an important role in the right to silence under section 7 of the *Charter*, has received considerable attention from the Court.[9] Particularly in the July 2009 decisions in *Grant*[10] and *Suberu*,[11] the Court provides much guidance on the term's definition. Yet what is not so clear is that these cases are not about detention powers. Rather, they address the question as

---

3   *Dedman v. The Queen*, [1985] 2 S.C.R. 2 [*Dedman*].

4   *R. v. Hufsky*, [1988] 1 S.C.R. 621 [*Hufsky*].

5   *R. v. Mellenthin*, [1992] 3 S.C.R. 615 [*Mellenthin*].

6   *R. v. Ladouceur*, [1990] 1 S.C.R. 1257 [*Ladouceur*].

7   *R. v. Mann*, 2004 SCC 52 [*Mann*].

8   *R. v. Clayton*, 2007 SCC 32 [*Clayton*].

9   *Charter*, above note 2.

10   *R. v. Grant*, 2009 SCC 32 [*Grant*].

11   *R. v. Suberu*, 2009 SCC 33 [*Suberu*].

to what rights a detained person has once they are, in fact, detained. A detention power, on the other hand, needs to focus upon a situation in which the state or an individual has the power, at law, to assume "control over the movement of a person by a demand or direction," not just whether the police did in fact detain a person in a given circumstance.[12] The failure to recognize the distinction can result in a misunderstanding of the principles at stake in any given situation.

A detention may be for varying amounts of time but generally we are here speaking of brief detentions that give rise to rights concerns. Different detention powers will sometimes be used in succession in that the exercise of one detention power might lead to the use of another or others. For example, the power to demand a roadside screening sample from a driver of a motor vehicle pursuant to section 254 of the *Criminal Code*[13] gives rise to a detention, which then gives rise to rights under sections 9 and 10 of the *Charter*.[14] But such a power does not give rise to the power to stop a motor vehicle. That is, a driver of a stopped motor vehicle might be detained for a roadside test; but the actual stopping of the vehicle by the police officer will need to be justified under some other power, such as the power to conduct a checkstop. That power arises under the common law as set out in the decision in *Dedman*.[15] In most impaired-driving checkstops, then, the *Dedman* power will be relied upon, followed by a detention under section 254(2) where that power so permits.[16] Of course, that second detention may then lead to a further detention for a breathalyzer test or an arrest under applicable police arrest powers based upon reasonable belief in impaired driving. Likewise, where the police do not employ a checkstop but rather conduct a random stop, the police will need to look elsewhere for their power to stop the vehicle, even though both kinds of stops may, in the right circumstance, lead to a section 254(2) roadside detention and demand.[17] The power to conduct a random stop, as we shall see, is less clear, although the Court has certainly discovered such a power in most of the provinces.[18] Understood properly, therefore, the power to detain that is present in section 254 of the *Criminal Code* will in many

---

12   *Thomsen*, above note 1 at para. 12.
13   *Criminal Code*, R.S.C. 1985, c. C-46.
14   *Thomsen*, above note 1 at 12; *Charter*, above note 2.
15   *Dedman*, above note 3.
16   *Criminal Code*, above note 13.
17   *Ibid.*
18   *Ladouceur*, above note 6.

cases actually operate as a power to further detain a suspect who was detained initially for some other reason and on some other power.[19]

Initially, it appears useful to separate this heading into stop powers and subsequent detention powers. In the *Criminal Code,* outside the impaired-driving context, there would appear to be few detention powers short of arrests themselves. There is, for example, a specific arrest power relating to apprehended terrorist activity which depends in part only on reasonable suspicion.[20] Significantly, there are detention powers in other federal statutes relating specifically to border crossings and customs.[21] Further, there are important detention powers in provincial legislation which in almost all cases will be centred on those that engage in various licensed or regulated activities or industries.

1) Statutory Motor Vehicle Detention Powers

Our focus here will be on motor vehicle legislation stop powers since they have received the most attention from the Court. In *Dedman* the Supreme Court faced an argument that section 14 of the then *Highway Traffic Act* of Ontario justified the checkstop in which Dedman was caught.[22] The section imposed a duty upon the driver of a motor vehicle to surrender his or her licence for inspection upon demand. It did not expressly provide a police power to stop the vehicle to ask to see the licence. The Crown argued that a police officer's power to stop a mo-

---

19 *Criminal Code*, above note 13.

20 See *ibid.*, s. 83.3(4), which permits an arrest without warrant where a peace officer:

(a) believes on reasonable grounds that a terrorist activity will be carried out; and

(b) suspects on reasonable grounds that the imposition of a recognizance with conditions on a person, or the arrest of a person, is necessary to prevent the carrying out of the terrorist activity.

21 See the *Customs Act*, R.S.C. 1985 (2d Supp.), c. 1, discussed in Section B(2)(b), below in this chapter.

22 R.S.O. 1970, c. 202, s. 14, as am. by S.O. 1979, c. 57, s. 2:

1) Every operator of a motor vehicle shall carry his licence with him at all times while he is in charge of a motor vehicle and shall surrender the licence for reasonable inspection upon the demand of a constable or officer appointed for carrying out the provisions of this Act.

2) Every person who is unable or refuses to surrender his licence in accordance with subsection 1 shall, when requested by a constable, give reasonable identification of himself and, for the purposes of this subsection, the correct name and address of such person shall be deemed to be reasonable identification.

tor vehicle for the purpose of inspecting a licence arose by implication from the driver's duty. The majority disagreed with the Crown, ruling that the section might imply a power to demand surrender of the licence for inspection, but whether such a power should extend, by further implication, to a power to stop a motor vehicle for such purpose was "doubtful."[23] Writing for the majority, Justice Gerald Le Dain also said:

> It would appear to involve an unusual extension of the rule of implied powers, as a matter of statutory construction. Such a power might exist as a matter of implication from the general nature of police duties, but that is a different basis. That is what I understand by common law authority for the exercise of police power. It may seem to come down to much the same thing in the end but the rule of statutory construction must not be distorted because of its application in a great variety of other statutory contexts. In any event, even assuming for the purposes of analysis that a power to stop a motor vehicle in order to demand surrender of a licence for inspection arises by implication from the terms of s. 14 of *The Highway Traffic Act*, and need not be grounded as a matter of common law on the general duties of police officers, it is a power that must be exercised for the purpose indicated in s. 14. It cannot be validly exercised for another purpose, using the purpose indicated in s. 14 as a subterfuge or pretext. In this case, it is clear from the findings of fact as set out in the stated case that while the police officer asked the appellant for his licence, the true purpose of the signal to stop was not to demand surrender of the licence for inspection but rather to determine whether there were grounds for a reasonable suspicion that the appellant had alcohol in his blood. That is clear from the following findings of fact: "Although police officers ask for valid driver's licences, they only do so to initiate conversation or contact to detect the drinking driver that they may not otherwise be able to detect" and "The only reason he was stopped was as part of the R.I.D.E. programme." I am, therefore, of the opinion that s. 14 of *The Highway Traffic Act* did not provide statutory authority for the signal to stop in the present case.[24]

Several significant findings appear in the above passage, at least some of which are now of doubtful validity. First, Justice Le Dain, for the majority, suggests that it is not appropriate to find by implication a power not expressly provided for in the statutory language. As we

---

23   *Dedman*, above note 3 at para. 62.
24   *Ibid*.

shall see, the Court later does exactly that in *Orbanski*.[25] Next, it is suggested that a power must be used for the purpose there stated, in this circumstance, to ask for the driver's licence, and not for another purpose, such as discovering evidence of impaired driving. We will see that the Supreme Court has held that it is a valid purpose to investigate the sobriety of the driver by way of provincial motor vehicle legislation.[26] Yet, as will be discussed below, while the Court in *Dedman* did go on to employ the common law to create a power to conduct impaired driving checkstops, it would also in a subsequent decision return to the theme that that power must be used only for that purpose and not to investigate other criminal offending.[27] We will discuss this common law power further, in Section C below in this chapter.

The Ontario legislature did not sit idly and accept the *Dedman* interpretation of section 14 and soon amended its Act. The issue then returned to the Court in *Hufsky* in 1988.[28] By this time, the legislature had added section 189(a) to the Ontario *Highway Traffic Act*[29] which now provided:

> (1) A police officer, in the lawful execution of his duties and responsibilities, may require the driver of a motor vehicle to stop and the driver of a motor vehicle, when signalled or requested to stop by a police officer who is readily identifiable as such, shall immediately come to a safe stop.

> (2) Every person who contravenes subsection (1) is guilty of an offence and on conviction is liable to a fine of not less than $100 and not more than $2,000 or to imprisonment for a term of not more than six months, or to both.

In *Hufsky*, Le Dain J. had little difficulty finding the stop, based as it was on this section, to be lawful:

> It [section 189(a)] does not specify that there must be some grounds or cause for stopping a particular driver but on its face leaves the choice of the drivers to be stopped to the discretion of the officer. In carrying out the purposes of the spot check procedure, including the

---

25   *R. v. Orbanski*, 2005 SCC 37 [*Orbanski*].

26   *Hufsky*, above note 4 at para. 13, and *Ladouceur*, above note 6 at 1287.

27   *Mellenthin*, above note 5.

28   *Hufsky*, above note 4.

29   R.S.O. 1980, c. 198, as am. by *Highway Traffic Amendment Act, 1981 (No. 3)*, S.O. 1981, c. 72, s. 2.

observation of the condition or "sobriety" of the driver, the officer was clearly in the lawful execution of his duties and responsibilities.[30]

We will return to this decision below for its important discussion on arbitrary detention, but for now note that the Court found that a stop conducted for the purposes of checking a driver's sobriety was authorized by the provincial statute, even though no express reference to sobriety or impaired driving appeared in the section. In doing so, it observed that the Crown relied upon the provincial statute, and not upon the common law power available since *Dedman*.

This gloss on the statutory language was accepted in the subsequent decision in *Ladouceur*.[31] At issue in *Ladouceur* was a "random" stop which did not involve an organized checkstop, such as those the Court had faced in the earlier decisions.[32] Describing the stop at issue as having a broad range of purposes, "to check for sobriety, for licences, insurance and the mechanical fitness of cars," Cory J., for the majority, nonetheless upheld the stop pursuant to section 189(a) as the Court had done in *Hufsky*. [33] The majority rejected the "reading down" of this language that had occurred in the Court of Appeal below, holding that there was no need to "qualify it in any way."[34] The Court refused, therefore, to see the section as requiring any kind of "cause" to exercise the stop.

While the Court, in *Mellenthin*,[35] recognized limits on the scope of the police actions that could be taken after the vehicle was stopped, it was later to read such a power expansively when deciding the case of *Orbanski*. There the Court was faced with the issue of the use of "field sobriety checks" in two cases arising from Manitoba. The Manitoba section being relied upon was a general stop provision that made no mention of sobriety checks.[36] The Court saw itself as interpreting the section of the Manitoba *Highway Traffic Act* as well as the overall legislative scheme in place to combat impaired driving which, of course, included the federal *Criminal Code* provisions relating to breath testing and roadside breath testing. The Court stressed the "operability" of that scheme, which it seemed to assume was similar across the country. That might not be a safe assumption. Describing the regulation of motor vehicles as affecting a "'liberty' interest in a general sense," the

30   *Hufsky*, above note 4 at para. 13.
31   *Ladouceur*, above note 6.
32   *Ibid.*
33   *Ibid.* at para. 30.
34   *Ibid.* at para. 63.
35   *Mellenthin*, above note 5.
36   *Highway Traffic Act*, C.C.S.M. c. H60.

Court said that it "cannot be equated to the ordinary freedom of movement of the individual that constitutes one of the fundamental values of our democratic society. Rather, it is a licensed activity that is subject to regulation and control for the protection of life and property."[37]

The interpretation of the regulatory scheme seems to have moved the Court to read in to the general stop power a statutory power to conduct roadside sobriety tests:

> [I]t is important to recognize that the need for regulation and control is achieved through an interlocking scheme of federal and provincial legislation. The provincial legislative scheme includes driver licensing, vehicle safety and highway traffic rules. At the federal level, the primary interest lies in deterring and punishing the commission of criminal offences involving motor vehicles. Control of drinking and driving is not confined exclusively to the laying of criminal charges after a criminal offence has been committed. Roadside screening techniques contemplated by provincial legislation provide a mechanism for combatting the continuing danger presented by the drinking driver, even if the driver may not ultimately be found to have reached a criminal level of impairment. Examples of such provisions in the Manitoba *Highway Traffic Act* applicable at the roadside include s. 263.1(1), which permits a peace officer to suspend a driver's licence if the officer has reason to believe that the driver's blood alcohol level exceeds 80 milligrams of alcohol in 100 millilitres of blood or if the driver refuses to comply with a demand for a breath or blood sample made under s. 254 of the *Criminal Code*. Hence, although the issues on these appeals arise in the context of criminal trials, their resolution must nonetheless take into account both federal and provincial legislative schemes. The Court must carefully balance the *Charter* rights of motorists against the policy concerns of both Parliament and the provincial legislatures.[38]

So, while stressing that it was a particular legislative scheme that was under consideration, the decision in *Orbanski* was a clear signal from the Court that, at least in the context of impaired driving, the policy of the law may be more important than what the statute actually says.

The ultimate issue the Court was analyzing in *Orbanski* was whether the stop power provided a limit on the right to counsel which was "prescribed by law" in the section 1 sense. Such a limit would have to be found by implication from the legislative scheme in existence at the

---

37   *Orbanski*, above note 25 at para. 24.
38   *Ibid*. at para. 27.

time of the offence. Relying on its earlier decision in *Therens,* the Court said that "a prescribed limit arose in these cases by necessary implication from the operating requirements of the governing provincial and federal legislative provisions."[39] Interestingly, the Manitoba legislature had in fact moved to expressly limit the right to counsel through a recent amendment to its *Highway Traffic Act.* [40] However, the new section did not apply to the cases before the court, since those cases had occurred before the amendment came into force. The Court in effect interpreted the general stop power in accord with the new law which expressly went much further.

What is not clear is how the decision applies in those provinces where there have not been legislative initiatives in this area. Relying on *Ladouceur,* the Court found that checking the sobriety of drivers is in fact a legitimate purpose for a stop under the general Manitoba stop power then in existence, as it had been under the Ontario legislation at issue in the earlier case.[41] Such a purpose was "necessarily implicit

---

39 *Ibid.* at para. 35. It is worth mentioning here that, in *Orbanski,* the Court also suggested that the justified limit on the right to counsel was only proportional (as required by s. 1 analysis) because the evidence obtained "can only be used as an investigative tool to confirm or reject the officer's suspicion that the driver might be impaired" [para. 58] and not as direct evidence to incriminate the driver. Since that time, most courts have held that this limitation on the use of the evidence applies to all evidence obtained during the initial interaction between the police and the driver including the result of the approved screening device (ASD) test. In Ontario see *R. v. Huff,* [1999] O.J. No. 5153 (S.C.J.), aff'd [2000] O.J. No. 3487 (C.A.), leave to appeal to the S.C.C. refused, [2001] 1 S.C.R. xvii, [2000] S.C.C.A. No. 562; *R. v. Cresswell,* [2002] O.J. No. 2492 (C.A.); and *R. v. Boothby,* [2001] O.J. No. 5078 (C.A.). Some courts in other provinces have adopted *Huff: R. v. Penner,* 2004 ABQB 98; *R. v. Lieskovsky,* 2004 ABPC 153; *R. v. Abercrombie,* 2007 ABPC 226; and *R. v. Ross,* 2009 BCSC 356. On the other hand, the Saskatchewan Court of Appeal has continued to insist that *Orbanski* does not prohibit use of the ASD result or even of statements of the accused when used by the Crown for the limited purpose of testing the credibility of the accused. See *R. v. Fox,* 2003 SKCA 79; *R. v. Beston,* 2006 SKCA 131; *R. v. Doell,* 2007 SKCA 61; and, most recently, *R. v. Gunn,* 2010 SKCA 44.

40 *Highway Traffic Act,* above note 36, s. 76.1(6): a peace officer is not required to inform a driver or passenger of his or her right to counsel, or to give the driver or passenger the opportunity to consult counsel, before doing anything subsection (4) or (5) authorizes. (Subsection (4) permits a peace officer to demand that a driver provide information and driving documents to the officer. It also permits the officer to conduct field sobriety tests or question the driver about his or her drinking. Subsection (5) permits the officer to request relevant information from the passenger of the vehicle.)

41 *Orbanski,* above note 25.

under the general statutory vehicle stop provision," according to the majority.[42]

In Newfoundland, the courts have not been fully accepting of *Orbanski*. There, the courts continue to be of the view expressed by the province's Court of Appeal in its 1996 decision in *Griffin*, prior to *Orbanski*, that the Newfoundland *Highway Traffic Act* does not allow a random stop of a motor vehicle. Rather, the law requires "articulable cause" to stop a motor vehicle.[43]

In *Griffin* the Newfoundland and Labrador Court of Appeal considered the effect of section 162 of the provincial *Highway Traffic Act*[44] and held that there must be an

> objective fact-based circumstance relating to the target vehicle which leads the officer to believe that it is necessary to act to achieve one or more of the purposes listed in relation to that vehicle. This would preclude a random stop.[45]

Interestingly, the court noted that "[t]here is very little consistency across the country with respect to the specific language used in provincial highway traffic legislation to potentially justify stopping of motorists by peace officers for various purposes."[46]

Currently, it apparently is still the view of the Newfoundland courts that there is no general random stop power in that province. For example, in 2008, well after *Orbanski*, one court said this:

> The stop by the police, in order to be lawful, must be justified by either statute or common law. In Newfoundland and Labrador, the police have no right to randomly stop motor vehicles except as part of a clearly identified program or ride spot check. The police must have articulable cause (see *R. v. Griffin* (1997) 111 C.C.C. (3d) 490 N.C.A.). Random stops in this province are arbitrary detention (see

---

42 *Ibid.* at para. 43.

43 *R. v. Griffin* (1996), 111 C.C.C. (3d) 490 (Nfld. C.A.), leave to appeal to S.C.C. refused, [1997] S.C.C.A. No. 32 [*Griffin*].

44 R.S.N.L. 1990, c. H-3: s. 162:

> Where a traffic officer reasonably considers it necessary
> (a) to ensure orderly movement of traffic;
> (b) to prevent injury or damage to persons or property;
> (c) to permit proper action in an emergency; or
> (d) to stop a motor vehicle on a highway to ensure that this Act
> and the regulations are being complied with, the officer may direct traffic according to his or her discretion, notwithstanding anything in this Part, and every person shall obey the officer's directions.

45 *Griffin*, above note 43 at para. 34.

46 *Ibid.* at para. 23.

R. v. *Ladouceur* [1990] 1 S.C.R. 1257 at p. 1277 S.C.C.; R. v. *Mellenthin* [1992] 3 S.C.R. 615).[47]

This is surprising given the general statements by the Supreme Court in *Orbanski*, but, nevertheless, the legislature in Newfoundland has not seen fit to amend its Act to react to *Griffin* in any way. It seems content with this result. The view seems to be that *Orbanski* has little application without a general and unlimited stop power in the provincial legislation.

Other courts of appeal have been more willing to read such legislation expansively. In Nova Scotia, for example, the Court of Appeal did imply a random stop power in *MacLennan*.[48] There, the court noted that, while there was no express stop power, the legislation did provide that the motorist must follow all "directions" given by a police officer.[49] The court had little difficulty in finding that such a general provision provided police in that province with a general power to stop vehicles arbitrarily:

> When this is read in the context of the common law authority of police to control traffic on the highways, other provisions of the *Motor Vehicle Act* and provisions of the *Criminal Code*, and note is taken of long standing customary practices, I am left in no doubt that s. 83(1) authorizes peace officers to require vehicles on the highway to come to a stop in response to an appropriate order, signal or direction.[50]

On the other hand, there remains a view that the power to stop vehicles randomly does require that the motor vehicle regulatory purpose must be the actual purpose of the police at the time. For example, in *Schaeffer* the Saskatchewan Court of Appeal held that where the police officer was relying on an unproven park bylaw that apparently prohibited vehicles in a park campground during the late-night hours, and where there was a factual finding at trial that the accused "was not stopped for purposes relating to vehicle or highway traffic safety," the highway traffic provision could not be relied upon to authorize the stopping of the vehicle.[51] In the absence of reliance on the *Highway Traf-*

---

47   R. v. *Tucker* (2008), 280 Nfld. & P.E.I.R. 169 at para. 17 (Prov. Ct.).

48   R. v. *MacLennan* (1995), 138 N.S.R. (2d) 369 (C.A.) [*MacLennan*].

49   *Motor Vehicle Act*, R.S.N.S. 1989, c. 293. s. 83, provided: "It shall be an offence for any person to refuse or fail to comply with any order, signal or direction of any peace officer."

50   *MacLennan*, above note 48 at para. 28.

51   R. v. *Schaeffer*, 2005 SKCA 33 at para. 23 [*Schaeffer*]. The [then] Saskatchewan *Highway Traffic Act* s. 40(8) provided:

> A peace officer who:

fic Act, then, the stop could be conducted only upon articulable cause of some offending pursuant to *Mann*, to be discussed fully below. The Saskatchewan Court followed *Schaeffer* in its decisions in *Houben*[52] and *Schell*.[53] In the former case, the court considered the Ontario Court of Appeal decision in *Brown* where it had said:

> The detention authorized by s. 216(1) of the HTA is circumscribed by its purpose. The detention is limited to the roadside and must be brief, unless other grounds are established for a further detention. The police may require production of the documents which drivers are required to have with them and may detain the vehicle and its occupants while those documents are checked against information available through the computer terminal in the police vehicle. The police may also assess the mechanical fitness of the vehicle, examine equipment for compliance with safety standards and from outside of the vehicle, make a visual examination of the interior to ensure their own safety in the course of the detention: *R. v. Ladouceur*, supra, at 1286-87; *R. v. Mellenthin*, [1992] 3 S.C.R. 615 at 623-24; *R. v. E. (G.A.)* (1992), 77 C.C.C. (3d) 60 (Ont. C.A.). More intrusive examinations or inquiries directed at matters not relevant to highway safety concerns are not authorized by s. 216(1) of the HTA: *R. v. Mellenthin*, supra.[54]

Significantly, the Ontario Court is careful to say that "more intrusive" examinations or inquiries are not authorized by the highway traffic legislation. These further examinations might, of course, be authorized by other powers such as those operative where the police obtain, during the statutorily authorized stop, reasonable cause to further detain under the authority of *Mann* or where they form a reasonable suspicion pursuant to the *Criminal Code*, section 254.[55]

There may be disagreement among members of the various courts of appeal as to the nature of the inquiries that can be undertaken pursuant to the highway traffic stop powers. As we have seen, the Supreme Court added "sobriety" to licensing and registration in *Hufsky* and *Ladouceur*, and, as the Court notes in *Brown*, mechanical fitness

---

    (a) is readily identifiable as a peace officer; and

    (b) is in the lawful execution of his or her duties and responsibilities; may require the person in charge of or operating a motor vehicle to stop that vehicle.

52 *R. v. Houben*, 2006 SKCA 129 [*Houben*].

53 *R. v. Schell*, 2006 SKCA 128 [*Schell*].

54 *Brown v. Durham (Regional Municipality) Police Force* (1998), 116 O.A.C. 126 at para. 24 [*Brown*].

55 *Criminal Code*, above note 13.

would seem to be a valid concern under the provincial stop powers.[56] In *Brown*, the Court labels these grounds to be "proper" and differentiates them from "improper" ones. But the basis of the distinction is not clear. It appears the Saskatchewan Court is of the view that the above listed purposes are the only proper grounds while the *Brown* Courts may view the criteria as more open-ended. It is to be noted that in *Schaeffer* and *Houben* the courts were dealing with stops that were found *not* to be for highway traffic purposes, while in *Brown* the court found that the stops were there for those purposes as well as other ones. So when does the purpose, not authorized for highway traffic purposes, override or overcome the proper purposes? It appears that, according to the Ontario Court of Appeal, this is where the highway traffic stop is used as a "ruse" for other purposes.[57] The court also said:

> I agree with this conclusion as long as the other purposes motivating the stop are not themselves improper. For example, the police are entitled on a s. 216(1) stop to require drivers to produce their licences. That requirement is consistent with the highway safety concerns which underlie the power granted by the section. In addition to ensuring that the driver is properly licensed, the police may wish to identify the driver for other purposes. It may be, as in this case, that the police are interested in knowing the identity of all those who are connected with what they believe to be organized criminal activity. The gathering of police intelligence is well within the ongoing police duty to investigate criminal activity. As long as the additional police purpose is not improper and does not entail an infringement on the liberty or security of the detained person beyond that contemplated by the purpose animating s. 216(1) of the HTA, I see no reason for declaring that a legitimate police interest beyond highway safety concerns should taint the lawfulness of the stop and detention. As the trial judge pointed out, known criminals should not be more immune from s. 216(1) stops than law abiding citizens who are not known to the police.[58]

We have discussed this same point above, in Chapter 2, Section B(2). As noted there, the Saskatchewan Court of Appeal has said that the improper purpose will invalidate the proper purpose where the lawful purpose is but a "plausible façade for an unlawful aim."[59] For now it is useful to see that both courts agree that the statutory powers must

---

56   *Brown*, above note 54.
57   *Ibid.* at para. 25.
58   *Ibid.* at para. 31.
59   R. v. *Ladouceur*, 2002 SKCA 73 at para. 66; see also R. v. *Dhuna*, 2009 ABCA 103.

include a lawful purpose which is part of the highway traffic scheme and which would appear to include licensing, registration, mechanical fitness, and sobriety of the driver.

Indeed, as noted, the Supreme Court has held that the extent of the inquiries that can be made during an impaired driving checkstop must be limited to the valid aims of a checkstop. In *Mellenthin*, where the officer enquired of a driver stopped in a checkstop as to what was in a gym bag in the front seat of the vehicle, an enquiry that led to the discovery of cannabis resin, the Court said:

> [T]he subsequent questions pertaining to the gym bag were improper. At the moment the questions were asked, the officer had not even the slightest suspicion that drugs or alcohol were in the vehicle or in the possession of the appellant. The appellant's words, actions and manner of driving did not demonstrate any symptoms of impairment. Check stop programs result in the arbitrary detention of motorists. The programs are justified as a means aimed at reducing the terrible toll of death and injury so often occasioned by impaired drivers or by dangerous vehicles. The primary aim of the program is thus to check for sobriety, licences, ownership, insurance and the mechanical fitness of cars. The police use of check stops should not be extended beyond these aims. Random stop programs must not be turned into a means of conducting either an unfounded general inquisition or an unreasonable search.[60]

In *Nolet*, the Supreme Court considered this question again and reaffirmed that "it is important not to encourage the establishment of checkstops where a nominally lawful aim is but a plausible facade for an unlawful aim."[61] As a practical matter, however, that decision is likely to make it more difficult to achieve that goal. The trial judge had found a search of a duffle bag in the cab of a truck to be predominantly for the purpose of pursuing a criminal investigation, and therefore had found it violated the *Charter* for the police to use a regulatory power aimed at driving offences to conduct that search. The Supreme Court rejected the "predominant purpose" approach in this context. They held that police officers were likely to be interested in both criminal and provincial infractions most of the time, and that the existence of some purpose outside the regulatory one did not invalidate the search.

---

60   *Mellenthin*, above note 5 at para. 15.
61   *R. v. Nolet*, 2010 SCC 24 at para. 36, quoting *Ladouceur*, above note 59 at para. 66. See a further discussion of this recent decision above in Chapter 2, Section C(1). In the interests of disclosure, note that Glen Luther, one of the authors of this book, was also one of the counsel for Nolet in front of the Supreme Court.

However, if the only requirement is that driving concerns be *among* the issues in a police officer's mind at the time of a search or detention, not necessarily the predominant one, then only in very rare circumstances will a random vehicle stop be perceived as a ruse. In fact such stops will have been extended beyond the original aims.

2) Other Statutory Powers of Detention

a) Screening Demands for Impaired Driving

As we have seen, the Supreme Court has found in a series of cases that section 254(2) of the *Criminal Code* contains within it a power of detention on less than reasonable grounds. The power to demand a screening breath test will result in a search (not our concern here) but also entails a detention which is part of the scheme and allows the demand to be made in the first place. In 2008 Parliament saw fit to amend the section in question, such that the statutory power to detain would now seem to be much broader than in existence when the Court's earlier decisions on the section were decided.

Section 254(2) currently reads as follows:

Testing for presence of alcohol or a drug

(2) If a peace officer has reasonable grounds to suspect that a person has alcohol or a drug in their body and that the person has, within the preceding three hours, operated a motor vehicle or vessel, operated or assisted in the operation of an aircraft or railway equipment or had the care or control of a motor vehicle, a vessel, an aircraft or railway equipment, whether it was in motion or not, the peace officer may, by demand, require the person to comply with paragraph (*a*), in the case of a drug, or with either or both of paragraphs (*a*) and (*b*), in the case of alcohol:

   (*a*) to perform forthwith physical coordination tests prescribed by regulation to enable the peace officer to determine whether a demand may be made under subsection (3) or (3.1) and, if necessary, to accompany the peace officer for that purpose; and

   (*b*) to provide forthwith a sample of breath that, in the peace officer's opinion, will enable a proper analysis to be made by means of an approved screening device and, if necessary, to accompany the peace officer for that purpose.[62]

---

62   *Criminal Code*, above note 13. Note also s. 254(3.3), which reads:

(3.3) If the evaluating officer has reasonable grounds to suspect that the person has alcohol in their body and if a demand was not made under para-

The earlier and narrower versions of this section were interpreted by the Court in *Therens* and in *Thomsen*, two cases that remain of significance in understanding sections 1, 9, and 10 of the *Charter*. *Therens* was also very significant in the interpretation of section 24 of the *Charter*. Here it is only the section 9 issue that is relevant.

The Court had little difficulty in these cases in holding that a detention occurs when a screening-device demand is made. Notably, this was contrary to its pre-*Charter* decision in *Chromiak*.[63] The nature of the demand pursuant to section 254(2), which has been upheld under section 9 and has been deemed to represent a constitutional exercise of police power as a section 1 limit on the right to counsel, has been found by the Court to be a detention of brief duration.

At the time of *Thomsen*, the section referred to a "road-side" screening device and the Court, in finding a section 1 limit on the right to counsel, said that "a limit prescribed by law within the meaning of section 1 may result by implication from the terms of a legislative provision or its operating requirements. It need not be an explicit limitation of a particular right or freedom."[64] The Court proceeded then to find that there was a limit on the right to counsel which arose by implication, since the "roadside screening device test is to be administered at roadside, at such time and place as the motorist is stopped, and as quickly as possible, having regard to the outside operating limit of two hours for the breathalyzer test which it may be found to be necessary to administer pursuant to section 235(1) of the *Code*."[65]

After *Thomsen*, the section was amended as Parliament authorized the screening device to be administered to airplane pilots and to operators of watercraft and thus the word "road-side" was removed. Nonetheless, in *Grant* (1991)[66] the Court found that the implicit limit on the right to counsel remained, finding no intention on the part of Parliament to move away from short detentions for screening purposes. The failure of the police to have the screening device available such that the test might be administered "forthwith" resulted, on the facts, in a failure to administer the test in accord with the section, and thus the right to counsel did indeed arise on the facts where the sample was provided

---

graph (2)(*b*) or subsection (3), the evaluating officer may, by demand made as soon as practicable, require the person to provide, as soon as practicable, a sample of breath that, in the evaluating officer's opinion, will enable a proper analysis to be made by means of an approved instrument.

63   *R. v. Chromiak*, [1980] 1 S.C.R. 471 [*Chromiak*].
64   *Thomsen*, above note 1 at para. 15.
65   *Ibid.* at para. 19
66   *R. v. Grant*, [1991] 3 S.C.R. 139, 67 C.C.C. (3d) 268 [*Grant* (1991)].

some thirty minutes after the demand. Presumably, also, the detention became unlawful.

Later, in *Bernshaw*,[67] a divided Court was faced with the suggestion that, since the police officer failed to delay the screening test for fifteen minutes to allow for the dissipation of mouth alcohol (which might have provided a false high reading), the result of the test could not form part of the reasonable grounds to demand the later breathalyzer test. Justice Cory, who formed part of the majority, held that, "This Court has in fact recognized that the ALERT [the screening device in use at the time] test must be administered immediately and that the detention under s. 254(2) is constitutionally justifiable under s. 1 of the *Charter* for the very reason that the detention is of such very brief duration."[68] To Cory J., a fifteen-minute delay was unnecessary. On the other hand, Sopinka J., whose judgment made up the balance of the majority, held that the word "forthwith" in the section did not mean "immediately" but rather its interpretation required that the particular facts be taken into account and that, where there was an indication of recent drinking, the officer would be acting in accord with the section to delay the test for fifteen minutes to allow the mouth alcohol to dissipate. Therefore, to Sopinka J., the section did in some circumstances authorize a somewhat longer detention. He further held that the right to counsel would be held in abeyance in such circumstances.

When one reviews the new version of the provision regarding the screening-device demand, set out above, one can see that Parliament has greatly expanded the circumstances in which such a demand and sample is authorized by the statute. No longer need the person be in care and control or driving the vehicle when the demand is made.[69] Rather,

---

67 *R. v. Bernshaw*, [1995] 1 S.C.R. 254 [*Bernshaw*].

68 *Ibid.* at para. 23.

69 The prior version of s. 254(2) was expressed in this way:

> (2) Where a peace officer reasonably suspects that a person who is operating a motor vehicle or vessel or operating or assisting in the operation of an aircraft or of railway equipment or who has the care or control of a motor vehicle, vessel or aircraft or of railway equipment, whether it is in motion or not, has alcohol in the person's body, the peace officer may, by demand made to that person, require the person to provide forthwith such a sample of breath as in the opinion of the peace officer is necessary to enable a proper analysis of the breath to be made by means of an approved screening device and, where necessary, to accompany the peace officer for the purpose of enabling such a sample of breath to be taken.

The requirement that the person receiving the demand be "operating a motor vehicle" or be in "care or control of a motor vehicle" resulted in demands being held unlawful in several cases when the demand was delayed. See, for example:

the section suggests that a screening demand may be made when an officer has a reasonable suspicion that the driver has alcohol in her body and that she was driving or in care and control of a vehicle within the past three hours. While the section continues to require that the test be administered "forthwith" upon the demand, the timing of the demand itself can seemingly be delayed for up to three hours. Of course, if the detention begins with the demand and the test is administered forthwith (within the limits of the cases above), it may be that the courts will remain of the view that the detention remains short-lived and is a reasonable limit on the right to counsel. On the other hand, as cases arise where the demand is delayed for extended periods, the courts may note that the "screening" nature of the test may be less clear and the need to limit the right to counsel for "operational" reasons may be less obvious than at the roadside. Of course, the section now also authorizes, in addition to the screening breath tests, physical tests for impairment by alcohol and for impairment by drugs. The length of these delays and the place of the right to counsel are yet to be authoritatively settled by the Court.

Where the detention is not "brief," the Crown and police run into problems on several fronts. Particularly as discussed above in *Grant* (1991), the Court has recognized that where the detention is more than brief the right to counsel arises.[70] Further, even if the police provide the right to counsel where the demand is delayed, the Court has found the demand or the test to be *not* conducted "forthwith" and therefore presumably the detention to be unlawful. This might be seen most clearly from the 2005 decision of the Supreme Court in *Woods*, where a demand at the police station more than an hour after the stop was held to be coercive (and thus not voluntary nor obtained by consent) and also unlawful.[71] Once the demand and resulting detention becomes unlawful, it would appear that the decision in 2009 in *Grant* —which holds that detentions that are unlawful are thus arbitrary — has significant application.[72] The crucial factual finding in such circumstances may be as to when the detention began rather than the question as to whether the sample was provided "forthwith."[73]

R. v. Woods, 2005 SCC 42 [*Woods*]; *R. v. Campbell* (1988), 44 C.C.C. (3d) 502 (Ont. C.A.); *R. v. Husulak*, 2006 SKQB 284; and *R. v. Good*, 2007 ABQB 696.

70   *Grant* (1991), above note 66.

71   *Woods*, above note 69.

72   *Grant*, above note 10.

73   For a general discussion of the new provision and the constitutionality of the new screening device and roadside sobriety tests, see R. S. Prithipaul, "Irrefut-

b) Customs Detentions

The main area of litigation around stops on less than reasonable grounds and outside the highway-traffic context has been that of customs. In a series of customs cases, the Supreme Court has dealt with the "reasonable suspicion" standard in the *Customs Act*. Generally, it is clear that, when one is crossing international boundaries, something less than reasonable grounds can justify a stop and a limited detention. In *Simmons*,[74] *Monney*,[75] and *Jacoy*,[76] the Court dealt with *Customs Act* searches. Currently, section 98 of that Act reads:

98. (1) An officer may search

(a) any person who has arrived in Canada, within a reasonable time after his arrival in Canada,

(b) any person who is about to leave Canada, at any time prior to his departure, or

(c) any person who has had access to an area designated for use by persons about to leave Canada and who leaves the area but does not leave Canada, within a reasonable time after he leaves the area,

if the officer suspects on reasonable grounds that the person has secreted on or about his person anything in respect of which this Act has been or might be contravened, anything that would afford evidence with respect to a contravention of this Act or any goods the importation or exportation of which is prohibited, controlled or regulated under this or any other Act of Parliament.

(2) An officer who is about to search a person under this section shall, on the request of that person, forthwith take him before the senior officer at the place where the search is to take place.

(3) A senior officer before whom a person is taken pursuant to subsection (2) shall, if he sees no reasonable grounds for the search, discharge the person or, if he believes otherwise, direct that the person be searched.[77]

As a review of the section shows, the legislation contemplates a search where the "officer suspects on reasonable grounds" that the person has

---

ably Guilty? A Brief Overview of the New Impaired Driving Amendments" ADGN/RP-216 (15 November 2008) (commentary on Quicklaw).

74   *R. v. Simmons*, [1988] 2 S.C.R. 495 [*Simmons*].

75   *R. v. Monney*, [1999] 1 S.C.R. 652 [*Monney*].

76   *R. v. Jacoy*, [1988] 2 S.C.R. 548 [*Jacoy*].

77   *Customs Act*, above note 21.

secreted on his or her person "anything that would afford evidence with respect to a contravention of" the *Customs Act* "or any goods the importation or exportation of which is prohibited, controlled or regulated under this or any other Act of Parliament." The detention aspect of this provision is presumably the length of time the detention takes the person away from their normal travel process and includes the time it takes to search the person. The statutory limit requires only "suspicion on reasonable grounds" before the person can be detained and subsequently searched. In fact, the Court authorizes a random albeit brief "detention" (and search) of all travellers although the source of such power is unclear. The Court seems of the view that such "detentions," being very brief, do not raise *Charter* concerns. Also, the statute requires that any search must be conducted within a "reasonable time," which again seems to limit the detention. In *Monney* the Court read this latter requirement in context when it held that a "passive bedpan vigil" of two hours was reasonable.[78]

The Court found in *Monney* that "border crossings represent a unique factual circumstance for the purposes of a s. 8 analysis,"[79] reasoning that presumably also applies to section 9. In the border-crossing context, "[n]ational self-protection becomes a compelling component in the calculus,"[80] according to the Court. The majority judgment in *Simmons*, written by Dickson C.J., held that there are three kinds of interactions with travellers in the customs context:

---

78   *Monney*, above note 75 at para. 53, where the Court said:

> On the question of whether the customs officers conducted the search within a reasonable time after the respondent's arrival in Canada, I agree with Weiler J.A.'s conclusion that the assessment of "reasonableness" must take into account not only any delay in the search process, but also the inherent time requirements of the particular search technique. Based on the evidence at trial, a delay of 30 minutes from the time a person is detained until the search begins is reasonable. In this case, however, the customs enforcement officers did not arrive until nearly two hours after the respondent was detained. As Weiler J.A. noted, however, while a delay at any point in the search process is an important consideration, it cannot be examined in isolation. Given the fact that a passive "bedpan vigil" is an inherently time-consuming process, I am of the opinion that the delayed response by the customs enforcement officers of one-and-a-half hours is not sufficient to establish that the search of the respondent was not conducted "within a reasonable time after his arrival in Canada" as required by s. 98(1) of the *Customs Act*.

79   *Ibid.* at para. 42.

80   *Simmons*, supra note 74 at para. 48, Dickson J., cited with approval in *R. v. Jacques*, [1996] 3 S.C.R. 312 at para. 18, Gonthier J., and in *Monney*, *ibid.* at para. 42.

It is, I think, of importance that the cases and the literature seem to recognize three distinct types of border search. First is the routine of questioning which every traveller undergoes at a port of entry, accompanied in some cases by a search of baggage and perhaps a pat or frisk of outer clothing. No stigma is attached to being one of the thousands of travellers who are daily routinely checked in that manner upon entry to Canada and no constitutional issues are raised. It would be absurd to suggest that a person in such circumstances is detained in a constitutional sense and therefore entitled to be advised of his or her right to counsel. The second type of border search is the strip or skin search of the nature of that to which the present appellant was subjected, conducted in a private room, after a secondary examination and with the permission of a customs officer in authority. The third and most highly intrusive type of search is that sometimes referred to as the body cavity search, in which customs officers have recourse to medical doctors, to X-rays, to emetics, and to other highly invasive means.

I wish to make it clear that each of the different types of search raises different issues. We are here concerned with searches of the second type and what I have to say relates only to that type of search. Searches of the third or bodily cavity type may raise entirely different constitutional issues for it is obvious that the greater the intrusion, the greater must be the justification and the greater the degree of constitutional protection.[81]

One can see, therefore, that the majority was of the view that the first category of search allows individuals to be questioned and even searched without, according to the majority, raising a constitutional issue.

This conclusion may now be somewhat suspect. After the Supreme Court judgments on section 9 in *Clayton*[82] and *Grant*,[83] the lawfulness of such state action seems essential to the constitutionality of that action. As we have seen, section 98 of the *Customs Act* requires the officer to have at least reasonable grounds to suspect that a relevant offence is being committed.[84] If there are no such grounds, one would assume that the resulting illegal search might support an argument based on sections 8 and 9 of the *Charter*. Having said that, it is to be noted that, if such a person is not detained in the meaning of section 9, then the

---

81   *Simmons, ibid.* at paras. 27-28.
82   *Clayton*, above note 8.
83   *Grant*, above note 10.
84   *Customs Act*, above note 21.

illegality of the state action is irrelevant to the analysis: if there is no detention at all, it cannot be an arbitrary detention.

We will return to these cases in Chapter 5 in an analysis of arbitrary detention and the right to counsel, but here it also worth mentioning that the majority in *Simmons* did find that individuals whose detentions fall within the second or third category are detained and therefore entitled to their right to counsel, even though they did admit the evidence in the given circumstance.

c) Wildlife Enforcement Detentions

Another area of statutory random stops that has been litigated in some provinces has been that of Wildlife Acts. In particular, Saskatchewan has been active in amending its *Wildlife Act* to authorize the random stopping of vehicles for the purpose of enforcing hunting and fishing regulations. The original legislation in that province read as follows:

> 49.2(1) Where due to the circumstances, the time or the location there could reasonably be expected to be a high incidence of offences against this Act or the regulations in any area, a wildlife officer may request or signal to the person in charge of or operating a vehicle or boat in the area to stop the vehicle or boat and may search it for evidence of an offence against this Act or the regulations and seize anything that may be evidence of such an offence.
>
> (2) The person in charge of or operating a vehicle or boat shall, upon being requested to do so by a wildlife officer pursuant to subsection (1), immediately bring the vehicle or boat to a safe stop, and the operator of the vehicle or boat shall, upon request, permit the wildlife officer to search the vehicle or boat.[85]

In *Denys* the Saskatchewan Court of Appeal threw the constitutional validity of this section into some doubt when it said:

> Since, in empowering wildlife officers to take action of this nature, the subsection does not expressly require the existence of reasonable and probable grounds to believe an offence has been or is being committed, it is constitutionally suspect, as are the actions of wildlife officers taken in exercise of the powers conferred by the subsection.[86]

The court noted that the section of the Act might be saved by section 1 of the *Charter*, though the justices did not find it necessary to make that decision on the case there presented. In a subsequent judgment, a

---

85   *The Wildlife Act*, R.S.S. 1978, c. W-13.1.
86   *R. v. Denys* (1995), 131 Sask. R. 251 at para. 28 [*Denys*].

provincial court judge did rule that a very similarly worded provision in the Saskatchewan *Fisheries Act*[87] was unconstitutional.[88] In analyzing whether such random stops could be "saved" under section 1, the trial judge noted the

> fact that the initial stop and the checks made were of the travelling public at random, that is, they were not made regarding persons engaged, or apparently engaged, in the regulated activity being monitored. This is a substantial and crucial difference between this case and those involving traffic stops for the purpose of monitoring driver's licences, vehicle registrations, the condition of drivers, etc.[89]

The judge also noted that the evidence before him showed that

> Overall, from 1993 to the present, 3971 vehicles were stopped on the highway. Ninety charges were laid for what could be called the primary purpose of the process, the conservation of the fishery by prevention of overfishing. That is a ratio of about 2.26 per cent of substantive charges to vehicles stopped and checked. Putting it another way, about 98 vehicles with no violations were stopped to discover 2 vehicles with a violation. The number of people involved is, of course, substantially higher.[90]

The Crown did not appeal the decision in *Stengler*, and the provincial government amended its *Wildlife Act* to remove the requirement in the stop power that required the stops to be in locations where there "could reasonably be expected to be a high incidence of offences against this Act or the regulations."[91] The current section, enacted in 2007, therefore allows random stopping of any vehicles for the purpose of enforcing the Act and does not seem to require any grounds for doing so.[92] The section would seem to be constitutionally invalid as allowing an arbitrary detention based on the above authorities.[93] Only section 1 can

---

87   *Fisheries Act*, S.S. 1994, c. F-16, s. 24.
88   *R. v. Stengler*, [2004] 3 W.W.R. 739 (Sask. Prov. Ct.) [*Stengler*].
89   *Ibid.* at para. 31.
90   *Ibid.* at para. 32.
91   *Wildlife Act*, above note 85.
92   *Wildlife Act, 1998*, S.S. 1998, c. W-13.2, as amended.
93   This issue has seemingly not arisen relating to arbitrary detention in other provinces, although similar issues have arisen in the context of the right to silence and the right to counsel in the context of wildlife investigations. See, for example: *R. v. Douglas*, 2002 BCPC 666; *R. v. Taylor*, 2001 BCPC 67; *R. v. Meise*, [1994] B.C.J. No. 876 (S.C.); *R. v. Calder*, [1988] N.S.J. No. 230 (Co. Ct.); *R. v. Lowe*, [2007] N.J. No. 456 (Prov. Ct.); *R. v. Sosnich*, 2003 ABPC 96. And, for Saskatchewan, see *R. v. Rutley*, 2004 SKPC 44.

save its constitutional validity, as occurred in *Ladouceur*[94] and *Hufsky*[95] with motor vehicle stops.

Recently, the British Columbia Court of Appeal in *Rice*[96] dealt with a similarly worded statute in that province. The court did not analyze the stop power but did hold that statutory-compelled statements under the same legislation were admissible given that the offences being investigated were not criminal in nature and that hunters voluntarily enter into the activity and thereby agree to the statutory compulsion that the statute requires. While it appears that in *Rice* the accused did not challenge the stop power and thus it was not at issue, there is, as was found in *Stengler,* a significant difference between a hunter who agrees to the regime set out for hunting regulation and a driver, not being a hunter, who does not. In other words, the stop power seemingly applies to all drivers while the statutory compulsion seems to apply only to hunters who have undertaken the regulated activity in question. If the Court of Appeal is correct in *Rice* about the admissibility of the compelled statements, which is not at issue here, the stop in question remains constitutionally suspect.

C. COMMON LAW POWERS OF DETENTION

1) Common Law Power for Investigative Detention: R. v. *Mann*

For a long time, there was a phrase in law-enforcement parlance that the law ignored. In various contexts, police were often heard to say that a given individual was a "person of interest" in their investigation. Until about the year 2000, the law had steadfastly been of the view that a citizen on the street had "the right to be let alone" and that, unless the police had "reasonable and probable grounds" to arrest an individual, they had no power to stop, question or search that person unless and until the individual voluntarily agreed to stop and subject him or herself to police interrogatories. On the other hand, in an influential 1991 article, Professor Alan Young argued:

> It is naive to believe that the state will restrict itself only to such non-invasive investigative procedures until such time as it acquires the requisite grounds to effect a proper arrest. Of necessity, the state

---

94   *Ladouceur*, above note 6.
95   *Hufsky*, above note 4.
96   *R. v. Rice*, 2009 BCCA 569.

will employ liberty-restraining practices of low visibility that manage to escape public and judicial scrutiny. In particular, the practice of brief investigative detention is carried out on a daily basis with little or no accountability. The police power to restrain liberty when the requisite grounds to effect an arrest are lacking is not a power that is recognized or accepted in the common law world; however, investigative detention is part and parcel of the routine activities of all police forces.[97]

The realization that such steps were a routine practice for police in Canada prompted Canadian courts to focus their attention on the issue. It was the Ontario Court of Appeal that first recognized the power for a "brief investigatory detention." In *Simpson*,[98] that court saw a need for the common law to recognize such a power, short of arrest, a power the U.S. Supreme Court had recognized in its 1963 decision in *Terry v. Ohio*[99] (which became known south of the border as the "stop and frisk" power). Ten years after *Simpson*, the Supreme Court of Canada also decided that it was time to begin to regulate an activity that the law had for too long ignored. One possibility open to them, in the face of police acting in the absence of any power, was to find the practice in violation of the *Charter* and put a stop to it. In fact, the Court took the opposite approach and created a power authorizing what the police were doing, though within some limits. In *Mann* the Court, for the first time, recognized and attempted to delineate this common law power to detain on less than a reasonable belief in criminal offending.[100]

The 2004 decision in *Mann* represented a major step in the creation of police powers at common law, a step not yet fully understood nor fully clarified. The *Waterfield* test for the creation of common law powers was once again invoked by the Court as it took a major step in the creation of police powers, seemingly on the basis that Parliament was not interested and, with a sort of reverse logic, that the Court needed to start regulating actions that are occurring with or without parliamentary action. How far the Court went, though, remains an area of confusion and disagreement among the various appeal court justices across the country.

In *Mann*, two police officers received a radio dispatch about a break and enter in progress. They were given a description of the suspect, in-

---

97 Alan Young, "All Along the Watchtower: Arbitrary Detention and the Police Function" (1991) 29 Osgoode Hall L.J. 329.

98 *R. v. Simpson* (1993), 12 O.R. (3d) 182 [*Simpson*].

99 392 U.S. 1 (1968).

100 *Mann*, above note 7.

cluding approximate height, weight, and age, his name, and a description of his clothing; he was also identified as Aboriginal. As the officers approached the scene of the reported crime, they observed the accused walking casually away. They stopped him and asked him to identify himself, in response to which he gave his name and date of birth. The officers then performed a pat-down search of his person. The accused was not connected with the break and enter, but in the course of the pat-down search one officer felt a soft object in his pocket and reached inside. The accused was found to be in possession of narcotics and was arrested for that offence. He argued that there had been a violation of his *Charter* rights: specifically, that the police had violated his section 9 right to be free from arbitrary detention by stopping him without any power to do so, and his section 8 right to be protected against arbitrary search and seizure.

Justice Frank Iacobucci, for the majority, suggested that the Court should *not* "recognize a general power of detention for investigative purposes"; instead, its "duty is to lay down the common law governing police powers of investigative detention in the particular context of this case."[101] Nonetheless, the majority did indeed go on to recognize that these officers had the power to detain Mann in the circumstances.[102] As noted above, the majority seemed of the view that the common law had an obligation to regulate this area; they noted that "the unregulated use of investigative detentions in policing, their uncertain legal status, and the potential for abuse inherent in such low-visibility exercises of discretionary power are all pressing reasons why the Court must exercise its custodial role."[103] In their judgment, the majority almost presupposes the existence of the power to detain in appropriate circumstances on this basis. Indeed, the major part of the judgment is focused on the limits of the power in question. Justice Iacobucci says:

> Police powers and police duties are not necessarily correlative. While the police have a common law duty to investigate crime, they are not empowered to undertake any and all action in the exercise of that duty. Individual liberty interests are fundamental to the Canadian constitutional order. Consequently, any intrusion upon them must not be taken lightly and, as a result, police officers do not have *carte blanche* to detain. The power to detain cannot be exercised on the basis of a hunch, nor can it become a *de facto* arrest.[104]

---

101 *Ibid.* at para. 17.
102 *Ibid.*
103 *Ibid.* at para. 18.
104 *Ibid.* at para. 35.

The Court acknowledges the American approach and the Ontario Court of Appeal's decision in *Simpson* that adopted "articulable cause" as a standard less than the reasonable grounds needed for an arrest. On the other hand, the majority in *Mann* is not satisfied either with the phrase articulable cause or with its common synonym, "reasonable suspicion," but rather is of the view that a better formulation would be "reasonable grounds to detain":

> The caselaw raises several guiding principles governing the use of a police power to detain for investigative purposes. The evolution of the *Waterfield* test, along with the *Simpson* articulable cause requirement, calls for investigative detentions to be premised upon reasonable grounds. The detention must be viewed as reasonably necessary on an objective view of the totality of the circumstances, informing the officer's suspicion that there is a clear nexus between the individual to be detained and a recent or on-going criminal offence. Reasonable grounds figures at the front-end of such an assessment, underlying the officer's reasonable suspicion that the particular individual is implicated in the criminal activity under investigation. The overall reasonableness of the decision to detain, however, must further be assessed against all of the circumstances, most notably the extent to which the interference with individual liberty is necessary to perform the officer's duty, the liberty interfered with, and the nature and extent of that interference, in order to meet the second prong of the *Waterfield* test.[105]

It is necessary to "unpack" the above quotation to determine what the Court was trying to say. By using the phrase "reasonable grounds to detain," the majority seemed to want to stress the stringency of the standard that they intend to employ. On the other hand, they acknowledge that the standard in question is less than reasonable grounds to believe and indeed can be seen as a standard of suspicion. We will discuss this requirement in Section C(1)(a) below. Further, the majority says that the suspicion must be of a recent or ongoing criminal offence. This requirement ought to operate to help keep the power confined within some limits, a point that is discussed in Section C(1)(b) below. In *Mann* itself, the information available to the officers was that there was an ongoing break and enter at a nearby business premise. Lastly, the majority states that the detention must, in all the circumstances, be "necessary" to the performance of the officer's duty. This latter requirement seems to require an objective assessment that the detention in the

---

105 *Ibid.* at para. 34.

circumstances was justifiable as a limit on the suspect's right to be let alone. This will be discussed in Section C(1)(c) below.

a) Reasonable Suspicion: *R. v. Mann*

As noted above, the Court in *Mann* adopted the phrase "reasonable grounds to detain" as the appropriate standard for an investigative detention. It appears that this language was chosen to stress that a multi-factorial approach is necessary to make the decision.

"Reasonable grounds to detain" were intended to include "reasonable suspicion," which appears to be the same standard as *Simpson's* "articulable cause." On the other hand, it also appears, based on the majority's judgment in *Mann,* that reasonable suspicion alone is not sufficient to allow a valid *Mann* detention. The majority held that the suspicion must be that the accused has a "nexus" to a recent or ongoing criminal offence and that the detention be "necessary" in the circumstances. One therefore needs to be somewhat careful in simply following cases on reasonable suspicion from other contexts, like the sniffer-dog cases[106] and those cases involving the assessment of the grounds under section 254 of the *Criminal Code* relating to roadside breath testing. One also needs to be cautious about relying on investigative-detention cases that pre-date *Mann.*

The reasonable suspicion standard has been discussed above in Chapter 2, Section C. The standard requires that the officer have a reasonable basis to suspect the individual. As recently stressed by the British Columbia Court of Appeal, "as is the case with the power of arrest, an officer invoking the power of investigative detention must subjectively believe that the requisite standard has been met, and the officer's belief must be objectively reasonable."[107] There the Court of Appeal majority found that the officer's suspicions were no more than a hunch. The majority said as follows:

> Mr. Justice Binnie, in *R. v. Kang-Brown*, 2008 SCC 18, [2008] 1 S.C.R. 456, had this to say about the difference between the reasonable suspicion required for an investigative detention, and the higher threshold of reasonable grounds to believe (i.e., credibly-based probability) required for an arrest:
>
> > 75 The "reasonable suspicion" standard is not a new juridical standard called into existence for the purposes of this case. "Sus-

---

106 *R.v. Kang-Brown*, 2008 SCC 18 [*Kang-Brown*]; and *R. v. A.M.*, 2008 SCC 19.

107 *R. v. Reddy*, 2010 BCCA 11 at paras. 66–67, citing *Mann*, above note 7 at para. 27, and *R. v. Greaves*, 2004 BCCA 484 at para. 33.

picion" is an expectation that the targeted individual is possibly engaged in some criminal activity. A "reasonable" suspicion means something more than a mere suspicion and something less than a belief based upon reasonable and probable grounds.

Appendix II sets out in table form the most important of the decisions on the issue. In *Bramley*[108] the Saskatchewan Court of Appeal found there to be a reasonable suspicion on the facts. It said that, in assessing the reasonableness of police suspicions, it is important to consider all the circumstances and not to look at any particular police assertion as to the probability it provides. Here the court was of the view that the following factors pointed to a reasonable suspicion even though each point alone could not be said to give rise to any probability of offending:

(a) The respondents lived in Surrey, British Columbia and were coming from that city. Constable Donison knew Surrey to be a known point of origin for illegal drugs.

(b) The respondents were traveling to Regina, a known destination point in the movement of illegal drugs.

(c) The respondents were driving a car which had been rented by a third party. Constable Donison understood this to be a practice used by drug traffickers.

(d) Mr. Bramley said he did not have enough money to rent a car, a $260.00 charge, but was nonetheless on a trip to Regina to visit friends.

(e) Mr. Bramley lived in Surrey but the renter of the vehicle, whom he identified as his wife, was noted on the rental agreement as being from Markinch, Saskatchewan. This is not the usual husband and wife arrangement.

(f) The rental agreement appeared to be improperly completed in that, on the endorsement concerning additional drivers, Mr. Bramley's name was in the place where the renter was to sign.

(g) Both Mr. Bramley and Mr. Schiller were described as being nervous when they were stopped. While acknowledging that people pulled over in traffic stops are often nervous at first, Constable Donison said such nervousness typically subsides as the stop progresses. In contrast, Mr. Bramley became more nervous over time.

(h) Between the time the respondents had sped past Constable Donison's parked cruiser and the time they were pulled over, Mr.

---

108 *R. v. Bramley*, 2009 SKCA 49 [*Bramley*].

Schiller had put his long hair up under his baseball cap. This was unusual and appeared to be an attempt by Mr. Schiller to make himself look more conservative.

(j) Both respondents had criminal records involving drug offence convictions. This included convictions, dated in Mr. Bramley's case, for possession for the purposes of trafficking in both Saskatchewan and British Columbia. (As noted earlier, counsel did not question or put in issue the propriety of Constable Donison asking Mr. Schiller, a passenger in the rental vehicle, for his driver's licence. The legality of that request is not an issue in this appeal.)[109]

Some may find offensive and parochial the finding that, because someone is from and coming from Surrey, British Columbia, and is driving to Regina, Saskatchewan, there may be a reasonable suspicion that he is a drug trafficker. In any event, while stressing the evils of drug trafficking, the court then says:

> In summary, but for the fact the respondents' investigative detentions were in respect of a *suspected* offence and thus unlawful as *per Nguyen*, a proper view of the evidence would have confirmed the validity of those detentions.[110]

b) *Mann*: The Nexus Issue

As we have seen, the *Mann* majority held that there must "a clear nexus between the individual to be detained and a recent or on-going criminal offence" for an investigative detention to be lawful. Many courts of appeal are not convinced and some have asked whether the police may detain where their suspicion relates not just to the suspect's involvement in a known crime but also to a circumstance where the existence of a crime cannot be said to be known but is rather only suspected.

This issue has come to the fore as the police have continued on the track of investigating suspected offending and making detentions in such circumstances. Indeed, the Royal Canadian Mounted Police (RCMP), Canada's national police force, has been active in attempting to use its various powers to combat smuggling activities of both drugs and weapons. Adopting practices from the American Drug Enforcement Agency, the RCMP has created various training programs for its officers to assist them in detecting contraband during various interactions with members of the public. Operation Convoy and Pipeline on the high-

---

109 *Ibid.* at para. 42.
110 *Ibid.* at para. 49.

ways and Operation Jetway at airports and bus depots are designed to discover smugglers by focusing on behaviours and attributes that are consistent with profiles that are thought to be indicative of smuggling activities. According to the RCMP website:

> In Sept. 1995, the Drug Enforcement Branch, HQ Ottawa launched an initiative now known as the Pipeline/Convoy Program. The program's focus was the detection and seizure of contraband moving across Canada in cars and transport trucks. In early 1998 Jetway, a sister program of Pipeline/Convoy, was developed to help target couriers with contraband who body pack, have checked and carry on luggage, who use other means of transportation such as air, bus and train and who forward mail and parcels through cargo and courier services.[111]

As noted in Chapter 2, Section C(2)(a), the RCMP practices received some attention in the sniffer-dog decision of the Supreme Court of Canada in *Kang-Brown*, where Binnie J., in partial concurrence, said:

> "Operation Jetway" is an RCMP program designed to curtail drug trafficking. It monitors the travelling public in transportation hubs such as airports and bus depots. It appears to be modelled on drug "courier" profiles developed since 1974 by the United States Drug Enforcement Administration. Police officers contend that certain types of behaviour, demeanour, dress and other visible personal characteristics of travellers may be indicative of criminal activity. [112]

While the police will rely on the various tools at their disposal to effect searches and arrests of smugglers, what is not clear is whether the *Mann* power is one of these tools when their suspicions are raised as a result of random stops of vehicles in particular. The power to use sniffer dogs and attempts to obtain consent from travellers are also employed.[113] While Binnie J. was not very happy with the Jetway practices of the police in *Kang-Brown*, the Court, as a whole, was very divided in this case and it is difficult to discern a majority view on most issues. Nonetheless, there are indications that the Court may not be very receptive to this type of investigative scheme, especially where it is a

---

111 Online: www.rcmp-learning.org/bestdocs/english/fsd/drugs/pipeline.htm (accessed 18 February 2010).
112 *Kang-Brown*, above note 106 at para. 47. See also Deschamps J., in dissent, at para. 109.
113 In relation to consent search and its limits, see, generally, Glen Luther, "Consent Search and Reasonable Expectation of Privacy: Twin Barriers to the Reasonable Protection of Privacy in Canada" (2008) 41 U.B.C. L. Rev. 1.

Mann-type detention that is employed. Of course, as noted in Chapter 2, *Mann* will in fact be used in many situations to further detain an individual who has been stopped for other reasons, which in many cases will involve reliance on the decisions on motor vehicle stops discussed above.

In particular, in *Grant* in 2009, the majority noted how the accused can often be seen as representing other members of the public who have been subjected to such activities by the police but who do not end up before the courts because the detention and search of them failed to yield the suspected evidence.[114] Such occurrences have become known as "false positives" although the extent of their occurrence is often difficult to discern and to prove.[115] The use of profiles by the police will also at times give rise to racial-profiling issues.

Pipeline/Convoy-type cases have been common in Saskatchewan, centring on the Trans-Canada Highway which crosses Canada's prairies. In *Bramley*, two officers stopped a vehicle for speeding and soon became suspicious that the driver and passenger were transporting drugs in their vehicle.[116] They employed a sniffer dog at the scene, and once the dog signalled the presence of drugs the officers opened the trunk of the vehicle, where they found the drugs for which they were looking. The Court of Appeal rejected the trial judge's exclusion of the evidence. In doing so, the justices asked themselves whether the power to conduct investigative detentions allowed the officers to *further* detain a statutorily stopped vehicle and its occupants for a suspected offence where the grounds arose after the valid motor vehicle stop. The *Bramley* court noted that, in its earlier decision in *Nguyen*, the majority had said: "Investigative detention will not avoid *Charter* challenge if its purpose is to determine whether a crime has been or is being committed as opposed to determining whether the detainee is linked to a recent or on-going crime."[117] In *Bramley*, then, the court held that it is "appropriate" to follow this *obiter dicta* from the earlier case, although it did not seem very happy with the result. The *Bramley* court said: "In other words, because the detentions of the respondents were conducted

---

114 *Grant*, above note 10 at para. 75, Charron J. and McLachlin C.J.C.

115 Reasonable suspicion, police profiling, and racial profiling are discussed in Chapter 2. See also Nathan J.S. Gorham, "Eight Plus Twenty-Four Two Equals Zero-Point-Five" (2003) 6 C. R. (6th) 257, where the author reviews so-called "pretext stops"; David M. Tanovich, *The Colour of Justice: Policing Race in Canada* (Toronto: Irwin Law, 2006), particularly chapters 3 and 4; and David M. Tanovich, "A Powerful Blow against Police Use of Drug Courier Profiles" (2008) 55 C.R. (6th) 379.

116 *Bramley*, above note 108.

117 *Ibid.* at para. 30, quoting *R. v. Nguyen*, 2008 SKCA 160 at para. 13 [*Nguyen*].

in relation to a *suspected* rather than a *known* offence, I shall take those detentions as having violated the respondents' rights as guaranteed by section 9 of the *Charter*."[118] It then noted:

> There are a number of considerations which suggest a police power to conduct investigative detentions in relation to suspected offences can be reconciled with the substance of s. 9 of the *Charter*. Accordingly, it may be appropriate for this Court, in a proper case, to revisit the question of whether investigative detentions can be lawfully conducted in respect of suspected, as opposed to known, offences.[119]

Some courts have been careful to look for the existence of a particular offence to which there is a recent nexus.[120] Others, however, seem to overlook this requirement.[121] One might speculate that this represents a failure to recognize that, although the Supreme Court in *Mann* recognized a power of investigative detention, as had the Ontario Court of Appeal in *Simpson*, the *Mann* decision did not simply adopt the *Simpson* approach.

In *Nesbeth* the Ontario Court of Appeal said: "While the court in *Mann* speaks of reasonable grounds to suspect that the individual is connected to 'a particular crime,' in my view, it is not necessary that the officers be able to pinpoint the crime with absolute precision."[122] This finding could be seen as suggesting a standard of suspicion in relation to the crime as well as the individual. In *Nesbeth*, when the police officer asked Nesbeth what he was doing, he ran away. The officer yelled "stop, police" but Nesbeth continued to run and actively attempted to impede the police in their attempt to catch him. The court, being not impressed with his attempt to flee, held that he was not in fact detained until he was eventually caught by the police, by which time they had formed the necessary reasonable suspicion to detain him based on his actions during the chase.

It would appear that, at the time the police initially sought to ask Nesbeth what he was doing, the facts known to the officers were that he was entering a stairwell in a building located in a high-crime area

---

118 *Bramley, ibid.* at para. 32.

119 *Ibid.* at para. 33.

120 See, for example, *R. v. Williams* (2007), 52 C.R. (6th) 98 (Ont. S.C.J.); *R. v. S.V.* (2005), 32 C.R. (6th) 389 (Ont. Ct. J.); *R. v. Cooper* (2005), 28 C.R. (6th) 338 (N.S.C.A.); or *R. v. Scott* (2004), 191 C.C.C. (3d) 183 (N.S.C.A.). See also Christina Skibinsky, "Regulating *Mann* in Canada" (2006) 69 Sask. L. Rev. 197.

121 See, for example: *R. v. Byfield* (2005), 74 O.R. (3d) 206 (C.A.), or *R. v. Chaisson* (2005), 200 C.C.C. (3d) 494 (Nfld. C.A.), rev'd on other grounds, 2006 SCC 11.

122 *R. v. Nesbeth*, 2008 ONCA 579 at para. 18.

late at night and in which they detected a smell of freshly smoked marijuana. While the court seemed of the view that, even though the police demand that the accused stop, if acceded to, would not have allowed a valid *Mann* detention, the police officer's unlawful intention to detain him before he fled did not attract a finding of unconstitutionality. The problem with this reasoning is surely that, unless the police had the requisite reasonable suspicion when they made the demand for the suspect to stop, he had the right to be let alone and therefore was within his rights to flee.[123]

Likewise, the Saskatchewan Court of Appeal has recently revisited its earlier decisions in *Nguyen* and *Bramley*. In *Yeh*[124] the majority held that *Nguyen* should not be followed. In the majority's view, *Mann* allows detentions where an offence is reasonably suspected as opposed to being known or reported. The dissenting justice, the author of the majority decision in *Nguyen*, was predictably not impressed and, in dissent, was decidedly of the view that the majority had expanded the reach of *Mann* beyond what is required or desirable. Interestingly, both the majority and the dissent use hypothetical situations to try to make their points.

The majority speaks of an individual in the early-morning hours putting a television in his car trunk when a police officer arrives on the scene. The majority use the example to suggest that the police must be able to inquire about the ownership of the television even though they do not "know" whether an offence has been committed by the television-toting individual. One wonders whether such police inquiries actually require a power in that brief inquiries of individuals on the street, to use the words of the Supreme Court, may not give rise to *Charter* concerns.[125]

In the dissenting justice's view, the *Mann* power does not require the offence to be known in the sense that the police know for certain that an offence has occurred, only that they form a belief that a given offence has occurred. On this view, "known" will always refer (and be referred on the facts of *Mann*) to a "reported" offence or to an offence observed by the police themselves. In this hypothetical case, have the

---

123   It is to be noted that in *Mann*, above note 7, the Supreme Court was clear that being in a high-crime area does not mean someone can be detained. At para. 47, the Court said: "The presence of an individual in a so-called high crime area is relevant only so far as it reflects his or her proximity to a particular crime. The high crime nature of a neighbourhood is not by itself a basis for detaining individuals."

124   *R. v. Yeh*, 2009 SKCA 112 [*Yeh*].

125   See *Suberu*, above note 11, and *Monney*, above note 75.

police found the person apparently committing an offence giving rise to the power to arrest under section 495(1)(b) of the *Criminal Code,* as discussed in Chapter 4? In her view, such a situation is not a realistic situation to discover what was intended by the Court in *Mann.* The dissent provides an example of what it means:

> For example, if an officer sees a woman lying on the ground crying and, seconds later, sees a man fleeing with a woman's handbag, it is probable that a trial judge would conclude that investigative detention was necessary to determine whether the detained person is linked to the recent, specific crime of theft. The arrest power under s. 495(1)(b) of the *Criminal Code* would not be available because the individual is not found committing or apparently committing an offence. An investigative detention power may be necessary, in such circumstances, to permit the police to determine whether the individual is linked to the recent crime of theft in the same way as with a reported crime. In such a case, the police need not wait for a crime to be reported if they observe, smell or hear something that causes them to believe that a particular crime has recently been committed or is being committed — assuming, of course, that the balance of the *Mann* criteria are satisfied.[126]

---

126 *Yeh,* above note 124 at para. 123. There, the dissent provides a useful catalogue of caselaw on *Mann:*

> [135] Since we are engaged in the exercise of interpreting *Mann,* it is important to review the decisions from across the country that have interpreted and applied this decision. First of all, it must be pointed out that none of the Courts have been asked to address the specific issues raised on this appeal. Thus, the most that can be accomplished by this exercise is to review the various fact patterns and extrapolate from the caselaw based on the language used and the result. The cases fall into three broadly based categories. The first category includes those cases where the Courts found that the detention was arbitrary and used the precise language of *Mann* to do so: *R. v. Ferdinand* (2004), 21 C.R. (6th) 65 (Ont. Sup. Ct.) at para. 37; *R. v. Calderon* (2004), 188 C.C.C. (3d) 481 (Ont. C.A.) at para. 69; *R. v. Bell,* 2004 ABPC 136, 123 C.R.R. (2d) 1 at para. 16; *R. v. Graham* (2004), 124 C.R.R. (2d) 121 (Ont. Ct. J.) at paras. 25-26; *R. v. Abraham,* 2004 MBQB 234, 7 M.V.R. (5th) 128 at para. 9; *R. v. A.B.,* [2004] O.J. No. 5660 (QL) (Ont. Ct. J.) at para. 22; *R. v. K.W.,* 2004 ONCJ 351 at para. 38; *R. v. S.V.,* 2005 ONCJ 410, 32 C.R. (6th) 389 at paras. 23-25; *R. v. Peters,* 2006 BCSC 1560, 147 C.R.R. (2d) 334 at para. 33; *R. v. Filli,* [2007] O.J. No. 3192 (QL), 2007 CarswellOnt 5281 (Ont. Sup. Ct.) at para. 74, affirmed by 2008 ONCA 649; *R. v. Barrett,* [2007] O.J. No. 3680 (QL), 2007 CarswellOnt 6899 (Ont. Sup. Ct.) at para. 55; *R. v. Ambrose,* 2008 NBPC 32 at paras. 30 and 36; and *R. v. Yaran,* 2009 ABPC 31 at paras. 94-95. (Ms. Skibinsky analyzes and categorizes many of these decisions in her article (see *Skibinsky, supra*).)

According to this view, then:

> The full *Mann* criteria are these. A police officer cannot detain some-
> one unless the following requirements of *Mann* have been met:
>
> > 1. the officer decides, based on all of the information available,
> > including a reported crime and what he or she hears, smells and
> > sees, that a crime has been recently committed, or is being com-
> > mitted;
> >
> > 2. the officer has a reasonable suspicion that there is a clear nexus
> > between the particular individual to be detained and the crime
> > identified by the officer; and
> >
> > 3. the detention is reasonably necessary given the totality of the
> > circumstances.
>
> If, in the exercise of the courts' supervisory power, a judge cannot
> conclude that these criteria were met before the person was placed
> under investigative detention, the detention will be found to be arbi-
> trary.[127]

It appears that *Mann* will continue to engender disagreement at least
until the Supreme Court has a chance to clarify its earlier decision.

---

[136] The second category of cases includes those decisions where the
Courts found there was no arbitrary detention and the fact patterns re-
semble most closely those of *Mann* either because the police had received
a tip or the police were investigating a particular crime: *R. v. Gomez*, 2006
BCPC 82; *R. v. Dykhuizen*, 2007 ABQB 489; and *R. v. Hanano*, 2007 MBQB 9,
210 Man.R. (2d) 250.

[137] The third category of cases encompasses those cases where the
Courts have not found the detention to be arbitrary and there was no
reported crime and the police were not engaged in investigating a particular crime: *R. v. Cooper*, 2005 NSCA 47, 195 C.C.C. (3d) 162; *R. v. Reid*,
[2005] O.J. No. 5618 (QL), 2005 CarswellOnt 7545 (Ont. Sup. Ct.); *R. v.
Duong*, 2006 BCCA 325, 142 C.R.R. (2d) 261; *R. v. Schrenk*, 2007 MBQB
93, [2007] 9 W.W.R. 697; *R. v. Lynds*, 2007 NSPC 47, 264 N.S.R. (2d) 24; *R.
v. Nesbeth*, 2008 ONCA 579, 238 C.C.C. (3d) 567, leave to appeal denied
[2009] S.C.C.A. No. 10 (QL); and *R. v. Pearson*, 2009 ABQB 382. Admit-
tedly, *Schrenk* is referred to with approval in the reasons of Binnie J. in
Kang-Brown at para. 94. Nonetheless, in my respectful view, insofar as
these decisions permit investigative detention without the police, and
subsequently, the trial judge, being able to say that the detention was in
relation to a particular recent or ongoing crime, these decisions are not in
keeping with *Mann*.

127 *Yeh, ibid.* at para. 143.

c) *Mann:* The Necessity Issue

In *Mann*, as we have seen, Iacobucci J. said:

> The overall reasonableness of the decision to detain . . . must further
> be assessed against all of the circumstances, most notably the extent
> to which the interference with individual liberty is necessary to per-
> form the officer's duty, the liberty interfered with, and the nature and
> extent of that interference, in order to meet the second prong of the
> *Waterfield* test.[128]

The second branch of the *Waterfield* test is described by him elsewhere
in the judgment in these terms: "[W]hether such conduct, albeit within
the general scope of such a duty, involved an unjustifiable use of powers
associated with the duty."[129] It would appear, therefore, that the *Mann*
majority felt the detention had to be necessary in the sense that it was
a justifiable use of power on the facts.

This latter requirement has been criticized elsewhere herein.
Above, in Chapter 2, Section A(4), it was suggested that at times it appears the courts have simply asked under *Waterfield* whether the police
need this power, and if so, they shall have it. The majority decision in
Yeh and that of the Ontario Court of Appeal in *Nesbeth* seem to fall into
the same trap by stressing the "importance of the community interest
served by allowing the police to pursue such practices."[130] On the other
hand, and in fairness to the *Yeh* court, the majority there found that
there was no reasonable suspicion on the facts before them. In the final
analysis, it may be the robustness of this standard that might be the ultimate test of whether investigative detentions go too far in entrenching
upon the so-called right to be left alone.

In days past, some Supreme Court judges criticized even the arrest
standard of reasonable grounds (or reasonable and probable grounds)
as not up to the task of adequately protecting the privacy of Canadians
under section 8 of the *Charter*. For example, in *Landry*, Justice Gérard
La Forest, in dissent, said, *inter alia*, about the then common law power
to enter a home to arrest on reasonable grounds:

> Let me first say something about the vagueness of the proposed test of
> "reasonable and probable cause" and the consequential danger of giv-
> ing the police power to enter into a private dwelling on that basis. The
> expression, no doubt, comprises something more than mere surmise,
> but determining with any useful measure of precision what it means

---

128 *Mann*, above note 7 at para. 34.
129 *Ibid.* at para. 24.
130 *Yeh*, above note 124 at para. 94.

beyond that poses rather intractable problems both for the police and the courts. If the principle in *Eccles v. Bourque* is to be extended to permit forcible entry into private homes, for the purpose of making arrests simply on the basis that a police officer has reasonable and probable cause, then as the Law Reform Commission put it in its working paper on *Arrest, supra*, at p. 115, it would allow him a "wide latitude based on vague, sometimes contradictory statements which provide police with few guidelines, individuals with few definable rights, and courts with little means of control"; see also John Manley's comment on *Eccles v. Bourque* in (1975), 7 *Ottawa L. Rev.* 649, at p. 656. I have found nothing in the cases or in learned commentaries that gives much assistance in giving more precision to the concept, the situations being so various. Because of the vagueness of the discretion it gives a police officer, that discretion is virtually uncontrollable. Small wonder, then, that the Law Reform Commission recommended the statutory reaffirmation of the traditional position.[131]

Of course, since that was said by the learned justice, we now have two standards that purport to be different in intensity and so the concern must be even greater. Nonetheless, the two standards seem to be here to stay. The challenge, then, is to ensure that both standards have real teeth and real value, thereby justifying the Supreme Court's faith that they can provide meaningful protection of constitutional rights.

2) Common Law Roadblocks: *R. v. Clayton*

After *Mann*, further issues reached the Supreme Court. As we have seen, in *Mann* the Court appeared to see itself as largely confirming what had already occurred in practice and been approved of in the lower courts, led by the Ontario Court of Appeal in *Simpson*. In *Mann*, the Court seemingly approved of *Murray*,[132] a prior Quebec Court of Appeal decision that had approved the use of a roadblock to block a main exit point following an armed robbery. Iacobucci J. said this about the Quebec case:

> The Court of Appeal of Quebec did not find it necessary to apply the articulable cause doctrine in *R. v. Murray* (1999), 136 C.C.C. (3d) 197. Relying upon the *Waterfield* test, Fish J.A. (as he then was) recognized a narrow police power at common law to set up immediate road

---

131 *R. v. Landry*, [1986] 1 S.C.R. 145 at para. 72 [*Landry*]. It is to be noted that *Landry* itself was later found to have countenanced an unconstitutional entry power in *R. v. Feeney*, [1997] 2 S.C.R. 13.

132 *R. v. Murray* (1999), 136 C.C.C. (3d) 197 [*Murray*].

blocks along an obvious avenue of escape from the scene of a serious crime. Fish J.A.'s comments on the exercise of this power focus specifically on its reasonable necessity in the totality of the circumstances (p. 205). The road block in *Murray* was set up immediately after the commission of a crime and was limited to an obvious escape route for the sole purpose of apprehending the fleeing perpetrators.[133]

A roadblock differs from a *Mann* stop since in a roadblock there is no individualized suspicion of a given car or its occupants, but rather a "generalized" suspicion that the suspect is going to be in one of the cars passing by and to be stopped in the roadblock. After *Mann*, it was not long before the Court itself allowed a form of roadblock after a report of gun crime.

In *Clayton*, the police received an emergency call reporting that about ten "black guys" were around a group of cars in a strip-club parking lot, and that four of them had guns "like glocks."[134] The caller described their vehicles. The police arrived at the scene minutes later and blocked both exits. The police officers at the rear exit stopped the next car to try to leave, though it did not match the description of any of the vehicles they had been given. After stopping the car, the officers observed that the two occupants were black. Some conversation between the police and the occupants ensued, which resulted in one of the occupants running away and then being apprehended: he was searched and was discovered to be carrying a gun. The other occupant was then also arrested and searched, and was also found to be armed. The two accused claimed that the detention and the searches violated their *Charter* rights. The Ontario Court of Appeal accepted this argument; however, the Supreme Court of Canada overturned that decision and found that there were no *Charter* violations.

Although the decision is difficult to understand and has been criticized,[135] the case is an important one. In *Clayton* a unanimous Court held that a police roadblock was a lawful exercise of police power in the circumstances. The question dividing the Court was why this was so. For the majority of six, Abella J. confined herself to the power at common law:

> The statement that a detention which is lawful is not arbitrary should not be understood as exempting the authorizing law, whether it is common law or statutory, from *Charter* scrutiny. Previous decisions

---

133 *Mann*, above note 7 at para. 29.
134 *Clayton*, above note 8 at para. 2.
135 See Steve Coughlan, "Common Law Police Powers and the Rule of Law" (2007) 47 C.R. (6th) 266.

of this Court are clear that where a detention by police is authorized by law, the law authorizing detention is also subject to *Charter* scrutiny: *R. v. Hufsky*, [1988] 1 S.C.R. 621; *R. v. Ladouceur*, [1990] 1 S.C.R. 1257. The courts can and should develop the common law in a manner consistent with the *Charter*: *Dagenais v. Canadian Broadcasting Corp.*, [1994] 3 S.C.R. 835, at pp. 875-78. The common law regarding police powers of detention, developed building on *R. v. Waterfield*, [1963] 3 All E.R. 659 (C.A.), and *Dedman v. The Queen*, [1985] 2 S.C.R. 2, is consistent with *Charter* values because it requires the state to justify the interference with liberty based on criteria which focus on whether the interference with liberty is necessary given the extent of the risk and the liberty at stake, and no more intrusive to liberty than reasonably necessary to address the risk. The standard of justification must be commensurate with the fundamental rights at stake.[136]

It seems that the majority is of the view that, once they have applied the *Waterfield* test to the facts, section 9 is satisfied. Oddly, section 1 seemingly gets lost in the analysis. It would seem from this that, once a common law analysis is completed, section 9 is satisfied even though the earlier cases would suggest that a stop without criteria is by its nature arbitrary and will be constitutional only when it can be justified under section 1 as a reasonable limit on section 9.

It may be that the majority is saying that the *Waterfield* test acts as a proxy for the section 1 analysis, although one would think it is preferable to say that section 9 is breached by the stop but that the power represents a reasonable limit under section 1 based on the *Waterfield* analysis. If a stop is justified by section 1, one can agree that the stop is constitutional and thus lawful. On the prior approach and because of its generalized nature, a justified roadblock was a constitutionally valid and lawful arbitrary stop.[137] On the *Clayton* reasoning, since the stop is lawful, the stop is therefore not arbitrary. Lost in the analysis is what

---

136   *Clayton*, above note 8 at para. 21.

137   It is to be noted that very recently in *Nolet*, above note 61 at para. 22, Binnie J., for a unanimous Supreme Court, seemed to revive the random equals arbitrary view when he said:

> A random vehicle stop on the highway is, by definition, an arbitrary detention: *Dedman v. The Queen*, [1985] 2 S.C.R. 2; *R. v. Hufsky*, [1988] 1 S.C.R. 621; *R. v. Ladouceur*, [1990] 1 S.C.R. 1257 (hereinafter "*Ladouceur (Ont.)*"); *Mellenthin*, and *R. v. Harris*, 2007 ONCA 574, 87 O.R. (3d) 214. The detention will only be justified under s. 1 of the *Charter* (*Hufsky*, at p. 637), if the police act within the limited highway related purposes for which the powers were conferred (*Ladouceur (Ont.)*, per Cory J., at p. 1287).

the word "arbitrary" means. Of course, Abella J. might simply be of the view that arbitrary means unlawful, full stop.

Justice Abella goes on to adopt the *Waterfield* analysis as set out in the court below, which she describes as containing "great clarity" and which requires "no further refinement." The Ontario Court of Appeal had said:

> The powers of police constables at common law, often described as the ancillary police power, as set out in *Waterfield* have been accepted by the Supreme Court of Canada as part of the Canadian common law in several decisions rendered both before and after the proclamation of the *Charter*: see e.g. *Knowlton v. The Queen* (1973), 10 C.C.C. (2d) 377 (S.C.C.) at 379-80; *Dedman v. The Queen* (1985), 20 C.C.C. (3d) 97 (S.C.C.); *R. v. Godoy* (1999), 131 C.C.C. (3d) 129 (S.C.C.) at 135-36; *R. v. Mann* [(2004), 185 C.C.C. (3d) 308 (S.C.C.)], at 320-1. The power of the police to detain for investigative purposes in some circumstances and the power to search as an incident of arrest are two of the better known examples of the exercise of the common law ancillary police power: *R. v. Mann, supra*; *R. v. Caslake* (1998), 121 C.C.C. (3d) 97 (S.C.C.) at 107-108.
>
> Where the prosecution relies on the ancillary power doctrine to justify police conduct that interferes with individual liberties, a two-pronged case-specific inquiry must be made. First, the prosecution must demonstrate that the police were acting in the exercise of a lawful duty when they engaged in the conduct in issue. Second, and in addition to showing that the police were acting in the course of their duty, the prosecution must demonstrate that the impugned conduct amounted to a justifiable use of police powers associated with that duty: *Brown v. Durham Regional Police Force* (1998), 131 C.C.C. (3d) 1 (Ont. C.A.) at 23-24.[138]

On the other hand, Abella J. disagrees with the appeal court's conclusion on the facts. While in agreement with the finding that the common law allowed such a stop of a motor vehicle, a power that "reaches beyond" the statutes, she disagreed with the Court of Appeal concerning whether this particular stop was justifiable. According to Abella J., quoting the trial judge, the police were "justified in stopping 'all vehicles' emerging from the parking lot and 'would have been dere-

---

138 *Clayton*, above note 8 at para. 22, quoting Doherty J.A. in *R. v. Clayton* (2005), 194 C.C.C. (3d) 289 at paras. 35–37 (Ont. C.A.) [emphasis deleted].

lict in their duties had they sat by and watched vehicles leave.'"[139] She stressed that

> The determination will focus on the nature of the situation, including the seriousness of the offence, as well as on the information known to the police about the suspect or the crime, and the extent to which the detention was reasonably responsive or tailored to these circumstances, including its geographic and temporal scope.[140]

Of course, in *Clayton* we are speaking of a roadblock of a single parking lot which was the result of a very recent 911 report alleging several weapons being brandished. Justice Abella held that, in all the circumstances, the roadblock was justified:

> The police had reasonable grounds to believe that there were several handguns in a public place. This represented a serious offence, accompanied by a genuine risk of serious bodily harm to the public. The police were entitled to take reasonable measures to investigate the offence without waiting for the harm to materialize and had reasonable grounds for believing that stopping cars emerging from this parking lot would be an effective way to apprehend the perpetrators of the serious crime being investigated.[141]

The majority stressed the "significant and undeniable danger" reported and that, even though the 911 report spoke only of four specific vehicles, which the accused were *not* in, the report did make the four reported vehicles part of a "larger scenario" and therefore the police roadblock was "reasonable and reasonably tailored"[142] to the situation reported. Thus, "[t]he initial stop was consequently a justifiable use of police powers associated with the police duty to investigate the offences described by the 911 caller and did not represent an arbitrary detention contrary to s. 9 of the *Charter*."[143]

For the minority, Binnie J., on the other hand, went to great lengths to analyze the circumstances from the point of view of the common law and then to subject the common law to a full *Charter* analysis. In the end, he, too, found that the roadblock was authorized by the common law and that the common law so recognized is *Charter*-compliant. In the process he described the area of police powers to be "beset with

---

139 *Clayton, ibid.* at para. 24.
140 *Ibid.* at para. 31.
141 *Ibid.* at para. 33.
142 *Ibid.* at paras. 36–40.
143 *Ibid.* at para. 41.

both uncertainty and controversy."[144] As we have seen, the judges all seem to agree that it is not their job to fully flesh out particular police powers. Such a job is for Parliament. Accordingly, then, the case does not provide much guidance for courts considering the effect of *Clayton* on other situations.

The Court seemingly denies that it is in the business of creating general police powers rather than approving the use of such power in particular circumstances. Justice Binnie's judgment is slightly more helpful, since he does discuss other situations in which the common law may authorize the use of a roadblock. He suggests, for example, that a prison break or a child kidnapping would likely give rise to a power to conduct a roadblock.[145] In deciding the case before him, he speaks of *Mann* as recognizing the "narrowly targeted police power of investigative detention based on 'individualized suspicion.'"[146] Describing the common law tendency to create police powers incrementally as the "least worst solution"[147] in the absence of parliamentary action, Binnie J. goes on to say that, on these facts

> it is of importance that the police were in fast pursuit (i.e., they ar-
> rived on the scene within five minutes of the 911 call) and limited
> their blockade to the parking lot of the premises identified by the 911
> caller. The police, in my view, had reasonable grounds to believe in
> these circumstances that a "serious crime had been committed" and
> that by means of a quick roadblock the perpetrators "might" be ap-
> prehended.[148]

How far *Clayton* goes in recognizing a police power to conduct a roadblock is difficult to say. The offence in question clearly related to firearms that had been brandished in public and the scope of the road-block was limited in the sense that it applied to a single parking lot. Thus, one can see *Clayton* as being limited to serious fact situations and roadblocks of limited scope.

However, the uncertain impact of *Clayton* can be seen by contrasting the majority judgment to that of the minority. The minority are quite clear as to what new common law power is being created:

> common law authority for the police (1) to form a blockade (2) on
> receipt of information the police consider reliable (3) about serious

---

144 *Ibid.* at para. 58.
145 *Ibid.* at para. 99.
146 *Ibid.* at para. 81.
147 *Ibid.* at para. 76.
148 *Ibid.* at para. 90

firearms offences underway or recently committed (4) limited to the premises where the offence allegedly occurred (5) sufficiently soon after the alleged incident to give police reasonable grounds for belief that the perpetrators may be caught.[149]

They acknowledge that such a specific power leaves other situations unsettled, and suggest that this is why parliamentary action, taking a broader view, would be desirable.

The majority judgment, on the other hand, is quite open-ended. It is not possible to identify *any* specific new power which they created. Rather, for them, the question was settled by the fact that what the police officers did was "reasonably necessary" given all the facts.[150] That is not a power at all: it is simply an after-the-fact assessment that what the police did was desirable and justifiable. That approach seems fundamentally at odds with the Court's stated position that "the police (and more broadly, the state) may act only to the extent that they are empowered to do so by law."[151] Indeed, more generally, "it impairs the right of citizens to know what the law is in advance and govern their conduct accordingly — a fundamental tenet of the rule of law."[152] That surely is a worrying result.

---

149 *Ibid.* at para. 89.
150 *Ibid.* at para. 41.
151 *Mann*, above note 7 at para. 15.
152 *R. v. Ferguson*, 2008 SCC 6 at para. 72.

CHAPTER 4

ARREST AND COMPELLING APPEARANCE

A. METHODS OF COMPELLING APPEARANCE

The topic of arrest — the first term in this chapter's title — will occupy a great part of the discussion below. It is necessary to recognize, however, that powers of arrest are part of a larger scheme for causing an individual who is alleged to have committed a crime to appear in court to face charges. It is for that reason that Part XVI of the *Code*, which contains the arrest powers, is actually entitled "Compelling Appearance before a Justice and Interim Release."[1]

The "compelling appearance" part of the chapter's title refers to powers of arrest but also to summonses, appearance notices, and other things. The "interim release" part refers to the various ways in which a person can, after arrest, nonetheless be released pending trial rather than held in custody. The most obvious of those ways is through the judicial interim-release portion of Part XVI, popularly referred to as "bail." That is not the only form of interim release, however, since non-judicial actors are also given a similar discretion. This chapter will

---

1   *Criminal Code*, R.S.C. 1985, c. C-46 [*Criminal Code*]. Part XVI is not limited to indictable offences, and indeed some of the arrest powers specifically are designed to cover any criminal offence. Nonetheless, note s. 795 of the *Criminal Code*, which provides, with regard to summary conviction offences, that:

> [t]he provisions of Parts XVI and XVIII with respect to compelling the appearance of an accused before a justice, and the provisions of Parts XX and XX.1, in so far as they are not inconsistent with this Part, apply, with such modifications as the circumstances require, to proceedings under this Part.

discuss the forms of interim release available prior to the bail-hearing stage, but the more complex topic of judicial interim release will be left for specialist volumes on that subject.[2]

As noted, arrest is the most well-known method of causing a person to appear in court to face charges, and the mental image most people have is probably that of a warrantless arrest. It is worth observing, therefore, that having warrantless arrest in mind as a model for that process is somewhat misleading. The most obvious actors in an arrest will be the police officers who take an accused into custody. That mental image therefore obscures the fact that the decision to make a person account for his actions to a court is generally not one made exclusively by a police officer. Rather, the decision that that is necessary must normally have been reached separately by both a police officer and a justice of the peace. Sometimes this decision by a justice of the peace will precede the police officer's interaction with the individual, sometimes it will follow it, but except in one instance – arrest without a warrant – it does occur at some point. Even in that case the accused person is then taken in front of a justice, though in a slightly different context.

Further, although the image of an arrest involves taking physical control of the accused person, that too is not the only model. Summonses and appearance notices consist of a written demand to the person to appear in court; in essence, because of the nature of the charges or the situation, it is reasonable to expect that the person will comply with the request that they appear. "Request" is not an entirely accurate word, since there are significant legal consequences for non-compliance, but at least initially the person is given the opportunity to comply voluntarily.[3]

These two considerations — whether the approval of the justice of the peace is sought beforehand or after the fact, and whether the individual is given an opportunity to comply or is physically compelled to appear — can be seen as creating a matrix of four possibilities, as set out in Figure 1 below. And, in fact, the four methods of compelling appearance — appearance notice, summons, arrest with a warrant, and arrest without a warrant — fit neatly into that matrix.[4]

---

2   See, for example, Gary Trotter, *The Law of Bail in Canada*, 2d ed. (Toronto: Carswell, 1999) [Trotter].

3   *Criminal Code*, above note 1, s. 145.

4   There are other mechanisms that are relevant to compelling appearance. For example, after an accused has been arrested and actually taken to a police lock-up, the officer in charge of the lock-up can release the person on either a promise to appear (Form 10) or a recognizance (Form 11): see *Criminal Code*, s. 498(1). These options, however, are more akin to the judicial interim-release provi-

Figure 1: CompellingAppearance Matrix

	Justice of the Peace confirmation first	Justice of the Peace confirmation second
Give written notice	Summons defined — s. 493, Form 6 lay information before JP — s. 504 issuance by JP — s. 507 issuance in private pros. — s. 507.1 contents — s. 509(1), (4), (5) service — s. 509(2), ss. 703.1-703.2 failure to comply — s. 145(4) expiry — s. 523, s. 730(2)	Appearance notice defined — s. 493, Form 9 availability — ss. 496-97 contents — s. 501 arrest for failure to comply — s. 502 failure to comply — s. 145(5) lay information before JP — s. 505 confirmation (or not) by JP — s. 508 expiry — s. 523, s. 730(2)
Take physical control	**Arrest with a warrant** availability — s. 504, s. 507(4), s. 512 contents — s. 511, 513 execution — s. 512, s. 511(3),(4) release after arrest — s. 499 take before J.P. — s. 503	**Arrest without a warrant** power — ss. 494-5 release — ss. 497-8 take before JP — s. 503 territorial validity — s. 703(1), (2)

It will be helpful at this point simply to "trace through" these various routes to compelling a person's appearance before a court. To some extent, this is an artificial division, since the routes overlap at many points or follow parallel paths: still, it is useful for purposes of clarity to examine the features of each route separately, to the extent possible. Following that we will look in greater detail at some specific issues within the compelling-appearance scheme.

The primary goal of this overview and subsequent consideration of specific issues is to examine the non-arrest methods of compelling an accused's appearance in court. Arrest will be the focus of the next section in this chapter.

---

sions, rather than the powers available to a peace officer in initiating contact with a person.

A point to note, which will be discussed in greater detail below, is that the *Code* provisions can be looked at as varying in the degree of intrusiveness with respect to individual liberty which they entail.[5] Most obviously, liberty is infringed less when an accused person is simply handed a piece of paper requiring him to appear in court on a particular date than when the police physically take control of him. More subtly, there is less of an infringement on liberty when *both* the police officer and the justice of the peace have considered beforehand whether the accused should be made to come to court, rather than the justice of the peace reviewing this decision after the accused has already been dealt with. On that basis, the matrix in Figure 1 above is least intrusive in the upper left (summons) and most intrusive in the lower right (arrest without a warrant). We shall deal with the sections in degrees of increasing intrusiveness.[6]

1) Summons

The issuing of a summons depends on two *Code* provisions: sections 504 and 507. Section 504 permits anyone to "lay an information" in front of a justice: that is, allege that a person has committed an offence.[7] Section 507 then permits the justice to decide what, if anything, to do about the allegation.

Under section 504, the information can be laid by a person having reasonable grounds, and must be in writing and under oath. The information must allege one of four things: 1) that the person committed an offence anywhere which can be tried in the province where the information is laid and that the person is in the territorial jurisdiction of the justice; 2) that the person committed an offence in the territorial jurisdiction of the justice, even if the person might no longer be in that jurisdiction; 3) that property was stolen in the territorial jurisdiction of the justice and the person has received it, anywhere, or finally; 4) that the person is in the territorial jurisdiction of the justice and is in possession of stolen property, wherever that property came from.

---

5   See Section B(3), below in this chapter.

6   Relevant to all of these approaches, see s. 20 of the *Criminal Code*, which provides that a warrant, summons, appearance notice, promise to appear, undertaking, or recognizance "may be issued, executed, given or entered into, as the case may be, on a holiday."

7   Section 504 deals with alleging that a person has committed an indictable offence. However, as noted in note 1, s. 795 of the *Criminal Code* makes Part XVI, "Compelling Appearance," applicable in the case of summary conviction offences, and so this section, and indeed all of the rules to be discussed, are equally applicable in the case of all crimes.

A justice has no discretion under section 504: she "shall receive the information." However, the fact that an information has been laid before a justice is, on its own, of no consequence. It is merely a step leading to the provisions which permit a justice to decide what, if anything, to do about the information.[8]

By far the most common next step is found in section 507, which is used when the information has been laid by a police officer (as is typically the case) or Crown prosecutor. Under that section the justice hears the allegations of the informant and of any witnesses (on oath), where he considers it desirable, and then decides what to do. Section 507(1)(b) permits a justice to issue a summons or warrant, but only "where he considers that a case for doing so is made out." In other words, the justice first decides whether the allegations actually justify requiring the person to attend court: if they do, the justice chooses between a summons or an arrest warrant. Section 507(4) directs the justice to issue a summons unless there are reasonable grounds to believe that it is "necessary in the public interest" to issue an arrest warrant. A summons or warrant can be issued even if the person could be arrested without a warrant; indeed, a justice is specifically barred from refusing to issue process on that basis.[9]

The alternative next step is found in section 507.1, which applies only in the case of a private prosecution, that is, an information laid by a member of the public. For the most part, the same rules apply,[10] but with some additional requirements. The primary difference is that, while informations laid by a police officer can go in front of any justice, an information laid by a private citizen must be considered at the later stages either by a provincial court judge or by a justice who has been designated by the chief judge of the provincial court to receive such informations.[11] That judge or justice has the same three choices — do nothing, issue a summons, issue a warrant – but there are a few other additional requirements. The judge or justice must also be satisfied that the attorney general has received a copy of the information and notice of the hearing. Further, if a judge or justice decides not to issue a summons or warrant, she endorses the information to this effect. This step will not only notify other judges or justices that the information has once been considered and rejected (since it is possible to bring a new

---

8   See Section B(1), below in this chapter.
9   See Section B(3), below in this chapter.
10   Indeed, s. 507.1(8) incorporates ss. 507(2)–(8).
11   In Quebec, the relevant court is the Court of Quebec rather than the provincial court.

application concerning the same offence[12]), it also starts a clock ticking. Six months from the date of that endorsement the information is deemed never to have been laid, unless the informant commences proceedings to compel the judge or justice to issue process.

There is one further noteworthy distinction between sections 507 and 507.1. The former refers to a justice hearing witnesses "where he considers it desirable or necessary to do so." The private-prosecution provision, on the other hand, states that "[t]he judge or designated justice may issue a summons or warrant only if he or she (a) has heard and considered the allegations of the informant and the evidence of witnesses."[13] It has been held that this creates an absolute requirement, in the case of private prosecutions, for witnesses to be called.[14] In addition, it has been suggested that a private informant should be sworn even when simply making allegations, and that where a private informant's allegations depend on information obtained from others, the informant should be expected to call those other witnesses.[15]

---

12   *Criminal Code*, above note 1, s. 507.1(7).
13   *Ibid.*, s. 507.1(3)(a).
14   *R. v. Edge*, 2004 ABPC 55 at para. 91 [*Edge*].
15   *Edge*, *ibid.* at para. 99. *Edge* contains, at paragraph 100, a useful summary of the approach to be taken in the case of private prosecutions:

- The receiving of an information is a ministerial act; the issuance of process is a judicial act. Where the informant is a private informant, the latter responsibility can only be exercised by a judge as defined in s. 507.1 or a justice who is designated pursuant to s. 507.1(10). Hereafter in these bullets, the judicial officer issuing process will be referred to as "judge" or "the judge."
- The judge who determines whether process must be issued must weigh two competing interests and perspectives: (a) the right of private informant to seek justice; (b) the right of the potential accused and that a person not be called before the court to respond to the charge without just cause. The public has an interest in both of those rights and that the process is balanced.
- These two competing interests are balanced by the judge applying the standard set out in s. 507.1(2), i.e. a case has been made out requiring an accused to be compelled to appear to answer to the charge. If so, a judicial officer shall issue a summons. A warrant can be issued where there are reasonable grounds to believe a warrant is necessary in the public interest: ss. 507.1(8) and 507(4).
- The informant bears the onus to establish that a summons or warrant should be issued. The onus is satisfied where there is a *prima facie* case that satisfies the elements of the offence charged.
- There are conditions that must be satisfied before the judge can issue process. The judge must be satisfied that the Attorney General has a copy of the information, notice of the hearing and had an opportunity to attend, cross-examine, and call relevant witnesses: ss. 507.1(3)(b)(c)(d).
- The judge may issue process only if he or she has heard and considered the allegations of the informant and the evidence of witnesses. This means

The contents of a summons are described in section 509.[16] It must be directed to the accused, describe the offence charged, and indicate a time and place for the accused to appear in court. It is to be served personally by a peace officer, or left at the accused's usual place of abode with a person over sixteen. The summons can also require the accused to appear at some other date for fingerprinting. In addition, the summons must indicate the consequences of failing to appear either for court or for identification purposes. In the former case, the accused will have committed an offence, and in the latter an arrest warrant can be issued.

A summons can be served anywhere in Canada and if served is effective no matter what territorial jurisdiction it was issued in.[17] However, a summons cannot be served outside the country without specific statutory authority, and so any such service will not give a court jurisdiction over the person.[18] Unless otherwise vacated, a summons, once served on an accused, remains in force until the trial is complete and the accused is acquitted, sentenced, or ordered held in custody pending sentencing.[19]

---

that a witness or witnesses must testify before process is issued. Where the informant has personal knowledge to prove the required elements, the informant's recorded testimony can satisfy that onus. However, where the proof relies upon the evidence of other witnesses, those witnesses should testify. Adjournments can be granted, in appropriate circumstances, to allow witnesses who can prove the required elements to attend. Where there is insufficient evidence to establish a *prima facie* case the justice will not issue process and the information will be endorsed to that effect.

- The judge does not weigh the evidence or consider any defences to the charge in coming to a determination whether a *prima facie* case exists. If a *prima facie* case has been established, the judge must issue process. The judge has some limited discretion not to issue process where he or she decides the charge is frivolous, vexatious, or abusive. There is also such discretion when the evidence is based upon the evidence of someone who is mentally disordered.

- The informant has six-months after process has been refused to appear before the same judge or another judge to request process be issued on the information. The new process request must be based upon new evidence. If process does not issue within six months the information is deemed never to have been laid: s. 507.1(5), (6).

16 See also Form 6.

17 *Criminal Code*, above note 1, s. 703.1

18 *R. v. R.J. Reynolds Tobacco Co. (Delaware)*, 2007 ONCA 749; *R. v. Shulman* (1975), 23 C.C.C. (2d) 242 (B.C.C.A.).

19 *Criminal Code*, above note 1, s. 523. Note that the summons continues to apply even if a new information is laid.

2) Arrest with a Warrant

Many of the rules that apply to summonses also apply to arrests with a warrant, since they are issued by the same route of laying an information under section 504 and process potentially being issued under sections 507 or 507.1. As noted above, justices are directed to prefer the use of a summons. However, even if a summons has previously been issued, or for that matter the accused has been released at some earlier stage (these possibilities are discussed below), an arrest warrant can be issued where there are reasonable grounds to believe it is necessary in the public interest.[20] Similarly, an arrest warrant may be issued where the accused fails to appear for court after other process has been used.[21]

Like a summons, an arrest warrant names the accused and briefly describes the offence.[22] An arrest warrant is directed to the peace officers within the territorial jurisdiction in which it is issued. It may be executed by one of those officers anywhere in the territorial jurisdiction of the issuing judge or justice, or anywhere in Canada in the case of fresh pursuit.[23] The warrant directs that the accused is to be arrested and brought before the issuing judge or justice or some other judge or justice having jurisdiction. The warrant remains in effect until it is executed.[24] It is possible for a judge or justice to delay execution of a warrant to allow an accused to turn himself in voluntarily; if the accused does so, the warrant is deemed to be executed.[25]

Once the accused has been arrested, two possibilities arise. A justice can, at the time of issuing the warrant, endorse it to allow the officer in charge of the lock-up to release the accused.[26] If that is the case, the officer in charge is entitled to release the accused on various conditions, ranging from a promise to appear to an undertaking with conditions to a recognizance.[27] If the warrant was not so endorsed, however, then the accused must be taken to a justice of the peace in accordance with

---

20   *Ibid.*, s. 512.
21   *Ibid.*
22   *Criminal Code*, above note 1, s. 511.
23   *Ibid.*, ss. 513 & 514. Note as well s. 703 of the *Criminal Code*, which provides that warrants issued by a court other than a provincial court may be executed anywhere in Canada. Section 703(2) provides that an arrest warrant issued by a provincial court judge or a justice may be executed anywhere in the province in which it is issued.
24   *Ibid.*, s. 511(2).
25   *Ibid.*, ss. 511(3) & (4).
26   *Ibid.*, s. 507(6).
27   *Ibid.*, s. 499.

Arrest and Compelling Appearance 153

section 503. That section requires that the accused be taken to a justice "without unreasonable delay" and in any case within twenty-four hours. It is important to recognize that the primary obligation created by this section is to avoid unreasonable delay. That is, a delay might well be unreasonable even though twenty-four hours has not passed: that time is better seen as creating the outer limit of possible reasonableness.[28] The twenty-four-hour limit does not apply where no justice is available within that time, but the unavailability must be based on some real obstacle, such as the accused being arrested in a remote area; an administrative decision not to have justices available on weekends, for example, could not justify non-compliance with the section.[29] This requirement of section 503 will be discussed at greater length below.[30]

Once an arrested accused is taken before a justice of the peace, the issue becomes one of judicial interim release, or bail, a subject that will not be pursued at any length in this book.[31]

3) Appearance Notice

An appearance notice is issued by a peace officer to an accused, requiring her to appear in court on a particular date. It is used as an alternative to the more intrusive route of actually arresting the accused and taking her into custody. Like a summons, it contains the accused's name, describes the offence, and sets out a date for the accused to appear in court.[32] Also like a summons, an appearance notice can require an accused to appear for fingerprinting, and must set out the consequences either of failing to comply with that requirement (a warrant will be issued) or of failing to appear in court on the specified date (the offence of failure to appear under section 145(5)).[33] Note, however, that these consequences flow only if the appearance notice is in fact confirmed later by a justice, an issue to be discussed shortly.

There are several circumstances in which an appearance notice might be used, all of which are aimed at minimizing the intrusiveness of police power. Section 495(2) of the *Code* directs a peace officer in certain circumstances not to use the power of arrest, even if it exists.[34]

---

28   R. v. Storrey, [1990] 1 S.C.R. 241 [Storrey].
29   R. v. Simpson (1994), 117 Nfld. & P.E.I.R. 110 (Nfld. C.A.), rev'd on the issue of remedy, [1995] 1 S.C.R. 449 [Simpson].
30   See Section B(4), below in this chapter.
31   For information on bail, see Trotter, above note 2.
32   *Criminal Code*, above note 1, s. 501.
33   *Ibid.*, s. 502.
34   See also Section B(4), below in this chapter.

Specifically, the *Code* discourages officers from arresting for summary conviction offences, for hybrid offences, or for indictable offences for which the method of trial is in the absolute jurisdiction of a magistrate. Put more simply, one might say that police are encouraged not to arrest in the case of less serious offences.[35] In those cases, rather than arresting, the peace officer is authorized to issue an appearance notice instead.[36] Further, even if the peace officer *does* arrest a person for one of those less serious offences, he can after the fact decide to issue an appearance notice rather than continue to hold the person in custody.[37] This might be appropriate, for example, where an immediate arrest was necessary in order to get control of a situation which then is defused and calms down.

It might be noted at this point that there is a situation which can be seen as even less serious than these less serious offences. Specifically, note that peace officers do not always have the power to arrest at all: if the offence is a summary conviction one and the officer did not find the accused committing it, then there is no power to arrest. This might be seen as the very least serious of situations, at least in the criminal context, in that not only is the offence itself minor, but there is less justification to intervene immediately because the offence itself is not ongoing. In these circumstances, even the relatively unintrusive method of issuing an appearance notice is not available. Rather, the only option available to an officer is to go to a justice in order to lay an information and seek a summons or warrant.

When a police officer has issued an appearance notice, a route parallel to the "section 504/507" route for issuing a summons or warrant is then followed. Under section 505, the police officer is required to lay an information relating to that offence (or another one) before a justice. This information is, according to the section, to be laid as soon as practicable and in any event before the time stated in the appearance notice for the accused to appear in court. As will be discussed further below, however, this requirement has not been interpreted strictly by courts. Once the information is laid, the justice of the peace considers it, under section 508. As with a summons or warrant, the justice of the peace is to hear the informant and can hear witnesses. The choices available to the justice at that stage are to cancel the appearance notice entirely, to confirm it, or to issue a summons or warrant in its place.[38]

---

35 See Section B(3), below in this chapter.
36 *Criminal Code*, above note 1, s. 496.
37 *Ibid.*, s. 497.
38 *Ibid.*, s. 508.

Note that an officer issuing an appearance notice is to request that the accused sign a duplicate of it, though the failure to sign does not invalidate the process.[39] Whether she signs it or not, the accused is to be given a copy of the appearance notice. Further, in seeking confirmation of the appearance notice in front of a justice, the police must prove at that point that a copy was given to the accused; that is, it is not sufficient only to prove service of the appearance notice in court, if the accused fails to comply with it.[40]

If confirmed, like a summons, an appearance notice remains in force until the trial is complete and the accused is acquitted, sentenced, or ordered held in custody pending sentencing.[41]

4) Arrest without a Warrant

Various powers of warrantless arrest are created in sections 494 and 495 of the *Code*: they will be discussed in greater detail below. It is sufficient to note here that they are given to both private citizens and to peace officers, and that their availability depends primarily on the type of offence and whether the person arresting has witnessed the offence or only believes on reasonable grounds that it has occurred. For purposes of tracing through the "route" for various methods of compelling appearance, there is for the most part no significant difference between an arrest without a warrant and with one. Although different *Code* sections govern the two situations, they describe essentially parallel routes.

As already noted, if an accused has been arrested with a warrant, he might nonetheless be released by the police rather than retained in custody, if the issuing justice has authorized this. Similarly, it was noted that a peace officer can, in the case of less serious offences, issue an appearance notice either as an alternative to an arrest without a warrant or following it. In addition to those possibilities, the officer in charge of a lockup to which a person arrested without a warrant has been taken also has the ability to release a person.[42]

---

39   *Ibid.*, s. 501(4).

40   *R. v. DeMelo* (1994), 92 C.C.C. (3d) 52 (Ont. C.A.).

41   *Criminal Code*, above note 1, s. 523. Note that the summons continues to apply even if a new information is laid.

42   *Ibid.*, s. 498. The officer in charge can release an accused in a broader range of circumstances than an arresting officer can, and is also permitted to impose greater restrictions on the accused's liberty in exchange for being released: see Section B(3), below in this chapter.

If the accused is released in any of these fashions in a situation where there was or could have been a warrantless arrest, then the police officer is directed to lay an information in front of a justice.[43] In that event, the ordinary rules about laying an information, discussed above, will apply. If the arrested person is not released, on the other hand, then, just as when an accused is arrested under a warrant, she must be taken under section 503 of the *Code* in front of a justice of the peace without unreasonable delay and in any case within twenty-four hours.

Arrest without a warrant can differ from the other methods of compelling appearance in one fashion, noted at the start: a justice does not oversee the officer's decision that the person should be made to come to court at all. This is quite surprising, at a conceptual level. The purpose of this review in other contexts is to "place a judicial officer between the informant and the defendant to ensure that the liberty of the subject was secure from unwarranted intrusion."[44] There is no obvious reason that those subject to arrest without a warrant — the *most* intrusive method of compelling appearance — should have the least protection in this regard, and yet "[t]he current statutory scheme actually provides greater procedural protection for those charged with an offence whom the police choose not to arrest or release."[45]

That is, in the case of a summons or warrant, section 507 permits a justice to decide that no case for issuing any process has been made out. In the case of an appearance notice, section 508(1)(c) gives the justice the power to cancel the appearance notice on the grounds that it ought not to have been issued. But, when an accused is arrested without a warrant and is *not* released on an appearance notice, no precise analogue to this supervisory function can be found. The officer must still lay an information under section 504 charging the accused with an offence, of course. However, although section 504 normally leads to a review under section 507, that latter section notes that it does not apply "if an accused has already been arrested." An accused is not entirely without options, but a review by a justice of the peace as to whether the charge was justified is not among them:

> It should be pointed out that the issue of whether the person arresting the accused had sufficient grounds to do so cannot be inquired into with a view to quashing the information charging the accused.

---

43   *Ibid.*, s. 505.

44   *R. v. Jeffrey* (1976), 34 C.R.N.S. 283 at para. 9 (Ont. Prov. Ct. (Crim. Div.)) [*Jeffrey*].

45   James Stribopoulos, "Unchecked Power: The Constitutional Regulation of Arrest Reconsidered" (2003) 48 McGill L.J. 225 at 252–53 [Stribopoulos].

That is not to say that the arrested accused could not sue the arresting party for false imprisonment and malicious prosecution where the arrest is without factual foundation. Additionally, an accused could attempt to establish that the arrest was arbitrary, thereby contravening s. 9 of the *Canadian Charter of Rights and Freedoms.*[46]

Nonetheless, the fact remains that, in the case of arrest without a warrant, no judicial screening mechanism is provided. Although the accused is brought to a justice, that justice will consider only whether the accused should be released pending trial, not whether the accused should have to face trial at all.

B. ISSUES WITHIN COMPELLING APPEARANCE

1) The Role of the Justice

A common feature to all of the methods of compelling appearance is the requirement for some person, at some point, to lay an information before a justice.[47] Several issues are worth noting in this regard.

The most important thing to stress about the process for laying informations and issuing process is its two-step nature. Many cases have noted the important distinction to be drawn between laying an information under section 504 and asking a justice to act on that information under section 507.

In the former task, the justice of the peace is acting "ministerially" or "administratively." That is, in receiving the information, the justice is making sure that it is valid on its face: that it is in writing, that it sufficiently describes the accused person so as to make him identifiable, that it alleges an offence known to law, that the jurisdictional requirements are met, and so on. Provided these technical requirements are satisfied, the justice has no choice but to accept the information.[48]

---

46   R. v. *Whitmore* (1987), 41 C.C.C. (3d) 555 at 561 (Ont. H.C.J.) [*Whitmore*], aff'd (1989), 51 C.C.C. (3d) 294 (Ont. C.A.) [*Whitmore* appeal]. The Court of Appeal accepted the trial judge's conclusions and added some observations of their own.

47   Form 2 in the *Criminal Code*, above note 1, sets out the format for an information: see s. 506.

48   See, for example *Re Watt*, 1999 YTTC 16 at para. 5:

> Mr. Watt (the informant) will recall that he placed this Information before Justice of the Peace Studds and the Information was sworn. That step in the process is referred to as receiving an Information or swearing an Informa-

However, that merely means that the first step has been taken — an information has been laid. Generally speaking, unless the justice carries on to issue a summons or warrant or confirm the appearance notice, there are no consequences for the accused from the simple fact that an information has been laid. It is at the second step, deciding whether process should be issued based on the information, that an accused begins to face potential consequences, and it is at this stage that a justice is required to act judicially.[49] Note that, although the wording of the section implies that the same justice undertakes both roles, this is not necessarily the case, and a second justice can decide whether to issue process based on an information laid before the first.[50]

This is one of the reasons that justices of the peace "occupy a critical role as the point of entry into the criminal justice system."[51] It is the role of the justice to act as a check on state power, in this particular context by preventing the police from bringing to court anyone they choose. However, institutional structures have not always made it easy for justices of the peace to genuinely play this role. The Supreme Court of Canada has noted that

---

> tion, and it is an administrative or ministerial act. It is not a judicial act. If, on the face of it, the wording of the Information appears to make out an offence known or recognized in law, the justice of the peace has no choice but to swear the Information. But that does not result in anything being done. The Information is merely sworn. In order for something to happen on the Information a judicial officer has to make a decision that process should issue, process meaning summons that should issue and the parties should be brought to court to answer to the charge.

In *Whitmore* appeal, above note 46, the Ontario Court of Appeal (although not making specific reference to the *Criminal Code* sections) observed at 296 that "the duty of the justice of the peace is, first, to determine if the information is valid on its face and secondly, to determine whether it discloses or there is disclosed by the evidence a prima facie case of the offences alleged." At the trial level in *Whitmore*, above note 46, Ewaschuk J. had suggested that a justice's role in deciding the facial validity of an information did not extend to such questions as whether it was duplicitous. However, his reasoning seems to depend in part on the fact that at the time many if not most justices would not have had legal training. With the changes in qualifications for justices of the peace since then (see below), it is not clear that the same rationale would still apply.

49 *Jeffrey*, above note 44; *Whitmore*, above note 46. See also *R. v. Jean Talon Fashion Centre Inc.* (1975), 22 C.C.C. (2d) 223 (Que. Q.B.). In *Whitmore* it is noted at 564 that the justice who "hears and considers ex parte the allegations of the informant," along with any witnesses, is required to act judicially: *R. v. Allen* (1974), 20 C.C.C. (2d) 447 (Ont. C.A.).

50 *R. v. Southwick* (1968), 1 C.C.C. 356 (Ont. C.A.); *Edge*, above note 14; *Re Willisko* (1980), 13 Alta. L.R. (2d) 298 (Q.B.).

51 *Ell v. Alberta*, 2003 SCC 35 at para. 5 [*Ell*].

the whole concept, that the office should stand as a safeguard of the civil rights of the individual against the exercise of arbitrary police power, is in many cases, and probably in most cases, little more than a sham. In saying this we do not want to be taken as condemning individuals. We are condemning a system under which many conscientious and dedicated individuals are required to work.[52]

As a result, in relatively recent years provinces have taken steps to improve the qualifications and other aspects of the role of the justice of the peace, in order to allow them to act more independently.[53] The Court has held that the concept of judicial independence does apply to justices of the peace because of the role they play. Legislative change has been intended to help protect that. Legislation varies from province to province, of course, but typically there are now two categories of justices of the peace: sitting and non-sitting, or presiding and non-presiding. We will not here pursue the details of each province's scheme,

---

52 *Ell, ibid.* at para. 6, quoting from the *Royal Commission Inquiry into Civil Rights: Report No. 1*, vol. 2 (Toronto: Queen's Printer, 1968) c. 38. Note as well this observation from the trial level in *R. v. Morton* (1992), 70 C.C.C. (3d) 244 at para. 10 (Ont. Ct. Gen. Div.), aff'd (1993), 83 C.C.C. (3d) 95 (Ont. C.A.) [*Morton*] dealing with the procedure for swearing informations in a jurisdiction where (as is often the case) a particular officer is designated as the court officer, responsible for swearing informations in front of a justice:

> Sergeant Neeson testified that he had sworn the information before the justice of the peace in this case. He indicated that in the course of his duties as a court officer, he would swear several informations on any given day. When this occurred, there would be a number of officers lined up to see the justice of the peace and they would get 10 or 15 seconds per information.

53 *Justice of the Peace Act*, R.S.A. 2000, c. J-4; *Provincial Court Act*, R.S.B.C. 1996, c. 379; *The Provincial Court Act*, C.C.S.M. c. C275 [enacted as: R.S.M. 1987, c. C275]; *Provincial Court Act*, R.S.N.B. 1973, c. P-21; *Justices Act*, R.S.N.L. 1990, c. J-6; *Justices and Other Public Authorities Protection Act*, R.S.N.L. 1990, c. J-7; *Justices of the Peace Act*, R.S.N.W.T. 1988, c. J-3, as am. by R.S.N.W.T. 1988, c. 39 (Supp.) in force 2 November 1992: SI-014-92; S.N.W.T. 1997, c. 3; S.N.W.T. 1998, c. 15; S.N.W.T. 2003, c. 9 in force 1 April 2003; S.N.W.T. 2003, c. 12; S.N.W.T. 2003, c. 31 in force 1 April 2004: SI-003-2004; S.N.W.T. 2007, c. 16; *Justices of the Peace Act*, R.S.N.S. 1989, c. 244, as am. by 1992, c. 16, ss. 71–76; 2000, c. 28, ss. 56–64; 2002, c. 10, ss. 7–9; 2007, c. 18, s. 1; *Justices of the Peace Act*, R.S.O. 1990, c. J.4 as am. by S.O. 1994, c.12, ss. 50–57; S.O. 1999, c. 12, Sch. B, s. 12; S.O. 2002, c. 18, Sch. A, s. 11; S.O. 2002, c. 17, Sch. F; S.O. 2006, c. 21, Sch. B, ss.1–19; 2007, c. 7, Sch. 20; S.O. 2006, c. 35, Sch. C, ss. 56(1) and (3); *Provincial Court Act*, R.S.P.E.I. 1988, c. P-25; *Summary Convictions Act*, R.S.Q. c. P-15, *Courts of Justice Act*, R.S.Q. c. T-16; *The Justices of the Peace Act, 1988*, S.S. 1988–89, c. J-5.1 (effective 1 May 1989), as am. by the S.S. 1997, c. 10; *Territorial Court Act*, R.S.Y. 2002, c. 217.

but the essential distinction that has been drawn has been to separate out those justices who are required to act judicially by issuing process such as summons, arrest warrants, or search warrants, and to create different qualifications for them: often the requirement that they have a law degree, among other things.

We will now consider in turn the ministerial and judicial aspects of the justice's role. First, note that section 504, dealing with the ministerial act of receiving the information, requires that it be laid by someone who "on reasonable grounds, believes that a person has committed an indictable offence." The question of what constitutes reasonable grounds has been discussed above, in Chapter 2, Section C(2).The point to note here is that the requirement that the informant personally *believes* is also crucial.

The laying of an information is an important point in the criminal justice process. It is the point at which, at least conceptually, the state ceases to investigate an offence and begins to try to prove that a particular person is guilty of it.[54] The rules therefore demand that the process of laying an information not, to the extent possible, merely be seen as a matter of paperwork to be got out of the way.

In *Pilcher*, for example, the accused, two police officers, were charged with theft of firearms.[55] At trial they called as their witness the police officer who had sworn the information. He testified that he had been instructed by a superior officer and a senior Crown attorney to go before a justice of the peace and lay the information, but that he was not given any details about it. His normal practice before swearing an information was to read the police reports and summaries of the investigation prepared by other officers, in order to have reasonable grounds to believe the offence had been committed. In this case he testified that he knew nothing beyond what was stated in the information itself. The trial judge held that, on these facts, the information was invalid and had to be quashed. The informant was entitled to rely on information provided by others in order to form reasonable grounds, but he was required to actually form them personally: simply being told by someone

---

54   See *Lindsay v. British Columbia (A.G.)*, 2005 BCSC 1494 at para. 11, where the court observes that: "The process set out in the *Code* (see, for example, s. 504 to s. 597.1 of the *Code*) establishes a finely tuned set of checks and balances which, coupled with a modicum of judicial discretion, work together to provide part of the process that leads to a just determination of a criminal proceeding" and concludes therefore that there are no alternative ways of commencing criminal proceedings.

55   *R. v. Pilcher* (1981), 58 C.C.C. (2d) 435 (Man. Prov. Ct.).

else that the grounds existed was not sufficient. As the Ontario High Court of Justice put it in *Peavoy*:

> Recognizing that the pressure of duties and administration upon police forces may quite naturally cause them, when under pressure, to manage the laying of informations as a form of routine 'paperwork,' I feel obliged to add the following comments. A person swearing an information, particularly a law enforcement officer, is not at liberty to swear the information in a perfunctory or irresponsible manner with a reckless disregard as to the truth of his assertion. To do so is clearly an affront to the Courts and is at variance with the right of the citizen to be left alone by the authorities unless there is reasonable and probable grounds for invading his liberty by compelling his attendance before the Courts. The police officer who does not satisfy himself that he can personally swear to the truth of the information according to its terms (i.e., personal knowledge or reasonable and probable grounds), yet does so, jeopardizes his personal position and also does a disservice to the upholding of law in the community. His oath must be beyond reproach. He need not, of course, have personal knowledge of all the facts or even most of the facts that support the allegation; indeed much of what would be available to him will, so far as he is concerned, be hearsay. He must, however, be satisfied, even if it be on the basis of reliable reports made by other persons in the course of an investigation, that there is some evidence to support the charge, that that evidence in fact constitutes reasonable and probable grounds for believing that the accused committed the offence and that he believes that the accused did so.[56]

Similarly, for the information to be valid on its face, it must adequately identify the accused. *Buchbinder* presented a rather odd situation in which the informant (the matter was a private prosecution) alleged that four RCMP members were in possession of documents which had been stolen from him, but he did not know the identity of the particular officers who had taken them. The information was laid against "an unknown person that can be pointed out": the informant's intention was then to rely on the power of a justice in section 507 to hear the evidence of witnesses, in order to compel testimony from a former RCMP superintendent who would be able to identify the particular officers.[57] The Court of Appeal held, however, that the information was fatally flawed, and so could not satisfy the earlier section 504

---

56   *R. v. Peavoy* (1974), 15 C.C.C. (2d) 97 at para. 39 (Ont. H.C.J.).
57   *Re Buchbinder and Venner* (1985), 47 C.R. (3d) 135 (Ont. C.A.).

stage: in that event there was no jurisdiction to issue subpoenas or otherwise call witnesses for a section 507 proceeding. It rejected the suggestion that there might be some sort of "halfway house" whereby an information that was not sufficient to allow process to be issued might be sufficient to allow a hearing to be held.

On the other hand, the court in *Buchbinder* did note that something less than the accused's name might be sufficient, and that an information could be valid as long as it sufficiently described the accused. Without deciding the point, the court seemed to suggest that a narrower description than "unknown person that can be pointed out" — something that identified where the officers worked, when they worked there, and other details — might be sufficient. In concluding that a name was not always necessary, the court held:

> If a description was given in an information that the accused was short, swarthy, had a prominent scar on his left cheek, and was referred to as "Marty," surely the Justice of the Peace could "receive" such an information and permit witnesses to be brought forth by the complainant who could further identify him for the purpose of greater specificity in the information and subsequent warrant or summons. An example closer to home would be the case of an unidentified police officer who commits an assault. The victim knows the force he belongs to, his rank and badge number, and states that he can identify him. Is the entire process of the law then to be frustrated because the Chief of Police refuses to tell the complainant the name of the police officer to whom that badge number was assigned?[58]

A further issue related to the justice's judicial function has to do with exercising the powers in the *Code* for a proper purpose. In particular, it was noted above that, when a summons is issued requiring an accused to appear in court on a particular date, that summons can require the accused to appear for fingerprinting or other identification purposes. In *Michelsen* the accused had been arrested, fingerprinted, and then released by a justice on a recognizance; subsequently, the police decided that they also wanted to obtain a palm print from him. They therefore obtained a summons from a justice which only required the accused to appear for the purposes of providing that palm print. The accused was successful in having that summons quashed. It was held that the only justification for a summons was as a method of compelling the accused to appear in court, a purpose that was already accomplished in this case by the recognizance he had signed. Without

---

58   *Ibid.* at 146–47.

that primary justification for a summons, the ancillary ability to compel the accused to appear for fingerprinting did not exist: the summons procedure was not intended to be an investigative technique.[59]

Sections 507 and 508 set out the justice's judicial function of deciding whether process should issue based on the information.[60] In 1986 the Law Reform Commission suggested that there was little authority on the issue of what standard a justice is to apply in deciding whether "a case for doing so is made out," as the *Code* requires. The commission concluded that it must be at least the reasonable grounds standard that would apply to a warrantless arrest, but that probably nothing more stringent is required.[61] Since that time, various courts have stated that a justice's task is to decide whether the information or the evidence presented discloses a *prima facie* case, which is a stricter standard than reasonable grounds.[62] It has been suggested that the standard is lower than that of a judge deciding whether to commit an accused at a preliminary inquiry.[63] Others suggest, however, that the standard *is* analogous to that for committing at a preliminary inquiry, although the rules of evidence are more relaxed.[64]

---

59   *Re Michelsen* (1983), 4 C.C.C. (3d) 371 (Man. Q.B.).

60   Note the quite fundamental point about acting judicially included in s. 507(5), namely, that a justice shall not sign a summons or warrant in blank.

61   The Law Reform Commission of Canada, *Arrest*, Working Paper 41 (Ottawa: Law Reform Commission of Canada, 1986) at 42 [LRC, *Arrest*].

62   *R. v. Morton* (1993), 83 C.C.C. (3d) 95 (Ont. C.A.), aff'g (1992), 70 C.C.C. (3d) 244 (Ont. Ct. Gen. Div.). The Court of Appeal does not discuss the justification for adopting the *prima facie* case standard, but that justification is considered at some length in the decision below, which it upholds. *Storrey*, above note 28, makes clear that the reasonable-grounds standard is a lower one than that of a *prima facie* case: see Chapter 2. See also *R. v. Fry* (1998), 38 R.F.L. (4th) 328 (B.C.C.A.), which upholds the lower court's decision based on the conclusion that process should issue only where a *prima facie* case is made out.

63   See the useful review of caselaw in *Re Sorenson*, [2001] B.C.J. No. 2114 (Prov. Ct.). See also *Re Lindsay*, 2005 BCPC 176 at para. 12, summarizing the conclusions in *Sorenson*:

1.   under s. 507 the justice of the peace "effectively fills the role of a grand jury," as regards the finding of grounds to issue a process;

2.   the threshold test is that there must be tangible evidence from which one might conclude that the offence has been committed by the person named in the information;

3.   the threshold test is lower than that required to commit on a preliminary inquiry;

4.   the test is "whether the information or the allegations of the informant and any evidence of witnesses . . . disclose a prima facie case . . ."

64   *Edge*, above note 14 at para. 63, quoting Quigley: "[He] seemed to agree with that approach but added the following at p. 231 of his text: 'The rules of evi-

The justice must consider the evidence not only of the informant but also of any witnesses who are called in deciding whether to issue process.[65] This requirement parallels, more or less, the obligation of a police officer to consider all the evidence known to her in deciding whether she subjectively has reasonable grounds.[66] However, the application for a summons or warrant is conducted on an *ex parte* basis, so as a practical matter the only witnesses likely to be called are those who can be expected to provide evidence which favours issuing some sort of process. Witnesses can be called even if they were discovered only after the laying of the information; the important question is what evidence is available at the time the justice decides whether to issue process. The *Code* makes the hearing of witnesses optional, not mandatory.[67]

The *Code* does not specify that this hearing must take place in *camera*, but caselaw has imposed that requirement for hearings held under both section 507 and section 507.1.[68] This has been justified in part on the basis that the statutory requirement for proceedings against an accused to take place in open court did not apply, since until a justice had decided whether to issue process there *was* no "accused." In addition, there was a much greater privacy interest to be protected at a stage where allegations which might turn out to be unfounded and not to justify the laying of charges were made.[69]

The holding that the standard for issuing process on an information is analogous to the test at a preliminary inquiry has an important element that should be noted. The standard for committal at a pre-

---

dence are relaxed for pre-inquiries, however, so that the justice is permitted to rely on hearsay or other evidence that might not be admissible at a trial or preliminary inquiry.'"

65 *Whitmore*, above note 46 at 568: "[A] justice acting under s. 455.3 must consider not only the allegations of the informant but also the evidence of other witnesses where they are called: *Re Tait* (1950), 11 C.R. 42 at 53 (B.C.C.A.)."

66 See Chapter 2.

67 Section 507(1)(a)(ii). There is authority suggesting that, although s. 795 of the *Code* makes s. 507 applicable to summary conviction offences, there is no authority for a justice to hear witnesses in considering such charges. See *Whitmore* (trial level), above note 46 at 564:

It is also interesting to note that, a justice determining whether or not to issue process in respect of a summary conviction offence has never had the jurisdiction to hear witnesses in addition to the informant: see s. 723 of the *Criminal Code* and *R. v. Sweeney* (1912), 19 C.C.C. 222 (N.S.S.C. in banco).

See also *Canada v. Galbraith*, 2001 BCSC 675; *R. v. Gibbs*, [2006] 3 C.T.C. 223 (B.C.S.C.).

68 See *Southam Inc. v. Coulter* (1990), 60 C.C.C. (3d) 267 (Ont. C.A.).

69 *Ibid.*

liminary inquiry has, somewhat unusually, been largely developed in the context of extradition hearings. In *Shephard*, the Supreme Court held that a justice is to commit for trial at a preliminary inquiry if "there is admissible evidence which could, if it were believed, result in a conviction."[70] That standard was taken to imply that a judge could not weigh the evidence presented and decide to reject any of it as unreliable. More recently, however, the Court has held that that cannot be the case. In *Ferras*, again an extradition case, the Court held it was "axiomatic that a person could not be committed for trial for an offence in Canada if the evidence is so manifestly unreliable that it would be unsafe to rest a verdict upon it."[71] Lower courts, even prior to *Ferras*, had concluded that essentially this same standard had to be applicable in the case of a decision by a justice whether to issue process based on an information. That is, although the question is whether a *prima facie* case has been made out, which in large measure requires the justice simply to accept the evidence presented, the justice is not simply a rubber stamp. Consequently there is a discretion to refuse to act "where the basis is abusive, frivolous, vexatious, or the informant is not credible because of mental disorder."[72] However, a justice is not entitled to consider issues such as whether the accused might have a defence to the charge.[73]

The judicial role in section 507 can be thought of in two quite different ways. First, without this step, the criminal process has not really been invoked at all: the laying of an information by itself does not mean that an accused has been "charged" in the sense in which that term is generally understood. For example, although the attorney general has the power to stay charges, this power cannot be exercised when the only step which has been taken is to lay an information under section 505: it is only after a summons or warrant has been issued that the power to stay exists.[74] Second, once the justice has acted judicially, the

---

70   *United States v. Shephard*, [1977] 2 S.C.R. 1067.

71   *United States v. Ferras*, 2006 SCC 33 at para. 40. The Court held as well, in the same paragraph: "Similarly, I take it as axiomatic that a person could not be committed to trial for an offence in Canada if the evidence put against the person is not available for trial."

72   See *Edge*, above note 14 at para. 73. See also *Marcotte v. Pelletier*, [1998] R.J.Q. 3186 (Que. S.C.).

73   *Edge*, above note 14 at para. 85.

74   *R. v. Dowson*, [1983] 2 S.C.R. 144. On the other hand, see also *Casey v. Automobiles Renault Canada Ltd.*, [1965] S.C.R. 607, where the Court held that an accused could sue for malicious prosecution in a case where the informant had laid the information but no process had yet been issued. The Court found there that the informant had done everything in his power to commence proceedings,

criminal justice process *has* begun: accordingly, there are a number of requirements for that step.

Sections 507 and 508 require that the justice "hear" the allegations of the informant. There is authority suggesting that this requirement is to be taken quite literally, and therefore that, beyond simply being sworn, the informant must actually testify in front of the justice.[75] Others take the view that it is sufficient for the justice to read the material filed and simply ask the informant whether it is true.[76] In any case, it is agreed that no very great level of formality is expected, evidence is not recorded, and so on, because the accused's interests will eventually be adequately protected by the trial process.[77] Nonetheless, it has been suggested that

> [i]n the vast majority of cases, the justice should question the informant, the more so where the informant has only hearsay knowledge of the charge, to decide whether process should issue. Often an inquiry of a few minutes will suffice. In other cases, the inquiry must be more detailed. If the justice is not satisfied that the informant has a sufficient factual basis justifying the issuance of process, the justice must hear the evidence of other witnesses. In such case, it is "necessary to do so" in accordance with s. 455.3(1)(a)(ii): *R. v. Ingwer* (1955), 113 C.C.C. 361 at pp. 365-6, [1956] O.R. 60, 22 C.R. 399 (Ont. H.C.J.), and *R. v. Jean Talon Fashion Center Inc.* (1975), 22 C.C.C. (2d) 223 at p. 228, 56 D.L.R. (3d) 296 (Que. Q.B.). Even though an informant might have sufficient grounds to justify process, the justice may still consider it "desirable" to hear the evidence of other witnesses, especially where the witnesses are alleged accomplices, of disreputable backgrounds, or closely associated to the accused.[78]

---

and was therefore liable in tort. Note, however, that the Court also seems to suggest on the facts that the justice had heard the informant and in some way acted judicially, even though he had not yet issued any process.

75 *Jeffrey*, above note 44 at para. 5: ". . . I cannot interpret 'hear' to mean 'see' or 'read'." See also *R. v. Brown* (1975), 28 C.C.C. (2d) 398 (Ont. Prov. Ct.). Note the observation in *Edge*, above note 14 at para. 43, however, that "[s]ome older jurisprudence support the view that the justice is only obliged to read the information and to ask the informant if the allegations are true: *Ex parte Archambault* (1910), 16 C.C.C. 433 (Que. K.B.) at p. 438; *R. v. Mitchell* (1911), 19 C.C.C. 113 (Ont. H.C.) at pp. 121-2; *Ex parte Dolan*; *Kay* (1911), 26 C.C.C. 171 (N.B.S.C.)."

76 See *R. v. Brar*, 2007 ONCJ 359, citing Roger E. Salhany, *Canadian Criminal Procedure*, 6th ed. (Aurora, ON: Canada Law Book, 1996) at 3-26.

77 *Morton*, above note 52; *R. v. Ingwer*, [1956] O.R. 60 (H.C.J.); *Edge*, above note 14.

78 *Morton*, *ibid.* at 565, citing Ewaschuk J. in *Whitmore*, above note 46 at 564–65 (H.C.J.).

It might seem to be difficult to reconcile these requirements with the reality that in many cases a single officer is responsible for swearing informations in front of a justice and that only a very short time might be available for each. In large part, the explanation can be found in the presumption of regularity, which imposes on an accused the onus of proving that the proper procedures were not followed. In *Morton*, for example, a court officer testified that when he laid informations in front of a justice, he would swear several informations on any given day, that there would be a number of officers lined up to see the justice of the peace, and that they would get ten or fifteen seconds per information. He also testified that he was always asked whether the information was true to the best of his knowledge but was only sometimes asked other questions. He further stated that he did not have any specific recollection of laying the information in that case.[79] On those facts, an objection to the validity of the information was rejected. It was held that the presumption of regularity required a judge to begin by presuming that the information *had* been properly issued. The court officer's testimony that he did not recall what had happened and that he was only sometimes asked questions did not rebut that presumption, in which case it remained intact; on that basis, the objection to validity was rejected. The court suggested that it did not intend to condone perfunctory or rudimentary hearings, but it must be said that this decision certainly does little to discourage them.

There are other factors that serve to limit the extent to which the justice's supervisory role is a real one. Most significantly, it is worth noting the consequences of a failure by the justice to actually perform that role: in a great many cases, there will be none. In *Pottle*, for example, the justice who issued the summons actually testified that she had not conducted the hearing that was required. The Court of Appeal held that this failure resulted in a loss of jurisdiction over the person, but not over the offence. The loss of jurisdiction over the person was of no consequence, since it was regained when the accused actually did appear for trial. In that event, it really made no difference that the justice had not performed the second, and one might think more important, of her two functions.[80]

The basis upon which this conclusion is reached depends, in fact, on the separation between the ministerial and judicial functions. On the one hand, the ministerial function only involves confirming the

---

79   *Morton, ibid.*

80   *R. v. Pottle* (1978), 49 C.C.C. (2d) 113 (Nfld. C.A.). See also *R. v. Hrankowski* (1980), 54 C.C.C. (2d) 174 (Alta. C.A.) [*Hrankowski*].

facial validity of the information: on the other hand, it actually *does* confirm that validity. In other words, once the ministerial stage has been properly complied with, the information is valid and remains so, despite any later failures at the judicial stage.[81] The general position of courts is that any errors are of no consequence if the accused does in fact appear in court, since it is not possible for an accused to make a "conditional appearance" simply to object to jurisdiction:

> The argument is also made that if an accused is not obliged to appear by reason of a defect in process, why should he not be entitled to appear solely to make this point and to obtain the Court's declaration on it in his favour. I appreciate the apparent logic of this submission but it appears to me that it overlooks one of the basic functions of process and that is to bring the accused before the Court. If this purpose is accomplished, and the objection is not based on jurisdictional grounds, the balance of policy considerations is in favour of holding that the Court does have jurisdiction, regardless of protest.[82]

This argument has been taken to apply not merely when there is some non-jurisdictional defect in the information itself, but also where there have been other errors at the preliminary stages.[83] Accordingly, where there is some problem with an appearance notice rendering it invalid but an information has been filed, it is possible for a summons later to be issued based on that information.[84] It would be the case, however, that an accused who did not respond to an invalid summons would not be guilty of the offence of failing to appear.[85]

---

81   To the same effect, see *R. v. Bachman*, [1979] 6 W.W.R. 468 at para. 14 (B.C.C.A.), where the issuing justice had not held the necessary hearing: "There may have been various reasons for this. I need not examine them or discuss them. Suffice it to say that he did not, apparently, hold the hearing contemplated by the section. The information did not thereby become a nullity. It remained valid."

82   *R. v. Gougeon* (1980), 55 C.C.C. (2d) 218 (Ont. C.A.) (*Gougeon*). Also quoted in *R. c. Manseau* (1992), 73 C.C.C. (3d) 476 (Que. C.A.). See also *R. v. Harnish* (1979), 49 C.C.C. (2d) 190 (N.S.S.C.A.D.) [*Harnish*].

83   In a similar vein, see s. 546 of the *Criminal Code*, above note 1, which provides that an irregularity in the substance or form of a summons or warrant does not affect the validity of a preliminary inquiry. See also *R. v. Curlew* (1981), 64 C.C.C. (2d) 211 (Nfld. C.A.).

84   See, for example, *R. v. McAskill* (1981), 58 C.C.C. (2d) 361 (N.S.S.C.A.D.), or *R. v. Thomson* (1984), 11 C.C.C. (3d) 435 (Alta. C.A.).

85   See, for example *R. v. Gray*, [1979] O.J. No. 1598 (H.C.J.). The problem with the information in that case was that it had not been sworn as soon as practicable after the appearance notice was issued, a question that will be pursued at greater length below. That fact did not mean that he could not still be tried for the

Note as well that, if a justice acts judicially and decides not to issue process, mandamus does not lie to require the justice to do so. Mandamus lies only to require someone to perform their legal duty; if the justice has actually performed his judicial duty, mandamus cannot be used as a method of review of the decision reached.[86] It could be that a justice who acts based on extraneous considerations has not really performed her duty, in which case a remedy might be available, but even then that remedy would amount only to ordering the justice to hear the matter again: mandamus cannot require a particular result.[87]

The justice's role is a supervisory one, though the exact nature of that supervision varies with the context. Where an appearance notice has been laid and taken to a justice, for example, the justice is authorized under section 508(1)(c) to cancel the appearance notice and cause the accused to be informed of that cancellation; in effect, in that instance the justice's decision does stop the process, subject of course to a new process being sought. Put another way, the justice says "yes" or "no" to the possibility of further proceedings in that context. On the other hand, when a peace officer lays an information and seeks a summons or warrant, the justice's role is somewhat more limited. The justice can refuse to issue a summons or warrant, but he cannot do anything further, such as cancelling the information. In effect, the justice can say "yes" to further proceedings, or can fail to say "yes", but cannot actually say "no." Rather, it is always open to the officer to take the same information before a different justice to seek a summons or warrant. As the Ontario Court of Appeal has held:

> In our view the determination which is made by the Justice under section 455.3(1) [now section 507(1)] is a determination, to be made judicially, whether on the evidence which is placed before him upon that hearing a case for the issue of a summons has been made out. It has no further effect. If he refuses to issue a summons, the information still stands, and the complainant is entitled to attend before the same or another Justice of the Peace on a subsequent occasion with

---

offence of impaired driving with which had had been charged. However, when he did not appear for trial, the judge had no authority to issue a warrant for his arrest based on non-attendance. See also *R. v. Legge* (1990), 112 N.B.R. (2d) 11 (Q.B.), where the accused was not guilty of failing to appear, on the basis that the appearance notice had not been confirmed in a timely manner.

86   *R. v. Coughlan, Ex parte Evans*, [1970] 3 C.C.C. 61 (Alta. S.C); *R. v. Jones, Ex parte Cohen* (1969), 2 C.C.C. 374 (B.C.S.C.) [*Jones*].

87   *Jones, ibid.*; *Re Blythe* (1973), 113 C.C.C. (2d) 192 (B.C.S.C.).

additional evidence, and to request the issue of a summons on the basis of the evidence which is presented on that subsequent day.[88]

However, note as well in this context section 507.1, dealing with informations laid by private citizens. In those cases, if a justice decides not to say "yes," then she endorses the information to that effect. Such an information is deemed not to have been laid six months from the date of the endorsement unless the informant commences proceedings to require a summons or warrant to be issued.[89] Further, the *Code* specifically requires that any further application on the same information requires the informant to bring forward new evidence.[90]

2) Charge Screening

In principle, there is a further way in which a peace officer's decision whether to lay charges can be assessed by another person. Crown prosecutors also engage in the process of "charge screening," though the way in which it is conducted varies from province to province.

There is no dispute that, at some stage, a Crown prosecutor should consider the charges which are proposed or have been laid, and decide whether to proceed with the matter. This question is a broader one than that before the justice of the peace, which is whether a *prima facie* case can be made out. Crown prosecutors certainly are looking at whether there is a reasonable prospect of conviction; however, they are typically looking as well at whether it is in the public interest to proceed with the charges. That is, in a variety of circumstances it might be possible to obtain a conviction but preferable not to. Further, having this second look at the charges, by an independent Crown, can help to provide greater accountability. It should be noted, of course, that having the decision whether to lay charges initially made by independent peace officers also helps guarantee accountability.[91]

---

88 *R. v. Allen* (1974), 20 C.C.C. (2d) 447 at para. 6 (Ont. C.A.) [*Allen*].

89 *Criminal Code*, above note 1, s. 507(5).

90 *Ibid.*, s. 507(7). There is a certain ambiguity in the fact that new evidence is explicitly required for a reapplication in the case of a private prosecution. *Allen*, above note 88, had also referred in passing to a need for new evidence in the case of reapplications by a peace officer, though no *Criminal Code* section sets out any such requirement. Other cases have spoken about a peace officer re-applying before a different justice without specifically calling for new evidence: see, for example, *Whitmore*, above note 46.

91 See Law Reform Commission of Canada, *Controlling Criminal Prosecutions: The Attorney General and the Crown Prosecutor*, Working Paper 62 (Ottawa: Law Reform Commission of Canada, 1990). [LRC, *Controlling Criminal Prosecutions*].

The real question, therefore, is not whether Crown prosecutors should review the decision of police officers, but *when*. In most provinces, police lay the charges and only afterward do Crowns review them and potentially withdraw the charges. In three provinces, however — New Brunswick, Quebec, and British Columbia — the screening happens before the charges are laid.[92]

Briefly put, the advantage of pre-charge screening is the possibility of avoiding technical errors, as well as the stigma of laying charges that will later be withdrawn. The major potential disadvantage is that it is less open and accountable, since the decision not to proceed with a charge will have been made privately. The advantages and disadvantages of post-charge screening are essentially complementary to those: it is more open and accountable, but potentially less efficient.

The Supreme Court has held that either procedure is acceptable. It is important, the justices found, that the decision of the Crown prosecutor is truly independent of the police decision, and is made objectively. However, pre-charge screening does not necessarily lead to a loss of objectivity, and its absence does not guarantee objectivity.[93]

In any case, it has been argued that practical considerations mean that charge screening, whether it happens pre- or post-charge, is of limited value in restricting the number of charges which actually go to court. Crown prosecutors have access to limited information, and often are not in a good position to seriously assess the strength of their case until much later in the process.[94]

3) Restraint in Compelling Appearance

The general purpose of the compelling-appearance section of the *Criminal Code* is, of course, to see to it that an accused who is charged with an offence will actually appear in court to face the charges laid. However, woven throughout the provisions is the assumption that this result should be assured by the least intrusive means possible; indeed, the arrest provisions fall under the subheading "arrest without warrant and release from custody." If necessary, a person will be arrested and held in custody until the time of trial; preferably, the accused will be released after arrest, or if possible not arrested in the first place. Most notably, that philosophy is reflected in the "ladder" approach of the bail provisions, which start from a presumption of release on an undertak-

---

92 R. v. Regan, 2002 SCC 12 [Regan]. See also LRC, Controlling Criminal Prosecutions, ibid.

93 Regan, ibid. at para. 70.

94 Stribopoulos, above note 45 at paras. 64–66.

ing without conditions, and which require the Crown to justify each greater restriction, in turn.[95] This book will not discuss the standards or procedures at a bail hearing, but the same philosophy can be observed at the earlier stages of the process of compelling an accused's appearance.

In particular, there are a series of points where release, or an approach that prefers the less intrusive of two options, is specifically preferred by the statutory scheme. In the order they will be discussed here, these are:

- Section 507(4), preferring the use of a summons to an arrest warrant;
- Sections 507(6) and 499, permitting the release on conditions by police of a person who has been arrested under a warrant;
- Section 495(2), directing a peace officer to use an appearance notice rather than to arrest without a warrant in certain cases;
- Section 497, directing an officer to release an accused on an appearance notice in certain cases even if an initial arrest was necessary;
- Section 498, allowing the officer in charge of a police station to release an arrested person on certain conditions without waiting to take that person to a justice for a bail hearing; and
- Section 503(2) and (2.1), allowing a peace officer or the officer in charge to release an arrestee on conditions without waiting to take that person to a justice for a bail hearing.

To begin with the most minimally intrusive approach to compelling appearance, let us look at the situation when a peace officer approaches a justice of the peace first to lay a charge. In that event, the justice decides under section 507 not only whether to compel the accused's appearance at all but also the means for doing so. That section provides that, if grounds for compelling the accused's appearance have been made out, the justice is to issue a summons. The only exception to this rule is if the evidence led when laying the summons shows "reasonable grounds to believe that it is necessary in the public interest to issue a warrant for the arrest of the accused."[96]

The phrase "necessary in the public interest" is worth pausing to take note of. That phrase had appeared in section 515 of the *Criminal Code*, the bail provisions, as a tertiary ground justifying detaining an accused in custody pending trial. The primary and secondary grounds were that the accused would not otherwise appear for trial and that

---

95   *Criminal Code*, above note 1, s. 515.
96   *Ibid.*, s. 507(4).

the accused's detention was necessary for public safety. In *Morales*, the Supreme Court struck down the public-interest criterion, holding that it was unconstitutionally vague.[97] The question therefore arises as to whether the same conclusion ought to follow in the context of section 507(4), or for that matter in other related sections which refer to the same consideration.

Although the matter has not been considered by the Supreme Court, general opinion seems to favour the constitutionality of the provision, once it is interpreted properly. It has been held that the result in *Morales* does not lead to the conclusion that the phrase "public interest" will necessarily be unconstitutionally vague; rather, its meaning and validity will depend on the context in which it occurs.[98] The specific constitutionality of the phrase in section 507(4) was raised in *Budreo*, where the accused argued that the section did violate the *Charter* on the grounds set out in *Morales*. The trial judge rejected the challenge, though in doing so he read "public interest" in a narrow fashion. The judge distinguished the use of the criterion in the two sections. Specifically, in section 515(10) the public-interest criterion had been used as a third, and separate, ground for detention beyond guaranteeing the accused's appearance and preventing the commission of more offences. It was in that context — of what concerns *other* than those could justify the accused's detention — that the phrase had been found to offer insufficient guidance.

In section 507(4), on the other hand, the "public interest" was not an additional and residual criterion: it was the *sole* criterion. The judge held that it ought to be interpreted in a narrow fashion, related to the justifiable reasons for detaining an accused. That is, the trial judge held that the only grounds which would mean that it was in the public interest to issue a warrant rather than a summons were that the accused otherwise would not appear or might commit another offence if a summons were used. The "public interest" was to be interpreted as shorthand for the primary and secondary grounds which had been upheld in *Morales*.[99]

This reasoning appears to have been accepted by the Ontario Court of Appeal when it heard the case as well. It is not absolutely clear, however, whether the court interpreted the section to apply that way in general, or only in the particular context of its interaction with the recognizance provisions in section 810.1 of the *Code*. It held:

---

97   *R. v. Morales*, [1992] 3 S.C.R. 711 [*Morales*].
98   *R. v. Farinacci* (1993), 86 C.C.C. (3d) 32 (Ont. C.A.).
99   *R. v. Budreo* (1996), 104 C.C.C. (3d) 245 at para. 177 (Ont. Ct. Gen. Div.).

67 . . . Under s. 507(4), the justice is to compel the defendant's attendance by means of a summons only, unless the allegations of the informant or the evidence "discloses reasonable grounds to believe that it is necessary in the public interest to issue a warrant for the arrest of the accused." Because a hearing under s. 810.1 can only result in the defendant being required to enter into a recognizance, the circumstances in which it would be "necessary in the public interest" to issue an arrest warrant will be limited to cases where that process is necessary to preserve the integrity of the s. 810.1 proceedings. The justice will require the informant to make out a case that the defendant will not otherwise attend court or that the defendant poses an imminent risk to the safety of children, which s. 810.1 is designed to protect.[100]

In any case, a sensible reading of "public interest" in section 507(4) is that offered in the trial court, namely, that it is limited to considerations of making sure the accused attends trial or to prevent further offences in the interim. On that basis, the section would not be unconstitutionally vague.[101]

It is not entirely clear who bears the burden of showing compliance with section 507(4), or what type of evidence is necessary. In *Brown*, for example, the accused had agreed to surrender himself to the police, but his lawyer had subsequently written a letter offering to make arrangements for the accused to come to court without being arrested. The police officer did not reply to the accused's counsel's letter, and instead prepared a report to the Crown suggesting that the accused be arrested based on his non-appearance. A justice did issue a warrant and the accused was arrested, but he objected that section 507(4) had not been complied with. The trial judge concluded that, because there was no evidence of the allegations placed before the justice, the warrant had to be presumed to have been properly issued "unless there is evidence before the court that the justice improperly issued the warrant."[102]

On the other hand, in *Gagnon* the police recommended an arrest to the Crown, and the Crown agreed but recommended a subsequent release on an undertaking to appear. The trial judge found this warrant to have been improperly issued, because the accused had given notice

---

100 *R. v. Budreo* (2000), 142 C.C.C. (3d) 225 at para. 67 (Ont. C.A.).

101 Note as well that since *Morales*, above note 97, Parliament inserted a new "public interest" criterion into s. 515(10), which includes more specific criteria. That section was subsequently upheld by the Court: *R. v. Hall*, 2002 SCC 64. It is possible that that later decision could have an impact on the meaning of the phrase in s. 507(4).

102 *R. v. Brown*, 2004 BCPC 290 at para. 17.

of his intention to challenge the claim that a warrant was required "[y] et there is no explanation of the basis for the existence of the reasonable and probable grounds required by s. 507(4)."[103] Nothing in the facts showed why a warrant would be necessary, and the recommendation of release on an undertaking implied the opposite. In that event, the warrant was found to have been improperly issued.

In the normal course of events, a warrant will name or describe the accused, name the charge for which he is sought, and order that he be arrested and brought before "the judge or justice who issued the warrant or some other judge or justice having jurisdiction in the same territorial division."[104] This wording does not, it has been held, allow an issuing judge to insist on an accused being brought before her personally: the "or" means that the police must take the accused before *some* justice with jurisdiction within the time period allowed.[105]

Note in addition the possibility provided for in section 511(3), which is to allow the justice to delay the execution of a warrant, in order to give an accused the opportunity to surrender herself. If an accused does so, the warrant is deemed to be executed. On the other hand, section 512 allows a justice to issue a warrant (or summons) when the accused has previously been dealt with on some other basis, such as an appearance notice. Section 512 also refers to the public interest as the criterion to be applied by the justice in deciding, but in this context that phrase has been interpreted to give a justice "residual powers to be exercised in the public interest."[106] For example, where an accused who is already in custody is not brought to court at a scheduled time, the public-interest criterion has been held to justify the issuance of an arrest warrant, despite the fact that the accused is actually in custody, as a means of retaining jurisdiction over the person.[107]

A further example of the potential restraint in the use of arrest powers is found in section 507(6), which also applies once a warrant has been issued. That section allows the justice (except in the case of

---

103 *R. v. Gagnon*, [1994] B.C.J. No. 818 at para. 22 (Prov. Ct.).

104 *Criminal Code*, above note 1, s. 511.

105 *R. v. Davidson*, 2004 ABCA 337. See Section B(4), below in this chapter.

106 *Ex parte Chung* (1975), 26 C.C.C. (2d) 497, (B.C.S.C.), aff'd (1976), 26 C.C.C. (2d) 497 (B.C.C.A.); *R. v. Horton*, [2002] O.J. No. 1219 (Ont. S.C.J.).

107 See also *Criminal Code*, above note 1, s. 485(2), which provides :

(2) Where jurisdiction over an accused or a defendant is lost and has not been regained, a court, judge, provincial court judge or justice may, within three months after the loss of jurisdiction, issue a summons, or if it or he considers it necessary in the public interest, a warrant for the arrest of the accused or defendant.

section 469 offences) to endorse the warrant, authorizing the accused to be released after arrest by an officer in charge. The officer in charge is authorized to release on a number of bases: simply on the basis of a promise to appear, on a recognizance without sureties in an amount not exceeding $500, or, in the case of an accused who does not ordinarily reside in the province or within two hundred kilometres, on a recognizance without sureties in an amount not exceeding $500 accompanied by the deposit of a sum not exceeding five hundred dollars. In addition, the officer in charge can require the person to enter an undertaking as a condition of release. That undertaking can include a variety of conditions:

(a) to remain within a territorial jurisdiction specified in the undertaking;
(b) to notify a peace officer or another person mentioned in the undertaking of any change in his or her address, employment or occupation;
(c) to abstain from communicating, directly or indirectly, with any victim, witness or other person identified in the undertaking, or from going to a place specified in the undertaking, except in accordance with the conditions specified in the undertaking;
(d) to deposit the person's passport with the peace officer or other person mentioned in the undertaking;
(e) to abstain from possessing a firearm and to surrender any firearm in the possession of the person and any authorization, licence or registration certificate or other document enabling that person to acquire or possess a firearm;
(f) to report at the times specified in the undertaking to a peace officer or other person designated in the undertaking;
(g) to abstain from
   (i) the consumption of alcohol or other intoxicating substances, or
   (ii) the consumption of drugs except in accordance with a medical prescription; and
(h) to comply with any other condition specified in the undertaking that the officer in charge considers necessary to ensure the safety and security of any victim of or witness to the offence.[108]

This is a broad range of options, though, as is appropriate to the intermediate stage, it is narrower than the range eventually open to the justice at a bail hearing. Both the accused and the Crown have the ability

---

108 *Criminal Code, ibid.*, s. 499(1)(c).

to apply to a justice to modify an undertaking entered into before an officer in charge.[109]

In addition to these rules governing the context of pre-arrest and arrest with a warrant, there are a number of provisions that attempt to impose restraint on the use of arrest without warrant powers. A set of largely parallel provisions affect a peace officer's abilities at the time of arrest, post-arrest, and after the accused is taken to the police station.

The easiest starting point is in section 495, the arrest-powers section itself. Section 495(1) creates a number of warrantless-arrest powers (see the discussion in Section C(2)(b)(iii) below). Between them, sections 495(2) and 495(3) have an impact on how peace officers should exercise their powers that is not easy to encapsulate in a few words. On the one hand, the sections do not actually take away the power to arrest. On the other hand, they do make clear that an officer is wrong to arrest in some situations. That is, section 495(2) says that an officer "shall not arrest" if particular conditions (which will be discussed below) are met. However, section 495(3) carries on to say that the officer is "deemed to be acting lawfully and in the execution of duty" even if she does arrest despite section 495(2). Accordingly, section 495(2) is not actually a limit on the ability to arrest: it is in some ways merely guidance intended to increase restraint in the exercise of those powers.

That said, it is worth pausing to note that the exact impact of sections 495(2) and 495(3) is not entirely clear. It can be seen as merely guidance in some contexts.[110] The primary impact of 495(3)(a) in the criminal law context is to prevent an accused from invoking non-compliance with section 495(2) as a justification for resisting an arrest. One clear effect — perhaps the only clear effect — of section 495(3) is that an accused who resists an officer who is ignoring section 495(2) will nonetheless be guilty of resisting.[111] However, saying that an officer is deemed to be acting in the execution of duty does not necessarily amount to saying that the arrest was lawful for all purposes:

> The purpose of Subsection (3) is to make it impossible for a person
> to invoke the illegality of an arrest by reason of Subsection (2) as a

---

109 *Ibid.*, s. 495(3)(4).

110 It has been described as "a mere paper restriction": *R. v. Prince* (1981), 61 C.C.C. (2d) 73 (Man. Prov. J. Crim. Div.).

111 *R. v. Schwartz* (1998), 51 C.R.R. (2d) 277 at para. 47 (B.C. Prov. Ct.) [*Schwartz*]; *R. v. McKibbon* (1973), 12 C.C.C. (2d) 66, (B.C.C.A). See also *R. v. Munson*, 2003 SKCA 28 and the cases listed at para. 58, or *R. v. Adams* (1972), 21 C. R.N.S. 257 (Sask. C.A.).

defence in criminal proceedings, not to render such an arrest lawful; otherwise there would be no purpose to Subsection (2).[112]

In some cases, police officers have arrested an accused because they were acting on the basis of a particular policy: to arrest all impaired drivers, or all those charged with spousal assaults, or all street prostitutes, for example. Such policies have come under criticism from courts, since they conflict with the discretion whether to arrest or not given by the word "may" in section 495(1), and can conflict with the criteria set out in section 495(2). Accordingly, some courts have found that such arrests were not lawful, and that they amounted to a violation of the right to be free from arbitrary detention.[113]

Further, section 495(3) actually distinguishes two situations. In the case of proceedings under the *Code* or other Acts of Parliament, the rule above prevails automatically. However, the section provides that, for other proceedings, the rule prevails "unless in any such proceedings it is alleged and established by the person making the allegation that the peace officer did not comply with the requirements of subsection (2)."[114] In other words, in a civil action the arrest might be illegal, though the burden of showing that the officer was not authorized to arrest will fall on the claimant. In essence, then, section 495(3) means that, if there has been non-compliance with section 495(2), an accused could on the same set of facts be guilty of resisting arrest but bring a successful "false arrest" tort claim.[115]

In any event, section 495(2) applies in the case of arrests for relatively less serious offences: summary conviction offences, hybrid offences, or indictable offences that are in the absolute jurisdiction of a magistrate. In the case of those offences, presumptively a peace officer should not arrest. However, the section carries on to set out two bases which could displace that presumption: that an arrest is necessary in

---

112 *Schwartz, ibid.* at para. 47.

113 See, for example, *R. v. Labine*, [1987] B.C.J. No. 567 (Co. Ct.); *Schwartz, ibid.*; *R. v. Pithart* (1987), 34 C.C.C. (3d) 150 (B.C. Co. Ct.).

114 *Criminal Code*, above note 1, s. 495(3)(b). In *Schwartz, ibid.* at para. 47, the trial judge noted that the *Charter* is not an Act of Parliament, but rather an imperial act, and relied on this as a justification for finding that non-compliance with s. 495(2) was of consequence. This rationale does not seem to have been more generally adopted.

115 On the other hand, see also *R. v. Hall*, [1996] B.C.J. No. 348 (Prov. Ct. (Crim. Div.))[*Hall*], where the trial judge was persuaded that, on the facts of the case, ss. 495(3) and 498(3) meant that the accused would be precluded from obtaining a civil remedy because the police had acted outside of s. 495(2) but nonetheless in good faith. The judge relied on the likely denial of a civil remedy as one justification for granting a stay of proceedings in the criminal matter.

the public interest, or that an arrest is necessary to make the person attend court.[116] An assessment of whether section 495(2) should act to limit section 495(1) in a particular case rests on an examination of "all of the circumstances existing at the moment of arrest which were apparent to the police officer."[117]

Once again we have, in this subsection, a potentially problematic reference to the public-interest criterion which was found unconstitutionally vague in *Morales*. In this context, the *Code* carries on to give some guidance. Section 495(2) says that the public interest in this context includes:

> the need to
> (i)   establish the identity of the person,
> (ii) secure or preserve evidence of or relating to the offence, or
> (iii) prevent the continuation or repetition of the offence or the commission of another offence.

It has been held that an open-ended reference to the public interest in section 495(2) would violate the *Charter*; however, if the section is read as being limited to the specific considerations listed, then it is constitutional.[118] In essence, the section complies with the *Charter* if "includes" is read as "means." This approach is similar to that noted above as a way of ensuring *Charter* compliance in the case of section 507(4).

---

116 Section 495(2) is phrased as a double, and sometimes triple, negative, which makes it difficult to follow. In fact the relevant restrictions are phrased in this fashion:

> (2) A peace officer shall not arrest a person without warrant . . . where
> (d) he believes on reasonable grounds that the public interest, having regard to all the circumstances including the need to
> (i)   establish the identity of the person,
> (ii) secure or preserve evidence of or relating to the offence, or
> (iii) prevent the continuation or repetition of the offence or the commission of another offence,
> may be satisfied without so arresting the person, and
> (e) he has no reasonable grounds to believe that, if he does not so arrest the person, the person will fail to attend court in order to be dealt with according to law.

117 *R. v. Sieben* (1989), 51 C.C.C. (3d) 343 (Alta. C.A.) [*Sieben*].

118 *R. v. Fosseneuve* (1995), 43 C.R. (4th) 260 (Man. Q.B.) [*Fosseneuve*]. The Alberta Court of Appeal in *Sieben*, *ibid.*, had held that the public interest was not limited to the specific criteria listed, but that decision predates *Morales*, above note 97, and so is unlikely to be followed on this point. See also the discussion of *R. v. Saxby*, 2006 ABPC 201 [*Saxby*], below, concerning the similar provision in s. 498.

Section 495(2) deals with a decision by a peace officer not to arrest at all (in which case section 496 authorizes the use of an appearance notice). Section 497 carries on to create almost the same rule, but applies after an arrest has actually occurred. Even if that initial decision to arrest was made, the *Code* directs an officer to release the person as soon as possible, either by releasing them with the intention of later seeking a summons, or by issuing an appearance notice. Exactly as in section 495(2), this preference for release applies to summary conviction, hybrid, and absolute jurisdiction offences.

Also, as in section 495, section 497 contains exceptions to that preference, and non-release is still possible. Non-release can be justified based either on the need to keep the person in custody or simply to have their release determined at a later stage of the process.[119] The latter option could be useful because of the greater ability, at later stages, to impose conditions making the accused's appearance in court that much more likely. An arresting officer has no ability to impose conditions or really do anything but issue an appearance notice as a way of binding the accused; later stages permit the imposition of conditions, the use of recognizances, sureties, and so on.

Non-release can be justified on the same grounds as in section 495(2)(d) and (e): the need to ensure the accused's attendance and the public interest. However, section 497 adds one further public-interest criterion: the need to ensure the safety and security of any victim or witness to the offence.[120] Seemingly, this additional exception is meant to reflect the difference between not arresting in the first place (section 495(2)) and arresting but then immediately releasing (section 497); in any case, where there is a need to ensure the safety of victims, the officer will have arrested, and so the issue is whether subsequently to release. If this is the rationale, however, it is not immediately clear that the section achieves its goals. Section 495(2)(d) and (e) are, in effect, the criteria that *preserve* the officer's arrest power. If preserving the safety of victims is meant to be a justification for making an arrest, then it ought to be listed in one of those two subsections.[121]

---

119 *Criminal Code*, above note 1, s. 497(1.1)(a).

120 *Ibid.*, s. 497(1.1)(a)(iv).

121 Some mention should be made here of the Supreme Court's decision in *R. v. Moore*, [1979] 1 S.C.R. 195, since it runs against the general spirit of s. 495(2). The accused had ridden his bicycle through a red light and was witnessed doing so by a police officer. The accused refused to stop when asked to do so by the police officer and was ultimately charged with an offence. However, he was not charged with going through the red light: rather, he was charged with obstructing an officer in the execution of duty, on the basis that he refused to give his name to the officer when the officer requested it. The issue in the case

As with other sections structuring discretion, there is authority holding that police will be acting unreasonably if they fail to release based on considerations other than those set out in the section.[122]

Assuming an accused is arrested and not released by the arresting officer, then a further pre-bail hearing opportunity for release arises with the officer in charge of the station to which the accused is taken.[123] The arresting officer had a power to release applying only to relatively minor offences and allowing the imposition of nothing more than a requirement to appear in court; the bail hearing will apply to all offences, and will feature a full range of potential restrictions on the accused's liberty in exchange for release. The officer in charge has a power that falls in between these two extremes: it applies to a broader but still limited range of offences, and it allows for the imposition of some but not all restrictions.

An officer in charge can release an accused arrested for the same range of offences as an arresting officer, but also for any offence for which the potential sentence is five years or less. The officer in charge can release with the intention of seeking a summons, or based on a promise to appear (though not by issuing an appearance notice). In addition, the officer in charge can release the person on a recognizance

---

was whether the officer had the authority to demand Moore's name; in essence, the court held that s. 495(2) gave the officer that power. The Court held that the officer's only potential arrest power was under s. 495(1). However, since riding through a red light was a summary conviction offence, s. 495(2) would apply. In that case, the officer "had no power to arrest the accused for such offence unless and until he had attempted to identify the accused" (*Moore, ibid.* at 204). That in turn meant that the officer was acting in the execution of duty in demanding the accused's name, and therefore that the accused was guilty of obstructing the officer.

Moore runs against the general trend of obstruction cases: more commonly courts conclude that, in the absence of a clear and express power to compel a person to provide information to the police, a person does not obstruct in refusing to do so. See, for example, *R. v. Greaves*, 2004 BCCA 484 at para. 49: "Generally, a person cannot then be convicted of obstructing a police officer in the execution of duty for simply refusing to say or establish who he or she is when asked to do so" [citations omitted]. See also *R. v. Guthrie* (1982), 69 C.C.C. (2d) 216 (Alta. C.A.), or *R. v. Fraser*, 2002 NSPC 6. There has been a tendency to try to limit *Moore's* application. *R. v. Sandy*, 2007 ABPC 173 at para. 73, for example, cites *Guthrie* for the proposition that "the ruling in *R. v. Moore* . . . is limited to situations in which the requesting peace officer has, as a result of seeing the individual commit some act, reasonable and probable grounds to believe that that individual has committed an offence, the *actus reus* of which is the act the peace officer saw the individual commit."

122 See *R. v. Korecki*, 2007 ABPC 321.
123 *Criminal Code*, above note 1, ss. 498 and 503(2).

of up to $500. In the case of a person who resides out of province or more than 200 kilometres away, the officer can in addition require a deposit of up to $500.[124] The same exceptions to release based upon appearance-in-court and public-interest criteria as in section 497(1.1) apply here.[125]

This greater grant of power to the officer in charge reflects the expanding seriousness of the decision being made. An arresting officer can release only in the least serious cases, where release with nothing seriously binding the accused to appear is appropriate; an officer in charge can release for more serious offences, but with correspondingly greater "pull" on the accused.

Just as noted concerning section 495(2) above, the fact that section 498(2) sets out specific criteria justifying the detention of an accused means that those must *be* the criteria applied. Accordingly, a general policy not to release particular types of accused —those who are intoxicated, for example — does not take priority over the requirements of the *Code*. In addition, the existence of this release power on the part of the officer in charge has been held to impose an obligation on the police: that is, given that the officer in charge has the ability to release a detainee, the detainee is entitled to have that question considered. This includes, it has been held, a minimal duty of fairness, requiring that the officer in charge at least briefly and informally look at the detainee, talk to the detainee, and give the detainee the opportunity to be heard.[126]

---

124 Section 498(1) provides that the officer in charge can:

    (c) release the person on the person's entering into a recognizance before the officer in charge or another peace officer without sureties in an amount not exceeding $500 that the officer directs, but without deposit of money or other valuable security; or

    (d) if the person is not ordinarily resident in the province in which the person is in custody or does not ordinarily reside within 200 kilometres of the place in which the person is in custody, release the person on the person's entering into a recognizance before the officer in charge or another peace officer without sureties in an amount not exceeding $500 that the officer directs and, if the officer so directs, on depositing with the officer a sum of money or other valuable security not exceeding in amount or value $500, that the officer directs.

125 *Criminal Code*, above note 1, s. 498(1.1).

126 *Hall*, above note 115. See also *R. v Miller*, 2005 SKPC 100, which also finds that an accused is entitled to have a decision made by the officer in charge as to whether he should be detained, rather than have his detention continue based on a general policy. Both Hall and Miller were intoxicated and were kept in custody in accordance with policies to let such detainees "sleep it off" before being released. In *Miller*, the judge noted that if the accused had been taken in front of the officer in charge, it might have been discovered that there was some person

On the other hand, there is authority suggesting that the criteria listed in section 498(1.1), and specifically the considerations concerning the public interest, should not be seen as exhaustive of the possible justifications for the officer in charge to decline to release. It has been argued that other legal powers, such as that in provincial legislation allowing intoxicated persons to be taken into custody, might justify detention independently of the public-interest criteria specifically mentioned in section 498(1.1).[127] Two points can be made about this argument. First, it is not necessarily inconsistent with the suggestion in the previous paragraph that detainees cannot be kept in custody on the basis of a general policy to retain all intoxicated persons. Rather, it could simply mean that the detainee's drunkenness would be a legitimate consideration — part of "all the circumstances" — in making a discretionary decision.[128] However, it is inconsistent with the suggested interpretation of section 495(2) which limited the public interest to only the listed factors, as a way of avoiding the section being vague and therefore unconstitutional.[129]

This dilemma can be reconciled without the need to read "public interest" as something broader than the specific criteria listed in section 498(1.1), and yet still allow police to hold intoxicated detainees until it is safe to release them. The general obligation in section 498 is to release the detainee "as soon as practicable." Some courts have held that, where police decide not to release an intoxicated person, they have not actually decided to detain the person. In such cases, the police might not, for example, intend to take the person in front of a justice of the peace eventually: rather, he is simply being held until he is sober enough to be released. In that event, the person is in fact being released as soon as practicable, and so no justification for detention in section 498(1.1) needs to be found at all.[130]

---

into whose custody he could safely be released. However, the judge concluded that Miller had not shown that he was *not* taken before the officer in charge, and so no arbitrary-detention *Charter* violation had been demonstrated. To similar effect, see *R. v. Wilson*, 2003 ABPC 167.

127 *Saxby*, above note 118.

128 See, for example, *R. v. Coulter*, [2000] O.J. No. 3452 (Ct. J.) [*Coulter*].

129 See *Fosseneuve*, above note 118.

130 See, for example, *Coulter*, above note 128; *R. v. Smith*, 2005 ABPC 202; or *R. v. Campbell*, [1995] O.J. No. 2975 (Gen. Div.). In the latter case, this argument was offered as one reason making it unnecessary to decide whether s. 498(1.1) should be found vague based on *Morales*, above note 97. Nonetheless, the judge went on to hold that he would not have found the section vague, since the words "public interest" did not appear alone, as in *Morales*, but in the context of the enumerated criteria.

Note that there is, in effect, the possibility of review of any release conditions imposed in an undertaking by an officer in charge. Both the accused and the Crown are entitled to apply to a justice for an order which will replace that undertaking.[131]

In addition to the various release points in sections 495, 496, and 498 already discussed, a further power to release on conditions rather than detain the person pending appearance in front of a justice is found in section 503(2). This section applies to both ordinary peace officers and the officer in charge. The primary difference between the release power in this section and those just discussed is the range of offences to which it applies. The earlier release powers governed relatively less serious offences; this power is available following an arrest for any offence except those most serious ones listed in section 469 of the *Code*.

It was observed in the discussion of section 498 that, as the range of offences for which the accused could be released grew, so did the range of conditions which could be imposed in exchange for that release. The same trend continues here. In the case of minor offences, it can simply be appropriate to decide whether detaining the accused is or is not worthwhile. When more serious offences are at stake, the balance is more difficult: detention might not be necessary, but an unconditional release might also be inappropriate. Section 503(2) therefore permits a more measured and restrained approach than simply detaining everyone for whom unconditional release is not appropriate, and permits it at an earlier stage than the accused's appearance before a justice. As the Ontario Court of Appeal explained in *Oliveira*:

> Although the promise to appear and other similar mechanisms for release by the police introduced into the *Criminal Code* by the *Bail Reform Act*, S.C. 1970-72, c. 37, gave the police broad powers of release, those powers were deficient in that they did not permit the police to impose conditions as a term of the release. Unless the police were satisfied that the arrested person should be released without any conditions, they had to detain that person pending appearance before a justice of the peace. The justice of the peace could then release that individual on the appropriate bail conditions. This shortcoming was eventually cured by amendments that gave a peace officer who released the person on a promise to appear, the power to require that

---

131 *Criminal Code*, above note 1, ss. 499(3) & (4). The Crown is required to give the accused three days' notice if seeking a variation of the undertaking at some point prior to the accused's appearance in court. An accused is entitled to bring such an application at her first appearance, or at any point prior to or following that time: *R. v. Paul*, 2007 ONCJ 615.

person to enter into an undertaking before being released: *Criminal Code*, s. 503(2). That undertaking could contain one or more of the conditions set out in s. 503(2.1) of the *Criminal Code* and is aptly described as "police bail . . . "[132]

Section 503(2.1) permits a wide range of conditions, but in fact we have looked at them before: the list of conditions here is identical to that in section 499, permitting an officer in charge to release a person who has been arrested under a warrant. They allow release on a more nuanced basis than "promise you will appear or don't be released," but still consist of a smaller range of options than those eventually available to a justice in a bail hearing. Just as with release by an officer in charge under section 498, both the accused and the Crown have the right to apply to a justice to replace an undertaking entered into before a peace officer under section 503(2.1).[133]

There are some issues worth noting in the interplay between these various provisions giving release powers to arresting officers and officers in charge. For example, on a literal reading of section 495(2), it would seem to apply to any arrest made under section 495(1). However, there is some authority suggesting a different reading. Section 495(1) (discussed at greater length below) allows a peace officer to arrest if she: a) has reasonable grounds to believe that an indictable offence has occurred; b) finds a criminal offence being committed; or c) reasonably believes there is a warrant for the accused's arrest. Some lower courts have held that the requirement to release in section 495(2) applies only to arrests made on the former two grounds. In the third case, where an arrest is made because a warrant exists, it has been suggested that the justice's ability under section 507(6) to endorse the warrant takes priority; more specifically, if the justice did *not* endorse the warrant allowing the accused to be released, then the officer is not entitled to release based on the factors in section 495(2).[134]

It is not clear that this authority ought to be followed. First of all, of course, a literal reading of the section suggests otherwise, and the literal reading ought to prevail. Second, *Gamracy* makes clear that an arrest under section 495(1)(c) is *not* an arrest based on the warrant, but rather is a warrantless arrest; in that event there is no reason in princi-

---

132 *R. v. Oliveira*, 2009 ONCA 219 at para. 6.
133 Just as in s. 499(3), the Crown must give three days' notice to the accused unless the application is made at the accused's appearance in court: ss. 503(2.2) & (2.3). See also *R. v. Hill*, 2005 NSPC 50.
134 See *Wall v. British Columbia*, [1995] B.C.J. No. 1697 (S.C.), or *Ilnicki v. Macleod*, 2003 ABQB 465.

ple that any conditions in the warrant should bind an officer, since the officer is not acting upon it.[135] Further, as a practical matter, an officer who arrests based on section 495(1)(c) might know only of the existence of a warrant, and will not necessarily know anything about its contents — such as, for example, whether it has been endorsed or not. Finally, although section 495(2) places the least ability in the hands of an officer to impose restrictions on the accused, it is applicable to the narrowest range of offences. The circumstances in which a warrant is likely to be issued, on the other hand, embrace a broader range of offences. An endorsement under section 507(6) relates back to release by an officer in charge under section 499. That section covered a "midrange" set of options, dealing with a balanced approach to something more than simply the least serious offences. It is not clear that it is relevant to the "all or nothing" option governing section 495.

4) Non-compliance with Time Limits

As noted above, the statutory scheme for compelling appearance envisions the likelihood that most accused will not be held in custody until the time of their trial. The officer first dealing with the accused might not arrest in the first place or, having arrested, might release the accused on an appearance notice. Once the accused is taken to the police station, the officer in charge might release the accused on an appearance notice, promise to appear, or undertaking. Either of those officers might release the accused on certain limited conditions. But if neither officer opts for release, the accused must be taken to a justice, at which point a bail hearing considering whether the accused will be released, and if so on what terms, will be held.

Out of this scheme, there arise three important time limits relating to the interaction between a justice of the peace and the officers who are seeking to compel the accused's appearance in court. First, when an appearance notice has been issued (or the accused has been released on a promise to appear or on an undertaking by the officer in charge), an information must be laid in front of a justice "as soon as practicable."[136] Second, such an information is, as an outer limit, required to be laid "in any event before the time stated in the appearance notice . . . for his attendance in court."[137] Finally, when an accused has been arrested without a warrant, the accused is to be brought before a justice "as soon

---

135 *R. v. Gamracy*, [1974] S.C.R. 640 [*Gamracy*].
136 *Criminal Code*, above note 1, s. 505.
137 *Ibid.*

as practicable and in any case within twenty-four hours," caselaw has discussed all three of these requirements.

Note first that the "as soon as practicable" and "before the time stated" requirements in the case of an appearance notice (or release under sections 497 or 498) are independent of one another.[138] Accordingly, the former requirement can fail to be met even if there is an information in court when the accused appears.[139] This is consistent with the purpose of having an information laid in front of a justice at all, which is to allow a justice to decide whether to confirm the appearance notice or not.

It has been held that the "as soon as practicable" requirement with regard to appearance notices is mandatory for some purposes but merely directory for others. If no information is laid after an appearance notice has been issued, then the accused cannot be found guilty of the offence of failing to comply with an appearance notice.[140] Nor could a warrant be issued for the accused's arrest in the event of non-compliance with the appearance notice or a failure to appear.[141] These are not trivial points. It means, for example, that an accused might be not guilty of failing to appear for fingerprinting even if the appearance notice has been confirmed, if this review was not undertaken soon enough.[142]

However, although the requirement is mandatory in those contexts, it is merely directory with regard to the validity of the information itself. That is to say, even if not laid as soon as possible, the information will still be valid. This result flows from the purpose of the section in the statutory scheme. It is not meant to prevent prosecutions from taking place if the time limit is not met. Rather, its purpose is to guarantee that there will be a prompt opportunity for judicial review of the appearance notice, to see whether it should be cancelled. Non-compliance with the "as soon as practicable" time limit therefore does not lead to the information's invalidity.[143] In this event, a court will have lost jurisdiction only over the person, and this can be regained if the person does in fact appear in court on the required date.[144] That means that the accused is still obliged to face the charge in the information; how-

---

138 *R. v. Naylor* (1978), 42 C.C.C. (2d) 12 (Ont. C.A.) [*Naylor*].

139 See, for example, *R. v. Taylor*, 2005 BCSC 1257 [*Taylor*], where the accused was, on 12 June, released on a promise to appear in court on 16 September. The information was not laid before a justice until 14 September, and this was found to violate the "as soon as practicable" requirement.

140 See *Criminal Code*, above note 1, s. 145.

141 See *ibid.*, ss. 512 and 803(3).

142 See, for example, *Taylor*, above note 139.

143 *Gougeon*, above note 82 at paras. 35–36.

144 See the discussion above and the authorities cited in footnotes 80–85.

ever, since jurisdiction over the person was attained only through the accused's actual appearance, he is not bound by the conditions in any undertaking which had been issued.[145]

This leads to the question of what "as soon as practicable" means. It does not, it has been held, mean "as soon as convenient," because that would be too lax. Such a requirement might allow unduly restrictive terms of release to be imposed by an officer in charge under section 498 which would then not be reviewed sufficiently soon.[146] On the other hand, it is less strict than "as soon as possible." There is no hard and fast numerical formula determining the meaning of the phrase, and so the analysis will turn largely on the facts of each individual case.[147] That said, the practicable time for laying the information does not vary according to the degree of restriction placed on the accused's release, nor on whether she is released by way of appearance notice, promise to appear, or an undertaking to the officer in charge.

The same conclusion, that the information remains valid despite the deadline not being met, has been reached with regard to the obligation to swear an information before the time stated for the accused's appearance. One might have argued that there was a difference between the two situations, since in the previous case there would have been an information in court but in the latter the accused would appear and no charge would have been laid at all. However, it has been held that the same reasoning applies, and that an information can still be laid under section 504 even though the accused has already appeared in court. Concluding otherwise, it has been held, would amount to allowing the section to create a statutory limitation period for the trial of a criminal offence, which was not the intention of the section.[148]

More complex is the time limit for taking an arrested accused before a justice of the peace, found in section 503. First, note that different interests are at stake. In the previous case, it was simply a matter of an information being laid with respect to an accused who has been released. In this context, the accused has not been released, and so the deadline actually concerns a review of his liberty. It has been noted that

145 R. v. Oliveira, [2007] O.J. No. 2394 (S.C.J.).

146 R. v. Marshall, [2003] O.J. No. 5501 (Ct. J.).

147 Taylor, above note 139 at para. 24. Periods of eight, nine, and ten days have been seen as falling within the "as soon as practicable" limit; see Naylor, above note 138; R. v. Wetmore (1976), 18 N.S.R. (2d) 292 (S.C.A.D.); and Harnish, above note 82. However, sixteen days has been seen as too long: Hrankowski, above note 80.

148 R. v. Markovic (2005), 200 C.C.C. (3d) 449 (Ont. C.A.).

Section 503 may be one of the most important procedural provisions of the *Criminal Code*. The liberty of the subject is dominant. A person not convicted of an offence should never be held in custody except in accordance with constitutionally valid provisions of the *Criminal Code* or other legislation . . . The paramountcy of the liberty of the subject has been recognized in English law from the earliest times. Freedom is a fundamental right. It is not to be taken away except in strict accordance with the law.[149]

The *Code* creates two separate deadlines in this regard. The first applies when a justice is available within a period of twenty-four hours. In that case, section 503 provides that the person "shall be taken before a justice without unreasonable delay." The section carries on to say "and in any event within that period," but caselaw has made very clear that the intention is *not* to say that the police may hold the accused for twenty-four hours before taking him to a justice. Rather, "the police must take the person before a justice without unreasonable delay and . . . the twenty-four hours is simply the outer limit of the time span."[150] In other words, once twenty-four hours have passed, the delay is (in the normal case) necessarily unreasonable, but it will frequently have become unreasonable well before then. There is a possible exception to that requirement, however, which is found in subsection 503(b). That section simply requires that a person be taken before a justice of the peace "as soon as possible" in any case where "a justice is not available within a period of twenty-four hours."[151]

Four issues need to be discussed: 1) What does "without unreasonable delay" mean in this context?; 2) What does it mean to say that a justice is not available?; 3) What is the impact of taking the accused before a justice?; and 4) What are the *Charter* implications of a failure to comply with the requirements of this section?

---

149 *Simpson*, above note 29 at paras. 36–37.

150 *Storrey*, above note 28 at para. 31, relying on *R. v. Koszulap* (1974), 27 C.R.N.S. 226 (Ont. C.A.).

151 *Criminal Code*, above note 1, s. 503(1)(b). There is virtually no caselaw interpreting the meaning of "as soon as possible" in s. 503(1)(b) in comparison to "without unreasonable delay" in s. 503(1)(a). This is in part due to the fact that very little consideration has been given to s. 503(1)(b) at all, though see the cases discussed below. There is some suggestion that "as soon as possible" implies a greater sense of urgency than does "without unreasonable delay," but it would of necessity be a greater urgency only after a longer time has already passed, since seemingly it will be a period of more than twenty-four hours. See *R. v. Warren*, [1994] N.W.T.J. No. 82 at para. 150 (S.C.).

In general, it has been held that "without unreasonable delay" is intended to convey a relatively short period, similar to "as short as reasonably practicable" or to "forthwith."[152] However, further guidance comes from the Court's decision in *Storrey*: at a minimum, that case seems to demonstrate that an accused need not be taken before a justice at the absolute first moment that it might be possible to do so. Rather, inherent in the concept of "without unreasonable delay" seems to be the notion that *some* delay will be reasonable.

In *Storrey*, the accused had been arrested in Windsor, Ontario at 7:25 p.m., and the police wanted to conduct an identification parade, or lineup. The complainants in the case lived in Michigan and so had to be brought to the jurisdiction to view the lineup; that did not occur until the following day. Immediately following the lineup, the accused was taken in front of a justice, a total of some eighteen hours after his arrest. The Court found that, in the circumstances of the case, this was not an unreasonable delay. It concluded first that it was open to the police, having arrested a person, to continue their investigation. To be sure, the police must already have had reasonable grounds for arrest before arresting, but that does not mean that a continued investigation to gather more evidence, or potentially to exonerate the accused, is not permitted. In some cases, therefore, that continued investigation can justify a delay in taking the accused to a justice. In *Storrey* itself the delay was based on the investigative needs of the particular case: the Court stressed the lack of alternatives to a lineup in the specific case and the fact that the complainants lived out of the jurisdiction.

Storrey has not been taken to mean that, as a general proposition, the investigative needs of the police trump the rights of the accused under section 503. It has been held that, even if an investigation is ongoing, the police must be able to offer some reasonable explanation for why the accused needs to be in custody while this occurs.[153] Even where that is necessary — that the accused is being questioned, for example — the police do not have carte blanche. In *C.K.* the accused, two sisters, were arrested at 7:00 a.m. one morning but not taken to a justice until after 9:00 a.m. the next day. The reason for this delay was that the police were interrogating the girls until 6:00 p.m. and were unable to persuade the "after hours" justice to hear the matter. That justice did not regard the matter as an emergency: tellingly, the police had begun trying to arrange for an after-hours justice at about 1:00 p.m. on the first day, at a point when taking the accused to a justice during normal

---

152 *R. v. C.K.*, 2005 ONCJ 462 [*C.K.*].
153 *R. v. Clarke* (2003), 184 C.C.C. (3d) 39 at para. 185 (Ont. S.C.J.) [*Clarke*].

hours was still feasible.[154] The trial judge noted that throughout this time the accused were being held ten minutes away from a courthouse where any number of judges and justices were available; the fact that the police wanted to continue their investigation did not justify delaying matters past 5:00 p.m., when justices ceased to be available.[155]

Similarly, in *Clarke* three accused were arrested at different points on the same day but were not taken before a justice until the following morning. As a result of being held overnight, all three accused were strip-searched. The judge noted in that case that the nature of the investigation being conducted by the police did not justify the overnight detention. Documents were found on one of the three accused which justified some delay in order to question him concerning them. However, to the extent that those documents raised the possibility that some further charge might be laid, that point could be pursued at a later time. Though some delay was justified to question the one accused about the documents, the existence of the documents did not justify an overnight detention for all three accused, particularly since the other two never were asked about them. Related to that point, although the police wanted to bring all three accused before a justice together, there was no need to do so. Accordingly, that desire did not justify delaying the bail hearing.

C.K. suggested as a general rule that "anyone arrested in the early morning should be brought to court during its sittings on the same day, absent a very good explanation."[156] In addition, that case offered some suggestions for deciding what would be a reasonable delay in each case. Courts should consider how necessary the investigative procedure was to the investigation: the stronger the case already, the less justification for delaying taking the accused before a justice.[157] In *Storrey* the lineup might provide evidence of guilt but also might have exonerated the accused. Also, a lineup takes a discrete amount of time: once it is done, it is done. In *C.K.*, on the other hand, the reason for the delay

---

154 *C.K.*, above note 152. Note as well that, even if the police are properly investigating, this will not justify a detention beyond the twenty-four-hour outside limit: *C.K.*, *ibid.*, and also *R. v. Dann*, 2002 NSSC 37.

155 To similar effect, see *R. v. Mangat* (2006), 209 C.C.C. (3d) 225 (Ont. C.A.) [*Mangat*].

156 *C.K.*, above note 152 at para. 41.

157 *C.K.*, *ibid.* at para. 42, where the judge suggests that courts ask, "Was it, like *Storrey*, a step to determine whether they had the right man — whether a charge would proceed at all — or was it a procedure to simply gather more evidence in respect of a charge that would be proceeding in any event?" This advice should be understood in light of the prior finding in *Storrey*, that if the police had not already had reasonable grounds to arrest when they did arrest, there would have been an arbitrary detention on that basis.

was the desire of the police to continue interrogating the accused. The judge suggested that in such cases the right to silence should be taken into account: "[O]nce the right to silence was asserted and the police were given a reasonable opportunity to persist and persuade a change of heart (as the law now permits), delay beyond that point for further interrogation was unreasonable."[158] The length of a "reasonable opportunity," of course, might be quite extensive given the subsequent decision of the Supreme Court of Canada in *Singh*, but that case did not raise the issue of the interplay between questioning and the requirements of section 503.[159]

Other factors besides the nature of the investigation can also be relevant to how long it takes to bring an accused before a justice, and what will be seen as reasonable. In *Clarke*, for example, the three accused were held overnight but were still taken to a justice within the twenty-four-hour time frame.[160] Nonetheless, the delay was found to be unreasonable. In part, the overnight detention resulted from the fact that bail court had closed at 3:00 that day. The trial judge concluded that the police could have been finished any investigations justifying delay by roughly 4:00 p.m.; even though the bail court might have been closed by that point, the judge noted that "[i]t is hard to accept that, in a city of 2.5 million people, a justice of the peace was not available."[161] Also in that case, it was significant that there was no need for a contested bail hearing, since the accused had agreed to the terms which the police wanted as conditions of their release. Most of those terms could have been imposed by the officer in charge (see Section B[3], above), but the police were requesting a surety in an amount great enough that only a justice could make such an order. Nonetheless, the trial judge suggested that, given the consent nature of the order, it would have been feasible to release the accused on the terms sought by the Crown and on an undertaking to appear in front of a justice the following morning to add the surety. If that had been done, the overnight detention (and consequent strip search) would have been unnecessary.

Other rights can also be relevant to deciding the amount of delay which will be seen as unreasonable. Strip searches, for example, are sometimes justifiable, but they have been recognized as particularly invasive. One context in which they are allowed is when an accused

---

158 *C.K.*, *ibid.* at para. 43.

159 *R. v. Singh*, 2007 SCC 48 [*Singh*].

160 *Clarke*, above note 153. Two of the three were within the twenty-four-hour period, and one was outside it.

161 *Clarke*, *ibid.* at para. 189. See also the discussion below of the interplay between s. 503 and a purported lack of resources.

will be intermingling with other prisoners, such as, for example, when being held overnight before being taken before a justice. Some courts have held that this possibility of a strip search creates an added obligation on police to be expeditious in taking accused persons before a justice, to avoid the necessity of holding them overnight.[162]

Where the police do fail to bring an accused before a justice in the specified time period, it is irrelevant whether this has happened deliberately or negligently.[163] In addition, it is not relevant that the accused was unlikely to be released if actually taken in front of a justice.[164] As has been said, "[w]hat s. 503(1) guarantees to the accused is the opportunity to seek release from custody without unreasonable delay."[165]

As noted above, the general obligation is to bring an accused before a justice without unreasonable delay, with twenty-four hours set as an outer limit on reasonableness unless a justice is "not available" in that period of time. If a justice is not available, something more than twenty-four hours might consequently be reasonable.

It is necessary to consider the second question posed above, the meaning of "not available" in this context. Mere administrative issues will not be sufficient to meet this criterion: "[A] lack of resources or a failure to apply resources effectively, cannot be used as a justification."[166] That is, the fact that particular courts might not be sitting and so it is not possible to proceed in a routine fashion is not, by itself, sufficient to say that a justice is "not available." In *Simpson*, for example, the accused was arrested in St. John's on a Sunday, but as the following Monday was a holiday and the provincial court was closed, she was not taken before a justice until Tuesday, forty-eight hours after her arrest. The Newfoundland Court of Appeal concluded, with no difficulty, that the "not available" exception did not apply. There were Provincial Court judges in St. John's, as well as fifty-five justices of the peace: the fact that the

---

162 *Clarke, ibid.; R. v. S.F.*, [2003] O.J. No. 92 (Ct. J.).
163 *R. v. E.W.*, 2002 NFCA 49 [*E.W.*]; *Clarke*, above note 153. See also *R. v. Dumont*, 2005 BCPC 204 at para. 50:

> . . . I do not believe that Constable Gill nor any of the other police officers deliberately planned to defeat the rights of the accused under s. 503 of the *Criminal Code*. I do think, though, that the police utterly failed to give the rights of the detainees anything like the priority which is required by the legislative provisions. The attitude disclosed by the evidence is altogether too casual, subordinating the s. 503 requirements to other considerations related to the police investigation.

164 *R. v. MacPherson* (1995), 100 C.C.C. (3d) 216 (N.B.C.A.) [*MacPherson*].
165 *E.W.*, above note 163 at para. 18.
166 *Clarke*, above note 153 at para. 192.

courts were not open did not mean no one was available.[167] Similarly, in *MacPherson* the province of New Brunswick had not, at the time, created a system by which judges were available on weekends. The Court of Appeal there concluded that this was a systemic defect which had routinely resulted in violations of section 9, and did not fall within the meaning of a justice not being available: it commented that "justice does not stop on weekends."[168]

Simpson and *MacPherson* both dealt with "system-wide" failures, but the same principle applies in individual cases. In *C.K.* the police chose to keep questioning the two accused past the time when bail court would close, and were unable to persuade the after-hours justice (before the court had closed) that hearing the matter was an emergency. As noted above, the officers' desire to continue questioning the accused did not make the delay reasonable, nor did it mean that a justice was not available.[169]

The third question to be considered is the impact of taking an accused before a justice. Specifically, of course, the effect is that there will be a bail hearing and the accused will either be detained or will be released on some basis. It is also possible that the accused will be ordered remanded for up to three days before the bail hearing takes place, if the Crown is seeking to show cause why he should be detained.[170] The broader, more conceptual point, however, is that once the accused is taken before a justice, she has "come into the judicial sphere and out of the hands of the investigating authorities."[171]

Put another way, if the accused is remanded into custody, then he should be transferred to a prison: that is the authority given to a justice by the *Code*.[172] He should *not* be returned to police custody for whatever investigation had been going on to continue. As the Ontario Court of Appeal noted in *Precourt*:

> When the accused has been taken before a judicial officer and remanded on an information the investigative process incidental to arrest, previously referred to, has terminated, a decision to invoke the

---

167 *Simpson*, above note 29.
168 *MacPherson*, above note 164 at para. 13.
169 *C.K.*, above note 152 at para. 35: "At its highest, the Crown/police position is that a justice was not available when they were ready to take the accused before a justice. The defendants were being held 10 minutes or less from the courthouse in which any number of judges and justices were sitting from 9 a.m. onwards. A justice was most definitely available within twenty-four hours."
170 *Criminal Code*, above note 1, ss. 515 & 516.
171 *R. v. Ansari*, 2008 BCSC 1492 at para. 48 [*Ansari*].
172 *Criminal Code*, above note 1, s. 515(5).

machinery of the criminal law to try the accused has been made, and he is thereafter under the jurisdiction of the Court.[173]

The court added that, in appropriate circumstances, police could still interview the accused or conduct an identification parade, but that, nonetheless, the accused was to be held in a separate location following her remand. Some delay — for example, to allow other accused also to be dealt with in court — might be justified, but the requirement to take the accused to prison "forthwith" meant that it must be done as soon as possible in the circumstances.

If the accused cannot immediately be transported to a prison, she must nonetheless be treated differently following the appearance before a justice. It has been held, for example, that

> The general police investigative power to interrogate the accused person has terminated. The right to question the accused in the absence of counsel without his consent and the use of police persuasion to convince the accused to waive his or her right to silence do not exist at this stage, because the accused is under the jurisdiction of the court.[174]

Further, if an accused is not taken immediately to prison, he must be given an opportunity to consult with counsel, in order to be informed of the change in his status, and the police no longer have the right to interrogate the accused as though he is in investigative custody.[175]

In *Ansari*, for example, the accused was not taken before a justice until more than twenty-four hours had passed, and even then the hearing was conducted only by telephone. The trial judge noted that the effect was that "the police simply took the accused back to cells as if nothing of any importance had happened, and had another go at him."[176] The accused, who had been actively seeking an opportunity to speak with his lawyer again, obtained none of the protections which ought to have flowed from being taken in front of a justice. The justice had recommended to the police that they should let the accused contact his lawyer, but had behaved as though the accused were still under the authority of the police, rather than having passed into judicial hands. The trial judge found this to be a serious breach of section 9.

Finally, then, we arrive at the fourth question, the *Charter* implications of non-compliance with this requirement of section 503. Some

---

173 R. v. *Precourt* (1976), 18 O.R. (2d) 714 at 725 (C.A.) [*Precourt*].

174 R. v. *Daunt*, [2005] Y.J. No. 23 at para. 143 (S.C.) [*Daunt*].

175 *Daunt*, ibid.

176 *Ansari*, above note 171 at para. 54.

older caselaw had suggested that failure to meet the deadline would not necessarily result in an arbitrary detention: that is, these cases held out the possibility that there could be unreasonable delay in taking an accused before a justice, but that this unreasonable delay did not make the detention arbitrary. If there was a valid explanation for the delay, it had been suggested, then the detention, although unlawful, would not be arbitrary.[177]

This argument appears now to be foreclosed by the Supreme Court's decision in *Grant*. In that case the Court notes that the question of whether an unlawful detention was necessarily an arbitrary one had not been settled, and that earlier caselaw had held out the possibility of unlawful but non-arbitrary detentions. *Grant* specifically rejects that possibility, holding that "a detention not authorized by law is arbitrary and violates s. 9."[178] It follows, therefore, that unreasonable delay in taking an arrested person before a justice will be a *Charter* violation.[179]

The remedy for such a violation will be settled under section 24 and will depend on the particular circumstances of the case.[180] In *Simpson*, in the context of a systemic failure to provide the possibility of bail hearings within twenty-four hours, the trial judge ordered a stay of proceedings; this decision was upheld by the Supreme Court of Canada. Stays have also been granted as a remedy in other cases which are not reflections of any systemic failure.[181] Other cases have excluded evidence that was obtained as a result of the detention.[182] Yet other courts have given the accused no remedy despite a finding of a breach: if no evidence was discovered as a result of the arbitrary detention and the

---

177 See, for example, *R. v. Tam* (1995), 100 C.C.C. (3d) 196 (B.C.C.A.).

178 *R. v. Grant*, 2009 SCC 32 at para. 54 [*Grant*].

179 The issue of the proper remedy for a s. 9 violation can also arise in contexts related to s. 503 but not specifically based on it. In each of *R. v. Cutforth* (1987), 40 C.C.C. (3d) 253 (Alta. C.A.), and *R. v. Weaver*, 2005 ABCA 105, the accused was arrested and eventually released without being taken in front of a justice at all: both accused had been intoxicated when arrested and were held overnight for that reason. Each accused was held longer than necessary for that purpose, and so s. 9 violations were found.

180 It is interesting to note that a recent series of trial decisions in Saskatchewan have entered stays as a remedy in cases where an accused has been initially detained for a breath test but then held overnight in cells, in violation of the *Code* release provisions. In these decisions, trial judges have quite explicitly pointed to the goal of changing this improper police practice as a justification for the remedy of a stay. See *R. v. Fox*, 2007 SKPC 61; *R. v. Holbrook*, 2008 SKPC 133; and *R. v. Poletz*, 2009 SKPC 121. Note that the Crown chose not to appeal any of these trial decisions.

181 See, for example, *R. v. Gagea*, [1989] Y.J. No. 90 (S.C.), or *Hall*, above note 115.

182 *Mangat*, above note 155; *C.K.*, above note 152.

test for a stay is not met, the accused might not receive any relief.[183] Still other cases have taken the arbitrary detention into account on sentencing, imposing a significantly shortened period of imprisonment.[184]

5) Lineups and Time Limits

One particular investigative technique that can have an impact on the length of a reasonable delay is an identification parade, or lineup. In *Storrey*, for example, the Court relied on the wish of the police to conduct a lineup as part of the justification for holding an accused overnight. That case made clear the point noted above, that the police can continue their investigation although they had already arrested the accused, and specifically stated that "[t]he constable can put him up on an identification parade to see if he is picked out by the witnesses."[185] Other cases have made statements suggesting that the police have some sort of authority to place an accused in a lineup.[186]

On the other hand, the Court has also explicitly noted, in *Ross*, what appears to be the contrary of this view: there, it held that there is no statutory legal obligation to participate in a lineup, either statutorily or by judicial creation.[187] An accused *can* be compelled to allow her picture to be taken, and that picture could later be used for a photo lineup.[188] However, there is no basis upon which an accused can be forced physically to participate in a lineup.

That is not to say that an accused would always be well advised not to participate. The underlying rationale of asking a witness to identify the accused from a group of others is to protect the accused's interests. If an accused refuses to participate in the lineup, a less favourable method of identification might be used as an alternative. In *Marcoux*, the accused refused to take part in a lineup, and so the police instead conducted a "showup": the witness was allowed to see the accused and only one other person in a hallway, and then subsequently was shown the accused alone and asked whether he could identify him.[189] The

---

183 *Clarke*, above note 153; *E.W.*, above note 163.
184 *MacPherson*, above note 164.
185 *Storrey*, above note 28 at para. 26, quoting *Dallison v. Caffery*, [1964] 3 W.L.R. 385 at 398 (C.A.).
186 See, for example, *Precourt*, above note 173.
187 *R. v. Ross*, [1989] 1 S.C.R. 3 [*Ross*].
188 *Identification of Criminals Act*, R.S.C. 1985, c. I-1, s. 2.
189 *R. v. Marcoux*, [1976] 1 S.C.R. 763.

Court did not question the appropriateness of this action, and indeed in *Storrey* it seems also to affirm this type of action as appropriate.[190]

Conceptually, then, one might argue that an accused who is participating in a lineup is doing so voluntarily. Indeed, in *Ross* the Court stressed the importance of allowing an accused the opportunity to have access to counsel before a lineup is conducted, precisely so that he will have the ability to make an informed choice. The obligation to "hold off" (see Chapter 5, Section C[3][c]) was triggered by the accused's request to speak to counsel, and the lineup was among the evidence-gathering techniques foreclosed to the police in the interim. If the delay involved in taking an accused before a justice were analyzed from this perspective, on the assumption that an accused had consented to the delay, it might well have an impact on what period of time was seen as reasonable. Alternatively, it seems equally plausible that many accused who end up in lineups, particularly those who have not requested counsel, are simply unaware that they have no obligation to participate. In either case, this question seems not to arise in the caselaw very often.

In fact, the question of the interaction between lineups and reasonable delay has never seriously been analyzed, and it is an area that would benefit from more judicial attention. Although the Court has held that an accused has no legal obligation to participate in a lineup, it has suggested that this is distinct from the accused having a positive right to refuse to participate, a point it takes to be unsettled.[191]

Presumably, the Court has in mind some type of analogy to the right to silence: that if an accused has a positive right to refuse to participate, then non-refusal could not be made the subject of comment even in circumstances like those in *Marcoux*. In that case, the accused had objected to the admission of evidence about his refusal to participate in a lineup, but the Court held that the evidence was admissible since he had specifically criticized the police for using a showup rather than conducting a lineup.

Since *Marcoux* is a pre-*Charter* case, it is an open question as to what conclusion would be reached today; on the same facts, a court might well find a violation of *Charter* rights. This conclusion could be based either on a violation of section 7 or on the more direct ground that admitting identification evidence created in an unfair way would violate the accused's right to a fair trial. In *Walker*, for example, the accused was subpoenaed to a co-accused's preliminary inquiry, at which

---

190 *Storrey*, above note 28 at para. 32: "This is clearly not a case where the victim could, for example, be taken to the place of employment of the suspect to see if an identification could be made."

191 *Ross*, above note 187 at 13.

point several witnesses saw him in the hallway outside the courtroom and pointed him out to police; this method of identification was held to violate his *Charter* rights and the evidence was excluded.[192]

One might well argue that the circumstances should be seen as analogous to the Court's reasoning in *Turcotte*: if it would be "a snare and a delusion" to say that an accused has the right to silence but then to use that silence as evidence of the accused's guilt, then equally it would be objectionable to say that an accused has no obligation to be in a lineup but then place the accused in a worse position for refusing.[193] On the other hand, one might also analogize to *Singh*. That case seems to limit the extent to which the right to silence can be asserted as a positive protection, in the face of acquiescence to a police investigative technique.[194]

Entirely apart from the question of a *Charter* violation, there is increased skepticism over identification evidence since *Marcoux* was decided. The Sophonow Inquiry, for example, laid down a number of guidelines for identification parades and photo lineups, which have been referred to with approval by the Supreme Court in *Hibbert*.[195] Pre-trial identification evidence, however gathered, now tends to be evaluated against those criteria and to be treated more carefully. In *F.A.*, for example, a witness was shown a lineup of only two people and was told that suspects were in the group; the Ontario Court of Appeal found that convicting the accused based on the identification evidence in that case was unreasonable.[196] In *Miaponoose*, the police created a ruse whereby they drove the accused past the complainant in the case, who was waiting to see whether she could identify him. She did, but the Ontario Court of Appeal described that evidence as "very dubious and of very little weight" and once again overturned the conviction as unreasonable. It also noted:

> [I]t is crucial that procedures which tend to minimize the inherent dangers of eyewitness identification evidence be followed as much as possible in any given case . . . In all cases, the suspect should be presented to the complainant in circumstances that minimize any suggestion that the police believe the suspect is the offender.[197]

---

192 *R. v. Walker*, [2005] O.J. No. 6159 (S.C.J.).
193 *R. v. Turcotte*, 2005 SCC 50 at para. 44.
194 *Singh*, above note 159.
195 *R. v. Hibbert*, 2002 SCC 39.
196 *R. v. F.A.* (2004), 183 C.C.C. (3d) 518 (Ont. C.A.).
197 *R. v. Miaponoose* (1996), 110 C.C.C. (3d) 445 at paras. 17 and 28 (Ont. C.A.).

The procedures used in *Marcoux* seemingly would not meet today's standards, and so the impact of that case as an incentive for an accused to agree to take part in a lineup is very much up in the air.

6) Appearance by Telecommunications

It is possible for the accused's appearance in front of a justice to take place by telephone rather than in person. Section 515(2.2) creates a presumption that the appearance will take place in person but allows for appearance by "any suitable telecommunication device . . . that is satisfactory to the justice." This wording gives the discretion over the method of appearance in an individual case to the justice, not to the police, nor to be settled by a written policy.[198] Section 515(2.3) mandates that, if evidence is to be heard, the matter can take place electronically only if both the prosecutor and accused consent, unless the matter is to be heard "by closed-circuit television or any other means that allow the court and the accused to engage in simultaneous visual and oral communication." This would seem clearly to indicate that the accused's consent is not required in the case of other bail hearings, though there is some suggestion otherwise.[199] At a minimum it requires "an exercise of judicial discretion ensuring that there will be no compromise of the rights of the accused by virtue of the character of the hearing."[200] It does seem evident that the potential for appearance by means of a telecommunication device should be relevant to the issues of whether there has been "unreasonable delay" or whether a justice was available within the relevant time frame.[201]

C. ARREST

Several issues need to be discussed in looking at powers of arrest. First, we shall consider the meaning of the word "arrest" itself, which allows a determination of whether a particular person has or has not been ar-

---

198 *Ansari*, above note 171 at paras. 33 and 38.
199 See *R. v. Wright*, 2002 BCPC 488, for the argument that the accused's consent is not required under s. 515(2.2). See *Ansari*, above note 171 at para. 37, for the view that there is a "strong argument" the section does mean that the accused's consent is required.
200 *Ansari*, above note 171 at para. 37.
201 This appears to be an implicit argument in the related Youth Court cases LSJPA 0936, 2009 QCCQ 7069; LSJPA 0937, 2009 QCCQ 7070; LSJPA 0938, 2009 QCCQ 7071.

rested. Following that we shall consider the circumstances in which various persons are authorized to make arrests. This will entail discussion of "citizen's arrest" and arrests by peace officers. In the latter case, there are powers of arrest both with and without warrants.

1) Definition of "Arrest"

Powers of arrest for criminal law purposes are now set out statutorily, in section 494 for private citizens and in section 495 for peace officers. However, the concept of an arrest was initially a common law one. Partly because of this history, the meaning of the word "arrest" is actually drawn from the common law.

The definition of "arrest" in Canadian criminal law stems from the 1970 decision of the Supreme Court in *Whitfield*.[202] In that case, a police officer saw Whitfield, the accused, in a car and stopped at a stoplight. The officer knew that there was a warrant for Whitfield's arrest and went over, telling the accused to remain. Whitfield in fact tried to drive away, though he was not immediately able to flee because of other traffic. At one point the officer managed to reach in through the open window of the accused's car, grab Whitfield's shirt, and say to him, "You are under arrest." Shortly thereafter the accused was able to accelerate and drive away, breaking free from the officer, who fell to the ground and suffered minor injuries. The accused was not, as one might have expected, charged with resisting arrest. It would seem unambiguously true that he was guilty of that offence, and in the eyes of the dissenting judges in the case that would have been the proper charge. In fact, though, he was charged with "escaping lawful custody." He could be guilty of that offence, of course, only if he was actually "in custody" when the officer was reaching through the open car window and gripping his shirt. That is the conclusion that the majority reached.

The majority concluded that there was no distinction to be drawn between being arrested and being in custody. In essence, they held, the two states were the same:

> There is no room for what seems to be a new subdivision of "arrest" into "custodial" arrest and "symbolical" or "technical" arrest. An accused is either arrested or he is not arrested. If this accused was arrested, he escaped from lawful custody . . .[203]

---

202 *R. v. Whitfield*, [1970] S.C.R. 46 [*Whitfield*].
203 *Whitfield, ibid.* at 48.

That, then, led to the question of exactly what constitutes an arrest. The Court held that an arrest could be accomplished in one of two ways:

> [A]n arrest consists either of (i) the actual seizure or touching of a person's body with a view to his detention, or (ii) the pronouncing of "words of arrest" to a person who submits to the arresting officer.[204]

Both of these definitions of arrest create some oddities in practice. The former fixes the point of arrest quite precisely — almost too precisely, in a sense, since it is capable of making the process of arrest appear to be a game of tag.[205] If the person arresting can touch the arrestee, the arrest is made, but if the arrestee can dodge successfully, he is not guilty of the offence of escaping lawful custody. This is essentially the fact pattern in *Asante-Mensah*, to be discussed in a moment.[206]

In contrast, the latter basis for arrest is not always precise enough, because it might not be clear whether the words that preceded an arrestee's submission constituted "words of arrest." "Words of arrest," in the second branch of the test, is not interpreted narrowly. As a result, it is not always easy to know whether someone has been arrested or instead has had their liberty restrained in some other way.

These two branches of the definition of arrest are worth discussing separately.

a) Touching with a View to Detention

Asante-Mensah was primarily about the use of force, in particular in the context of arrest by private citizens. However, the facts neatly illustrate the use of the definition of arrest. The accused was a "scooper": that is, a taxi driver who picked up fares at the Toronto International Airport even though he was not licensed to do so. Security guards at the airport arrested him on a number of occasions, though he fled each time. Their power to arrest actually flowed from provincial legislation, but that did not matter in terms of deciding the factual question of whether the accused was arrested or not: the Court held that "arrest" is a term of art

---

204 *R. v. Latimer*, [1997] 1 S.C.R. 217 at para. 24 [*Latimer*], characterizing the result in *Whitfield*, above note 202.

205 In *R. v. Asante-Mensah*, 2003 SCC 38 at para. 45 [*Asante-Mensah*], the Court quotes with approval from *Genner v. Sparks* (1704), 6 Mod. Rep. 173, 87 E.R. 928 at 929 (Q.B.): "[I]f here he had but touched the defendant even with the end of his finger, it had been *an arrest*" [emphasis in original].

206 In *Asante-Mensah*, *ibid.* at para. 45, the Court notes that "[t]here is no doubt the appellant understood the significance of the inspector's touch because, according to the trial judge, he made every effort to avoid being touched."

and that the definition from *Whitfield* therefore applied when the word was used in the provincial statute.[207]

The case concerned three particular charges. In the first two, the accused had been tapped on the shoulder by a security guard before fleeing; he was convicted of escaping lawful custody in connection with both of those incidents. The third incident went as follows:

> 15 Later in the afternoon of July 25, 1991, another incident at the airport led to charges against the appellant of dangerous driving, use of a weapon in committing an assault, and escaping lawful custody. The charges arose in this way. A different inspector, aware of the appellant's previous arrest the same day, saw the appellant's taxi "trolling" past the arrivals level at Terminal 3. He stepped out in front of the appellant's taxi with his hand raised, holding his badge, and ordered the appellant to stop. The appellant kept on coming and, to avoid personal injury, the inspector jumped onto the hood of the appellant's car, from where he was dislodged as the appellant accelerated to get clear of the terminal. The inspector had made no physical contact to arrest the appellant. There was clearly no submission by the appellant to the inspector's authority. The trial judge held that no arrest had occurred and, having a reasonable doubt on other aspects of the evidence, dismissed all charges in connection with this incident.

In the first two incidents, the accused had been under arrest from the moment he was first touched; in the third, in the absence of any touch or submission, he was not arrested at all.

Although an arrest begins instantaneously, as it were, the Court describes it as a continuing act, in the sense that the accused remains in the state of arrest from the moment of the touch (or submission) "until the person so restrained is either released from custody or, having been brought before a magistrate, is remanded in custody by the magistrate's judicial act."[208] This definition, it should be observed, is the counterpart to the observation in Section B(4) above that once the accused is taken before a justice, she has "come into the judicial sphere and out of the hands of the investigating authorities."[209]

In the particular context of *Asante-Mensah*, the continuing nature of an arrest helped the Court reach the conclusion that a private citizen arresting under provincial legislation was entitled to use force to effect

---

207 *Asante-Mensah, ibid.* at paras. 28 and 41.
208 *Asante-Mensah, ibid.* at para. 33, quoting *Holgate-Mohammed v. Duke*, [1984] A.C. 437 at 441 (H.L.).
209 *Ansari*, above note 171 at para. 48.

the arrest.[210] The arrest was initiated by a touch, but the power to arrest was not exhausted once the touch was made: that is, the arrest was not over. Rather, the security guard was entitled to use necessary force to achieve the purpose of the arrest: to deliver the accused to a peace officer. To conclude otherwise, the Court held, would be to resurrect the "custodial arrest" and "technical arrest" distinction which had been rejected in *Whitfield*.

b) Words of Arrest plus Submission and "De Facto Arrest"

It should be said at the start that "words of arrest and submission" can, in many cases, be a perfectly sensible definition of arrest leading to no ambiguity, and justified on a policy basis. It is entirely correct that in many cases the police might say words to the effect of "you are under arrest — get in the car," following which the arrestee might act as requested. Similarly, arrests often occur while an accused is already in custody, in a police interview room, being questioned. It would be useless formalism to insist that in such cases there was some requirement for the police to touch the person as well as to pronounce the words of arrest. Indeed, to insist on some form of touching would be inconsistent with the principle of restraint in compelling appearance discussed above. The policy argument in *Whitfield* — that police are entitled to use force to effect an arrest but that the law should not encourage its use — has some validity.[211] Similarly, as the Court has noted, the legal authority to use force if necessary often makes it in fact unnecessary to do so, because it leads an accused to choose to submit.[212] It is also preferable from the perspective of the accused, in many cases, since the fact of being arrested triggers the various rights in section 10 of the *Charter*: an accused who submits in the face of clear words of arrest is more clearly immediately entitled to those rights.

The potential difficulty arises because of the point noted above: that "words of arrest" are not restricted to the words "you are under arrest." Rather, any words that convey to the accused the meaning that he is under arrest will be sufficient. Specifically, police need not use the word "arrest" itself. The important issue is:

> the substance of what the accused can reasonably be supposed to have understood, rather than the formalism of the precise words used . . . .

---

210 The issues arose because the arrest was not made under the *Criminal Code*. Had it been, even a private citizen authorized to arrest would be entitled to use necessary force by virtue of s. 25: see the discussion in Chapter 2.

211 *Whitfield*, above note 202 at 50.

212 *Asante-Mensah*, above note 205 at para. 57.

> The question is . . . what the accused was told, viewed reasonably in all
> the circumstances of the case.[213]

Again, this is not necessarily problematic in every case. "Don't go anywhere, I've got you, you can't leave, I am charging you with theft," or
something similar, would seem to be a pretty unambiguous way of
communicating to a shoplifter that she was under arrest.

The difficulty that arises on the second branch of *Whitfield*, and
on the rule that no particular words are absolutely required, is that in
some circumstances it allows courts to in essence rewrite reality. The
concept of "*de facto* arrest," which the Supreme Court essentially created in *Latimer*, allows courts to rely on the second definition in *Whitfield* as a basis for characterizing something, after the fact, as an arrest,
even if it was not meant to be one at the time.

In *Latimer*, the police had formed the view that the accused was
responsible for his daughter's death. They decided that they wanted
to take him into custody in order to question him about that: significantly, they consciously decided *not* to arrest him. Instead, they simply
wanted to detain him for questioning, and that was what they told him:
"You are being detained for investigation into the death of your daughter Tracy."[214] The important and awkward point here is that the police
did not have the power to detain Latimer — or anyone — for investigation. No such power existed; but, nonetheless, the police had not *asked*
the accused to come for questioning, they had insisted upon it, and
had told him that he was now in custody. That is, the police had set
out to do — and, one might think, had done — something they had no
legal authority to do. Not surprisingly, therefore, the accused brought
a *Charter* application, claiming that there had been a violation of his
right not to be arbitrarily detained. In his view, he had been detained
and there was no lawful authority for the detention, and so his section
9 right was violated.

The Court rejected this section 9 claim. It held that there had been
a legal authority for the accused's detention and that that authority was
the law of arrest. The Court acknowledged that the officers had decided
not to arrest the accused, and that in taking him into custody they had
used the word "detention" rather than "arrest." Nevertheless, the Court
concluded: "[N]otwithstanding what the *intention* of the officers may
have been, their conduct had the *effect* of putting Mr. Latimer under

---

213 *Latimer*, above note 204 at para. 24, quoting *R. v. Evans*, [1991] 1 S.C.R. 869 at
888 [*Evans*].
214 *Latimer, ibid.* at para. 8.

arrest."[215] The Court supported this claim based on the second branch of the *Whitfield* test. The accused had certainly submitted to the police, because he had gone with them at their request. So, if there were words of arrest, the second branch was made out. And, as noted above, the Court concluded that the precise words did not matter: rather, the issue was "what the accused can reasonably be supposed to have understood." On the facts of the case:

> Mr. Latimer was told that he was being detained, and that he would be taken back to North Battleford to be interviewed. The police officers informed him of his right to silence and his right to counsel. They accompanied him back into his house while he changed his clothes, telling him that they were doing so because he was now in their custody.[216]

This amounted to "words of arrest." the Court ruled. Since it was coupled with the accused's submission, there was a "*de facto* arrest." On the particular facts of *Latimer*, "accidental arrest" would be a better description: the officers did not mean to arrest the accused, tried not to, but did so despite their best intentions. The Court then carried on to find that the prerequisites to a legal arrest were also made out: in that event there was no arbitrary detention.

In *Latimer*, telling the accused that he was being detained for investigation and would be taken to the police station for questioning and of his right to counsel constituted "words of arrest."[217] Other courts have found the "words of arrest" requirement to be satisfied, despite no explicit arrest, when an accused was told by a customs officer that he could not leave, or was told by a police officer that he was required to accompany the officer to a vehicle.[218]

Applying the *Whitfield* definition of arrest in the way *Latimer* does — that is, to apply the concept of arrest despite the intentions of the police — is not clearly a sensible policy. Normally, the purpose the police have in mind is seen to be quite important to settling whether their behaviour is authorized by law or not (see Chapter 2, Section B(2)). Having an improper purpose in mind, or even just the wrong purpose, has often been taken to render illegal the use of some power: for example, in *Caslake*, a search that could have been made properly as a search incident to arrest was found to be illegal because the officer's

---

215 *Ibid.* at para. 24 [emphasis added].
216 *Ibid.* at para. 25.
217 *Ibid.*
218 See *R. v. Grossman*, [1998] B.C.J. No. 62 (S.C.) and *R. v. Tipewan*, [1998] S.J. No. 238 (Q.B.) [*Tipewan*] respectively.

purpose in conducting the search had been to produce an inventory of the contents of the vehicle.[219] If the concept of *de facto* arrest is accepted, however, then the police purpose is apparently simply irrelevant in this context.

Treating the police purpose as irrelevant is questionable. It is noteworthy, after all, that the police had in Latimer's case set out to violate his rights. Their conscious intention had been to do something they had no authority to do.

One could argue for this approach by suggesting that it properly focuses on the perspective of the accused, and that it is the accused's perspective that matters most in deciding whether she is arrested. Such an argument would be consistent with the Court's much more recent decision in *Grant* on the test for deciding whether an accused had been psychologically detained: "whether the reasonable person in the individual's circumstances would conclude that he or she had been deprived by the state of the liberty of choice."[220] That is similar to the test relied on in *Latimer*: "what the accused can reasonably be supposed to have understood."[221] This test might also be seen as asking what a reasonable person in the accused's circumstances would have concluded. On the other hand, the Court later described its decision in *Latimer* in these terms: "It was concluded that he submitted to go with the police because he understood that he was under compulsion to do so."[222] That formulation is subjective rather than objective, though in any case it still looks at the matter from the perspective of the accused.[223]

However, there are practical differences between asking whether there was a psychological detention and asking whether there was an arrest. In the former case, the issue is whether the accused had been detained at all. That question settles whether the accused "gets in" to section 9 in the first place: if there was no detention at all, there cannot have been an arbitrary detention. In that event, focusing on the accused's perspective is a way of protecting the accused's rights: a person who reasonably believes that the state is interfering with his liberty be-

---

219 *R. v. Caslake*, [1998] 1 S.C.R. 51.

220 *Grant*, above note 178 at para. 44.

221 *Latimer*, above note 204 at para. 24.

222 *Asante-Mensah*, above note 205 at para. 46.

223 This is not absolutely the case, however. The Court does not explicitly say whose perspective matters most. It relies on the quote from *Evans*, above note 213, that "the substance of what the accused can reasonably be supposed to have understood, rather than the formalism of the precise words used . . . The question is . . . what the accused was told, viewed reasonably in all the circumstances of the case." Looking at "what the accused was told" might be adopting a police-centric viewpoint.

comes entitled to the constitutional protections that accompany inter-ferences with liberty.

In the latter case, however, the situation is more or less reversed. A potential *de facto* arrest will of necessity involve a detention, since the accused will have submitted (*not* "consented") to an interference with liberty.[224] In that circumstance, there is no question that the accused *might* be entitled to section 9 protection. The only impact that rechar-acterizing the nature of the interference from "detention" to "arrest" can have is to help turn the detention from an unauthorized one to an authorized one: in other words, to make it non-arbitrary.[225] So, in the latter case, the accused's reasonable belief, a belief likely created by the police, is being used to deny her rights, not obtain them for her.

This makes *Latimer* difficult to reconcile with the later decision in *Grant*. If the behaviour of the police would make a reasonable person think that he had to comply with their demands, *Grant* says that that person is someone in need of *Charter* protection and so should have the benefit of section 9. If the behaviour of the police would make a reason-able person think that he had to comply with their demands, *Latimer* says that that person has been arrested and so might forfeit the benefit of section 9. *Grant* says that a person who submits to demands which lacked legal authority should be protected by the *Charter*; *Latimer* says that a person who submits to demands which lacked legal authority has infused those demands with legal authority by submitting.

Further, the *de facto* arrest test asks only whether the accused thought he had a choice about going with the police: that he "under-stood that he was under compulsion to do so." That is, it does not re-quire the accused to be wondering whether she was *arrested* or not. The Court has noted that people often comply with police demands even

---

224   See *R. v. C.G.B.*, [1997] B.C.J. No. 1884 (S.C.) for an example of a case where the trial judge found that the facts amounted to *at least* a psychological deten-tion and possibly a *de facto* arrest. The trial judge noted that the latter finding was not necessary to reach the conclusion that the accused ought to have been informed of his right to counsel. See also *Tipewan*, above note 218.

225   It is not sufficient on its own, of course, since, as noted in *Latimer*, above note 204, the arrest must still be a legal one, but it does help render the interference with liberty an authorized one. Nonetheless, it is possible for a court to find that there has been a *de facto* arrest but then conclude that that arrest was unlaw-ful because no reasonable grounds for it existed: see, for example, *R. v. Budden*, 2005 ABQB 314 [*Budden*]. Similarly, if there were a lawful *de facto* arrest, the police would then be required to comply with their obligations under s. 10 of the *Charter*. In *Latimer* itself, the Court concluded that this had happened, but that will not necessarily be the case: see, for example, *R. v. Godwin*, [2003] A.J. No. 1005 (Prov. Ct. (Crim. Div.)).

when they in fact have no obligation to do so, because people are quite reasonably not aware of the exact limits of police power:

> Most citizens are not aware of the precise legal limits of police authority. Rather than risk the application of physical force or prosecution for wilful obstruction, the reasonable person is likely to err on the side of caution, assume lawful authority and comply with the demand.[226]

This means, of course, that "submission" in the abstract should not be equated to "submission to an arrest."

To some extent, the need for the concept of *de facto* arrest has been diminished. At the time *Latimer* was decided, police had no power to detain a person for investigative purposes. In effect, that was the "problem." If the police were not acting lawfully, then there might have been a section 9 violation; concluding that there was a *de facto* arrest was a way of finding that the police had acted lawfully. Since that time the Court has created a power of investigative detention, with its decision in *Mann* (see the discussion in Chapter 3). That power does not permit the police to detain for questioning in all circumstances and it would not, for example, have been available in the circumstances in *Latimer*. Nonetheless, it is a further power that can be relied on to justify police interference with liberty as not being unlawful. In that event, Crown prosecutors will sometimes not need to argue *de facto* arrest as a way to justify police action, because that action will be more easily justified on other grounds.[227]

One final observation on this subject should be made, which is that it is not at all clear that "*de facto* arrest" is always used as a term of art. In *Latimer*, the phrase was used to mean that "the accused understood he had been placed under arrest and complied." In other cases, the same phrase is used but seemingly not with the same meaning. In *Mann*, for example, in cautioning that the power of investigative detention does not give the police carte blanche to detain, the Court noted that "[t]he power to detain cannot be exercised on the basis of a hunch, nor can it become a *de facto* arrest." Picking up on this point, the Ontario Court of Appeal in *Suberu* held:

---

226 *R. v. Therens*, [1985] 1 S.C.R. 613 at 644, quoted in *Grant*, above note 178 at para. 30.
227 On the other hand, the relationship between possible *de facto* arrests and possible investigative detentions can be a messy one to sort out on individual facts: see, for example, *R. v. Cunanan*, [2008] O.J. No. 1259 (S.C.J.), or *Budden*, above note 225.

54 The police activity during the brief interlude contemplated by the words "without delay" must be truly exploratory in that the officer must be trying to decide whether anything beyond a brief detention of the person will be necessary and justified. If the officer has already made up his or her mind that the detained person will be detained for something more than a brief interval, there is no justification for not providing the individual with his or her right to counsel immediately. To echo the words of R. v. Mann, supra, in those cases, the investigative detention is a *de facto* arrest.[228]

The courts in these cases clearly do not mean that "the accused understood he had been placed under arrest and complied"; indeed, they are not considering the accused's understanding at all. They are simply referring to a detention that is of such duration that the infringement on the accused's liberty is equivalent to an arrest.[229]

2) Powers of Arrest

a) Private Citizens and Peace Officers

Understanding the current state of powers of arrest requires a certain knowledge of its history. Today, the vast majority of arrests are conducted by professional police officers. However, this is a situation of the exception having swallowed the rule. As the Supreme Court has noted: "The concept of 'arrest' by private citizens is as old as the common law. It predates the rise of the modern police force."[230]

It will be necessary to discuss powers of arrest both by private citizens and by peace officers. It is worth pausing, however, to discuss exactly what it means to say that someone is a peace officer as opposed to a private citizen, since it makes a difference at many points. It has already been observed that, although anyone may lay an information, informations laid by private citizens are treated differently from those laid by peace officers. Similarly, although the *Code* offers a number of protections to anyone exercising powers, some protections are provided only to peace officers.[231] And, as we will discuss below, different arrest

---

228 *R. v. Suberu* (2007), 218 C.C.C. (3d) 27 (Ont. C.A.). The result in that case was affirmed by the Supreme Court of Canada, though for quite different reasons: *R. v. Suberu*, 2009 SCC 3.

229 See also *R. v. Lauten*, [1998] B.C.J. No. 226 (S.C.).

230 *Asante-Mensah*, above note 205 at para. 36.

231 For example, although s. 25(1) permits anyone authorized to act under the *Criminal Code* to use reasonable force, the use of force likely to cause grievous bodily harm or death is limited in s. 25(4) to peace officers and those assisting them. See Chapter 2, Section B(1).

powers are available depending on whether the person arresting is a peace officer or a private citizen.

It would be more accurate to say, though, that different powers are available to a person depending on whether she is, at the relevant time, acting as a peace officer or not. That is, the world does not simply divide into peace officers and non-peace officers: rather, the same person can fall into either category depending on the exact circumstances. In part, this is reflected in the fact that arrest powers are not, strictly speaking, divided into those available to peace officers and those available to private citizens. Although some arrest powers are limited to peace officers, the others are available to "anyone": that is, to peace officers and non-peace officers alike. While it is convenient to think of and refer to the latter as powers of "citizen's arrest," that is not really accurate. A person who is a peace officer could, if necessary, rely on the citizen's arrest powers.

In addition, a person might be a peace officer in some circumstances but not in others. Although the term is defined in the *Criminal Code*, the Supreme Court has observed that it is not really meant as a status:

> On the level of principle, it is important to remember that the definition of "peace officer" in s. 2 of the *Criminal Code* is not designed to create a police force. It simply provides that certain persons who derive their authority from other sources will be treated as "peace officers" as well, enabling them to enforce the *Criminal Code* within the scope of their pre-existing authority, and to benefit from certain protections granted only to "peace officers."[232]

"Peace officer" is defined in section 2 of the *Code*. The definition includes a police officer, of course, but is much broader. It also includes officers appointed under various other acts, such as the *Customs Act*, the *Immigration and Refugee Protection Act*, the *Corrections and Conditional Release Act*, and the *Fisheries Act*. It includes the pilot in command of an aircraft, members of the Canadian Forces who are appointed as military police, and "a mayor, warden, reeve, sheriff, deputy sheriff, sheriff's officer and justice of the peace."[233]

However, the definition of peace officer does not constitute a blanket inclusion of all those listed individuals as people having a peace officer's powers under the *Code* at all times. Some limits are explicitly built in: customs officers have that status only while enforcing the relevant statutes, a pilot is a peace officer only while the aircraft is in

---

232 *R. v. Nolan*, [1987] 1 S.C.R. 1212 at para. 19.
233 *Criminal Code*, above note 1, s. 2.

flight, and so on. Further, the Court concluded in *Nolan* that the definition ought not to be given the broadest interpretation possible.

In *Nolan*, a military police officer appointed under the *National Defence Act* observed the accused driving on the base (and in fact leaving the base) at a speed of 50 km/h in a 15-km/h zone. The military officer stopped the accused and made a breathalyzer demand; the issue in the case was whether the accused had been arbitrarily detained. The accused was a civilian and so was not himself subject to the *Code of Service Discipline*; he therefore argued that the military police had no power to stop him.

The Nova Scotia Court of Appeal had relied on the definition of "peace officer" in section 2 of the *Code* to find that the military officers did have the power to stop the accused, and qualified as peace officers "against the world." At the time, the definition referred to "officers and men" of the Canadian armed forces who were "(i) appointed for the purposes of section 134 of the *National Defence Act*."[234] The Court of Appeal held that the accused had been appointed under that section, and since they therefore met the definition of "peace officer" they had the powers of peace officers in every context.

The Supreme Court held that this would amount to Parliament having created a national police force and was too expansive an approach to interpreting the definition. Rather, it held, to have been appointed for "the purposes" of the *National Defence Act* did not merely mean that the military police had been appointed under that section. It meant that they were peace officers when they were acting to fulfill the purposes of the *National Defence Act*: that is, when they were dealing with people who were themselves subject to the *Code of Service Discipline*.

On the other hand, the Court did not adopt the most restrictive interpretation of "peace officer" either. Although not willing to allow military police to qualify as peace officers against everyone at all times, the Court held that on the facts of this case, the military police stopping the accused were peace officers. An alternative part of the definition was that military police were peace officers when "employed on duties that the Governor in Council . . . has prescribed to be of such a kind as to necessitate that the officers and men performing them have the powers of peace officers." Those duties included the powers needed for the maintenance or restoration of law and order, the protection of property, and the protection of persons; stopping drunk drivers fell within those purposes. In addition,

---

234 The section now reads "officers and non-commissioned members of the Canadian Forces who are (i) appointed for the purposes of s. 156 of the *National Defence Act*."

the regulations required that the military police officer be following a specific order or practice, but this was met by the obligations imposed under the *Trespass Regulations*. Accordingly, the officers in this case did qualify as peace officers for the purpose of stopping the accused on these facts, even though he was a civilian.

The Court reached a similar conclusion in *Decorte*, where it found that two First Nations constables were acting as peace officers in stopping a driver as part of a Reduced Impaired Driving Everywhere (RIDE) program, even though they did not stop him on the reserve. The officers were not police, though they had the powers of police officers in carrying out their duties. They were appointed as First Nations constables for the Fort Williams Reserve, but that did not mean, the Court held, that they could exercise their powers only within the territorial limits of the reserve; rather, they had been empowered by statute to act "in relation to" the community they served. In this case the checkstop had been set up just outside the reserve, and so they were acting within their authority.[235]

A similar conclusion was reached in *Roberge*. Peace officers are appointed within a particular jurisdiction: depending on the force, that might be for a particular city or for an entire province. Normally, a peace officer out of her jurisdiction loses the status of peace officer and would have to rely on the citizen's arrest power, if an arrest power existed at all. This was the argument in *Roberge*, where a Quebec police officer pursued a taxi driver into New Brunswick. However, an exception is made in the case of fresh pursuit. The Supreme Court held that a peace officer who had lawful authority to arrest a person in one province retains the status of peace officer in another province so long as "the pursuit had commenced lawfully in his jurisdiction and as long as such pursuit is fresh."[236] On the other hand, it also held:

> The police officer should endeavour to contact the local peace officers as soon as is possible, even during the pursuit, circumstances permitting. Once the local authorities have taken over the pursuit, he ceases to be a peace officer and becomes then a person assisting peace officers.[237]

---

235 *R. v. Decorte*, 2005 SCC 9.

236 *R. v. Roberge*, [1983] 1 S.C.R. 312 [*Roberge*]. The particular finding in that case was that the peace officer is still protected under s. 25(4) for the use of force likely to cause death or grievous bodily harm.

237 *Ibid.* at 332.

b)   Statutory Powers to Arrest

Beyond the issue of whether, as a matter of fact, an accused was arrested is the question of whether that arrest was lawful. Arrest can be made either with a warrant or without one.

Where a peace officer wishes to arrest a person with a warrant, she must lay an information before a justice under section 504 of the *Code*, then under section 507 seek a warrant. Section 507(4) requires the justice to issue a summons unless it is shown that there are reasonable grounds to believe that a warrant is necessary in the public interest. The warrant can authorize the officer in charge to release the person following arrest on conditions, rather than keeping him in custody until a bail hearing. Failing that, the warrant requires the person to be brought before a justice to answer to the charge. These issues have all been dealt with at length in Sections A(2), B(1), and B(3) above.

The issue that needs to be discussed at length here is the other arrest option, arrest without a warrant. Warrantless powers of arrest are also set out in the *Criminal Code*, specifically in sections 494 and 495.[238] The latter section sets out powers of arrest available only to peace officers. The powers in the former section are more broadly available: some to "any one" and others to property owners or their delegates. They are often referred to colloquially as the powers of "citizen's arrest," and that is not inaccurate, in the sense that they are available to private citizens. As noted above, though, in occasional fact situations peace officers might not be able to rely on section 495 but could rely on section 494. Since they too fall within "any one," they are also entitled to use these powers.[239]

As a preliminary observation, note that the Court has, broadly speaking, adopted the view that these arrest powers must be kept within their defined limits. That is, unless an arrest power has been specifically prescribed by the *Criminal Code* or some other statute, then no arrest power exists. This point is made clear in *Sharma*. The accused there was issued a ticket for selling flowers without a licence, contrary to a city bylaw. When he refused to leave the street, the officer arrested

---

238   There is authority suggesting that one remaining common law power of arrest still exists, which is an arrest for an apprehended breach of the peace: see Chapter 2, Section B(1)(c).

239   See, for example, *Roberge*, above note 236, where the Court observes that a peace officer might pursue someone across a provincial border and, once there, call on local police for help. At that point the original officer becomes only a citizen, but could rely on the citizen's arrest power in s. 494(1)(b). See also *R. v. Huff* (1979), 50 C.C.C. (3d) 324 (Alta. C.A.) [*Huff*]. In addition, see *R. v. Reddy*, 2007 BCPC 384 [*Reddy*], where an off-duty peace officer was entitled to rely on the citizen's arrest power.

him and charged him with obstructing an officer in the execution of duty. The Court held that the officer was not permitted to act in that fashion. The only mechanism provided for enforcement of the bylaw was to issue a ticket, and the officer had not been obstructed in doing that. Further, the officer was not permitted to "manufacture" an arrest power for himself by ordering the accused to stop violating the bylaw and then arresting him under the *Criminal Code* for failing to comply.[240] Indeed, even where the underlying bylaw does contain an arrest power, that means a peace officer would have the right to arrest the accused only for violating the bylaw: it does *not* permit an arrest for obstruction.[241]

We will begin with a brief overview of the individual warrantless powers of arrest, then return to consider each of them individually in greater depth.

i)   Overview of Arrest Powers

There are two initial distinctions to be noted in the arrest provisions. The first is that between an "indictable offence" and "criminal offence." An indictable offence is one that may be prosecuted by indictment: "may" be as opposed to "must" be, and therefore this category includes hybrid offences.[242] The category of "criminal offence," on the other hand, includes all offences in the *Criminal Code*. Put another way, "indictable offence" means indictable or hybrid offences, and "criminal offence" means indictable, hybrid, or summary conviction offences. An arrest power for criminal offences is therefore the broader one.

Second, it is necessary to distinguish between the arrestor finding a person committing an offence, and the arrestor having reasonable grounds to believe that someone has committed an offence. The former requires that the arrestor has actually witnessed the offence being committed.[243] The latter category is a broader one, since it requires only reasonable belief, not personal knowledge (see the discussion in Chapter 2, Section C(2)).

---

240   R. v. *Sharma*, [1993] 1 S.C.R. 650 [*Sharma*]. ·

241   R. v. *Fraser*, 2002 NSPC 6.

242   See *Huff*, above note 239. See also the *Interpretation Act*, R.S.C. 1985, c-I-21, s. 34(1):

> Where an enactment creates an offence, (a) the offence is deemed to be an indictable offence if the enactment provides that the offender may be prosecuted for the offence by indictment . . . .

243   The situation is somewhat more complicated than that, of course: see Section C(2)(b)(ii), below in this chapter. ·

Earlier in this chapter we discussed the principle of restraint in compelling appearance: the notion that the ability of the state to interfere with individual liberty should be constrained to the extent consistent with achieving the goal of public safety. Clearly, that consideration is also relevant here. Generally speaking, to allow an arrest power for criminal offences is more intrusive than to allow one only for indictable offences. Similarly, to allow an arrest on reasonable grounds is more intrusive than an arrest power based on a "finds committing" standard. The most intrusive possible arrest power, then, would be one that allowed arrest based on reasonable grounds to believe that the accused has committed any criminal offence. Appropriately, then, that is the one arrest power that is *not* created in any part of section 494 or 495.

Section 494(1) set out the powers of arrest available to anyone. There are two.

First, anyone may arrest someone whom he finds committing an indictable offence. Note that, as is appropriate to counterbalance the fact that this arrest power is the one most broadly available (that is, to anyone), it combines the more limited options, in order to maintain restraint. That is, it is available only for some offences, not all, and it requires the stricter "finds committing" standard.[244]

The second arrest power available to anyone depends on another arrest power already existing in someone else's hands: it is in effect a helping provision. That is, anyone may help arrest a person who is fleeing a valid arrest by someone else. Specifically, anyone may arrest if they have reasonable grounds to believe two things: that the person to be arrested has committed a criminal offence, and that that person is escaping from and being freshly pursued by someone with lawful authority to arrest him.[245]

Section 494(2) sets out specific arrest powers for those with an interest in property, and for their delegates: that is, "a person authorized by the owner or by a person in lawful possession of property." This power allows the arrest of anyone the arrestor finds committing a criminal offence on or in relation to the property. Although nominally available to any property owner, realistically this arrest power is most frequently used by private security guards, bouncers, and so on.

Anyone other than a peace officer who arrests a person is required to "forthwith deliver the person to a peace officer."[246]

---

244 *Criminal Code*, above note 1, s. 494(1)(b).
245 *Ibid.*
246 *Ibid.*, s. 494(3).

The warrantless powers of arrest exclusively available to peace officers are set out in section 495. There are limits on these powers, some of which were discussed in Section B(3) above. In general terms, however, peace officers are given quite broad powers of arrest. Really, there is only one circumstance in which peace officers cannot arrest, which is the situation that on the "finds committing/reasonable grounds" and "indictable/criminal" matrix would be the most intrusive. That is, if a peace officer has only reasonable grounds to believe an offence was committed, and the offence was only a summary conviction one, then no power of arrest exists: in those circumstances the only option available is to lay an information before a justice and seek a summons or warrant.

More specifically, section 495 creates three warrantless arrest powers for peace officers. The first relates to the more restricted category of indictable offences: a peace officer may arrest a person who "has committed an indictable offence" or whom he on reasonable grounds believes has committed or is about to commit an indictable offence. These requirements are not immediately very obviously distinguishable, and we will discuss in more detail below the differences between them. The second arrest power relates to the broader category of criminal offences: in this case, a peace officer can arrest only if he finds the person committing the offence. The final warrantless arrest power allows a peace officer to arrest a person if he has reasonable grounds to believe that there is a warrant for that person's arrest.

The arrest powers given to peace officers are subject to the terms of sections 495(2) and (3), imposing some limits on them: see the discussion in Section B(3) above.

Finally, note that it is of some importance for police, in the course of making an arrest, to be specific about the particular power upon which they are relying and the basis for the arrest. This issue will be pursued further in Chapter 5, dealing with the right under section 10(a) of the *Charter* to be informed of the reason for an arrest. Beyond that, however, later consideration of whether an arrest was valid or not will depend on the actual basis upon which the police purport to rely. That is, "[a]n arrest stated to be for one described offence cannot be validated by a later reliance upon another offence for which it might have been, but was not, made."[247]

---

247 *Huff*, above note 239. See also *Dumbell v. Roberts*, [1944] 1 All E.R. 326 (C.A.).

ii) Citizen's Arrest

Today the vast majority of arrests are made by peace officers, but the Supreme Court has noted that "it is the peace officer's powers which are in a sense derivative from that of the citizen, not the other way around."[248] That citizen's arrest power itself "is in direct descent over nearly a thousand years of the powers and duties of citizens in the age of Henry II in relation to the 'King's Peace.'"[249] The primary citizen's arrest power is to arrest a person one "finds committing" an indictable offence. The meaning of "finds committing" in the citizen's arrest context was reviewed at length by the Alberta Court of Appeal in R. v. Abel.[250] The accused in that case, Abel, believed that a person who had lived in his house, Holl, had stolen his rifle. After attempting in other ways to have the rifle returned, Abel went with several friends to Holl's residence. They entered, an altercation in which Holl was struck with a tire iron ensued, and after Holl was tied up he told Abel where to find the rifle, which was hidden in another location. Abel and his friends then recovered the rifle and took Holl to an RCMP station. Charges were laid against most participants, but Abel and his friends argued that they had acted with legal authority, specifically that they were performing a citizen's arrest. They argued that they had found Holl committing the offence of possession of stolen property.

The central question was whether on these facts the "finds committing" standard was met: the Court of Appeal held that it was not. First, the court noted that the citizen's arrest power in the Code was a codification of the power that had existed at common law: that power had insisted on a strict immediacy requirement. To have a power to arrest, the private citizen must have been "present when any felony is committed."[251] So, for example, a person finding a thief with stolen vegetables one field away from where they had been stolen had not found the person committing the theft.[252] Similarly, a person learning, at 3:00 p.m., that someone in his house had committed an offence at 1:00 p.m. had no power to arrest.[253]

---

248 *Asante-Mensah*, above note 205 at para. 40.
249 *Asante-Mensah*, ibid. at para. 36, quoting from R. v. Lerke (1986), 24 C.C.C. (3d) 129 (Alta. C.A.).
250 *R. v. Abel*, 2008 BCCA 54 [*Abel*].
251 William Blackstone, *Commentaries on the Laws of England*, vol. 5 (Oxford: Clarendon Press, 1769), quoted in *Asante-Mensah*, above note 205 at para. 37, and in *Abel*, ibid. at para. 32.
252 *R. v. Curran* (1828), 172 E.R. 472.
253 *Downing v. Capel* (1867), L.R. 2 C.P. 461.

The common law standard, the Court of Appeal held, was still reflected in the *Criminal Code* provision. It, too, requires that the person arresting witness the offence. Witnessing the offence, however, does not require that the arrestor witness every element of the offence. First, the arrestor is required only to "see at least the essential features of the offence."[254] Further:

> 13 It is not necessary for a citizen making an arrest under s. 494(1) (a) to have personal knowledge of all the factors that lead him to conclude *that the person is "in the process" of committing an offence*; it can be deduced from a series of circumstances that a person is apparently in the process of committing an offence, and that offence must be apparent to a reasonable person in the same circumstances.[255]

The court noted as well that the French version of the section in the *Code* referred to a person "qu'elle trouve en train de commetre un acte criminal," which also conveyed a sense of immediacy. In addition, it referred to various other statutes setting out a "finds committing" arrest standard. These were relevant, the court held, because "Parliament clearly intended the words 'finds committing' to have the same meaning whenever used in authorizing an arrest without warrant."[256] Some of these statutes described the standard, in French, as "en flagrant délit d'infraction," which is captured in the English as "caught red-handed."[257] It is clear, therefore, that "finds committing" sets a standard requiring a close temporal connection between the commission of the offence and the arrest, and requires that the arrestor be present at and witness the offence.

---

254 *Abel*, above note 250 at para. 50, quoting Laskin J. (as he then was) concurring in *R. v. Dean*, [1966] 3 C.C.C. 228 at 236 (Ont. C.A.) [*Dean*].

255 *Abel*, *ibid.* at para. 54, quoting *R. v. Sirois*, [1999] J.Q. no 1079 (C.A.) [emphasis in *Abel*]. So, for example, in *R. v. Gonzalez*, [1996] O.J. No. 761 (Prov. Div.) [*Gonzalez*], one security guard saw the accused hide an item on his person, and so he radioed to another security guard closer to the exit. Although the second security guard saw the accused commit the offence in the sense that he saw him leave the store while he in fact had the item, this did not count since the second security guard did not personally know that the accused had the item or that he had not paid.

256 *Abel*, *ibid.* at para. 61.

257 *Abel*, *ibid.* at para. 62. In *Abel* itself, the Court of Appeal held that the "finds committing" standard was not met. The accused reasonably believed Holl had stolen his rifle but did not find him in possession of it, and had no knowledge as to where he might have hidden it in order to justify finding him in constructive possession under s. 4(3)(1)(ii) of the *Code*.

An important point to note here is that the person arresting must not only have witnessed the offence: she must also have made the arrest at the time of witnessing it. Nonetheless, even at common law some gap in time between commission and arrest was permissible, so long as the person who committed the offence was being pursued throughout:

> The learned Judges present were clearly of opinion that the conviction was lawful: for, as he had been seen in the out-house, *and was taken on fresh pursuit* before he had left the neighbourhood, it was the same as if he had been taken in the out-house, or in running away from it, *that it was all one transaction.*[258]

On the other hand, an unjustified delay can cause the right to arrest to lapse. In *Twan*, for example, a store security guard stopped a customer who had left the store without paying for a newspaper and asked her to return to sign a trespass notice. She went with the guard and produced identification showing her name and address, and she was then permitted to leave temporarily to pick up food she had already ordered. When she returned, the detainee was asked to sign the trespass notice but refused to do so; she was told that she would therefore have to wait for the police to arrive. Upon being told that this could take as much as five hours, the detainee began to leave but was physically restrained. The Court found that the arrest occurred at this point, but that there was no justification for it.[259]

There is an area in the jurisprudence around section 494(1)(a) which remains ambiguous. Although the section clearly states that the power therein allows a person to arrest someone he "finds committing" an offence, some courts have held that in fact a reasonableness standard applies. That is, a literal interpretation suggests that the arrestor must be correct: the person arrested must actually have been committing an offence, or no arrest power arises. A reasonableness standard would mean that the arrest would be legal if the arrestor reasonably believed she had found the person committing an offence.

---

258 *R. v. Howarth* (1828), 168 E.R. 1243, quoted in *Abel, ibid.* at para. 36 [emphasis in *Abel*]. See also *Reddy*, above note 239, where the accused was an off-duty police officer who was threatened with a sword. The officer fled to safety initially then pursued the person who had brandished the sword, coming upon him minutes later, after on-duty police officers had arrested him. The court held that he was acting under the "finds committing" arrest power, though he then used excessive force.

259 *Twan v. Hudson's Bay Company* (2008), 93 O.R. (3d) 582 (S.C.J.).

The argument for this position is based on combining section 494(1)
(a) and section 25 of the *Code*. Section 494(1)(a) creates the "finds committing" citizen's arrest power. Section 25 states that:

> 25. (1) Every one who is required or authorized by law to do anything
> in the administration or enforcement of the law
>
>   (a)   as a private person . . .
>
> is, if he acts on reasonable and probable grounds, justified in doing
> what he is required or authorized to do . . .

Combining these, some courts have concluded that a person who has
reasonable grounds to think that a person has committed an offence is
therefore authorized to arrest.[260]

However, other courts have questioned this conclusion, for several
reasons. It has been observed that, at common law, there was a distinction between the arrest powers of a private citizen and those of a peace
officer:

> At common law a police constable may arrest a person if he has rea-
> sonable cause to suspect that a felony has been committed although
> it afterwards appears that no felony has been committed, but that
> it is not so when a private person makes or causes the arrest, for to
> justify his action he must prove, among other things, that a felony has
> actually been committed.[261]

That is not to say that reasonable grounds are not relevant at all, but
they are not sufficient on their own. It is still necessary that a crime
was actually committed by someone, even if not, as it transpires, by the
person arrested.[262]

---

260 See, for example, *Karogiannis v. Poulus*, [1976] 6 W.W.R. 197 (B.C.S.C.), or
Dendekker v. F.W. Woolworth Co., [1975] 3 W.W.R. 429 (Alta. S.C.). This result
is similar to that in *R. v. Biron*, [1976] 2 S.C.R. 56 [*Biron*], which interprets the
"finds committing" standard in the context of peace officer arrest powers to
mean "apparently finds committing": this issue will be discussed in Section
C(2)(b)(iii), below in this chapter. *Biron* is sometimes offered as a further justification (as in *Karogiannis*) but it is not the primary argument for this interpretation.

261 *Walters v. W.H. Smith & Son Ltd.*, [1914] 1 K.B. 595 at 602, quoted in *Kovacs v.
Ontario Jockey Club* (1995), 126 D.L.R. (4th) 576 (Ont. Ct. Gen. Div.) [*Kovacs*].
Note that (as was discussed in Chapter 2, Section B(1)) most of the relevant
cases on this section arise from private law actions for false imprisonment or
false arrest where the defendant relies on legal authority as the defence.

262 See *Williams v. Laing* (1923), 55 O.L.R. 26 at 28 (S.C.A.D.), quoted in *Kovacs*,
ibid. at para. 57: "The law is quite clear that in order to succeed in establishing

Many courts have concluded that this distinction between private citizen's arrest and peace officer arrests survives into the *Criminal Code* provisions. On this view, the law is that two distinct things must be proven:

> a private person who arrests an individual must satisfy the court on
> a balance of probabilities:
>
> (a) that someone committed an indictable offence, and
> (b) that the private person effecting the arrest had reasonable
>   grounds for believing and did believe the person arrested
>   had committed that indictable offence.[263]

This same result has been taken to follow from the combined reading of section 494(1)(a) and section 25. Section 25 invokes the "reasonable ground" standard when the person is already authorized to act by some other section, but it does not itself authorize anything. Accordingly, the preconditions in section 494(1)(a) must be satisfied before any question of reasonableness arises:

> The legally authorized action with which we are concerned in Section
> 449 [now 494] is the arresting without warrant of a person found
> committing a crime. Proof of the commission of a criminal act by
> someone is thus essential. There can be no doubt if there is no crime,
> there can be no justification.[264]

Only after that condition is satisfied do reasonable grounds enter, in the form of reasonable grounds to believe that it was the accused who committed the offence.

Finally, it is worth observing that a great deal of the caselaw on citizen's arrest, since it arises from tort actions for false imprisonment, has to do with shoplifting cases. In such cases, the two questions of whether an offence was committed at all and whether there are reasonable grounds to believe that the person arrested committed it tend to merge into a single question, for practical purposes: "In those cases there is usually no proof of a crime committed unless it is proof of the

---

this defence the appellants must prove first that the crime they suspected had
   actually been committed, not necessarily by the person detained, but by some
   one, and that they had reasonable ground for suspecting the person detained."
263 *Parlee (Guardian ad litem of) v. Port of Call Holdings Ltd.*, 2000 BCSC 548 at para.
   11. Adopting the same view, see *Kovacs*, above note 261; *Banyasz v. K-Mart Canada Ltd.* (1986), 57 O.R. (2d) 445 (Div. Ct.); and *Hayward v. Woolworth* (1979), 8
   C.C.L.T. 157 (Nfld. S.C.T.D.).
264 *Smart v. Sears Canada* (1987), 36 D.L.R. (4th) 756 (Nfld. C.A.).

crime committed by the person arrested."[265] Accordingly, many of those decisions seem to overlook that the first question is a separate one to be answered. In that event, they are of less precedential value than those cases that are careful to consider the two issues distinctly.

As a closing comment on the "apparently finds committing" standard in citizen's arrest, note that nothing in the discussion of reasonable grounds in any of the cases suggests that this standard *replaces* the strict immediacy requirement discussed above.[266] That is, to say that the arrestor need only have reasonable grounds to believe the person committed the offence is to say that if, given the facts immediately observed by the arrestor, it was reasonable for him *to believe that he had found the person committing the offence*, then section 494(1)(a) authorizes the arrest. Reasonable grounds alone will not do.[267]

The citizen's arrest power in section 494(1)(b) is based only on reasonable grounds, though it also depends on a prior arrest power in someone else's hands already existing. Specifically, that section gives an arrest power to anyone who on reasonable grounds believes two things: that the person to be arrested has committed a criminal offence, and that that person is escaping from and freshly pursued by someone who has lawful authority to arrest that person.

One issue that arises here is that this arrest power is based on reasonable grounds rather than the "finds committing" standard. We have discussed in Chapter 2 the meaning of "reasonable grounds," and that discussion would apply here. There are some specific observations worth making about the operation of the standard in this particular context.

First, note the significance of the fact that a person is running away — or perhaps more accurately, note the significance it does *not* have. Flight by a suspect can contribute towards creating reasonable grounds to believe that that person has committed an offence. However, it is not by itself sufficient to establish reasonable grounds. Section 494(1)(b) separates out as two distinct inquiries that (i) the suspect has committed an offence and (ii) the suspect is escaping. If the latter were suf-

---

265 *Briggs v. Laviolette* (1994), 21 C.C.L.T. (2d) 105 at para. 14 (B.C.S.C.).

266 If it did, then the result in *Abel*, above note 250, for example, would not only be different, there really would have been no dispute in the first place: Abel was acknowledged to have reasonable grounds to believe that Holl was in possession of the stolen rifle, but that was not sufficient because the standards was "finds committing."

267 See, for example, *Gonzalez*, above note 255 at para. 18: "Reasonable grounds in that s. [s. 494(1)(b)] includes what an arrestor is told. The 'reasonable grounds/ apparently' test for 'finds committing' requires that the arrestor have all the knowledge from his own senses, excluding everything he has been told."

ficient to create reasonable grounds for guilt, these two requirements would be collapsed into one.[268] In *Volker*, for example, a security guard saw a suspect standing by a car in a parkade, and a moment later the suspect ran off. The court held that this gave that security guard reasonable grounds to believe that the suspect was trying to escape. However, relatively few other facts were known to the accused, and he was found not to have reasonable grounds to believe the suspect had committed a criminal offence.[269]

More specifically, the fact that a person is fleeing a police officer is not sufficient, on its own, to create reasonable grounds. In *Gladue*, for example, two police constables were responding to a call that there had been a stabbing at an outdoor festival. As they approached the scene, they saw their corporal, with his gun drawn, chasing the accused, who was coming toward them. They drew their own guns and ordered the accused to lie down. He did not, with the result that they used force to take control of him, and he was charged with resisting an officer in the execution of duty. The accused was acquitted, on the basis that the police officers had had no power to arrest and so were not acting in the execution of duty.

The court noted the limited information known to the arresting officers. The call they had received had said only that there had been a stabbing. The stabber had not been identified, nor described in any way, such as by height, weight, race, gender, or clothing. There had been no indication that the stabber was fleeing or had fled the festival. The only information they acted on was that the accused was being chased by another officer. The court rejected the suggestion that "whenever a police officer sees a superior officer chasing someone, that police officer is entitled to step in and arrest the person being chased" and acquitted the accused.[270]

That does not mean that reliance on others is not allowed: it will necessarily be the case if the person is arresting based on reasonable grounds. In *Kendall*, for example, the head of security for a department store thought she observed two customers hiding items in their clothes. She made a coded message over the store's public-address system which informed other employees that she was observing potential shoplifters; she then specifically pointed out the suspects to two employees and instructed them to keep an eye on her and the suspects. When she later arrested the two accused after they left the store, the two employees

268   R. v. *Gladue*, 2002 ABQB 519 at para. 29 [*Gladue*].
269   R. v. *Volker*, [1994] B.C.J. No. 3134 (Prov. Ct.) [*Volker*].
270   *Gladue*, above note 268 at para. 40.

assisted her. In fact, the two suspects had not been shoplifting, and so their false arrest claim against the head of security succeeded: no offence had been committed, which was essential to her authority to arrest under section 494(1)(a). The two employees who assisted, however, were protected by section 494(1)(b): what they had been told gave them reasonable grounds to believe that the suspects had committed an offence.[271]

The two issues of "escaping from" and "freshly pursued" are also worth considering. The Ontario Court of Appeal held in *Dean* that these terms ought not to be given a narrow interpretation.[272] However, that decision long predates the *Charter*, and it should be noted that giving the terms a broad interpretation amounts to authorizing more widespread interferences with individual liberty: accordingly, it is not clear that that interpretive approach is in general the right one.

On the other hand, *Dean*'s specific interpretation of "escaping from" still seems sensible. In that case, the accused had rushed out of a coffee shop without paying his bill. Two staff members pursued him to the door and then flagged down a passing police car; that officer caught the accused and brought him back to the coffee shop. After the accused had refused several times to pay the bill, the officer arrested him. The court held that on these facts the officer was authorized under what is now section 494(1)(b). On one view, the accused was no longer "escaping" by the time he was arrested, since the officer had caught him and brought him back. However, the court held that the officer certainly had been in compliance with the "escaping from and freshly pursued by" requirements at the point he had first caught the accused, and so could have arrested him then. Holding that he had lost that arrest power by taking the accused back to the coffee shop to try to sort things out would require an officer "to arrest first and inquire afterwards, hardly a desirable procedure."[273]

Frequently the proof that someone is escaping will be that they are actually running away, coupled with the inference that this is being done to avoid arrest.[274] What appears to be more important than the physical activity is the intention behind it, however. For example, in

---

271   *Kendall v. Gambles Canada Ltd.*, [1981] 4 W.W.R. 718 (Sask.Q.B.). The court held that those facts also gave the employees reasonable grounds to believe the suspects were escaping from someone with authority to arrest.

272   *Dean*, above note 254.

273   *Ibid.* at para. 8.

274   In *Volker*, above note 269 at para. 47, for example, the security guard testified that he thought "why else would he run" when the accused fled, which the court took to be a reasonable inference that the accused was "escaping."

Matthews the detainee had been in an altercation with picketers while on his way into a movie theatre. The police had been called and an officer was at the front of the movie theatre when the movie ended a few hours later. The accused went to the back door of the theatre and found the detainee there, waiting for his wife and son to return with the car. Although the detainee testified that he had left that way in order to avoid further confrontation, the court held that it was reasonable of the accused to infer that the detainee had left by the back door in order to escape detection and not talk to the police. In that event there were reasonable grounds to think he was escaping from someone with authority to arrest him.

The meaning of "fresh pursuit" has been discussed by the Supreme Court of Canada, though not strictly in the context of section 494(1)(b). However, there is a common law exception to the rules around police entry into a dwelling house to effect arrest, which allows the police to enter in cases of "hot pursuit."[275] In defining "hot pursuit" the Court held:

> Generally, the essence of fresh pursuit is that it must be continuous pursuit conducted with reasonable diligence, so that pursuit and capture along with the commission of the offence may be considered as forming part of a single transaction.[276]

Seemingly, this meaning of "fresh pursuit" ought to be equally applicable in the context of section 494(1)(b).

However, "fresh pursuit" in the context of section 494(1)(b) does not require that the capture be by the same person who begins the pursuit at the commission of the offence: indeed, by definition it will not be. Therefore, the real requirement is that someone who had authority to arrest has begun a fresh pursuit, though not finished it.

The initial pursuit need not be of any particular duration. In *Dean*, for example, the staff of the coffee shop pursued the accused only as far as the door of the coffee shop when he fled without paying, because they were then able to flag down a police car. Nonetheless, this satisfied

---

275 *R. v. Macooh*, [1993] 2 S.C.R. 802 [*Macooh*]. *Macooh* was an exception to rules that have since been found to violate the *Charter*: see *R. v. Feeney*, [1997] 2 S.C.R. 13 [*Feeney*]. However, *Feeney* referred to and upheld the "hot pursuit" exception to the new rules formulated in that case. Subsequently Parliament has created a warrant scheme which explicitly creates an "exigent circumstances" exception, but the common law hot-pursuit exception has also survived. See the discussion in Chapter 2, Section B(1)(d).

276 *Macooh*, *ibid.* at para. 24, quoting from Roger E. Salhany, *Canadian Criminal Procedure*, 5th ed. (Aurora, ON: Canada Law Book, 1989) at 44.

the "freshly pursued" requirement and clothed the officer with power to arrest.

On the other hand, in *Gonzalez*, one store security guard radioed to another that the accused had hidden an item on his person. The second security guard saw the accused leave the store without paying. The second guard chased the accused down the street and caught up with him. As discussed above, the second security guard had no "finds committing" power, because he was dependent on what the first guard had told him to believe the accused had committed an offence. Those facts did give him reasonable grounds to believe that the accused had committed an offence, satisfying part of section 494(1)(b). However, no evidence was led that the first guard had attempted to catch the accused personally, and so it was not established that he was being freshly pursued.

Similarly, the pursuit, if commenced at one point, must still be ongoing to constitute fresh pursuit. In *Lawson* a taxi driver dropped off a passenger who did not pay; after some attempts to get into the rooming house to which the passenger had fled, the taxi driver left to get the police. The Court held that the taxi driver had had the authority to arrest the passenger, but the police did not have authority under section 494(1)(b): the taxi driver had abandoned his pursuit in order to get the help of the police.

One might be tempted to argue that there is a certain formalism or technicality in the distinctions between some of these cases. In *Dean* the coffee-shop staff were lucky enough to find a police officer on the street; in *Lawson* the taxi driver had to seek one; in *Kendall* the other store employees were authorized to arrest on reasonable grounds because the first security guard also stepped out of the store; in *Gonzalez* quite similar reasonable grounds were not enough because the first security guard was not shown to have stepped outside the store. However, there is in fact an important principle at play. Of the three citizen's arrest powers, two (section 494(1)(a) and section 494(2)) require that the arrestor find the accused committing the offence. The section 494(1)(b) power relaxes that standard to reasonable grounds, but does so because of the urgency in the situation: because it is a fast-developing situation, quick decisions need to be made. For that reason, it makes sense to be careful about interpreting the requirements in a way that reflects the urgent nature of the situation. If there is time to leave and seek the police, or if no one is actually pursuing the accused, then it is sensible to conclude that there *is* time for more measured reactions, and therefore that the ordinary arrest rules should apply.

The final citizen's arrest power is in section 494(2) and is reserved for "(a) the owner or a person in lawful possession of property, or (b) a person authorized by the owner or by a person in lawful possession of property." It permits such a person to arrest someone "whom he finds committing a criminal offence on or in relation to that property." "Property" is defined in section 2 of the *Code* to include both real and personal property.[277]

This power is often used by security personnel in stores as the authority for arresting shoplifters, but it is not limited to that situation. In *Dean*, discussed above, for example, the accused left a coffee shop without paying his bill. A waitress and a cashier were there, and the court held that they were both persons "in lawful possession of property": they "were found in complete control of the premises serving the customers and collecting payment therefore."[278] In *Cunningham*, the two accused were officers in charge of a ship that made trips up and down the Red and Assiniboine rivers; they were authorized under the section to arrest a youth who threw a rock at the boat from shore, breaking a window.[279]

The final point to note about citizen's arrests is the obligation in section 494(3) to "forthwith deliver the person to a peace officer." Arrest involves an imposition on liberty, and citizen's arrest is arguably the most difficult to control. In order to see to it that the detention lasts no longer than necessary, the accused is to be handed over to a state actor, the police.

"Forthwith" in this context does not mean immediately. Rather, it means as soon as "reasonably possible or practicable under all the circumstances." In *Cunningham*, for example, the accused arrested a youth who had thrown a rock and broken a window in the cruise ship they were taking up the Assiniboine River. They radioed the police, who indicated that they could not come to the scene and instructed the accused to bring the youth to the dock from which they had departed. The return voyage took ninety minutes, and the boy was confined in the wheelhouse the entire time, with his ankles tied together. Nonetheless, the court held that this met the "forthwith" requirement: the accused had acted as instructed, and had returned without stopping and with all reasonable speed.

Even if "forthwith" does not mean "instantly," however, it does require a timely delivery. In *Corbett*, the accused was assaulted by the

---

277 *Criminal Code*, above note 1, s. 2.
278 *Dean*, above note 254 at para. 11.
279 R. v. *Cunningham* (1979), 49 C.C.C. (2d) 390 (Man. Co. Ct.).

complainant while she was in his apartment. He and a friend were able to subdue her, and restrained her with tape and by tying her up. However, they did not then call the police, and she was not freed for several hours, until the police arrived after she was able to dial 911. The accused might, on these facts, have had the right to arrest the complainant. However, the court held that there was not even an air of reality to the claim that the accused was acting with lawful authority, because of the extended detention.[280]

iii) Peace Officer Arrests

Section 495(1) contains a number of different arrest powers given only to peace officers. For a full understanding of the powers, it is important to recall that they are all subject to sections 495(2) and (3), which attach some limits to their proper use: that issue is discussed in Section B(3) above. Here, we shall discuss at greater length the nature of the arrest powers themselves.

a. Section 495(1)(a)

Section 495(1) is limited to arrests for indictable offences. It appears to create three separate arrest powers, though they are closely related. The section allows a peace officer to arrest:

> a person who has committed an indictable offence or who, on reasonable grounds, he believes has committed or is about to commit an indictable offence.

As a practical matter, it is the middle of these three powers — a person "who, on reasonable grounds, he believes has committed" an indictable offence — that is the most used. We shall discuss each of them in turn.

On a literal reading, a power to arrest anyone who *has committed* an indictable offence would be extraordinarily broad. As the British Columbia Court of Appeal has noted, if these words were to be read in isolation from the rest of the subsection, then

> the arresting officer would not have to believe or even possess reasonable grounds for believing that the arrestee had in fact committed an offence. So long as that fact could subsequently be established, the arrest would be lawful.[281]

---

280 R. v. *Corbett*, 2004 BCCA 378.
281 R. v. *Klimchuk* (1991), 67 C.C.C. (3d) 385 at 404 (B.C.C.A.) [*Klimchuk*].

That literal approach to the section would in many cases render the "reasonable grounds" standard redundant, since arrests made without them might still be valid. Indeed, an arrest on reasonable grounds would become relevant only in cases where it transpired that the arrestee had *not* in fact committed the offence. It would also allow *post facto* justification for the use of police powers, which is generally an undesirable approach.[282]

Properly, the British Columbia Court of Appeal held that such a broad reading could not be justified. Rather, it concluded, the words must be understood by looking at the arrest powers available to peace officers as a whole. Section 495(1)(b) deals with arrests made while an offence is actually taking place: that is, the officer finds the person committing the offence. Section 495(1)(a), the court ruled, brackets that by providing an arrest power where an indictable offence has already been committed or is about to be committed. However, the words "has committed" should be understood, in essence, to mean "has just committed": that is, the officer witnessed the offence, but it was completed before she had a chance to intervene. The court held:

> Looking in particular at the first part of s. 495(1)(a), a peace officer is entitled to arrest a person who has committed an indictable offence. Before such an arrest can be made, the peace officer must know that the arrestee has committed an indictable offence. In order for him to know that, he must have witnessed the indictable offence occurring. Correctly construed, then, this first part of the provision covers those few situations where the arresting officer, having personally witnessed the commission of an indictable offence, could not prevent it or perfect an arrest before its completion. In such circumstances, s. 495(1)(b) would no longer apply because the offence was no longer being committed.[283]

Read in this way, the "has committed" standard is not a dilution of the "reasonable grounds" standard, permitting arrests on lesser grounds

---

282 See *Canada (Combines Investigation Branch, Director of Investigation and Research) v. Southam Inc.*, [1984] 2 S.C.R. 145 at 160, speaking in the context of searches:

> Such a *post facto* analysis would, however, be seriously at odds with the purpose of s. 8. That purpose is, as I have said, to protect individuals from unjustified state intrusions upon their privacy. That purpose requires a means of *preventing* unjustified searches before they happen, not simply of determining, after the fact, whether they ought to have occurred in the first place. This, in my view, can only be accomplished by a system of *prior authorization*, not one of subsequent validation. [emphasis added].

283 *Klimchuk*, above note 281 at 405–6.

and allowing them to be justified after the fact. Rather, as is appropriate, "has committed" will be a *stricter* standard than reasonable grounds.[284] This approach is consistent with the relationship between section 495(1)(a) (generally speaking, arrests on reasonable grounds) and section 495(1)(b) (arrests based on the "finds committing" standard): it has been observed that the latter standard is stricter than the former.[285]

Klimchuk also notes the relationship of the rest of section 495(1)(a) to the "has committed" standard:

> The remainder of s. 495(1)(a), that is, everything after the first "or," covers those situations in which the officer did not personally witness the indictable offence or in which the indictable offence has not yet occurred. In those cases the officer is entitled to arrest if he believes on reasonable grounds that such offence has been or is about to be committed.[286]

The primary arrest power in section 495(1)(a) is the second one, the authorization given to a peace officer to arrest a person "who, on reasonable grounds, he believes has committed" an indictable offence. The most important issue to understand in looking at the power is the meaning of "reasonable grounds to believe." However, that issue was discussed at length in Chapter 2. Accordingly, only a brief summary of the power need be given here.

The leading decision on the application of this portion of section 495(1)(a) is *Storrey*.[287] In that case, the Court noted that the purpose of the standard in the arrest provision was to strike the appropriate balance between the individual's right to liberty and the need for society to be protected from crime. It stated that reasonable and probable grounds must be established in front of a justice to obtain a search warrant, and that "it is even more important for the police to demonstrate that they have those same reasonable and probable grounds" in the case of warrantless arrests.[288]

A peace officer requires more than suspicion to arrest a person. On the other hand, the standard is short of a *prima facie* case. In addition, the fact that a person is later found to be not guilty does not mean that no reasonable grounds existed for the arrest:

---

284 The approach in *Klimchuk, ibid.*, has been referred to with approval in *Abel*, above note 250, and in *R. v. M.D.* (1994), 40 B.C.A.C. 101 (C.A.).

285 See *R. v. Janvier*, 2007 SKCA 147 at para. 28 [*Janvier*].

286 *Klimchuk*, above note 281 at 406.

287 *Storrey*, above note 28.

288 *Storrey, ibid.* at para. 14.

The question of reasonable and probable grounds depends upon a *bona fide* reasonable belief in a state of facts that, if true, would justify the course taken. That the supposed fact proves not to exist does not render the belief unreasonable.[289]

The Court also noted in *Storrey* that reasonable grounds consist of two components: the subjective and the objective. A peace officer must personally believe, on reasonable grounds, that the accused has committed the offence in question. In addition, however:

it must be objectively established that those reasonable and probable grounds did in fact exist. That is to say a reasonable person, standing in the shoes of the police officer, would have believed that reasonable and probable grounds existed to make the arrest.[290]

Finally, recall several other points about reasonable grounds which were discussed in greater length in Chapter 2: they must be specific to the offence for which the accused is arrested, they can be based on hearsay, and one officer is entitled to arrest on the basis that another officer meets the requirements for an arrest under section 495(1)(a).

The final arrest power in section 495(1)(a), an arrest on the basis that there are reasonable grounds to believe a person is "about to commit" an indictable offence, has received very little judicial attention. The reason for this is very likely that the words "about to commit" do not admit of any real ambiguity: they require a very close temporal connection. "About to commit" is obviously a much stricter test than "will commit at some point," and no real attempt to stretch its meaning seems to have been made.

Nonetheless, there are one or two observations that might be made about this arrest power. First, recall that reasonable grounds must be specific to the charge to be laid, or the issue in question. That is, of course, equally true in the "about to commit" context. In *Warford*, for example, the police received a reliable tip that the accused would be trafficking in narcotics at a particular nightclub on a particular date at an approximate time, and would be travelling there in a particular vehicle. The police stopped the accused on the date in question in the vehicle in question, at the time suggested, and while the accused was driving a route that was consistent with travelling to the nightclub. The Court of Appeal held that this did constitute reasonable grounds to believe that the accused was about to commit the offence of trafficking in narcotics; the fact that the police did not believe they had enough

---

289 *R. v. Grotheim*, 2001 SKCA 116 at para. 42.
290 *Storrey*, above note 28 at para. 16.

evidence to obtain a search warrant for the accused's home did not interfere with this conclusion.[291]

A second issue is worth noting in connection with the "about to commit" standard. Recall that an arrest made on one basis cannot later be justified on the grounds that arrest on a different basis would have been permissible.[292] In many factual situations, particularly those that are fast-evolving, this limitation can be of some significance. In *Jensen v. Stemmer*, for example, the police had attended at the home of a couple because the husband had reported to them that his common-law partner had threatened to kill him. The police interviewed both parties and told them that one of the two would have to leave the residence; they testified that they did this because they were afraid the situation would spiral out of control. Eventually, the police arrested the wife for uttering a threat. In upholding a finding of wrongful imprisonment, the Manitoba Court of Appeal noted that the power to arrest on the "about to commit" basis could be quite relevant in the domestic-dispute context: however, it was not the basis upon which the police had in fact purported to arrest. In that event the claimant had been wrongly imprisoned.[293]

b.   Section 495(1)(b)

Section 495(1)(b) allows a peace officer to arrest "a person whom he finds committing a criminal offence." The essential difference between the arrest powers in subsection (a) and (b) was laid out by the Court in *Biron*.[294] Where section 495(1)(a) primarily rests on arrests based on reasonable grounds,

> [p]aragraph (b) applies in relation to any criminal offence and it deals with the situation in which the peace officer himself finds an offence being committed. His power to arrest is based upon his own observation. Because it is based on his own discovery of an offence actually being committed there is no reason to refer to a belief based upon reasonable and probable grounds.[295]

Despite this difference, however, the Court held that section 495(1)(b) is equally to be decided based on the circumstances known to the peace officer at the time of the arrest. More specifically, the Court concluded that the "finds committing" standard does not require that the person

---

291 R. v. Warford, 2001 NFCA 64.
292 *Huff*, above note 239.
293 *Jensen v. Stemmer*, 2007 MBCA 42.
294 *Biron*, above note 260.
295 *Ibid.* at 72.

arrested was *in fact* committing the offence: rather, it is sufficient if she was "apparently" committing it.

This question arose in *Biron* because the accused was charged with two offences: causing a disturbance by shouting, and resisting a peace officer in the execution of duty. Biron was arrested at a bar during a raid to check for firearms and illegal liquor; he was uncooperative and refused to give the police his name. He was passed through several police officers before eventually getting into a scuffle with the officer who attempted to put him in the police wagon. He was acquitted of the causing a disturbance charge because there was no evidence that he had been shouting. He appealed his conviction on the other charge based on that finding. Specifically, he argued that, since he had *not* been committing an offence, the officer therefore could not have found him committing one. In that event the officer did not have the power to arrest under section 495(1)(b) and so was not acting in the execution of duty.

The majority of the Court rejected this argument. They held that Biron's argument would create an unworkable situation. Therefore, they concluded that it was not actually necessary that the accused was committing an offence — merely that it appeared to the peace officer that he was doing so:

> The power of arrest which that paragraph gives has to be exercised promptly, yet, strictly speaking, it is impossible to say that an offence is committed until the party arrested has been found guilty by the courts. If this is the way in which this provision is to be construed, no peace officer can ever decide, when making an arrest without a warrant, that the person arrested is "committing a criminal offence." In my opinion the wording used in para. (b), which is oversimplified, means that the power to arrest without a warrant is given where the peace officer himself finds a situation in which a person is apparently committing an offence.[296]

On that approach, Biron was guilty; the arresting officer was justified in thinking that the accused had committed an offence even if, as it turned out, that was not proven.

Subsequently, in *Roberge*, the Court clarified its decision in *Biron*. In that latter decision, the Court held that it was not sufficient merely for a peace officer to claim that it had been apparent the accused had been committing an offence. Rather, what was required was that "it

---

296 *Ibid.* at 75.

must be 'apparent' to a reasonable person placed in the circumstances of the arresting officer at the time."[297]

Somewhat infelicitously, the Court then described the "finds committing" standard as "an officer acting 'on reasonable and probable grounds.'" It would be easy to mistake the intent behind this description, and take it to be a general statement that section 495(1)(b) requires a peace officer only to have reasonable grounds to believe that the accused has committed a criminal offence. If that were the intention, then the one exception to peace officer powers of arrest — where the offence was only a summary conviction one and the peace officer only had reasonable grounds to believe the accused had committed it — would no longer be an exception.

In fact, that is not the Court's intention. A peace officer still cannot, despite *Biron*, simply arrest on reasonable belief for summary conviction offences. A peace officer who arrives at the scene of a summary conviction offence and is reliably told that the accused committed it is still not empowered to arrest. Rather, *Biron* retains the notion that the peace officer's "power to arrest is based upon his own observation."[298] It merely means that those personal observations need only give the peace officer reasonable grounds to believe the accused has committed an offence, rather than requiring that the officer is ultimately proven to be correct in that assessment.

Courts of appeal certainly have held to the view that the relaxation of the "finds committing" standard in *Biron* has not reduced it to nothing but a reasonable grounds standard. The Saskatchewan Court of Appeal has affirmed that, even given *Biron* and *Roberge*, the "finds committing" standard remains stricter than the standard for arrest for an indictable offence under section 495(1)(a).[299] As the British Columbia Court of Appeal has put it, "the arresting officer must have reasonable grounds to believe that the person to be arrested is apparently in the process of committing a crime in his or her presence."[300]

The Nova Scotia Court of Appeal has suggested that, given the decisions in *Biron* and *Roberge*, three things must be established to meet the "finds committing" standard. First, it must be shown that the po-

---

297 *Roberge*, above note 236 at 324–25.

298 *Biron*, above note 260.

299 *Janvier*, above note 285 at para. 28. See also *R. v. Yeh*, 2009 SKCA 112.

300 *Abel*, above note 250 at para. 52, relying on *Roberge*, above note 236. See also *Janvier*, above note 285 at para. 22: "*Roberge* does not eliminate the distinction between 'has committed' in s. 495(1)(a) and 'finds committing' in s. 495(1)(b) but instead is directed to the belief the officer has as to the presence of the grounds for either type of offence in order to arrest."

lice officer's knowledge is contemporaneous to the event: "[U]nlike the reasonable and probable grounds standard, it is not enough to believe that an offence has taken place in the past or is about to take place."[301] Second, the officer must actually observe the commission of the offence, or detect it in some way, by seeing, hearing, or in some cases smelling it. Finally, "there must be an objective basis for the officer's conclusion that an offence is being committed."[302]

There is some reason to be doubtful that the Court adopted the right policy with its decision in *Biron*. Note first of all the difference between the decision in *Biron* and the "finds committing" power in the case of citizen's arrests. As pointed out in the discussion of that topic, the common law requirements around this power depended on proving two things: that an offence was actually committed, and that there was a reasonable basis for believing it was the accused who had committed it. The approach in *Biron* departs from this, by giving up the requirement that an offence has actually been committed.

Further, as the dissent in the case observes, it is useful to distinguish two separate considerations. On the one hand, there is the question of whether a peace officer should forfeit the protection of section 25 to use reasonable force where she is "authorized by law to do anything in the administration or enforcement of the law." There are good policy reasons to think that an officer who reasonably believes she has the power to arrest should not forfeit that protection in civil proceedings even if the arrest later turns out not to have been authorized.[303]

That is quite a different question, however, from the issue of whether the accused should be guilty of resisting an officer in the execution of duty even though the officer was *not* acting in the execution of duty. In that context, the dissenting judges suggest:

> Our law has not, as I understand it, deprived the citizen of his right to resist unlawful arrest. His resistance may be at his own risk if the arrest proves to be lawful, but so too must the police officer accept the risk of having effected a lawful arrest.[304]

The decision of the majority in *Biron*, however, says that a person will be guilty of the offence of resisting arrest even if the arrest turns out to be unlawful.

---

301 *S.T.P. v. Canada (Director of Public Prosecutions Service)*, 2009 NSCA 86 at para. 20 [*S.T.P.*].

302 *S.T.P.*, *ibid.* at para. 22.

303 Indeed, s. 25(1) specifically says a person "is, if he acts on reasonable grounds, justified in doing what he is required or authorized to do."

304 *Biron*, above note 260 at 65.

These first two points are related in some sense. Note that *Biron* (abandoning the "an offence was actually committed" requirement) was decided in the context of whether the accused was guilty, whereas the great majority of citizen's arrest cases (retaining the requirement) were decided in the context of whether the person who made the arrest was protected from tort liability. It must surely seem surprising that a person's financial interest in compensation has received greater protection than his liberty interest.

A final reason to think that *Biron* was decided incorrectly — and indeed that it should be reversed — is that it is a pre-*Charter* case. Specifically, the *Charter* , in section 10(a), guarantees anyone arrested the right to be informed of the reason for the arrest. The Court has noted that there are two rationales for this right, the second of which is to permit the arrestee to exercise the right to consult with counsel effectively. However, that is not the primary justification:

> The right to be promptly advised of the reason for one's detention embodied in s. 10(*a*) of the *Charter* is founded most fundamentally on the notion that one is not obliged to submit to an arrest if one does not know the reasons for it.[305]

That is, the Court has specifically acknowledged that a person is entitled not to submit to — is entitled to resist — an arrest in some circumstances. Even more particularly, one must consider for what purpose an accused is entitled to be told the reason for the arrest. It would make little sense to say that as long as an accused was told of the reason for the arrest the accused must then submit to it, even though it was patently unlawful. Rather, it would make more sense to assume that one is entitled to know of the reason precisely because one is not obliged to submit to an unlawful arrest. That conclusion is the opposite of that reached in *Biron*.

To a small extent, the Court has already limited the impact of *Biron*. In *Sharma*, as recounted earlier, the accused was a flower vendor operating without a licence. A passing police officer gave him a provincial offence ticket and ordered him to pack up and move on. When the officer returned later, the accused was still selling flowers, and the officer arrested him for obstructing an officer in the execution of duty. In fact, the bylaw under which the provincial offence ticket was issued was found to be *ultra vires*, and so the accused was acquitted on that charge. The Crown argued that he was nonetheless guilty of the obstruction charge, on the *Biron* argument: although the accused had not

---

305 *Evans*, above note 213 at para. 31.

been committing the offence, it appeared to the officer that he was doing so, and so the arrest was valid. The Court rejected this argument and the analogy to *Biron*:

> *Biron* deals with apparent perpetration of an offence, not apparent offences, and as such it cannot be relied upon to confer on police the power to charge someone with obstruction where there is an apparent violation of a law which itself is invalid.[306]

It is not entirely clear that the distinction between "apparent perpetration of an offence" and "apparent offences" is a sensible one. From the perspective of the officer, the situation is the same: a law is in place and the accused appears to be violating it. Indeed, since the validity of a law will only ever be determined after the fact, this approach violates the rationale offered in *Biron* for adopting the "apparently finds committing" standard: that otherwise it would be impossible to say at the time of the arrest whether the power existed or not.[307] The most sensible conclusion to draw, however, is not that *Sharma* was wrongly decided. Rather, it is that *Biron* overestimates the extent to which this should really be a concern.[308]

c.   Section 495(1)(c)

Section 495(1)(c) seems, at first glance, a bit of an oddity. It allows a peace officer to arrest, without a warrant, anyone for whom he has reasonable grounds to believe that an arrest warrant exists. Although this might seem unusual, however, it reflects a sensible policy. In effect, it can be seen as simply an elaboration of the arrest power on reasonable grounds in section 495(1)(a) (though it is not necessarily limited to indictable offences). If a warrant for the person's arrest has been issued, then an information has been laid before a justice alleging that that person has committed an offence, and the justice has decided that it is in the public interest to issue a warrant rather than a summons. In

---

306 *Sharma*, above note 240 at para. 32.

307 *Biron*, above note 260 at 75: "If this is the way in which this provision is to be construed, no peace officer can ever decide, when making an arrest without a warrant, that the person arrested is 'committing a criminal offence.'"

308 The Court in *Biron*, *ibid.*, seems to have been influenced by the feeling that although Biron was acquitted of the causing a disturbance charge, he was "really" guilty of it. It states: "That he was justified in so thinking is shown by the fact that, at trial, Biron was convicted of the offence of causing a disturbance, and that his appeal from conviction resulted from the fact that the information charged only causing a disturbance 'by shouting,' which 'shouting' the judge on appeal found was not established by the evidence." The argument is not made explicitly, of course, and would be quite problematic if it were.

those circumstances, one can argue that there are "judicially certified" reasonable grounds to believe that the person has committed an offence.[309]

In essence, the only real thing to recognize about section 495(1)(c) is that it is exactly what it says: a power to arrest without warrant. In *Gamracy*, for example, the officer was at the accused's home to arrest him, but he knew only that there was a warrant for the accused's arrest, not the offence for which the warrant had been issued.[310] He also did not have a copy of the warrant with him. The Court held that the officer had complied with his obligations under the *Code*. He had the power to arrest without a warrant under section 495(1)(c), since he had reasonable grounds to believe that a warrant was in existence. He also complied with his obligation under section 29 to tell the accused the reason for the arrest when he told him merely that he was arresting him on the basis that a warrant existed. See the discussion of this issue in Chapter 2, Section B(1)(b).

At least two things are required to comply with section 495(1)(c): a reasonable belief that there is an arrest warrant, but also a reasonable belief that the person arrested is the person for whom the warrant was issued. In *Burke*, for example, the officer was carrying out an arrest under section 495(1)(c), and the accused insisted that the warrant was in fact for his brother, not for him. The Court upheld the trial judge's decision that the arrest was not legal, on the basis that on the particular facts of case the necessary reasonable grounds were not established.[311] As with section 495(1), the relevant beliefs must have been subjectively held by the officer, but must also have been objectively reasonable.[312]

Note as well that section 495(1)(c) is specific in stating that the warrant must be "in any form set out in Part XXVIII" and also must be in force within the territorial jurisdiction in which the person is found. The former requirement was significant in *Luc*, where a peace officer purported to rely on section 495(1)(c) to make a warrantless arrest on

---

309 LRC, *Arrest*, above note 61 at 23–24. The Law Reform Commission recommended retention of this warrantless arrest power. Note, however, that it also adopted the view that the standard a justice must apply in deciding whether to issue process based on an information was the same reasonable-grounds standard as for warrantless arrests. Not all authorities agree that the standard to be applied by a justice is as high as that: see the discussion in Section B(1), above in this chapter.

310 *Gamracy*, above note 135.

311 *R. v. Burke*, 2009 SCC 57.

312 *R. v. Hiltz*, [1991] N.S.J. No. 389 (S.C.A.D.).

the basis that an immigration warrant existed for the accused.[313] The Court of Appeal noted that the warrants in Part XXVIII depend upon the commission or apprehended commission of an offence under the *Code*. An immigration warrant does not depend on an offence having been committed, and is not listed in Part XXVIII: it therefore could not found an arrest under section 495(1)(c).

---

313 The case is further complicated by the fact that the immigration warrant was not in fact for the accused at all, but rather for someone with a superficially similar name, and the officer had made a mistake.

CHAPTER 5

THE IMPACT OF THE *CHARTER*

A. INTRODUCTION

It is trite to observe that the *Charter* has had a dramatic impact on criminal law and procedure. Of course, that has been true in the areas of detention and arrest as much as in other areas. In particular, the most relevant rights have been those specified in section 9 and section 10. Section 9 provides that "[e]veryone has the right not to be arbitrarily detained or imprisoned." Section 10 provides that several rights arise when a person is either arrested or detained, the most important of which are "to be informed promptly of the reasons therefor" and "to retain and instruct counsel without delay and to be informed of that right."

It is interesting to note that the impact of the *Charter* has been different in kind depending on whether one is speaking of detention or arrest. In the case of section 9, *Charter* caselaw has tended to focus on whether a power to detain exists or not. Indeed, rather paradoxically, court decisions dealing with section 9 have more often than not resulted in an expansion of police powers, rather than imposing limits on them. Section 10 of the *Charter*, on the other hand, has had no significant impact on the circumstances in which police (or anyone else) can or cannot arrest. Rather, the effect of section 10 has been to add additional obligations on the police when they make an arrest. Those obligations include both rights the police must extend to the accused at the time of the arrest as well as information which the accused is entitled to be told.

We shall discuss sections 9 and 10 in that order.

B. SECTION 9 — ARBITRARY DETENTION

Section 9 jurisprudence has, on the whole, been very late developing. There were several cases in the early days of the *Charter* that began to develop an understanding of what "arbitrary detention" might mean. However, those cases did not create an overall framework for analyzing a section 9 claim, in the way that frameworks were laid down for other rights, such as those in sections 7 or 8. Some relevant questions seem never to have been explicitly asked, and a number of questions were left deliberately unanswered. Individual cases decided that a particular accused had or had not been arbitrarily detained, but without offering much guidance for future cases.[1] It is really only with the Supreme Court's 2009 decision in *Grant* that a real structure, as opposed to a series of unrelated decisions, has emerged.[2]

Several factors contributed to the relative neglect of section 9. In part, the relatively limited utility of the section to an accused meant that it was not often argued. The first cases dealing with detention were a trio of vehicle-stop cases: *Dedman*,[3] *Hufsky*,[4] and *Ladouceur*.[5] Aspects of these cases will be dealt with in greater depth below, but the important point to note here is not so much the section 9 analysis as the section 1 analysis. The last of the three, *Ladouceur*, created a power for any police officer to, in the words of the dissent, "stop any vehicle at any time, in any place, without having any reason to do so."[6] The Supreme Court did find that any such stop would be an arbitrary detention and would violate section 9; the majority also held, however, that this violation was saved under section 1. Given this start to section 9 jurisprudence, it is not surprising that defence counsel would infrequently find it worthwhile to devote a great deal of time to developing an arbitrary-detention argument.

Further, defence counsel could resort to other *Charter*-based arguments that were more likely to be fruitful. If a detention was made in accordance with a statutory scheme (for example, dangerous-offend-

---

1   See, for example, *R. v. Hawkins*, [1993] 2 S.C.R. 157 [*Hawkins*], and *R. v. Chaisson*, 2006 SCC 11.

2   *R. v. Grant*, 2009 SCC 32 [*Grant*].

3   *R. v. Dedman*, [1985] 2 S.C.R. 2 [*Dedman*].

4   *R. v. Hufsky*, [1988] 1 S.C.R. 621 [*Hufsky*].

5   *R. v. Ladouceur*, [1990] 1 S.C.R. 1257 [*Ladouceur*].

6   *Ibid.* at 1264.

er legislation),[7] then a challenge could likely be made based on life, liberty, and security of the person under section 7, or based on cruel and unusual punishment under section 12. If the detention was a more discretionary one, of a vehicle or a pedestrian, then sections 8 or 10 are likely to be relevant. Specifically, if the person was detained and searched, then an argument concerning unreasonable search would likely be made. If the person was detained and made an incriminating statement, then an argument based on the right to be informed of the reason for arrest or the right to counsel would likely be made. A "pure" section 9 claim would probably be necessary only if the person was detained but was not searched and made no statement; in that event, it would actually be unlikely that any useful remedy would flow to the accused even if a violation was made out. As a result, section 9 has tended to be secondary to most analyses — sometimes supporting a claim of a pattern of violations, but not very often significant all on its own.

Nonetheless with *Grant*, a framework for evaluating section 9 claims has now been created. Given that section 9 protects against arbitrary detention, it is not surprising that the two central issues are: 1) what is a detention; and 2) when is a detention arbitrary?

1) What Is a "Detention"?

A definition of detention was first offered among the very earliest *Charter* cases. In *Therens*, the Supreme Court was called upon to decide whether an accused stopped for a breathalyzer demand was entitled to the right to counsel: since section 10(b) says that an accused is entitled to be informed of the right to counsel "on arrest or detention," that amounted to the question whether a breathalyzer stop fell within the meaning of the word "detention." Although it might seem obvious that being required to stay in the company of police for an extended period of time is a detention, the pre-*Charter* decision *Chromiak* had concluded that a person who while stopped performed roadside sobriety tests and complied with a demand for a breath sample was *not* detained.[8] In *Therens*, the Court reversed that conclusion, and its reasoning is instructive in a number of regards.

One of the most significant aspects of *Therens* is its general approach to *Charter* rights, rather than the particular finding it made about the meaning of detention. It had been argued that in using the word "detention" the drafters of the *Charter* should be taken to have

---

7   *R. v. Lyons*, [1987] 2 S.C.R. 309 [*Lyons*].
8   *R. v. Chromiak*, [1980] 1 S.C.R. 471 [*Chromiak*].

known of and to have relied on pre-*Charter* cases: in essence, that in using the word "detention" the legislators meant "detention as it was interpreted in *Chromiak*." The Court rejected this as an approach to interpreting the *Charter*. The *Charter*, it held, was "a new affirmation of rights and freedoms and of judicial power and responsibility in relation to their protection" and accordingly had to be interpreted afresh.[9] In particular, the Court was quite willing to allow the word "detention" to have a broad meaning, in part because any rights based on it were subject to a section 1 analysis.[10]

A second important point to note is an argument that was rejected as not relevant to interpreting the meaning of detention. Section 10(c) of the *Charter* guarantees the right "to have the validity of the detention determined by way of *habeas corpus* and to be released if the detention is not lawful." It had been argued that this demonstrated that the word "detention" was meant to be limited to infringements of liberty of a long enough duration that a challenge by way of *habeas corpus* was practical. In *Therens*, however, the Court held that the term "detention" covered a wide variety of situations of varying duration, and the fact that *habeas corpus* "may not be possible in some cases, because of the limited duration of the detention, is not, in my respectful opinion, a reason for limiting the meaning of the word 'detention' to detentions of a certain duration."[11]

Finally, *Therens* offered an approach to understanding what detention means: not so much a definition as a purposive reading of the purpose of the right. The term appears both in section 9 and in section 10. *Therens* was talking about the meaning of the word in the latter context, but the Court did soon thereafter hold that the same definition applied to both sections.[12] First, the Court noted:

> In its use of the word "detention," s. 10 of the *Charter* is directed to a restraint of liberty other than arrest in which a person may reasonably require the assistance of counsel but might be prevented or impeded from retaining and instructing counsel without delay but for the constitutional guarantee.[13]

---

9   *R. v. Therens*, [1985] 1 S.C.R. 613 at 638 [*Therens*]. This passage, and indeed all the reasoning about the meaning of the word "detention," occurs in the dissenting judgment of LeDain J. This aspect of his reasons was adopted by the majority.

10   *Therens, ibid.* at 639.

11   *Ibid.* at 641.

12   *Hufsky*, above note 4 at 632.

13   *Therens*, above note 9 at 641–42.

Based on this, the Court distinguished three different situations, all of which would fall within the meaning of "detention." The first was where a person was subject to physical constraint. In those circumstances, similar to an arrest, the person should be seen as detained. Second, a person would also be detained when given an order if there are legal consequences for non-compliance. It is, for example, an offence to refuse when a police officer makes a breathalyzer demand, as in *Therens*. The Court held that it would be inaccurate to describe the person to whom the demand was made as free to refuse to comply. In that event, the person is detained.

In fact that second category — detention by legal compulsion — was sufficient to settle the issue in *Therens*. The Court went on, however, to create a third category of detention: psychological detention. It held:

> [I]t is not realistic, as a general rule, to regard compliance with a demand or direction by a police officer as truly voluntary, in the sense that the citizen feels that he or she has the choice to obey or not, even where there is in fact a lack of statutory or common law authority for the demand or direction and therefore an absence of criminal liability for failure to comply with it. Most citizens are not aware of the precise legal limits of police authority. Rather than risk the application of physical force or prosecution for wilful obstruction, the reasonable person is likely to err on the side of caution, assume lawful authority and comply with the demand. The element of psychological compulsion, in the form of a reasonable perception of suspension of freedom of choice, is enough to make the restraint of liberty involuntary. Detention may be effected without the application or threat of application of physical restraint if the person concerned submits or acquiesces in the deprivation of liberty and reasonably believes that the choice to do otherwise does not exist.[14]

The Court conveniently summarized its various conclusions from *Therens* in the subsequent case *Thomsen*:

> 1. In its use of the word "detention," s. 10 of the *Charter* is directed to a restraint of liberty other than arrest in which a person may reasonably require the assistance of counsel but might be prevented or impeded from retaining and instructing counsel without delay but for the constitutional guarantee.
>
> 2. In addition to the case of deprivation of liberty by physical constraint, there is a detention within s. 10 of the *Charter*, when a police

---

14   *Therens, ibid.* at 644.

officer or other agent of the state assumes control over the movement of a person by a demand or direction which may have significant legal consequence and which prevents or impedes access to counsel.

3. The necessary element of compulsion or coercion to constitute a detention may arise from criminal liability for refusal to comply with a demand or direction, or from a reasonable belief that one does not have a choice as to whether or not to comply.

4. Section 10 of the *Charter* applies to a great variety of detentions of varying duration and is not confined to those of such duration as to make the effective use of *habeas corpus* possible.[15]

It has also been made clear that this definition applies only to relations between individuals and the state in circumstances that are closely similar to the investigation of a criminal offence. Deprivations of liberty can occur in other contexts, such as schools, where students often feel, or indeed are, compelled to go to or remain in various locations. These do not qualify as "detention" for *Charter* purposes.[16] Similarly, persons who face routine questioning by customs officials at the border are not free to leave, but this too does not qualify as a detention within the meaning of sections 9 and 10. On the other hand, those people who are taken out of the normal course of activity and subjected to a strip search *are* detained.[17]

Practically speaking, detention by physical constraint and detention by legal compulsion have provided no real challenges in application. Psychological detention, on the other hand, has been a very difficult issue for courts to come to grips with. This is not surprising, since almost by definition a psychological detention involves the police acting in circumstances where they have no specific power to act: if they did have such power, then "detention by legal compulsion" would be in issue.

Claims of psychological detentions have tended to fall into one of two scenarios. First, in the course of a formal investigation, a person might be taken (or invited) to the police station to answer questions. In some cases, in the course of questioning, a person who initially was merely a witness comes to be a suspect. Although the person might well at some point be placed under arrest, there is no immediate need to do so since the person is already sitting in a room with the police. Thus, although the situation might in some abstract way have changed from a

---

15   *R. v. Thomsen*, [1988] 1 S.C.R. 640 at 649 [*Thomsen*].
16   *R. v. M.(M.R.)*, [1998] 3 S.C.R. 393 [*M.(M.R.)*].
17   *R. v. Simmons*, [1988] 2 S.C.R. 495 [*Simmons*].

voluntary attendance to a detention, there will probably be no obvious outward manifestation of that change. In such cases, there is not likely to be a section 9 issue, since any detention is probably lawful and therefore not arbitrary. However, when the person passes that metaphysical boundary between "not detained" and "detained," he is entitled under section 10(b) to have been informed of the right to counsel. Since on this scenario the person is already answering questions, the failure to comply with section 10 is potentially quite significant.

The second situation in which the question of whether a person has been psychologically detained has typically arisen has been in sidewalk encounters with police officers. Police not infrequently approach individuals on the street and ask them questions. Often this is done not in the course of investigating any particular offences, nor based on any particular suspicion about the person stopped. Also not infrequently, such sidewalk stops have led individuals to make incriminating statements, or have led to searches which have turned up narcotics or firearms. In these cases, the question of whether the person was or was not detained when being questioned by the police leads directly to, at least, the question of whether there was an arbitrary detention.

Guidelines for the former situation, the police-station detention, were offered by the Ontario Court of Appeal in its decision in *Moran*. In that case the accused had been having an affair with a woman who had been murdered. He spoke with the police twice, both times at the police station rather than at his house. The police had not ruled out suicide as an explanation for the death at the time of the interviews, and, although the accused was asked some questions about his whereabouts and his willingness to take a polygraph test, similar questions were asked of others. The questioning officer testified that he did not consider the accused a suspect at the time, though the accused testified that he felt pressured by some of the questions. In fact, he was not arrested until two months later, when other evidence had turned up. The Court of Appeal held that the trial judge was correct to find that the accused had not been detained during these interviews. In doing so, it articulated factors to be applied in determining whether a person interviewed at a police station was detained:

1. The precise language used by the police officer in requesting the person who subsequently becomes an accused to come to the police station, and whether the accused was given a choice or expressed a preference that the interview be conducted at the Police station, rather than at his or her home;

2. Whether the accused was escorted to the police station by a police officer or came himself or herself in response to a police request;

3. Whether the accused left at the conclusion of the interview or whether he or she was arrested;

4. The stage of the investigation, that is, whether the questioning was part of the general investigation of a crime or possible crime or whether the police had already decided that a crime had been committed and that the accused was the perpetrator or involved in its commission and the questioning was conducted for the purpose of obtaining incriminating statements from the accused;

5. Whether the police had reasonable and probable grounds to believe that the accused had committed the crime being investigated;

6. The nature of the questions: whether they were questions of a general nature designed to obtain information or whether the accused was confronted with evidence pointing to his or her guilt;

7. The subjective belief by an accused that he or she is detained, although relevant, is not decisive, because the issue is whether he or she reasonably believed that he or she was detained. Personal circumstances relating to the accused, such as low intelligence, emotional disturbance, youth and lack of sophistication are circumstances to be considered in determining whether he had a subjective belief that he was detained.[18]

Leave to appeal to the Supreme Court was refused.[19] As a result, the guidelines set down by the Ontario Court of Appeal have tended to be employed by other courts faced with similar questions, making *Moran* for a long time the leading case in this area. It is possible that it should still be regarded in that way, though there is some ambiguity.

Note first that other tests have been proposed by other courts of appeal for dealing with this scenario. The Newfoundland Court of Appeal, for example, in *Hawkins* proposed a test for detention that centred around the views of the investigator: that a detention commenced when "the investigator's approach to the encounter is changed from a questioning of the individual to an examination with an intent to charge him or her with the offence."[20] Based on that test, the court found *Hawkins* to have been detained.

---

18   *R. v. Moran* (1987), 36 C.C.C. (3d) 225 at 258 & 259 (Ont. C.A.).
19   *R. v. Moran*, [1988] S.C.C.A. No. 213.
20   *R. v. Hawkins* (1992), 14 C.R. (4th) 286 at 298 (Nfld. C.A.).

However, the Supreme Court reversed that result with a two-sentence decision which simply asserted that the accused had not been detained and offered no commentary at all on the test proposed.[21] That seemed to leave the *Moran* criteria to be applied.

A difficulty, however, is that the *Moran* criteria are not really of very much relevance to the other situation in which the question of detention most commonly arises, the sidewalk stop. The *Moran* criteria all presume that there is already some particular crime under investigation. In sidewalk stops, on the other hand, police are typically talking to individuals in the absence of knowledge that any particular crime has occurred. If they did have such a belief, then likely they would be proceeding under a *Mann* stop, and it would not be psychological detention in issue at all.

Although this situation was left largely without guidance for many years, the Supreme Court's decision in *Grant* sets out a definition which pays particular attention to the difficult issue of psychological detention in sidewalk-stop situations. In *Grant*, the accused was walking along a street. Two plainclothes officers decided that he looked suspicious because he stared at them and fidgeted with his clothes. They suggested to a uniformed officer that he have a chat with the accused, and that officer stepped out his car and blocked the accused's path, asking him what was going on and requesting identification. The two plainclothes officers then joined the uniformed one, identified themselves as police, and positioned themselves so as to obstruct the way forward. On further questioning, the accused admitted to having marijuana and a firearm, at which point he was arrested and searched. The trial judge found on these facts that this interaction with the police did not constitute a detention; the Court of Appeal disagreed. The Supreme Court upheld the notion that the accused was detained, but went further than that particular conclusion and laid down a general set of criteria to be used in determining the detention question.

The Court had earlier observed in *Mann* that not every delay caused by police would constitute a detention, and that not every person asked for identification by police or interviewed would necessarily be detained. This is, of course, a sensible position: police might well direct all witnesses to a traffic accident to stay to identify themselves so they can be asked at some later time what they saw, but no one would suggest that, for example, the right to counsel should arise in all such cases. In *Grant*, however, the Court was careful to try not to let this reasonable limitation on the rights that are related to detention become

---

21 *Hawkins*, above note 1.

a large enough exception that the section failed to provide protection when it actually should. The Court noted that one of the purposes of section 9 was to guard "against incursions on mental liberty by prohibiting the coercive pressures of detention and imprisonment from being applied to people without adequate justification."[22] The central concerns, the Court held, were to preserve the accused's ability to make an informed choice about whether to walk away, and about whether to speak to state authorities.

The Court concluded that the question of detention had to be decided based on an objective test, rather than a subjective one. It also decided that the subjective views of the police officers should not be determinative on the detention question, though they would be relevant at other stages, such as deciding whether evidence should be excluded. Consistent with this, the Court held that "focussed suspicion, in and of itself, does not turn the encounter [into] a detention. What matters is how the police, based on that suspicion, interacted with the subject."[23] Having downplayed the police perspective on the interaction, the Court settled on a detainee-centred objective test: whether a reasonable person in the detainee's position would conclude that she had no choice but to comply.

The Court discussed a number of factors that would be relevant to this objective analysis, and eventually summarized the test for psychological detention:

> 1. Detention under ss. 9 and 10 of the *Charter* refers to a suspension of the individual's liberty interest by a significant physical or psychological restraint. Psychological detention is established either where the individual has a legal obligation to comply with the restrictive request or demand, or a reasonable person would conclude by reason of the state conduct that he or she had no choice but to comply.

> 2. In cases where there is no physical restraint or legal obligation, it may not be clear whether a person has been detained. To determine whether the reasonable person in the individual's circumstances would conclude that he or she had been deprived by the state of the liberty of choice, the court may consider, *inter alia*, the following factors:

> > a) The circumstances giving rise to the encounter as would reasonably be perceived by the individual: whether the police were

---

22 *Grant*, above note 2 at para. 20.

23 *Grant*, *ibid.* at para. 41. Note that minimizing the significance of focused suspicion is quite consistent with the Court's refusal to uphold *Hawkins*, above note 1.

providing general assistance; maintaining general order; making general inquiries regarding a particular occurrence; or, singling out the individual for focussed investigation.

b) The nature of the police conduct, including the language used; the use of physical contact; the place where the interaction occurred; the presence of others; and the duration of the encounter.

c) The particular characteristics or circumstances of the individual where relevant, including age; physical stature; minority status; level of sophistication.[24]

Based on these criteria, the Court held, the accused was detained. The initial questioning by the first officer would not be a detention, though the direction to the accused to keep his hands in front of him was ambiguous. When the other two officers took up positions behind the first, however, and the nature of the questioning changed from ascertaining the appellant's identity to determining whether he had anything that he shouldn't, it became clear that the accused was detained, and indeed detained from the time of the direction about his hands. Although the tone of the questioning officer was respectful, the power imbalance of a young inexperienced person faced with three physically larger officers made the encounter inherently intimidating.

At the time of this writing, *Grant* is a recent enough decision that there are no patterns in lower court applications to speak of. The Court did apply *Grant* itself in another decision handed down the same day, *Suberu*.[25] In *Suberu*, the police had responded to a call of two people using stolen gift cards at a liquor store; an officer who arrived encountered the accused, who was on his way out of the store. The accused said words to the effect of "he did this, not me, so I guess I can go," to which the officer replied, "Wait a minute, I need to talk to you before you go anywhere," and followed the accused outside. The accused sat in the driver's seat of a minivan and the officer engaged him in conversation, asking him questions about his connection to the events in the store, until eventually he arrested the accused. At trial and up to the Court of Appeal, the issue argued was whether the accused should have

---

24   *Grant, ibid.* at para. 44. It is arguable that *Grant* characterizes detentions slightly differently from *Therens*. *Therens* seemed to have created three categories: physical restraint, legal compulsion, and psychological detention. *Grant* characterizes legal compulsion as one of two branches of psychological detention. Whether this is different or not, it seems unlikely to have any practical consequences, since all three types of detention still exist.

25   *R. v. Suberu*, [2009] 2 S.C.R. 460 [*Suberu*].

been informed of his right to counsel. The Supreme Court concluded that the words "without delay" in section 10(b) meant immediately, and therefore that anyone who was subject to an investigative detention was immediately entitled to be informed of the right to counsel (see the discussion below). However, the majority of the Court concluded that Suberu had not, by the test in *Grant*, actually been detained, and therefore that there was no section 10(b) violation.

This is perhaps a surprising result. Justice Binnie, writing in dissent, noted that the accused's question to the officer amounted to asking "can I leave" and the officer's answer amounted to "no." In those circumstances, he found it hard to see how one could conclude that a reasonable person in the accused's situation would not have felt that he had been denied choice. Justice Binnie points to the fact that interpreting "without delay" to mean "immediately" removes any flexibility for the police around the issue of the timing of a *Charter* warning, and suggests that such flexibility must exist somewhere. He points to the danger that courts will avoid the consequence of being forced to find a section 10(b) violation by the stratagem of being overly strict in applying the test for whether a person has been detained. Certainly, this is a danger, and would be an unfortunate consequence. It would reflect the pattern that has arisen in search-and-seizure law of avoiding being forced to find that a search was unreasonable by adopting a narrow interpretation of reasonable expectation of privacy and thereby denying that a police investigative technique was a search at all.[26]

Justice Binnie's proposal, dissenting in *Grant*, had been to reduce the extent to which the test for detention was claimant-centred and incorporate more elements of the police perspective into the analysis. This suggestion would be closer to the approach of the Newfoundland Court of Appeal in *Hawkins*. Tim Quigley points out that to do so would be closer to the approach in *Moran*, which includes consideration of information known to the police.[27] Leaving the police perspective out also seemingly means that police can follow up on their suspicions about an individual without detaining her, so long as they are careful not to make their true intentions apparent to a reasonable person. It is certainly correct that one could incorporate such elements into the test; the effect of doing so, of course, is likely to be to reduce the number of situations that are held to be detentions. Further, reasoning that has relied on the police perspective has often incorporated an odd irony. If

---

26   See Steve Coughlan, "Arbitrary Detention: Whither — or Wither? — Section 9" (2008) 40 Sup. Ct. L. Rev. (2d) 147, pointing to the danger of this possibility.

27   Tim Quigley, "Was it Worth the Wait? The Supreme Court's New Approaches to Detention and Exclusion of Evidence" (2009) 66 C.R. (6th) 88.

the police do not see themselves as performing an investigative detention, for example, and are asking questions without reasonable grounds to suspect that there is a nexus between the detainee and a recent or ongoing offence, then relying on the police perspective means that there was no detention. This leads to the result that a section 9 violation is *less* likely to be found if the police are acting without legal authority. That is a counter-intuitive result.

It is in any case not entirely clear what the status of the *Moran* criteria is post-*Grant*. Many of the factors in the prior case are consistent with the approach in the latter, but not all: whether the police had reasonable and probable grounds to believe that the accused had committed the crime being investigated, for example, does not go to how a reasonable person in the accused's situation would perceive the situation. But the discussion in *Grant* is very much focused around sidewalk encounters, not interviews at the police station. Whether the police were providing general assistance or simply maintaining general order, for example, is not likely to be a relevant consideration in the latter context. It is arguable that *Moran* continues to be the leading authority on detentions in that situation, but more likely that *Grant* is now the governing test in all contexts.

2) When Is a Detention Arbitrary?

It now appears that the "arbitrariness" portion of section 9 claims is to be addressed by asking the following three questions: 1) Is the detention authorized by law?; 2) Is the law itself arbitrary?; and 3) Is the manner in which the detention was carried out arbitrary? A failure at any point along the way would lead to the conclusion that there was violation of section 9.

This structure is parallel to that created in *Collins* for assessing section 8 claims.[28] The Supreme Court has referred to the analogy to *Collins*, and it did so in the course of explicitly stating the first two of these rules. The third rule has been implicitly applied in many cases and serves a valuable function. This three-step analysis, then, represents the approach laid out in *Grant* combined with what *in fact* has tended to be done in analyzing section 9 claims, though no case has stated precisely these terms to date.

---

28   See *R. v. Collins*, [1987] 1 S.C.R. 265 at para. 23 [*Collins*]: "A search will be reasonable if it is authorized by law, if the law itself is reasonable and if the manner in which the search was carried out is reasonable."

The first question, whether the detention is authorized by law, sounds like an obvious step. The equivalent point for section 8, that "unreasonable search" and "unlawful search" mean the same thing, was established in some of the earliest *Charter* decisions about unreasonable search and seizure.[29] However, *Grant* is the first case to make fully clear that the same approach applies to section 9. In fact, the failure to have established this point earlier means that much section 9 caselaw prior to 2009 is not entirely reliable.

It is important to see that the first question includes two conclusions: that if the detention *is* authorized by law it passes the first stage, but also that if it is *not* authorized by law it fails the first stage. The first half of that equation had never really been controversial. As noted above, the requirement of finding a detention lawful as a means of avoiding a section 9 violation had led to the creation of new common law powers of detention. For that reason and others, the rule that "a lawful detention is not an arbitrary one" was used routinely (though, of course, this rule is subject to the second step — that the law itself is not arbitrary). The controversial point was the second half of equating "arbitrary" and "unlawful": that a detention would be arbitrary simply because it failed to comply with the law. In fact, many courts had denied that that was so. In *Duguay*, for example, the Ontario Court of Appeal had held that a police officer might arrest someone on grounds that fell just short of being reasonable, and that such an arrest "though subsequently found to be unlawful, could not be said to be capricious or arbitrary."[30] The Supreme Court did not comment in any way on this issue when it upheld the result in *Duguay*, but the appeal dealt only with the issue of exclusion of evidence and so this point did not arise.[31] On other occasions, the Court deliberately left the issue aside. In *Lat-*

---

29   See *R. v. Kokesch*, [1990] 3 S.C.R. 3, and *Collins, ibid.*

30   *R. v. Duguay* (1985), 45 C.R. (3d) 140 at 148 (Ont. C.A.) [*Duguay*]. It is probably fair to say that the majority opinion among courts of appeal had been that unlawfulness did *not* automatically amount to arbitrariness. See, for example, *R. v. Campbell*, 2003 MBCA 76 at para. 42:

> In summary, appellate courts in Canada have accepted the proposition that an unlawful arrest will not necessarily constitute an arbitrary detention. What must be determined is whether the arrest was 'capricious, despotic or unjustified,' or whether there were 'near grounds' or articulable cause for the detention.

See also *R. v. Ingle*, 2007 BCCA 445, and *R. v. Perello* (2005), 27 C.R. (6th) 19 (Sask. C.A.).

31   *R. v. Duguay*, [1989] 1 S.C.R. 93.

imer, for example, it commented that "[u]nlawful arrests may be inherently arbitrary . . . [but] it is not necessary to address that question."[32]

With *Grant*, however, the Court has now fully and consciously committed itself to both halves of the equation: unlawful detentions are arbitrary, and vice versa. It held:

> A lawful detention is not arbitrary within the meaning of s. 9 (*Mann*, at para. 20), unless the law authorizing the detention is itself arbitrary. Conversely, a detention not authorized by law is arbitrary and violates s. 9.[33]

In fact, the Court had said something similar two years earlier in *Clayton*.[34] There, however, the observation was made in passing, without reference to the fact that this was a point deliberately left undecided in earlier cases. In *Grant*, the Court refers explicitly to that unsettledness and commits itself, referring explicitly to the analogy to section 8 in doing so:

> [56] This approach mirrors the framework developed for assessing unreasonable searches and seizures under s. 8 of the *Charter*. Under *R. v. Collins*, [1987] 1 S.C.R. 265, and subsequent cases dealing with s. 8, a search must be authorized by law to be reasonable; the authorizing law must itself be reasonable; and the search must be carried out in a reasonable manner. Similarly, it should now be understood that for a detention to be non-arbitrary, it must be authorized by a law which is itself non-arbitrary.

The Court here, in the final sentence, states both the first and second step of the analytical structure suggested above: both "is the detention authorized by law" and "is the law itself arbitrary." The way of assessing the second of these questions was in fact one of the earliest aspects to be decided about section 9 — before this analytical structure existed. However, the question of how to tell whether a law is arbitrary was essentially decided by the Court more than twenty years before *Grant*, in *Hufsky*.

---

32 *R. v. Latimer*, [1997] 1 S.C.R. 217 at para. 26 [*Latimer*].
33 *Grant*, above note 2 at para. 54.
34 *R. v. Clayton*, 2007 SCC 32 at para. 19 [*Clayton*]:

> If the police conduct in detaining and searching Clayton and Farmer amounted to a lawful exercise of their common law powers, there was no violation of their *Charter* rights. If, on the other hand, the conduct fell outside the scope of these powers, it represented an infringement of the right under the *Charter* not to be arbitrarily detained or subjected to an unreasonable search or seizure.

In *Hufsky*, the Court was concerned with a provincial highway traffic act provision which permitted police to stop vehicles at random. It had no difficulty concluding that the accused, stopped under this power, was detained. The Court did not specifically ask whether his detention was authorized by law, though of course it was, by the relevant highway traffic act. The issue was whether his detention under this power was arbitrary. The Court held that it was. The statute did not create any criteria as to which cars could be stopped and left the matter entirely in the discretion of the individual police officer. The Court found this to be arbitrary and set out the definition that led it to this conclusion: "A discretion is arbitrary if there are no criteria, express or implied, which govern its exercise."[35] It also carried on to find that section 9 violation to be justified under section 1, but nonetheless it established that definition of "arbitrary."

This definition has applied by the Court in a number of other cases. First, and unsurprisingly, it was used in other vehicle-stop cases.[36] In *Swain*, in dealing with a law that required the automatic detention of a person found not guilty by reason of insanity, the Court noted: "The duty of the trial judge to detain is unqualified by any standards whatsoever. I cannot imagine a detention being ordered on a more arbitrary basis."[37] In *Pearson* and in *Morales*, the Court used this definition to assess aspects of the *Code*'s bail provisions.[38] In *Lyons* it was used to assess the dangerous-offender provisions.[39]

The important point to note is that the Court has not merely said that not being governed by any criteria is *one* way to be arbitrary. Rather, it actually does intend that "not governed by any criteria" is the definition of "arbitrary." In *Lyons*, for example, the accused challenged the dangerous-offender provisions of the *Code* under sections 7, 9, and 12. The Court rejected the section 9 claim, noting that the provisions did set out criteria governing when an offender could be designated as dangerous. It carried on to say: "If these criteria are themselves unconstitutional, it is because they otherwise fail adequately to safeguard the liberty of the individual, not because they are arbitrary."[40] On this

---

35   *Hufsky*, above note 4 at 633. The Court reaffirmed this criterion much more recently: see *R. v. Nolet*, 2010 SCC 24 at para. 22.

36   *R. v. Wilson*, [1990] 1 S.C.R. 1291; *Ladouceur*, above note 5; *R. v. Macooh*, [1993] 2 S.C.R. 802; and *R. v. Mellenthin*, [1992] 3 S.C.R. 615.

37   *R. v. Swain*, [1991] 1 S.C.R. 933 at 1012.

38   *R. v. Pearson*, [1992] 3 S.C.R. 665 [*Pearson*]; *R. v. Morales*, [1992] 3 S.C.R. 711 [*Morales*].

39   *Lyons*, above note 7.

40   *Lyons*, *ibid.* at 347. *Lyons* was actually decided prior to *Hufsky*, above note 4, but is consistent with the approach articulated in the latter case.

approach, the section 9 question reduces to whether criteria exist at all: if there are, the detention is not arbitrary. Questions relating to the *content* of the criteria would fall to be decided under some other section, such as section 7 or 12.[41]

This is unproblematic as far as it goes. The difficulty is that is does not go quite far enough. The Court has, in *Grant*, explicitly adopted analogues of the first two questions from *Collins*. It would be best to explicitly adopt the third question as well, and acknowledge that "is the manner in which the detention was carried out arbitrary" is not merely a question that many courts have asked, but one that should be asked.

This point can be seen most easily by thinking about racial profiling. Because of the roving random-stop power upheld in *Ladouceur*, or based on various pieces of provincial legislation, police have the authority to stop any car they like, without the need to point to a reason for the stop. One cannot say, therefore, that in stopping a vehicle because of the race of the driver, the police will have acted arbitrarily, at least based on the tools for assessing that question so far: the stop will have been lawful, and the law itself will not have been arbitrary. Nonetheless, it seems obvious that if *anything* ought to violate a rule against arbitrary detention, it would be racial profiling. Clearly, then, something more is needed.

In fact, the Supreme Court has noted this point in passing, though it has never developed it. But in *Ladouceur*, having upheld the very broad roving random-stop power, the Court observed that if the power to make such stops was used based on race, that misuse of the power would constitute a *Charter* violation.[42] Similarly, in *Storrey* the Court held:

> [T]here is no indication that the arrest was made because a police officer was biased towards a person of a different race, nationality or colour, or that there was a personal enmity between a police officer directed towards the person arrested. These factors, if established, might have the effect of rendering invalid an otherwise lawful arrest.[43]

---

41   See also *Pearson*, above note 38 at 699–700, and *Morales*, above note 38 at 740–41 and 747, for other instances where the fact that the provisions had some criteria led directly to the conclusion that the provisions did not violate s. 9.

42   In fact, this point is made in the dissenting judgment and attributed to the majority: "[R]acial considerations may be a factor too. My colleague states that in such circumstances, a *Charter* violation may be made out." *Ladouceur*, above note 5 at 1267.

43   *R. v. Storrey*, [1990] 1 S.C.R. 241 at 251–52 [*Storrey*].

These observations suggest that an equivalent to the third step in *Collins*, specifically "is the manner in which the detention was carried out arbitrary," should be seen as the third part of the analysis.

This question would, of course, be different from the question whether there were no criteria governing the exercise of discretion. It would, however, be capturing a different necessary part of the "arbitrariness" analysis, which is whether a power was used based on improper criteria. In this it would still be parallel to the approach in *Collins*, in which the "reasonableness" analysis relies on different criteria at the second and third stages. As a matter of fact, many lower courts have relied on essentially this criterion in deciding that an accused has been arbitrarily detained, though they have not formulated it as the third part of a test.

In *Brown v. Durham (Regional Municipality) Police Force*, for example, the Ontario Court of Appeal found that a stop made using the *Highway Traffic Act* would not violate section 9 even if the police had other purposes beyond highway traffic ones for making it. It carried on to say:

> If, however, one of the purposes motivating a stop and detention is improper, then in my view the stop is unlawful even if highway safety concerns also factor into the decision to make the stop and detention.[44]

The court continued:

> While I can find no sound reason for invalidating an otherwise proper stop because the police used the opportunity afforded by that stop to further some other legitimate interest, I do see strong policy reasons for invalidating a stop where the police have an additional improper purpose. Highway safety concerns are important, but they should not provide the police with a means to pursue objects which are themselves an abuse of the police power or are otherwise improper. For example, it would be unacceptable to allow a police officer who has valid highway safety concerns to give effect to those concerns by stopping only vehicles driven by persons of colour. Section 216(1) of the HTA does not, in my view, authorize discriminatory stops even where there is a highway safety purpose behind those stops.[45]

---

44   *Brown v. Durham (Regional Municipality) Police Force* (1998), 131 C.C.C. (3d) 1 at para. 34 (Ont. C.A.) [*Brown*]. Note that this approach seems to have been endorsed by the Supreme Court: see the discussion of *Nolet*, above note 35, in Chapter 2, Section B(2).

45   *Brown, ibid.* at para. 38.

This reasoning was adopted and applied in *Khan*, one of the few successful racial-profiling claims.[46]

Other cases have relied on "improper purpose" as a basis for finding a section 9 violation. In *Herter*, for example, the trial judge found that a peace officer arbitrarily detained the accused by keeping him in the "drunk tank" for over seven hours. It was not that there was no justification for doing so, in the sense that the accused was not intoxicated: he was. However, the trial judge concluded that the officer had acted in this way solely out of frustration at the accused's uncooperativeness.[47]

The third step, "is the manner in which the detention was carried out arbitrary," would therefore play a valuable role, and the need for it has been recognized. The three-step analysis of arbitrariness posed at the start of this section sets out a helpful analysis which incorporates the actual practice of many courts. It would be useful if the Supreme Court clearly articulated not only the first two steps but also the third.

C. SECTION 10 — THE RIGHT TO BE INFORMED OF THE REASONS FOR DETENTION AND THE RIGHT TO COUNSEL

1) Introduction

Section 10 of the *Charter* reads as follows:

Everyone has the right on arrest or detention

(a) to be informed promptly of the reasons therefor;

(b) to retain and instruct counsel without delay and to be informed of that right; and

(c) to have the validity of the detention determined by way of habeas corpus and to be released if the detention is not lawful.

---

46 The trial judge held: "The police stopped him for an improper purpose. Mr. Khan was targeted for this stop because of racial profiling, because he was a black man with an expensive car." *R. v. Khan* (2004), 189 C.C.C. (3d) 49 at para. 68 (Ont. S.C.J.).

47 *R. v. Herter*, 2006 ABPC 221, rev'd 2007 ABQB 756. The reversal is difficult to understand, given that it seems to amount to simply reversing the trial judge's findings of fact with no reference to standard of review: see Steve Coughlan, "*R v. Herter*: Annotation" (2007) 53 C.R. (6th) 287 at 288–89.

While the section 10(c) right to *habeas corpus* is beyond the scope of this book — our primary focus is "on the street encounters" — the rights under subsections 10(a) and (b) are intricately entwined with the section 9 right relating to arrest and detention.[48] Indeed, breaches of these two rights may well in themselves result in the arrest and detention being held unlawful. In Chapter 3, we discussed the concept of "detention" which triggers the applicability of the section 10 rights. We will not repeat that discussion here. It is worth saying, though, that subsection 10(a) and (b) rights have been treated as "gateway" rights in the sense that the Court has indicated that their purpose is to ensure that suspected persons are able to enjoy their other rights. By informing suspects why they are detained or arrested and allowing them to speak to counsel, suspects are able to enjoy their rights, in particular their right to silence in regard to the matter under investigation.

Therefore, based on the detention of the suspect, the suspect needs to be placed in a position to decide whether to exercise the right to silence in the face of police suspicion and desire to secure evidence. Having said that, there are significant situations in which the Court has determined that section 1 of the *Charter* legitimately limits the right to counsel, a subject covered in Chapter 3. The Supreme Court has generally limited the right to counsel in "screening" situations in impaired-driving cases. Further, as discussed in Chapter 2 , the issue as to whether these rights apply to non-police detentions has not been settled. Below, we will offer additional comments on this issue.

It is worth recognizing the interaction between sections 9 and 10. Earlier in this chapter we discussed section 9, which deals with whether there was any legal authority to detain or arrest the individual. If there was not, then there will already have been a violation of the accused's *Charter* rights, and so she will potentially be entitled to a remedy. Whether there was legal authority or not, however, the mere fact of arrest or detention triggers the rights in section 10(a) and (b). The police must then (in accordance with the requirements to be discussed below) inform the person of the reason for the detention and the right to counsel.

As a practical matter, this often means that there will be violations of both section 9 and section 10 on a single fact pattern. Where the police have crossed the line from legitimate conversation to psychological detention, they will often not have had legal authority and so will have

---

48   See, generally, Tim Quigley, *Procedure in Canadian Criminal Law*, 2d ed. (Toronto: Thomson Carswell, 2005) c. 15.2, and Robert J. Sharpe, *The Law of Habeas Corpus*, 2d ed. (Oxford: Clarendon Press, 1989) (new edition expected October 2010). See also *May v. Ferndale Institution*, 2005 SCC 82.

arbitrarily detained the accused in violation of section 9. Precisely because they were trying to skirt the line of detention, they will not have said to the accused "you are detained" at all, and typically will not in those situations have told the accused of the right to counsel: accordingly, there will be violations of subsections 10(a) and (b) as well.

On the other hand, it is also quite possible for the rights to be violated independently. An accused might be explicitly but unlawfully arrested or detained and given his section 10 rights, in which case there is a violation only of section 9. Alternatively, an accused might have been lawfully arrested or detained but there could be some failure to comply with the requirements of section 10, a scenario discussed below.

The most obvious "triggers" for section 10 are a formal arrest, made under one of the powers set out in the *Criminal Code*, or a detention of the sort discussed in Chapter 3. For some time it had remained unclear whether an investigative detention under *Mann* triggered the right to counsel; however, in R. v. *Suberu* the Supreme Court of Canada decided authoritatively that such detentions do trigger section 10.[49]

Although initial arrests and detentions are the most obvious triggers, they are not the only ones. For example, in R. v. *Evans*,[50] the accused had been arrested on a marijuana charge and taken to the police station for questioning. In fact, the real interest of the police was a murder for which they believed Evans's brother to be responsible, and they hoped to elicit information from Evans. When the accused was arrested, he was properly told of the reason, in accordance with section 10(a). As the interview continued, however, the police began to form the view that Evans himself was likely responsible for the murder.

In those circumstances, the Court held that the accused's section 10 rights were, in essence, retriggered. It stated that, when there is a "fundamental and discrete change in the purpose of the investigation, one involving a different and unrelated offence or a significantly more serious offence than that contemplated at the time of the warning," then the police must restate the accused's right to counsel.[51] The rationale for this rewarning is that the nature of the accused's jeopardy has changed, and so the accused's initial decision as to whether it was necessary to consult counsel might equally change.

The Court found what might be seen as a specific instance of this retriggering in R. v. *Burlingham*.[52] In that case, the accused was arrested for murder and questioned over the weekend. He had been properly

---

49   *Suberu*, above note 25.
50   R. v. *Evans*, [1991] 1 S.C.R. 869 [*Evans*].
51   *Ibid.* at 893.
52   R. v. *Burlingham*, [1995] 2 S.C.R. 206 [*Burlingham*].

cautioned at the time of his arrest and indeed had spoken with counsel. At a certain point in the interrogation, he was offered a plea bargain. The Court held that this constituted the kind of situation envisioned in *Evans*, and therefore that the accused's section 10(b) right to consult with counsel arose again at that point.

2) Section 10(a) — Right to be Informed of the Reasons for Detention

The section 10(a) right to be to be "informed promptly of the reasons" for an arrest or detention did not get very much attention in the early *Charter* cases. It was a right that was recognized at common law. In *Christie v. Leachinsky*, the House of Lords set out the following on the point:

> 1. If a policeman arrests without warrant on reasonable suspicion of felony, or of other crime of a sort which does not require a warrant, he must in ordinary circumstances inform the person arrested of the true ground of arrest. He is not entitled to keep the reason to himself or to give a reason which is not the true reason. In other words, a citizen is entitled to know on what charge or on suspicion of what crime he is seized.

> 2. If the citizen is not so informed, but is nevertheless seized, the policeman, apart from certain exceptions, is liable for false imprisonment.

> 3. The requirement that the person arrested should be informed of the reason why he is seized naturally does not exist if the circumstances are such that he must know the general nature of the alleged offence for which he is detained.

> 4. The requirement that he should be so informed does not mean that technical or precise language need be used. The matter is a matter of substance, and turns on the elementary proposition that in this country a person is, *prima facie*, entitled to his freedom and is only required to submit to restraint on his freedom if he knows in substance the reason why it is claimed that this restraint should be imposed.

> 5. The person arrested cannot complain that he has not been supplied with the above information as and when he should be, if he himself

produces the situation which makes it practically impossible to inform him, *eg*, by immediate counter-attack or by running away.[53]

The House was decidedly of the view that such a rule was necessary to protect the person arrested and particularly to allow the person arrested to determine whether the arrest was lawful:

> If another person has a lawful reason for seeking to deprive him of that liability, that person must as a general rule tell him what the reason is, for, unless he is told, he cannot be expected to submit to arrest or be blamed for resistance. The right to arrest and the duty to submit are correlative.[54]

Of course, the information thus provided allows the arrested person to know on what ground they are arrested and assists in their decision as to whether they should remain silent in the face of the allegation in question.

Before the enactment of subsection 10(a), the Supreme Court had thrown some doubt on whether Canadian law required full compliance with the law set out in *Christie*. In *R. v. Gamracy*,[55] the accused was arrested and told that he was being arrested on a warrant which the officer did not have with him; nor did the officer know for what offence the warrant had been issued. Nonetheless, the Court found compliance with subsection 29(2) of the *Criminal Code* which says:

> 29(2) It is the duty of every one who arrests a person, whether with or without a warrant, to give notice to that person, where it is feasible to do so, of
>
>> (*a*) the process or warrant under which he makes the arrest;
>> or
>> (*b*) the reason for the arrest.

The majority in *Gamracy* held that advising the suspect that there was a warrant for his arrest was sufficient compliance with the section and that, though *Christie* was

> no doubt an interesting one in the English context and naturally entitled to the greatest respect, I think it should be said that such cases afford no assistance in determining the true meaning and effect to be

---

53 *Christie v. Leachinsky*, [1947] 1 All E.R. 567 at 572–73 (H.L.), Simon L.J. [*Christie*].
54 *Ibid.* at 578, Lord DuParcq.
55 *R. v. Gamracy*, [1974] S.C.R. 640 [*Gamracy*].

given to ss. 450(1) and 29 of the Canadian *Criminal Code* and I do not think that any further comment is necessary.[56]

The arrest in *Gamracy* was, according to the Court, warrantless since the officer did not have the warrant with him and thus only section 29(2)(b) was applicable. The section was to be read disjunctively and so the officer met its requirements by telling the accused he was being arrested because there was a warrant for his arrest. Accordingly, the officer was in the execution of duty when he arrested the accused, who was therefore convicted of assaulting the officer when he resisted the arrest. The dissenting justices disagreed with the majority that informing the accused that there was a warrant without also telling him what the warrant was for was sufficient compliance.

Caselaw surrounding section 10(a) casts severe doubt on whether *Gamracy* should still be seen as good law. After the *Charter* came into force, the majority of the Supreme Court of Canada in *Evans* said in relation to subsection 10(a):

> The right to be promptly advised of the reason for one's detention embodied in s. 10(a) of the *Charter* is founded most fundamentally on the notion that one is not obliged to submit to an arrest if one does not know the reasons for it: *R. v. Kelly* . . . . A second aspect of the right lies in its role as an adjunct to the right to counsel conferred by s. 10(b) of the *Charter.* As Wilson J. stated for the Court in *R. v. Black* . . . . "[a]n individual can only exercise his s. 10(b) right in a meaningful way if he knows the extent of his jeopardy." In interpreting s. 10(a) in a purposive manner, regard must be had to the double rationale underlying the right.[57]

Therefore, in the majority's view, the double rationale included encouraging submission to lawful arrests and allowing meaningful exercise of the right to counsel. An accused who is merely told that the reason for her arrest is that there is a warrant might have had the first of these rationales satisfied, but certainly not the second. Indeed, it has specifically been held that section 10(a) reflects the right set out in *Christie*, which *Gamracy* had distinguished.[58]

---

56 *Ibid.* at 645.

57 *Evans*, above note 50 at 886–87, McLachlin J. citing *R. v. Kelly* (1985), 17 C.C.C. (3d) 419 at 424 (Ont. C.A.) [*Kelly*]; and *R. v. Black*, [1989] 2 S.C.R. 138 at 152–53 [*Black*].

58 *R. v. Nguyen*, 2008 ONCA 49 at para. 16 [*Nguyen*].

The Court's decision in *Evans*[59] also casts more light on the content of and approach to section 10(a). Evans was described by the Court as a youth (but who would appear to have been twenty years old on the date of his arrest) and as of "borderline" intelligence, being mentally the age of a fourteen year old. On the facts in *Evans*, although they found several breaches of the right to counsel, the majority ruled that the police had complied with section 10(a) since, in its view, Evans had understood why he was arrested and why he was being investigated. The accused had originally been told that he was arrested for drug offences when in fact he was being investigated in relation to a homicide. His section 10(b) right was violated, because he ought to have been rewarned of the right to counsel when the nature of his detention changed. However, the majority found no violation of section 10(a), the right to be informed of the reason for the detention. They held that, by the time the relevant statements had been made, the accused was aware that it was in fact the homicide that the police were interested in. To them, the crucial issue was

> what the accused can reasonably be supposed to have understood, rather than the formalism of the precise words used . . . . The question is whether what the accused was told, viewed reasonably in all the circumstances of the case, was sufficient to permit him to make a reasonable decision to decline to submit to arrest, or alternatively, to undermine his right to counsel under s. 10(b).[60]

Sopinka J., in dissent in relation to subsection 10(a), was not so accepting of the accused's understanding. He held that, because the police had not been as explicit in explaining that it was not the drug charge in which they were interested as they had been in originally concocting the drug charge as the reason for his detention, the accused's section 10(a) right had been breached. To the dissenting justice, the purpose of subsection 10(a) was "to enable the person under arrest or detention to immediately undertake his or her defence, including a decision as to what response, if any, to make to the accusation."[61]

Subsequent to *Evans*, the Supreme Court has seemingly continued to downplay the effect of subsection 10(a). In *R. v. Latimer*,[62] discussed in Chapter 4, the Court stressed that subsection 10(a) required only "that a person 'understand generally the jeopardy' in which he or

---

59   *Evans*, above note 50.
60   *Ibid.* at 888.
61   *Ibid.* at 875.
62   *Latimer*, above note 32.

she finds himself or herself,"[63] and therefore it was acceptable on the facts that Latimer knew he was being investigated in relation to his daughter's death and that he "was in an extremely grave situation as regards his daughter's death."[64] On the other hand, the Court did suggest that "it would be a gross interference with individual liberty for persons to have to submit to arrest without knowing the reasons for that arrest."[65]

Later still, the Court, upon creating the power of investigative detention in *Mann*, made clear its view that "[a]t a minimum, individuals who are detained for investigative purposes must therefore be advised, in clear and simple language, of the reasons for the detention."[66] The Ontario Court of Appeal then seemed to inject new life into subsection 10(a) in *R. v. Nguyen* where it held:

> It is clear, therefore, that while the main purpose of s. 10(a) is to inform an individual of why he or she is being detained, it also has an important secondary aspect as an adjunct to the right to counsel conferred by s. 10(b). Specifically, the purpose of s. 10(a) is also to inform an individual of the extent of his or her jeopardy such that he or she can exercise the right to counsel conferred by s. 10(b) in a meaningful way.[67]

The Court stressed that, "[o]nce detained, an individual is at the mercy of state actors" and that "the breach of the obligation to provide that information cannot be considered a trivial matter." [68]

Generally, it is significant to note that, like subsection 10(b), discussed below, subsection 10(a) has an informational component. Unlike section 10(b), though, that is all section 10(a) is. The Supreme Court has generally been of the view that it is the accused's understanding of her jeopardy that is necessary and that the police need not say any particular thing to the accused as long as it is reasonable to find that the accused did understand. Therefore, it seems clear that, if the police mislead the accused about the extent of his jeopardy and it is not reasonable to conclude that the accused nonetheless understood his

---

63   *Ibid.* at para. 28, quoting *R. v. Smith*, [1991] 1 S.C.R. 714 at 728 [*Smith*]. In *Smith* the Supreme Court held that an accused was not denied his s. 10(a) rights when the police failed to inform him that his victim had died. The Court was of the view that "Smith was aware that his situation was one of the most grave seriousness" (para. 33).

64   *Ibid.* at para. 31.

65   *Ibid.* at para. 28.

66   *R. v. Mann*, [2004] 3 S.C.R. 59 at para. 21 [*Mann*].

67   *Nguyen*, above note 58 at para. 20.

68   *Ibid.* at para. 21.

jeopardy, there will be a breach of the accused's section 10(a) right. In *Smith,* the Court said as much when it concluded:

> The fact that the accused knew that he was in jeopardy for a most serious offence distinguishes this case from one in which the description given minimizes the legal consequences of the acts committed by the person under detention. In such cases the description by the police may allay the concerns that the detainee might otherwise have. It would then be wrong for the court to conclude that the detainee ought to have inferred from the circumstances the extent of his or her jeopardy.[69]

The right under section 10(a) is intimately connected with the right to counsel since, unless the accused understands her jeopardy, she is in no position to decide whether to seek counsel. Further, a waiver of the right to counsel may be invalid where there is a breach of section 10(a).[70] Further, as noted in Chapter 3, in many situations, an accused's detention will in fact be a series of discrete detentions based on the successive use of different police powers. One would assume that, at least as an officer proceeds to a different and discrete investigation, section 10(a) may well reapply and require additional information to be given to the accused. On the other hand, given the approach to section 10(a) exhibited in the above cases, the issue will normally turn not on what the police say, but rather on what the accused can reasonably be taken to have understood in the circumstances.

3) Section 10(b) — The Right to Counsel

a) Introduction

Section 10(b) creates the right upon arrest or detention to "retain and instruct counsel without delay and to be informed of that right." Detention, which includes arrest, is discussed in Section B(1) above.

The content of the right to counsel has been the subject of considerable discussion by the Supreme Court. Generally, the Court has held that the right to counsel has an informational component and an implementational component. Recently, in *Suberu* the Court has made clear that the right to counsel does arise upon investigative detention.[71] Further, the issue of waiver of the right has received attention and needs to be contrasted with the suspect's responsibility to be reason-

---

69   *Smith*, above note 63 at 730.
70   *Ibid.*
71   *Suberu*, above note 25.

ably diligent in her attempt to contact counsel. We will also address issues around non-state actors and whether they have an obligation to provide the right to counsel.[72]

---

72 In *R. v. Luong*, 2000 ABCA 301 at para. 12 [*Luong*], the Alberta Court of Appeal provided a useful review of the caselaw concerning the right to counsel. The court there suggests that the 10(b) issues are largely fact driven enquiries:

For the assistance of trial judges charged with the onerous task of adjudicating such issues, we offer the following guidance:

1. The onus is upon the person asserting a violation of his or her *Charter* right to establish that the right as guaranteed by the *Charter* has been infringed or denied.

2. Section 10(b) imposes both informational and implementational duties on state authorities who arrest or detain a person.

3. The informational duty is to inform the detainee of his or her right to retain and instruct counsel without delay and of the existence and availability of Legal Aid and duty counsel.

4. The implementational duties are two-fold and arise upon the detainee indicating a desire to exercise his or her right to counsel.

5. The first implementational duty is "to provide the detainee with a reasonable opportunity to exercise the right (except in urgent and dangerous circumstances)." *R. v. Bartle* (1994), 92 C.C.C. (3d) 289 (S.C.C.) at 301.

6. The second implementational duty is "to refrain from eliciting evidence from the detainee until he or she has had that reasonable opportunity (again, except in cases of urgency or danger)." *R. v. Bartle, supra*, at 301.

7. A trial judge must first determine whether or not, in all of the circumstances, the police provided the detainee with a reasonable opportunity to exercise the right to counsel; the Crown has the burden of establishing that the detainee who invoked the right to counsel was provided with a reasonable opportunity to exercise the right.

8. If the trial judge concludes that the first implementation duty was breached, an infringement is made out.

9. If the trial judge is persuaded that the first implementation duty has been satisfied, only then will the trial judge consider whether the detainee, who has invoked the right to counsel, has been reasonably diligent in exercising it; the detainee has the burden of establishing that he was reasonably diligent in the exercise of his rights. *R. v. Smith* (1989), 50 C.C.C. (3d) 308 (S.C.C.) at 315-16 and 323.

10. If the detainee, who has invoked the right to counsel, is found not to have been reasonably diligent in exercising it, the implementation duties either do not arise in the first place or will be suspended. *R. v. Tremblay* (1987), 37 C.C.C. (3d) 565 (S.C.C.) at 568 [*Tremblay*]; *R. v. Ross* (1989), 46 C.C.C. (3d) 129 (S.C.C.) at 135; *R. v. Black* (1989), 50 C.C.C. (3d) 1 (S.C.C.) at 13; *R. v. Smith, supra*, at 314; *R. v. Bartle, supra*, at 301 and *R. v. Prosper* (1994), 92 C.C.C. (3d) 353 (S.C.C.) at 375-381 and 400-401. In such circumstances, no infringement is made out.

It is worth noting at the outset that the caselaw to date has mainly focused on accused persons consulting with a lawyer on the telephone while in police custody; at this initial investigative stage, the accused's principal concern often will be to receive immediate advice. There is less clarity in the cases about whether the accused has the right to have counsel present during questioning by the police. Since the issue has received little attention in the cases, it is largely unsettled. Having said that, it is submitted that in the absence of some compelling reason to the contrary, accused persons should be seen as having the right to have counsel present during investigative procedures, whether those procedures involve questioning by the police or involve other investigative steps requiring the accused's presence or participation. As we will see, this will normally not be feasible during breath-test procedures and it seems very unlikely that such procedures need be delayed while counsel makes its way to the police station. On the other hand, in most other situations there appears no significant or sufficient impediment to allowing counsel to observe and indeed actively assist the accused during police investigative steps.

This issue was dealt with by the Supreme Court of Canada in *Ross* where the issue was the applicability of the right to counsel prior to the accused participating in a police lineup conducted to establish the accused's identity as the offender. There the Crown argued that the accused did not have the right to have his counsel present during the police lineup. The Court seemingly made the assumption that that submission was correct but went on and stressed that "[e]ven if the appellants could not have their lawyers present during the line-up, this does not imply that counsel is of no assistance to a suspect."[73] Throughout the caselaw, the Court has consistently found that where the police undertake investigative steps that involve the accused, there will be a

---

11. Once a detainee asserts his or her right to counsel and is duly diligent in exercising it, (having been afforded a reasonable opportunity to exercise it), if the detainee indicates that he or she has changed his or her mind and no longer wants legal advice, the Crown is required to prove a valid waiver of the right to counsel. In such a case, state authorities have an additional informational obligation to "tell the detainee of his or her right to a reasonable opportunity to contact a lawyer and of the obligation on the part of the police during this time not to take any statements or require the detainee to participate in any potentially incriminating process until he or she has had that reasonable opportunity" (sometimes referred to as a "*Prosper* warning"). *R. v. Prosper, supra,* at 378-79. Absent such a warning, an infringement is made out.

73   *R. v. Ross,* [1989] 1 S.C.R. 3 [*Ross*].

legitimate scope for legal advice even if that advice is predictable.[74] The sense of confidence that exists between counsel and an accused should not be lightly assumed to be a matter of routine that might be overcome by various legal requirements of police advice. Indeed, it is clear that in most cases that access to legal advice will result in the court assuming that thereafter the accused is aware of his rights and that additional informational obligations in relation to subsequent rights, such as the right to silence, will not be required. For example, in *R. v. Meyers*,[75] the Newfoundland and Labrador Court of Appeal held that counsel ought to have warned the accused that he had the right to silence. Given that conclusion, the allowance of a prior telephone call to counsel was sufficient, not just in terms of the content of what the accused might say, but also in terms of the possibility that his voice itself might be used as evidence against him.

b) Informational Duties

The most obvious informational duty in section 10(b) is that explicitly stated in it: the right "to retain and instruct counsel without delay *and to be informed of that right.*" Jurisprudence from the Supreme Court, however, has made clear that the police do not satisfy their informational duties by informing an accused of the simple fact that she has the right to counsel. In *R. v. Brydges*[76] the Court found that subsection 10(b) also contained the right to be informed of the existence of whatever legal-aid and duty-counsel systems are in place in the province of arrest. Later, in *R. v. Bartle*,[77] the Court held that the information a suspect is entitled to receive from the police includes any 1-800 number that is provided by the legal-aid plan in place in that jurisdiction.

In practice, as a result of the Supreme Court decisions, police forces have created cards which are to be read to suspects upon arrest and detention. The typical police card in use in Canada reads as follows:

> You have the right to retain and instruct a lawyer without delay. This means that before we proceed with our investigation you may call any lawyer you wish or a lawyer from a free legal advice service immediately. If you want to call a lawyer from a free legal advice service, we will provide you with a telephone and you can call a toll-free

---

74 See, for example, *Simmons*, above note 17, where the Court noted that an accused detained for a customs search would have benefited from contacting counsel, if for no other reason than to be assured that the customs officers actually did have the power they purported to have: see para. 55.

75 *R. v. Meyers*, 2008 NLCA 13.

76 *R. v. Brydges*, [1990] 1 S.C.R. 190 [*Brydges*].

77 *R. v. Bartle*, [1994] 3 S.C.R. 173 [*Bartle*].

number for immediate legal advice. If you wish to contact any other lawyer, a telephone and telephone books will be provided for you. If you are charged with an offence, you may apply to Legal Aid for assistance. Do you understand: (*Record answer*) Do you want to call a free lawyer or any other lawyer? (*Record answer*).[78]

One can see that this police service has removed any reference to duty counsel, which is replaced here with "free legal advice service," presumably to make the information more accessible to the average detained person. Further, it is to be noted that the above card makes it part of the informational component that the police ask both of the questions set out therein. A failure to ask the second question as to whether the accused wants to call counsel means that without more there is neither a waiver of the right nor an assertion of the right. In many cases, the accused will assert their right to speak to counsel even if not asked and occasionally it appears the police will proceed to facilitate contact with counsel even in the absence of an express assertion by the accused. Nonetheless, it appears that, if the police do not ask the accused whether she wants to call counsel, the proper conclusion *should* be that the right to counsel is breached where the police proceed with their investigation, since the informational component has not been satisfied. As noted below, the Supreme Court has tended not to look at the issue in this way but rather has suggested that only where the accused asserts her right to counsel (with or without being asked) do the implementational duties arise.[79] In *Latimer* the Court explained:

---

78   The text of this card comes from the Calgary Police Service and was the card in use as of January 2010. Immediately following the informational component the Calgary card says this:

> Police Instructions: Where detainee wants to call a lawyer, read to detainee at time that detainee is provided access to a phone: All persons detained in police custody have the right to immediate legal advice regardless of their financial status. Detained persons also have the right to choice of counsel. You may choose to use the free legal advice number listed below, or the telephone books provided to contact a lawyer of your choice. The free legal advice number is (provide appropriate number):
> * Adults: All times — 1-866-653-3424
> * Youth: All times — (403)-297-4400

79   See the passage from *R. v. Baig,* [1987] 2 S.C.R. 537 [*Baig*], quoted below at note 108. See generally Steve Coughlan, "When Silence Isn't Golden: Waiver and the Right to Counsel" (1991) 33 Crim. L.Q. 43. An example of a failure to ask an accused whether he wants to call counsel appears to be *R. v. Elliott,* [1989] N.S.J. No. 54 (Co. Ct.), where it was found there was no breach of the right to counsel where the police only allowed the accused to contact counsel once they arrived at the police station which was some distance away. The justice held that the

The informational component of s. 10(b) is of critical importance because its purpose is to enable a detainee to make an informed decision about whether to exercise the right to counsel, and to exercise other rights protected by the *Charter,* such as the right to silence. In *R. v. Brydges,* [1990] 1 S.C.R. 190, this Court engrafted two requirements upon the informational component: first, information about access to counsel free of charge provided by provincial Legal Aid where an accused meets financial criteria with respect to need, and second, information about access to duty counsel, who provide immediate and temporary legal advice to all accused, irrespective of financial need.

However, *Brydges* only required that information be provided about the existence and availability of duty counsel; there is no doubt that the appellant was told about duty counsel here, and so *Brydges* is satisfied. *Bartle* imposed the additional requirement that persons be informed of the means necessary to access such services. However, whether the police have met this burden in a particular case must always be determined with regard to all the circumstances of that case, including the duty counsel services available at the time of arrest or detention.[80]

Apposite here is the statement by Lamer J. in *Bartle* as follows:

Under these circumstances, it is critical that the information component of the right to counsel be comprehensive in scope and that it be presented by police authorities in a "timely and comprehensible" manner: *R. v. Dubois,* [1990] R.J.Q. 681 (C.A.), (1990), 54 C.C.C. (3d) 166, at pp. 697 and 196 respectively. Unless they are clearly and fully informed of their rights at the outset, detainees cannot be expected to make informed choices and decisions about whether or not to contact counsel and, in turn, whether to exercise other rights, such as their right to silence: *Hebert.* Moreover, in light of the rule that, absent special circumstances indicating that a detainee may not understand the s. 10(b) caution, such as language difficulties or a known or obvious mental disability, police are not required to assure themselves that a detainee fully understands the s. 10(b) caution, it is important that the standard caution given to detainees be as instructive and clear

---

failure to allow the accused to request counsel resulted in no obligation on the arresting officer to afford him a reasonable opportunity to do so "at the point of detention."

80 *Latimer,* above note 32 at paras. 33–34.

as possible: *R. v. Baig*, [1987] 2 S.C.R. 537, at p. 540, and *Evans*, at p. 891.[81]

The majority did also say that:

> If the circumstances reveal, however, that a particular detainee does not understand the standard caution, the authorities must take additional steps to ensure that the detainee comprehends the rights guaranteed by s. 10(b), and the means by which they can be exercised.[82]

It is to be noted that in *R. v. Grouse* the Nova Scotia Court of Appeal held that the informational component does not need to include any advice about the right to choose counsel because

> the authorities do not require more, no additional information would be conveyed by adding more express information about counsel of choice and doing so would not help fulfil the purpose of the informational component of s. 10(b).
>
> The cases from the Supreme Court of Canada make it clear that there are three elements of the informational duty. The detained person must be told: (1) that they have the right to retain and instruct counsel without delay; (2) about access to counsel free of charge where the individual meets prescribed financial criteria set by provincial legal aid plans; and (3) about access to duty counsel and the means available to access such services: *Bartle* at 194-195; *Latimer* at para. 33. The additional requirement advocated by the appellant is not supported by authority.[83]

It has also not been decided that the informational component should contain information about the right to consult counsel in private, although it has been suggested that this might be useful.[84] The issue of privacy is discussed further in Section C(3)(c) below.

There have been cases where the accused may not have understood the information provided. In such situations it appears that, if the in-

---

81 *Bartle*, above note 77 at para. 19. In *Baig*, above note 79 at 540, the Court expressly adopted the statement in *R. v. Anderson* (1984), 10 C.C.C. (3d) 417 (C.A.), wherein that Court said at 431:

> . . . I am of the view that, absent proof of circumstances indicating that the accused did not understand his right to retain counsel when he was informed of it, the onus has to be on him to prove that he asked for the right but it was denied or he was denied any opportunity to even ask for it. No such evidence was put forth in this case.

82 *Bartle*, *ibid.* at para. 39.
83 *R. v. Grouse*, 2004 NSCA 108 at paras. 22–23.
84 See: *R. v. Parrill* (1998), 169 Nfld. & P.E.I.R. 28 (Nfld. C.A.) [*Parrill*].

formation was clear and full, the informational component will have been honoured unless the police should have known that there was a defect in understanding.[85] Often this will depend upon what the police know about the accused and on what the accused said to the police. In *R. v. Evans* the Supreme Court of Canada said this on the point:

> I am satisfied that the police did not comply with s. 10(b). It is true that they informed the appellant of his right to counsel. But they did not explain that right when he indicated that he did not understand it. A person who does not understand his or her right cannot be expected to assert it. The purpose of s. 10(b) is to require the police to communicate the right to counsel to the detainee. In most cases one can infer from the circumstances that the accused understands what he has been told. In such cases, the police are required to go no further (unless the detainee indicates a desire to retain counsel, in which case they must comply with the second and third duties set out above). But where, as here, there is a positive indication that the accused does not understand his right to counsel, the police cannot rely on their mechanical recitation of the right to the accused; they must take steps to facilitate that understanding.[86]

As noted above, in *Evans* the accused had a mental deficiency bordering on mental retardation, and so the Court stressed that, since the police were aware of his mental incapacity, they were required to take "special care" in the circumstances.[87]

In *R. v. Burlingham* the Supreme Court suggests that further information must be given where confusion about the right to counsel is caused by the police in their questioning of an accused. There, in regard to the accused's misunderstanding, the Court said that he need

---

85   In *R. v. Chisholm*, 2001 NSCA 32, the Court of Appeal found a breach of the right to counsel since the officer did not understand the difference between legal aid and duty counsel and failed to clearly inform the detainee of the 1-800 number that was available for the latter.

86   *Evans*, above note 50 at 891.

87   *Evans*, *ibid.* at 890. In *Latimer*, above note 32, the Court also said at para. 38:

> I hasten to add that there will be cases in which it will be necessary to provide more information to an accused or detained person than was provided to Mr. Latimer about the means to access duty counsel. For example, a young person, or even more obviously an individual who is visually impaired, may require more assistance from the police than Mr. Latimer. As well, someone whose facility in the language of the jurisdiction is not sufficient to understand the information provided about duty counsel may require more explicit information than was provided to Mr. Latimer. This list of examples should not be taken to be exhaustive.

not have accepted the advice of a "random lawyer"[88] instead of that his own lawyer, who knew the facts of the case but was unavailable on the weekend:

> When it is evident that there is such a misunderstanding, the police cannot rely on a mechanical recitation of the right to counsel in order to discharge their responsibilities under s. 10(b): *R. v. Evans* . . . . They must take positive steps to facilitate that understanding. In the case at bar, not only did the police fail to take affirmative steps to clear up the appellant's confusion, but they also in fact created this confusion in the first place.[89]

The Court in *Burlingham*[90] found the confusion to be at least partly created by what the police said to the accused about counsel. It held that the police must refrain in their interaction with the accused from "belittling" counsel so as to undermine the advice given by counsel, especially in the context of police interrogations. The police were found to have done so during their interrogation of the accused in a case where the arrest occurred on a weekend and the chosen counsel was known to be unavailable. The Court was of the view that

> s. 10(b) specifically prohibits the police, as they did in this case, from belittling an accused's lawyer with the express goal or effect of undermining the accused's confidence in and relationship with defence counsel. It makes no sense for s. 10(b) of the *Charter* to provide for the right to retain and instruct counsel if law enforcement authorities are able to undermine either an accused's confidence in his or her lawyer or the solicitor-client relationship.[91]

In *R. v. Edmonson* the Saskatchewan Court of Appeal explained this requirement and suggested that

> the test is whether the remarks in issue, viewed in the context of the interview as a whole, served to so belittle counsel, with the express goal or effect of undermining the accused's confidence in and relationship with counsel, as to have violated the accused's right to counsel and vitiated his choice to remain silent.[92]

The Court of Appeal stressed that this requirement is about more than the right to silence including the common law confession rule, and

---

88   *Burlingham*, above note 52 at para. 16.
89   *Ibid.* at para. 18.
90   *Ibid.*
91   *Ibid.* at para. 14.
92   *R. v. Edmonson*, 2005 SKCA 51 at para. 38.

its decision shows that the right to counsel may play a significant role in the context of those issues as well as be an issue on its own. Those issues are beyond the scope of this discussion but on the facts the Court found that the actions of the police were not sufficient in all the circumstances to breach either the right to counsel or the right to silence.

In *R. v. Whittle*, a case in which the accused was mentally ill, the Supreme Court found section 10(b) to have been satisfied since the accused was fit to stand trial:

> In exercising the right to counsel or waiving the right, the accused must possess the limited cognitive capacity that is required for fitness to stand trial. The accused must be capable of communicating with counsel to instruct counsel, and understand the function of counsel and that he or she can dispense with counsel even if this is not in the accused's best interests. It is not necessary that the accused possess analytical ability. The level of cognitive ability is the same as that required with respect to the confession rule and the right to silence. The accused must have the mental capacity of an operating mind as outlined above.[93]

The *Youth Criminal Justice Act* contains a special provision on the right to counsel which specifies obligations relating to informing an accused young person of the right to counsel and provides the right to have a parent or guardian present. In addition, the section requires a written waiver of the rights it details.[94]

The informational component of section 10(b), like that of section 10(a), may also apply on more than one occasion during an investigation. In *R. v. Black* the Supreme Court made the requirement clear that, where there is a change in the investigation (in this case an investigation of an aggravated assault became an investigation of a murder), it was incumbent upon the police to reread the informational component to the accused.[95] As the majority of the Supreme Court explained in *R. v. Evans*:

> A second violation of the appellant's s. 10(b) right occurred when the police failed to reiterate the appellant's right to counsel after the nature of their investigation changed and the appellant became a suspect in the two killings. This Court's judgment in R. v. Black, *supra*, per Wilson J., makes it clear that there is a duty on the police to

---

93   *R. v. Whittle*, [1994] 2 S.C.R. 914 at para. 51.

94   *Youth Criminal Justice Act*, S.C. 2002, c. 1, s. 146. See, generally, *R. v. L.T.H.*, 2008 SCC 49.

95   *Black*, above note 57 at 153.

advise the accused of his or her right to counsel a second time when new circumstances arise indicating that the accused is a suspect for a different, more serious crime than was the case at the time of the first warning. This is because the accused's decision as to whether to obtain a lawyer may well be affected by the seriousness of the charge he or she faces. The new circumstances give rise to a new and different situation, one requiring reconsideration of an initial waiver of the right to counsel . . . . I add that to hold otherwise leaves open the possibility of police manipulation, whereby the police — hoping to question a suspect in a serious crime without the suspect's lawyer present — bring in the suspect on a relatively minor offence, one for which a person may not consider it necessary to have a lawyer immediately present, in order to question him or her on the more serious crime.[96]

The majority then made clear that:

I should not be taken as suggesting that the police, in the course of an exploratory investigation, must reiterate the right to counsel every time that the investigation touches on a different offence. I do, however, affirm that in order to comply with the first of the three duties set out above, the police must restate the accused's right to counsel when there is a fundamental and discrete change in the purpose of the investigation, one involving a different and unrelated offence or a significantly more serious offence than that contemplated at the time of the warning.[97]

A related question arose in R. v. Chalmers.[98] There the accused was suspected of having killed his wife and had agreed to take a polygraph test. He was told at the start of the test that he was not detained and that he was free to leave at any time. He was also told that he had the right to talk to a lawyer, that the officer would facilitate contact with counsel if the accused wished, and that this was an open offer. About three hours later, the accused confessed to the offence. The accused argued that this created a significant change in his jeopardy and that he ought to have been rewarned of the right to counsel at that point.

The Ontario Court of Appeal upheld the trial judge's decision that there was no violation of section 10(b). The accused had known from the start of the interview that he was a suspect and had been informed of his right to counsel in that context. He understood the position he

---

96 *Evans*, above note 50 at 892.
97 *Ibid.* at 893.
98 *R. v. Chalmers*, 2009 ONCA 268.

was in, and that did not change with the transition from being interviewed to being detained. In addition:

> [W]hile it is clear that the close factual connection relating the warning to the detention is all that is required to satisfy s. 10(b) where the warning is given before the detention, I note that the [sic] there was also a close temporal connection between the earlier warnings and the appellant's detention. He was initially cautioned between around 12:56 and 1:10 p.m., and was reminded again of his rights at 3:51 P.M., after the polygraph test and only about half an hour before the first confession. The final conversation about consulting a lawyer, before the admission, occurred only moments before that happened. The appellant never left the same interview room and he never dealt with anyone other than Det. Sgt. Murray during this time.[99]

In these circumstances there was no section 10(b) violation.

Finally, a valid waiver of the informational components of section 10(b) will be a rarity. Waiver of information duties will be discussed below, and is a difficult area. However, the Court has concluded that waiver will arise with regard to informational duties only in exceptional circumstances. The reason for this is quite straightforward. A valid waiver depends on the accused having been fully informed of the nature of the right he is waiving.[100] Only in unusual circumstances would an accused be fully informed of the content of the right without having been told of the informational components. This could happen, however: for example, when it becomes necessary to rewarn an accused in the middle of an interrogation because the nature of the jeopardy has changed. In such cases, it might be safe not to mention again the telephone number for duty counsel, for instance.

c)   Implementational Duties

As early as 1987, in *R. v. Manninen*, the Supreme Court ruled that section

> 10(b) imposes at least two duties on the police in addition to the duty to inform the detainee of his rights. First, the police must provide the detainee with a reasonable opportunity to exercise the right to retain and instruct counsel without delay. The detainee is in the control of the police and he cannot exercise his right to counsel unless the police provide him with a reasonable opportunity to do so. This aspect

---

99   *Ibid.* at para. 43.
100   *Bartle*, above note 77.

of the right to counsel was recognized in Canadian law well before the advent of the *Charter*.[101]

The Court then noted the second implementational duty:

> Further, s. 10(b) imposes on the police the duty to cease questioning or otherwise attempting to elicit evidence from the detainee until he has had a reasonable opportunity to retain and instruct counsel. The purpose of the right to counsel is to allow the detainee not only to be informed of his rights and obligations under the law but, equally if not more important, to obtain advice as to how to exercise those rights. In this case, the police officers correctly informed the respondent of his right to remain silent and the main function of counsel would be to confirm the existence of that right and then to advise him as to how to exercise it. For the right to counsel to be effective, the detainee must have access to this advice before he is questioned or otherwise required to provide evidence.[102]

The Court emphasized that the police had an obligation to "facilitate" contact with counsel where the desire to contact counsel is asserted by the detainee.[103]

While "urgency" in the police investigation has been recognized in *obiter* as allowing a delay in the implementational duties, police "expediency" is not to be considered urgent.[104] On the other hand, where the detainee deliberately obstructs the police or makes the investigation difficult, a court may find the accused to have not been reasonably diligent in attempting to contact counsel and, in any event, is unlikely to grant a section 24(2) remedy.[105] *Manninen* requires that the police, on assertion of the right by the suspect, refrain from asking questions of the accused until she has had a reasonable opportunity to speak to counsel. An important point to note here is that these correlative imple-

---

101 *R. v. Manninen*, [1987] 1 S.C.R. 1233 at 1241 [*Manninen*].

102 *Ibid.* at 1242–43. The obligation to not "elicit" evidence was discussed in the context of the s. 7 right of silence in *R. v. Broyles*, [1991] 3 S.C.R. 595 at paras. 31–34.

103 This requirement was stressed in the pre-*Charter* judgment in *R. v. Brownridge*, [1972] S.C.R. 926, where Laskin J., as he then was, in a minority concurring judgment, spoke of a "correlative obligation" upon the police to facilitate contact with counsel.

104 *Manninen*, above note 101 at 1244. In *R. v. Prosper*, [1994] 3 S.C.R. 236 [*Prosper*], the Court stated that the two-hour limit in s. 258 of the *Criminal Code* relating to breath tests is not sufficient to allow the police to deny contact with counsel at least in a jurisdiction without a duty-counsel program (paras. 42–45). For a useful review of the principles, see *R. v. Turney*, 2000 ABPC 206.

105 See *Tremblay*, above note 10.

mentational duties arise *only* where the accused expresses an interest in having counsel. All the informational duties arise automatically and for all accused, whether that person expresses an interest in counsel or not. In contrast, the duties to facilitate contact with counsel and to hold off from eliciting evidence do not arise unless they are triggered by the accused requesting counsel.

The "request" might be perfectly explicit. Manninen, for example, very specifically said, "I ain't saying anything until I see my lawyer. I want to see my lawyer."[106] However, a less straightforward expression of interest in counsel might also be sufficient. Brydges, for example, upon being told of the right to counsel, said, "Well. Do they have any free Legal Aid or anything like that up here . . . Won't be able to afford anyone, hey? That's the main thing."[107] The Supreme Court upheld the trial judge's finding that this equivocal response amounted to a request for counsel and therefore triggered the correlative duties.

However, even if the request can be equivocal, there must be some sort of assertion of the right by the accused, or the implementational duties do not arise. As the Supreme Court concluded in *Baig*:

[O]nce the police have complied with s. 10(*b*), by advising the accused without delay of his right to counsel without delay, there are no correlative duties triggered and cast upon them until the accused, if he so chooses, has indicated his desire to exercise his right to counsel.[108]

On the other hand, in *R. v. Weeseekase*,[109] where the accused was remanded and had been approached by a police officer about making a statement, the right to counsel did not arise, according to the Court. Weeseekase told the officer that she wanted to speak to her lawyer before making a statement and the officer asked the remand facility staff to assist her in doing so. Shortly thereafter, the officer received a phone call from staff saying that the accused had changed her mind and now wanted to give a statement. The officer postponed the meeting until the next day, at which point he asked her if she had contacted her counsel. She said she had left a message but had not spoken to him, but nonetheless wanted to give a statement. The Court of Appeal held that section 10(b) was not really relevant at all in these circumstances. It provides rights "on arrest or detention," but in this case the accused had been in

---

106 *Manninen*, above note 101 at 1241.
107 *Brydges*, above note 76 at 540.
108 *Baig*, above note 79 at 540, but see the discussion above at note 79 concerning the issue as to whether the police should be required to ask, as part of the informational component, the accused whether she wishes to contact counsel.
109 *R. v. Weeseekase*, 2007 SKCA 115 [*Weeseekase*].

custody for over a week, had already appeared in court twice, and had spoken to her lawyer on several occasions.[110]

In *R. v. Dombrowski*, the Saskatchewan Court of Appeal stated:

> The basic right to counsel under s. 10(b) of the *Charter* is now part of the supreme law of Canada and must be respected by the courts if it is to have any meaning for the average citizen. This right must also be respected and taken seriously by law enforcement officers. In this case, the arresting officers had no right to limit the appellant's opportunity to contact counsel until they returned to the detachment office. With the availability of a telephone at the business premises of Co-op Implements, there was no justification for limiting or delaying the opportunity. We appreciate that regard must be had to the circumstances of each case but in this case we hold that the incriminating evidence should be excluded under s. 24(2) of the *Charter*. To hold otherwise would whittle away the rights accorded to every citizen under s. 10(b). The admission of the oral statements would in the circumstances of this case bring the administration of justice into disrepute.[111]

In *R. v. Lewis*[112] it was held that an accused arrested at a train station was given the opportunity to consult counsel without delay even though he was not permitted to call until he was taken to the police station. The police station was only a few minutes away, he was arrested in a public part of the railway station, and there was no private phone available. The police did not interrogate the accused in the interim, and so had properly held off in that respect. Although they did search his knapsack before he called counsel, searches incident to arrest are not captured by the duty to hold off.

On the other hand, in *R. v. MacEachern*,[113] some of the same officers and the same dog stopped the accused in the train station. An officer touched the accused on the arm and directed him to the side of the station, saying to a shuttle bus driver, "He's not going anywhere." The officers asked for the accused's train ticket, boarding pass, and identification, in order to determine whether he was on a one-way trip,

---

110 But see *R. v. Ngo* (2003), 327 A.R. 320 (C.A.) where the Court held that the accused's right to counsel was breached when the police failed to allow access to counsel when questioning the accused even though the accused had been detained three days earlier (and presumably earlier provided his right to counsel) and was being held for transport from Vancouver to Calgary.

111 *R. v. Dombrowski*, (1985), 44 C.R. (3d) 1 at 9 [*Dombrowski*].

112 *R. v. Lewis*, 2007 NSCA 2.

113 *R. v. MacEachern*, 2007 NSCA 69.

had paid cash, and had purchased the ticket at the last minute. After getting this information, the police arrested the accused and informed him of his right to counsel, which the accused immediately indicated he wished to exercise. On these facts, the Court of Appeal held that the accused had been detained before the point at which he was arrested, and so should have been told of the right to counsel at that earlier point. Although this meant there had been a *Charter* breach, the Court of Appeal concluded that the evidence should not be excluded.

In *R. v. Montgomery* the accused was arrested in a parking lot on drug-trafficking charges but was not permitted to call counsel until several hours later, at the police station, although he had a cellphone with him and could have called immediately. The British Columbia Court of Appeal upheld the decision that there had been no violation of section 10(b):

> The police considered the arrest to be one of high risk. The appellant was believed to be associated with an organization that used violence. It would have been difficult for the police to ensure that the call was not used for an improper purpose and to provide the appellant with privacy at the scene of his arrest while ensuring that he was secure.

> The police station had only one private phone for conversations with lawyers, and the police had to deal with the three other men arrested with the appellant, as well as an unrelated matter. The trial judge made the finding of fact that the appellant was provided access to counsel as soon as was reasonably possible in all of the circumstances. I am not persuaded that the judge made a palpable error in making this finding.[114]

d) Reasonable Opportunity to Contact Chosen Counsel

Generally, the caselaw further allows detainees their choice of counsel, although in some circumstances the unavailability of counsel of choice may result in the detainee being required to contact other counsel. It would seem that this decision is based on whether the delay caused by the unavailability of counsel is unreasonable in the circumstances.[115]

---

114 *R. v. Montgomery*, 2009 BCCA 41 at paras. 35–36.

115 See *Manninen*, above note 101. The issue of choice of counsel is also recognized in the cases concerning waiver and reasonable diligence discussed in Sections C(3)(e) and (f), below in this chapter. See also notes 116 and 139, below. In *R. v. Traicheff*, 2007 ONCJ 564 at para. 27, the justice was of the view that the choice of counsel did require the police to inform the accused that his lawyer had not called back after twenty-three minutes; they should also have sought other

What is reasonable is fact specific but on at least two occasions the Supreme Court has suggested that this period would be as long as the next business day.[116] On the other hand, in impaired-driving cases involving breath tests, the Ontario Court of Appeal has held that if the counsel chosen is not available within the two-hour period, the suspect is required to contact counsel that is available.[117] The actual conclusion in these cases appears to be that the accused is not acting diligently when refusing to call duty counsel when the two-hour limit is approaching.

It is trite to note that the accused is not allowed only one call. Even before the *Charter* it was the case that the accused could make as many phone calls as necessary to obtain the advice which he seeks. In *R. v. Louttit* in 1974, the Manitoba Court of Appeal said: "The 'one phone call' rule is a fiction propagated by Hollywood. Reasonable conduct by the police is always required, and that may in appropriate circumstances require that a plurality of phone calls be permitted."[118] This position was expressly adopted by the Ontario Court of Appeal after the *Charter* in *R. v. Pavel*.[119]

In *R. v. Badgerow* the Ontario Court of Appeal found that the accused had been denied a reasonable opportunity to consult with counsel. The trial judge had found that this duty was satisfied, because the accused had replied "yes" when asked whether he was satisfied he had had an opportunity to speak with counsel. The accused then asked for another phone call, which request was ignored. In fact, the accused had spoken to a lawyer very briefly but that lawyer was only attempting to contact the accused's actual lawyer. The Court of Appeal held that the trial judge erred. The Court of Appeal acknowledged that exactly what the police must do to comply with section 10(b) varies from case

---

contact information for the lawyer before requiring that the accused choose another counsel. The two-hour limit was not yet close, although the justice did not exclude the evidence. Likewise, in *R. v. Davidson*, 2004 ABPC 62, the Provincial Court judge excluded the evidence where the accused did not have a reasonable opportunity to contact counsel of his choice (see para. 33).

116 See *Black*, above note 57 at 155, where the Court was of the view that a delay of eight hours was not unreasonable where the charge was first-degree murder. In *Burlingham*, above note 52, the Court held that, where the interrogation occurred on the weekend, the police should have waited until the Monday since they were aware that the accused's lawyer was unavailable until then. Similarly, in *R. v. Clarkson*, [1986] 1 S.C.R. 383 [*Clarkson*], the Court held that the police interrogation should have been delayed until the accused sobered up.

117 See *R. v. Richfield* (2003), 175 O.A.C. 54 at para. 12 (C.A.), and *R. v. Van Binnendyk*, 2007 ONCA 537 at paras. 9–10.

118 *R. v. Louttit*, [1974] M.J. No. 76 (C.A.).

119 *R. v. Pavel* (1989), 36 O.A.C. 328 (C.A.).

to case, and that the police "cannot be expected to be mind readers." Nonetheless,

> they are not entitled to ignore statements by an accused that raise a reasonable prospect that the accused has not exercised his or her s. 10(b) rights. Rather, where an accused makes such a statement, the police must be diligent in ensuring that an accused has a reasonable opportunity to exercise his or her rights, and may not rely on answers to ambiguous questions as a basis for assuming that an accused has exercised his or her rights.[120]

The Court of Appeal ordered a new trial.

It seems that the basic protection provided by the right to counsel is normally taken to be satisfied if the accused has had an opportunity to speak to a lawyer. However, in *R. v. Osmond*, the British Columbia Court of Appeal held that the right encompasses more than just that. The court held that the underlying purpose of speaking to a lawyer relates to the right to silence, but also that that is important in two ways. The accused is entitled to: "1. confirmation of the right to silence; and 2. advice on how to exercise that right."[121] In other words, an accused person might speak with a lawyer, but the advice received might be so insufficient that the accused's right to counsel has not been complied with. In *Osmond* the court found that a two-minute call with a "*Brydges* list" lawyer contracted by the province to provide immediate and free legal advice was insufficient where the accused was young and was being investigated for murder. Thus, the accused's confession was found to be obtained in breach of his right to counsel and was inadmissible.[122]

e) Duty upon Accused to be Reasonably Diligent

If the detained individual asserts the wish to speak to counsel, the duty of the detained individual to be reasonably diligent then arises. It seems generally true that, when there is a failure to be reasonably diligent in attempting to contact counsel, "the implementation duties either do not arise in the first place or will be suspended."[123] What the failure to be reasonably diligent means has engendered considerable confusion in

---

120 *R. v. Badgerow*, 2008 ONCA 605 at para. 46.

121 *R. v. Osmond*, 2007 BCCA 470 at para. 20.

122 See also *R. v. Beieril*, 2007 ONCJ 267, where the accused testified that the advice from duty counsel was that the accused should refuse the breath-test demand. The defence argued the defence of officially induced error. The defence was rejected in the circumstances.

123 *Luong*, above note 72 at para. 12.

the cases. Interestingly, the failure operates in a similar way as a waiver of the right to counsel. It allows the police to continue their investigation by asking questions of the accused or taking bodily samples or breath tests from the accused. Below we will discuss waiver but here it is to be noted that where the accused is found not to be reasonably diligent no breach will be found even though the accused never expressly waives her right to counsel and never speaks to counsel. Unfortunately, there do not appear to be the same protections in place in this area as there are in the waiver cases discussed below, in terms of the accused's need to understand the consequences of giving up his right.

In *R. v. Tremblay* the Court said:

> Generally speaking, if a detainee is not being reasonably diligent in the exercise of his rights, the correlative duties set out in this Court's decision in *R. v. Manninen*, [1987] 1 S.C.R. 1233, imposed on the police in a situation where a detainee has requested the assistance of counsel[,] are suspended and are not a bar to their continuing their investigation and calling upon him to give a sample of his breath.[124]

A majority of the Supreme Court applied this requirement on the facts of *R. v. Smith*.[125] In a plurality opinion, the majority was of the view that Smith's "most casual"[126] attitude to the exercise of his right to counsel resulted in the suspension of the right. At 9:00 p.m. at night, the accused decided not to call his lawyer when he found only his lawyer's office telephone number in the telephone book, and he thus advised the police that he would contact his lawyer in the morning. Despite the police requests that he try the number, the accused refused and simply told the police he would call the next day. On the facts, while the accused clearly asserted his desire to speak to counsel, he took no steps beyond looking in the phone book to attempt to do so, despite police encouragement. Here the "suspension" of the right operated so as to no longer require the police to hold off questioning the accused. Accordingly, in *Smith* the four-person majority held Smith's later statement to be admissible in evidence as not being obtained in breach of the right to counsel.[127]

To fully analyze the duty to be reasonably diligent, it is necessary to first discuss the principles applicable to the waiver of the right to counsel.

---

124 *Tremblay*, above note 10 at 439. See also *Ross*, above note 73 at 11, and *Black*, above note 57 at 154.
125 *R. v. Smith*, [1989] 2 S.C.R. 368.
126 *Ibid.* at 391, Sopinka J.
127 For a similar result, see *R. v. Payeur*, 2005 BCPC 155.

f)   Waiver of the Right to Counsel

As explained above, the section 10(b) law on the issue of waiver of the right to counsel was built upon the Supreme Court's earlier decisions relating to waiver of statutory protections.[128] Indeed, it is useful to note that waiver is not unique to subsection 10(b), since the issue arises throughout *Charter* jurisprudence and in particular in the context of so-called consent searches.[129] On the whole, it is true to say that upon detention, in the absence of a suspect actually receiving advice from counsel, there will be a breach of the right to counsel in the absence of a valid waiver unless the accused is not reasonably diligent in exercising the right. The caselaw at times has suggested that the actions of the accused might "impliedly" waive counsel but whenever the argument is made there tends to be confusion as to nature of the waiver requirement. In *R. v. Clarkson* the majority said:

> Given the concern for fair treatment of an accused person which underlies such constitutional civil liberties as the right to counsel in s. 10(b) of the *Charter*, it is evident that any alleged waiver of this right by an accused must be carefully considered and that the accused's awareness of the consequences of what he or she was saying is crucial. Indeed, this Court stated with respect to the waiver of statutory procedural guarantees in *Korponay v. Attorney General of Canada* . . . that any waiver ". . . is dependent upon it being clear and unequivocal that the person is waiving the procedural safeguard and is doing so with full knowledge of the rights the procedure was enacted to protect and of the effect the waiver will have on those rights in the process."[130]

In *Evans* the accused made an unsuccessful attempt to call his lawyer and then provided a written statement. The majority held that he had not implicitly waived his right to counsel. The Crown had stated that the appellant was given the choice of contacting his lawyer later or proceeding with the written statement, and that he agreed to continue

---

128   See *Korponay v. Canada (A.G.)*, [1982] 1 S.C.R. 41 [*Korponay*].

129   See, generally, in the context of waiver of the s. 8 right to be free from unreasonable search and seizure: *R. v. Borden*, [1994] 3 S.C.R. 145 at 164–65; *R. v. Wills* (1992), 7 O.R. (3d) 337 (C.A.); *R. v. Luc*, 2004 SKCA 117; *R. v. Perello*, 2005 SKCA 8; *R. v. Sewell*, 2003 SKCA 52; *R. v. Rutten*, 2006 SKCA 17; *R. v. Williams* (1995), 58 B.C.A.C. 53 (C.A.); and *R. v. Deprez* (1994), 97 Man. R. (2d) 272 (C.A.). See, generally, Glen Luther, "Consent Search and Reasonable Expectation of Privacy: Twin Barriers to the Reasonable Expectation of Privacy in Canada" (2008) 41 U.B.C. L. Rev. 1.

130   *Clarkson*, above note 116 at 394, citing *Korponay*, above note 128 at 49 [emphasis omitted].

with the written statement. It argued that this "cured" the earlier section 10(b) violations, with the result that the written confession was obtained in conformity with section 10(b) of the *Charter* as his actions amounted to an implicit waiver of his right to consul with counsel. The majority disagreed:

> Such an argument could only succeed if it were concluded that by making the written confession the appellant had waived his s. 10(b) right. In *Manninen, supra*, this Court held that a person may implicitly, by words or conduct, waive his or her rights under s. 10(b). The Court cautioned, however, that "the standard will be very high" (at p. 1244) and referred to its judgment in *Clarkson v. The Queen*, [1986] 1 S.C.R. 383, where it was held that for a voluntary waiver to be valid and effective it must be premised on a true appreciation of the consequences of giving up the right . . . . I am not satisfied that he appreciated the consequences of making the written statement and thereby waiving his right to counsel or, to put it another way, that he waived his right "with full knowledge of the rights the procedure was enacted to protect and of the effect the waiver will have on those rights in the process": *Korponay v. Attorney General of Canada*, [1982] 1 S.C.R. 41, at p. 49, as cited in *Clarkson v. The Queen*, supra, at p. 395 (emphasis deleted). Accordingly, I am of the view that the written statement was also taken in violation of the appellant's s. 10(b) right.[131]

In *Evans*, of course, the accused suffered from "subnormal mental capacity" and in *Clarkson* the accused was significantly intoxicated. These factors therefore cause some confusion for the situation of an accused who is not impaired by alcohol or drugs and who is of "normal" capacity. The Court, in stressing the incapacity issues present in the two cases, seemingly leaves open the possibility that an accused who knows he is allowed to wait to speak to counsel but who goes along with the police's desire to proceed to questioning waives his right to counsel.

On the other hand, in *Ross*, a case where there were no particular special circumstances about the accused, the Supreme Court was clear that an implicit waiver should not be found when the purpose of the right to counsel is "contradicted":

> [T]hat the accused did not refuse to participate in the line-up cannot by itself amount to a waiver of the right to counsel. The very purpose of the right to counsel is to ensure that those who are accused or detained be advised of their legal rights and how to exercise them

---

131 *Evans*, above note 50 at 893.

when dealing with the authorities. It would contradict this purpose to conclude that a detained or accused person has waived the right to counsel simply by submitting, before being instructed by counsel, to precisely those attempts to secure the detainee's participation from which the police should refrain. Here, the appellants were unable to make an informed decision about participating in the line-up because they were ignorant of their legal position, not having been advised by their lawyers. Nor did the police even give them the choice as to whether they should participate. In the circumstances, therefore, to conclude that the appellants had waived their rights by participating in the line-up would render the right to counsel nugatory.[132]

One particular circumstance in which the issue of waiver arises is where the accused seemingly changes her mind about contacting counsel. Of course, in this instance, the duty to hold off in the investigation would arise when the accused first asserted a desire to speak to counsel; accordingly, unless the accused either is not diligent in exercising the right or the accused waives counsel, the police cannot proceed to questioning or the taking of bodily samples. It therefore seems wrong to suggest that, where the accused has asserted a desire to speak to counsel, the police might be allowed to question the accused in the absence of an express waiver (and rely upon the accused's answers as implicitly waiving the right) since the duty to hold off squarely arises in such situations.

In *Prosper* the Supreme Court was clear that the burden to prove waiver is upon the Crown where the accused had initially asserted the right:

> Given the importance of the right to counsel, I would also say with respect to waiver that once a detainee asserts the right there must be a clear indication that he or she has changed his or her mind, and the burden of establishing an unequivocal waiver will be on the Crown: *Ross*, at pp. 11-12. Further, the waiver must be free and voluntary and it must not be the product of either direct or indirect compulsion. This Court has indicated on numerous occasions that the standard required for an effective waiver of the right to counsel is very high: *Clarkson v. The Queen*, [1986] 1 S.C.R. 383, *Manninen*, and *Evans*. As I said in *Bartle*, at pp. 192-94 and 206, a person who waives a right must know what he or she is giving up if the waiver is to be valid. [133]

---

132 *Ross*, above note 73 at 14–15.
133 *Prosper*, above note 104 at para. 44.

In addition, the Court went on to find that, where the accused has a change of mind, a further informational warning, now referred to in the caselaw as a "*Prosper* warning," must be provided:

> In circumstances where a detainee has asserted his or her right to counsel and has been reasonably diligent in exercising it, yet has been unable to reach a lawyer because duty counsel is unavailable at the time of detention, courts must ensure that the *Charter*-protected right to counsel is not too easily waived. Indeed, I find that an additional informational obligation on police will be triggered once a detainee, who has previously asserted the right to counsel, indicates that he or she has changed his or her mind and no longer wants legal advice. At this point, police will be required to tell the detainee of his or her right to a reasonable opportunity to contact a lawyer and of the obligation on the part of the police during this time not to take any statements or require the detainee to participate in any potentially incriminating process until he or she has had that reasonable opportunity. This additional informational requirement on police ensures that a detainee who persists in wanting to waive the right to counsel will know what it is that he or she is actually giving up.[134]

As can be seen in the above analysis, the role of duty counsel in the Canadian legal landscape has created issues with respect to the choice of counsel and the duty to be diligent in exercising the right to counsel. Duty-counsel schemes are designed to provide immediate legal advice by a lawyer, who is not intended to be the suspect's lawyer for any other purpose in the future but who can facilitate immediate legal advice to detained individuals. In *Bartle*[135] and *Prosper*[136] the Court declined to explicitly require governments to create duty-counsel systems, but it did point out the benefits to the police that such systems offered. The timely provision of legal advice to detained individuals in fact fosters efficient police investigations, and, depending on whether individuals are required to speak to duty counsel to the exclusion of their chosen private lawyer, ensures that police can proceed with their investigation with minimal delays. Indeed, given the implementational duty to hold off from eliciting evidence until an accused has had the opportunity to consult with counsel, combined with the fact that in the breathalyzer context the police need to conduct the test within two hours if they are to obtain the evidentiary advantage of a breathalyzer certificate,

---

134 *Ibid.* at para. 43.
135 *Bartle*, above note 77.
136 *Prosper*, above note 104.

provinces were left with little real alternative but to create duty-counsel systems.

The existence of a choice of counsel can be seen as allowing suspects to delay investigations. Nonetheless, the Supreme Court has recognized that choice of counsel is something of value in our system. Unfortunately, the Court has been somewhat inconsistent on this front. While asserting a right to choose counsel, the Court said in *Prosper* that the existence of a duty-counsel scheme in the jurisdiction of arrest or detention will be relevant to the issues in a breach-of-counsel case and in particular will be relevant where there is a concern about the two-hour limit in breath-test cases. Naturally, courts of appeal, as noted above, have taken this to mean that in some cases, where duty counsel is available, detained persons will be required to contact duty counsel to the exclusion of their counsel of choice where the counsel of choice is not easily and quickly reached.[137] There does not appear to be any informational requirement that ensures that accused persons are informed that their failure to speak to duty counsel might result in a court finding them to have failed in their duty to be reasonably diligent.

Further, in *R. v. Willier*,[138] a case involving a murder charge, the accused was unable to contact his counsel of choice on the weekend but did speak to duty counsel. The Alberta Court of Appeal held that the accused waived his right to speak to counsel of choice apparently by speaking to duty counsel and choosing thereafter to speak to the police. It found that he had been told he could wait until the next day to speak to his counsel of choice but chose not to do so. The oddity here is that there apparently was no express waiver by the accused of his stated desire to speak to his chosen counsel and yet the majority found a waiver despite also finding that he had acted diligently. In this situation it seems that, if the accused had refused to speak to duty counsel, there may have been a breach of his right to counsel if the police had proceeded to question him.

In some jurisdictions where the duty-counsel calls are handled by a central system operated by Legal Aid, the police have run afoul of the choice-of-counsel rule when they assume or force upon the accused an obligation to speak to the readily available legal-aid office. In *R. v. McLaren*, for example, a Saskatchewan Queen's Bench justice noted that, when read the informational component, the accused said he did not

---

137 *Ibid.*
138 *R. v. Willier*, 2008 ABCA 126, leave to appeal to S.C.C. granted, [2008] S.C.C.A. No. 390.

have a lawyer and would phone his wife. This was interpreted by the officer as the expression of a desire on the accused's part to consult with a lawyer. The officer advised him that telephone contact with Legal Aid would be made once they were at the police station. The judge found that "[t]he fact that he did not currently have a lawyer on retainer does not mean it can be assumed he waived choosing one and opted to retain a Legal Aid counsel."[139] Further, the justice noted that the practice of some police detachments to provide telephones without a dial and through which the police acted as "gatekeeper" raised concerns about the accused's ability to make a choice as to the counsel to which they wished to speak. He said:

> This does not mean that a detained person cannot elicit police assistance or that the police may not offer assistance. The implementational duties imposed on the police will need to be exercised in a wide variety of circumstances, one size will not fit all. The test will be what was or was not reasonable. To provide a phone book to one who cannot read or whose reading glasses are broken may well not constitute a reasonable opportunity. To fail to provide a phone book or a list of lawyers to one who is capable of using it and to fail to provide a phone with which a lawyer can be contacted without passing through a police intermediary as occurred in this case does not constitute the reasonable opportunity required by s. 10.[140]

---

139 R. v. McLaren, 2001 SKQB 493 [McLaren].
140 Ibid. at para. 23. See also R. v. Restau, 2008 SKCA 147, where the Saskatchewan Court of Appeal distinguished McLaren, ibid., and held that the police control of the telephone did not breach the right to counsel where the police conduct left it up to the appellant to choose his own counsel. In R. v. McLinden, 2004 ABPC 7, an Alberta Provincial Court judge held that the police should provide yellow and white pages to the accused in addition to the list of lawyers who in Alberta have volunteered to take after-hours calls (the Brydges [above note 76] list). To like effect in Saskatchewan, see R. v. Ryland, 2006 SKPC 22; and R. v. Brouillette, 2009 SKQB 422. McLinden was distinguished in R. v. McDonald, 2008 ABQB 113, where the justice held that two offers to allow the accused to use the phone books were acceptable even though the phone books were not actually provided. The Nova Scotia Provincial Court suggests that the Saskatchewan Court's approach to the issue is in error. In R. v. Collicutt, 2008 NSPC 45, the court said that the police were not, after business hours, required to look in the white pages to assist the accused to find the home number of the chosen lawyer in the absence of request by the accused to do so. This same court, though, found that there was such a duty where a senior officer suggested that they would not reach the chosen lawyer after hours and suggested the accused contact duty counsel: R. v. Buck, 2008 NSPC 67. This seems to suggest that McLaren, ibid., may be correct to suggest that, where the police "control" the phone, their actions may be seen to override the accused's choice of counsel and indeed result in a

Reasonable diligence was at issue in *R. v. Jones*. The facts are succinctly set out in the Alberta Court of Appeal's judgment:

> On arriving at the police station, the police officer took the appellant to a private phone room which contained a working telephone, phone books and a list of lawyers who had indicated their availability for consultation. The police officer explained the use of the phone, and told the appellant to knock on the door when he was finished.
>
> Seven minutes later, the appellant knocked on the door. The police officer noted that the appellant was not speaking on the phone, and entered the room. He asked the appellant whether the appellant had reached his lawyer. When the appellant responded that he had not been able to reach him, the police officer again advised the appellant about the available list of legal aid lawyers and the phone book and advised that he could contact another lawyer. The appellant responded that he did not wish to speak to anyone else; that he wished to speak only to the named lawyer. The appellant did not indicate that he required more time, and did not suggest that he required any assistance. The police officer assumed from the appellant's act of knocking on the door and the appellant's response that the appellant had terminated his efforts to reach a lawyer. The officer requested that the appellant accompany him to the breathalyser where the appellant provided samples of his breath for analysis.[141]

On these facts the Court of Appeal agreed with the trial judge that there was no violation of the accused's section 10 rights. The officer did not interrupt the accused, and it was the accused who had knocked on the door, suggesting his efforts were over. According to the majority, it would have been redundant for the officer to ask the accused whether he needed more time, and the officer did remind the accused of the existence of duty counsel. According to the Court of Appeal, the officer had done everything that could reasonably be expected, and if the accused had wanted further time, he had not been reasonably diligent in requesting it.

Again, one wonders whether it should not be required that the accused be informed of the need to be reasonably diligent in the exercise of his rights. This accused did in fact assert his desire to speak to his counsel of choice and had informed the police that he had been

---

conclusion that it was not the accused's lack of diligence that caused the failure to contact the accused's counsel of choice. The Nova Scotia court later excluded the evidence in *R. v. Buck*, 2009 NSPC 4. See also notes 115–17, above.

141 *R. v. Jones*, 2005 ABCA 289 at paras. 3–4 [*Jones*], leave to appeal to S.C.C. refused, [2005] S.C.C.A. No. 538.

unsuccessful in doing so. Once more, the accused's found lack of due diligence operates in the same way as a waiver of his right to speak to his counsel of choice. It may be that the police in such circumstances should be required to obtain a so-called *Prosper* waiver from the accused as found by the dissenting justice in *Jones*.

Jones was expressly followed by the Saskatchewan Court of Appeal in *R. v. Basko*.[142] There, the Saskatchewan Court of Appeal considered the circumstances in which a *Prosper* warning is necessary. In *Prosper*[143] the Supreme Court had stated that, if an accused who has expressed a wish to contact counsel and has been reasonably diligent in trying to do so subsequently expresses a desire to waive the right, the police are required to rewarn the accused of the right to counsel, and, in particular, their obligation to hold off from eliciting incriminating information until a reasonable opportunity has been provided applies in the absence of a *Prosper* waiver. In *Basko* the accused had been detained at a routine traffic stop and taken back to the police station for a breathalyzer test, where he had been properly informed of the right to counsel. He indicated he wished to speak to a lawyer and through the officers made three attempts in an eight-minute period to call Legal Aid. However, the phone was busy on each occasion and the accused then indicated that he knew what they would say, that he would call the next day, and that he wished to get it over with.

The trial judge concluded that in the circumstances the accused had been entitled to a *Prosper* warning; the police had not complied with this duty when the accused attempted to waive counsel, and as a result there was a section 10(b) violation. The Crown appealed, and the Summary Conviction Appeal Court ordered a new trial, on the grounds that *Prosper* had been decided with regard to a province which at the time did not have a twenty-four-hour duty-counsel system and that a *Prosper* warning was therefore not required in provinces which did have such arrangements for legal aid and in which the accused had been attempting to call duty counsel.

The Court of Appeal held that the Summary Conviction Appeal Court's reasoning was incorrect but upheld the result. In particular, it held that the requirement for a *Prosper* warning does apply in a jurisdiction with twenty-four-hour duty counsel; however, whether a *Prosper* warning is actually required in a particular case will depend on the facts. In this case, the court said, the accused unequivocally waived the right to counsel. The trial judge failed to consider whether there was

---

142 *R. v. Basko*, 2007 SKCA 111 [*Basko*].
143 *Prosper*, above note 104.

a legally constituted waiver, which was an error of law permitting the Summary Conviction Appeal Court to come to its own conclusion on the issue. There was no error in that there had been a waiver, and so the matter was returned to the trial court for a continuation of the trial. However, this is not consistent with *Jones* since that case was not decided on the basis of a valid waiver: rather, it was decided on the basis that the accused there had not been reasonably diligent in exercising his right to counsel. In *Prosper* reasonable diligence by the accused had been listed as a precondition before any obligation on the part of the police to rewarn arose. Indeed, it can surely be argued that, whether a court finds that the accused was not reasonably diligent or that she implicitly waived her right to counsel, the accused is in need of information advising of the need to be reasonably diligent on the one hand of the duty on the police's part to hold off in their investigation on the other.

This case therefore stands as a further example of the confusion that exists in Canadian law because of the basic inconsistency between stating, at one and the same time, that the standard for waiver is high (and that the onus to prove it is on the Crown)[144] and that an accused must be reasonably diligent in exercising the right to counsel (and has the burden of proving a *Charter* violation).[145] The two tests both apply to the same types of fact situations and can in many cases (though not here) equally be adopted as the "correct" method of analysis, but, frustratingly, they will lead to opposite conclusions.[146]

Of course, in *Prosper* the Supreme Court seemingly suggests that this additional component is required where "a detainee has asserted his or her right to counsel and has been reasonably diligent in exercising it, yet has been unable to reach a lawyer because duty counsel is unavailable at the time of detention." To suggest that the accused must be reasonably diligent and/or that duty counsel be unavailable before this obligation arises seems inconsistent with the right to choose counsel and the principle that an accused must know what they are giving up to waive the right. Unfortunately, nowhere in the informational component does there appear a need to provide explicit advice concerning the obligation to be reasonably diligent in attempting to contact counsel nor any advice as to the circumstances in which the accused will be required to abandon attempts to contact their own lawyer as opposed

---

144 *Ibid.* at para. 44.

145 This burden comes from *R. v. Collins*, above note 28 at 277, and the general principles underlying s. 24(2), which requires an accused to prove a breach of rights.

146 See Steve Coughlan, "*R. v. Basko*: Annotation" (2007) 52 C.R. (6th) 359.

to duty counsel. In the absence of such informational obligations, and if the *Prosper* waiver requirement is read narrowly, it appears from many of the above cases on the obligation to be reasonably diligent that the accused will indeed be giving up their right to consult with counsel in the absence of knowledge of what he or she is giving up. We therefore suggest that the courts should be grappling with why this requirement is necessary rather than focusing on the precise words used by the Supreme Court at a time when duty-counsel systems were in their infancy.

Standard police right-to-counsel cards may in fact be more clear and fair about this issue than the courts have been. For example, the Calgary Police Services card says about the *Prosper* warning:

> FORMAL WAIVER: Where a detainee indicates a desire to contact a lawyer and then changes their mind OR there are concerns that the waiver of the right to counsel was not clear and unequivocal. READ THIS: You have the right to a reasonable opportunity to contact a lawyer. I am obliged not to take a statement from you or ask you to participate in any process that might provide evidence against you until you are certain about whether you want to exercise this right. Do you understand? (*Record answer*) Do you want to waive your right to contact a lawyer? (*Record answer*).[147]

Of course, it is a good practice for the police to be clear about the waiver if they wish evidence subsequently obtained to be admissible. Such a practice also has the salutary effect of ensuring that an accused truly wishes to waive their right. The restatement of the obligation to hold off investigating pending the exercise of the right is a significant part of this process. Otherwise the questioning of the accused can be seen as coercive in the sense that many accused will feel obligated to answer since they have not received legal advice concerning the right to silence.

Finally, it is worth noting that a *Prosper* warning was at issue in *Weeseekase*,[148] though in quite different circumstances. According to the Saskatchewan Court of Appeal, where an accused had been in custody for nine days and had made two court appearances where she was represented by counsel, a *Prosper* warning was not necessary as the considerations in *Prosper* were not relevant in the circumstances. Her statement given to the police was therefore wrongly excluded at trial.

---

147 This is from the Calgary Police Service right-to-counsel card in use as of January 2010. See above note 78.
148 *Weeseekase*, above note 109.

g)   Is There a Right to Privacy in Consultation with Counsel?

The notion that an accused has the right to consult counsel *in private* has been asserted by most courts, although the precise nature of this requirement has remained unsettled. The Supreme Court has not squarely addressed the issue after enactment of the *Charter*. Earlier, the majority had held in R. v. *Jumaga*[149] that there was no obligation on the police to afford privacy in the absence of a request by the accused. On the other hand, post-*Charter* courts of appeal have established the right to consult counsel in private. In R. v. *Playford* the Ontario Court of Appeal dealt with the issue in this way:

> In my opinion, the right to retain and instruct counsel without delay carries with it the right to do so in privacy. It would defy common sense to expect an accused person to instruct counsel properly when his instructions can be overheard by other persons and in particular by police officers. Such lack of privacy might even seriously prejudice his ability to retain counsel. Retention of counsel usually requires some explanation by the accused of the circumstances which have led to his arrest.[150]

The Ontario court expressly agreed with the decision in R. v *Lepage*[151] where the Nova Scotia Appellate Division had distinguished the pre-*Charter* decision in *Jumaga*. In fact, the Appellate Division expressly adopted the dissenting judgment of Laskin C.J., who had said:

> [T]he fact that it may have to be limited in some cases does not call for an unqualified denial of any privacy in all cases. I do not think that it can reasonably be made a condition that an accused be shown to have asked for it before consideration is given to providing it. Once an accused has requested that he be permitted to consult counsel, that should carry with it, to the knowledge of the police, a right to have the consultation in private, so far as circumstances permit. The right to counsel is diluted if it can only be secured by adding request to request. I would not put the police in an adversary position on this question; they are better placed than the ordinary person (who has been detained or arrested and is in police custody) to recognize what the right to counsel imports, and they should be alert to protect that right as an important element in the administration of justice

---

149 R. v. *Jumaga*, [1977] 1 S.C.R. 486 [*Jumaga*].

150 R. v. *Playford* (1987), 40 C.C.C. (3d) 142 (Ont. C.A.) [*Playford*].

151 R. v. *Lepage* (1986), 32 C.C.C. (3d) 171 (N.S.C.A.) [*Lepage*].

through law, for which they are as much accountable as any others involved in the judicial process.[152]

The Nova Scotia Court also said:

> Even to obtain the minimal advice by means of a telephone a person detained or arrested must be free to discuss the circumstances of his detention with counsel. If he cannot do so for fear of making admissions in the presence of the police then, obviously, his right to instruct counsel has been limited. In such circumstances the right under the *Charter* has been violated. In my view, the right to privacy is inherent in the right to retain and instruct counsel under s. 10(b) of the *Charter*.[153]

In that case the officer stood five to six feet away while the accused called counsel from his own telephone. A breach of the right was found by the court.

The New Brunswick Court of Appeal summarized the position thus in *R. v. O'Donnell*:

> It is settled law that the right to retain and instruct counsel, under s. 10(b) of the *Charter*, includes a corollary right to consult in private. Without the requisite degree of privacy, the constitutional right to counsel becomes illusory. Although waiver of the right is a possibility, the issue does not arise in the present case. While the amount of privacy need not be great, at a minimum, an accused must be able to converse with his or her lawyer without the conversation being overheard. Moreover, those who exercise their right to counsel are not required to request privacy or greater privacy than what the police are willing to provide. Furthermore, the right to consult in private extends to legal advice that is sought over the telephone and it matters not whether the advice sought is of minimal scope (whether to provide breath samples).[154]

That court, though, stressed that the breach of privacy must be proven, which requires a factual finding that the police did in fact overhear the conversation with the lawyer for a breach to be found.[155] Further, in *R. v. Standish*, the British Columbia Court of Appeal found no breach of privacy where the accused required and obtained the assistance of the

---

152 *Jumaga*, above note 149 at 494–95, Laskin C.J. dissenting.
153 *Lepage*, above note 151 at 176–77.
154 *R. v. O'Donnell*, 2004 NBCA 26 at para. 4.
155 See also *Parrill*, above note 84.

police in placing calls to counsel, holding that privacy "starts after the accused reaches his lawyer to seek his advice."[156]

An inability to provide privacy until the accused has been transported to the police station is sometimes asserted by the police as the justification for delaying the accused's phone calls. In *R. v. Bohn*[157] the British Columbia Court of Appeal found a delay during the execution of a search warrant to have breached the right to counsel and that such a police justification to have been inadequate, seemingly finding that the accused should have been allowed to speak to counsel on an available cellphone. Even in the absence of a statement by the accused, the breach of section 10(b) was relevant to the exclusion of the real evidence discovered during the unconstitutional search.

Likewise, in *R. v. Luu*,[158] the two accused were arrested after a police officer detected a strong smell of marijuana coming from their residence when he went to ask them to move a car which was blocking a driveway. A struggle ensued but the officer was able to handcuff the couple and call for assistance. The accused asked to call a lawyer when they were informed of their section 10(b) rights, but the officer did not permit them to do so at the time. He testified that this was because he could not give them privacy at that location. The Court of Appeal held that this violated section 10(b): where no privacy is possible, a detainee should still be offered the option of contacting counsel immediately without privacy.[159]

Further, in *R. v. Patterson*,[160] where the police initially stopped an accused for driving without a licence but then arrested him for possession of a narcotic, the British Columbia Court of Appeal held that the trial judge had been wrong in concluding that the officer's safety justified the delay in allowing the accused to call a lawyer. The police had obtained a warrant to search Patterson's home, finding more narcotics there. As this was going on, they detained the accused for six and a half hours without letting him call counsel, eventually releasing him without laying charges. The Crown had argued that prior authorities supported the ability of the police to get a situation under control before letting an accused call counsel, but the court held that those authorities were not analogous.

---

156 *R. v. Standish* (1988), 41 C.C.C. (3d) 340 at 343 (B.C.C.A.) [*Standish*].

157 *R. v. Bohn*, 2000 BCCA 239.

158 *R. v. Luu*, 2006 BCCA 73.

159 See also: *R. v. Bui*, 2005 BCCA 482.

160 *R. v. Patterson*, 2006 BCCA 24.

On the other hand, in *R. v. Burley*[161] the Ontario Court of Appeal found no privacy violation in the case of an accused who was placed in a small ambulance attendant room at a hospital in order to contact counsel. He was alone in the room, the only officer present had told him that he would not be within earshot, and the accused did not suggest at the time that he was concerned about privacy or request an opportunity to make a second call. The court held that the accused's duty to be reasonably diligent in exercising the right to counsel was relevant in this context, and found that "[t]he belief of the accused that he could not retain and instruct counsel in private was not reasonable in the circumstances."[162]

4) Section 10 and Non-state actors

In Chapter 2, we discussed the issue of the *Charter*'s application to non-state actors,[163] noting the main authorities from the Supreme Court concerning when a private citizen is acting as an agent of the police. We made the point that, generally, the *Charter*, by way of section 32, applies only to "state" actors.

This issue also arises in the context of section 10 of the *Charter*. Do security guards, loss-prevention officers, and other private policing services need to inform detainees of their rights under section 10 to know why they are detained and provide them with information about and access to their right to counsel?

In this context it is clear that private non-state employees have been provided with the power of "citizen's arrest" and indeed in section 494(2) employees of property owners have been given specific powers to arrest in certain circumstances. The power of citizen's arrest is discussed at length in Chapter 4.[164] Does this grant of power mean that the *Charter* should apply where it might not otherwise apply?

The decision that is most often cited in answering the above questions positively is that of the Alberta Court of Appeal in *R. v. Lerke*,[165] a 1986 decision involving an arrest and search by a tavern supervisor at a licensed drinking establishment. The Court of Appeal said as follows:

> In my opinion the facts of this case do not raise the issue whether the *Canadian Charter of Rights and Freedoms* applies to the actions

---

161 *R. v. Burley*, (2004), 182 O.A.C. 395 (C.A.).

162 *Ibid.* at para. 28.

163 See Chapter 2, Section B(4).

164 See Chapter 4, Section C(2)(b)(ii).

165 *R. v. Lerke*, (1986), 24 C.C.C. (3d) 129 (Alta. C.A.) [*Lerke*].

of one private citizen to another. In my view the arrest of a citizen is a governmental function whether the person making the arrest is a peace officer or a private citizen. I reach this conclusion from a consideration of the long legal history of citizen's arrest from its common law origins to the statutory expression of the present powers of arrest contained in the *Criminal Code of Canada* or in the *Petty Trespass Act*.[166]

After a review of the history of citizen and police arrest powers, the court was of the view that "when one citizen arrests another, the arrest is the exercise of a governmental function to which the *Canadian Charter of Rights and Freedoms* applies."[167] Accordingly, the court found that section 8 protected Lerke from unreasonable search, and it excluded the marijuana found in his jacket pocket.

The issue of section 10's application to the situation was not addressed in *Lerke*. On the other hand, in *R. v. J. (A.M.)*,[168] the British Columbia Court of Appeal seemingly was of the view that a person other than a peace officer making a citizen's arrest is not required to give the accused the requisite *Charter* warnings. Likewise, in *R. v. Skeir*,[169] the Nova Scotia Court of Appeal, relying on the Supreme Court's analysis of the place of security guards in *R. v. Buhay*, held that the *Charter* did not require a store security guard to comply with section 10(b) of the *Charter*. Interestingly, the security guard did in fact read a form of the right to counsel to the accused although the content thereof did not comply with *Bartle*.[170]

In *R. v. Shafie*[171] the accused was charged with theft. The Crown sought to introduce a statement made by the accused to a private investigator in a private office. The investigator did not provide the accused with his section 10(b) rights. The Ontario Court of Appeal ruled that there was no need for the investigator to do so because the accused was not "detained" by the investigator:

[T]he weight of judicial opinion . . . is that actions that, at the hands of the police or other state or governmental agents, would be a deten-

---

166 *Ibid.* at 134.
167 *Ibid.* at 136.
168 *R. v. J.(A.M.)*, 1999 BCCA 366.
169 *R. v. Skeir*, 2005 NSCA 86.
170 There are several lower court judgments dealing with these issues which find that the *Charter* does not apply. See *R. v. Karook*, [2001] Q.J. No. 983 (C.S.) (citizen's arrest of impaired driver); *R. v. Anderson* (2007), 151 C.R.R. (2d) 168 (NL Prov. Ct.) (search by landlord); and *R. v. Boujikian*, [2006] O.J. No. 3611 (Ct. J.) (private investigator arrest for mischief).
171 *R. v. Shafie* (1989), 47 C.C.C. (3d) 27 (Ont. C.A.) [*Shafie*].

tion, do not amount to a detention within the meaning of s. 10(b) of the *Charter* when done by private or non-governmental persons.[172]

The court added later on the same page:

In my view, however, the question whether a person's s. 10(b) rights were infringed must be tested as at the time the alleged detention occurred. Any other conclusion would result in the judicialization of private relationships beyond the point that society could tolerate. The requirement that advice about the right to counsel must be given by a school teacher to a pupil, by an employer to an employee or a parent to a child, to mention only a few relationships, is difficult to contemplate.[173]

In *R v. Dell*[174] a bouncer detained a man after seeing him with cocaine. The Alberta Court of Appeal found that *Lerke* had not been overruled by the Supreme Court of Canada:

As I read *Buhay*, it does not determine that the *Charter* has no application to a citizen's arrest by a private person. *Buhay* involved a search and seizure, not a citizen's arrest, and *Lerke* was neither considered nor mentioned. There is but a passing reference to arrest in paragraph 31. The Supreme Court confirmed the existence of the government function exception in *Buhay*, noting that it may derive from an express delegation or an abandonment of state powers to a citizen.

---

172 *Ibid.* at 34.

173 *Ibid.* As noted in Chapter 2, the reference to a schoolteacher may now be in error since the *Charter* does seem to apply to school officials, though not every restriction on liberty in that context will be a "detention." See *M.(M.R)*, above note 16.

174 *R. v. Dell*, 2005 ABCA 246 [*Dell*]. In *Dell* the Court of Appeal says this about its previous judgment in *Lerke*, above note 165 at para. 12:

> *Lerke* has not been uniformly applied. Many lower courts have followed it, including: *R. v. Parsons* (2001), 284 A.R. 345, 2001 ABQB 42; *R. v. Jones*, [2004] N.B.J. No. 510, aff'd 2005 NBQB 14; *R. v. Voege* (1997), 31 M.V.R. (3d) 293 (Ont. C.J. Gen. Div.); *R. v. Dean* (1991), 5 C.R. (4th) 176 (Ont. C.J. Gen. Div.); and *R. v. Wilson* (1994), 29 C.R. (4th) 302 (B.C.S.C.). However, three appellate courts have held that the actions of private persons performing citizen's arrests are not subject to the *Charter*: *R. v. N.S.*, [2004] O.J. No. 290 (Ont. C.A.); *R. v. J.(A.M.)* (1999), 137 C.C.C. (3d) 213, 1999 BCCA 366; and *R. v. Skeir*, 2005 NSCA 86. In the first two decisions, the courts arrived at this conclusion on the basis that private persons (in N.S. a security guard and in J.(A.M.) victims of a burglary) do not become agents of the state when effecting a citizen's arrest. Notably, the specific government function exception relied on in *Lerke*, and recognized in *Buhay*, was not canvassed.

Moreover, the Supreme Court recently confirmed that the power of citizen's arrest, having its roots in a power derived from the sovereign or state, survives in s. 494 of the *Criminal Code: Asante-Mensah, supra*, at paras. 36–40. It follows that the power of citizen's arrest is a delegation by the sovereign or state to the ordinary citizen. The fact that the delegation is concurrent (to peace officers as well as to private citizens) and direct (from the sovereign to the citizen rather than from the police to the citizen) does not necessarily defeat the essence of the delegation.

Further support for the proposition that *Buhay* did not expressly overrule *Lerke* is found in *Asante-Mensah*, a case heard and decided by the Supreme Court shortly after *Buhay*. The Court declined

> to address the question whether a citizen's arrest could be construed as state action for purposes of the *Charter*, as held by the Alberta Court of Appeal in *Lerke, supra*, at p. 134 and, if so, what consequences might flow from that ruling: at para. 77.[175]

The Court, though, proceeds to distinguish *Lerke* on the basis that the common law power to conduct an investigative detention does not arise from statute. In the majority's view, the fact that the investigative detention by a bouncer was not an arrest meant he was not relying on the statutory power to arrest and thus *Lerke* did not apply. The problem, of course, is that the bouncer's action can for the same reason be seen as illegal and indeed may constitute an assault or a false imprisonment. We pointed out in Chapter 2 that the power to investigatively detain can be given only to the police at common law.[176]

The problems with the *Dell* approach are exhibited by the decision *R. v. Castor*.[177] There the accused, while being questioned by a store security guard, tried to walk away and shook his fist at the guard. He then was arrested by the guard and he resisted that attempt. The guard attempted to handcuff the accused and was punched by the accused. The Provincial Court judge ruled that questioning was at most an investigative detention but once the accused shook his fist at the security officer the officer had reasonable grounds to believe the accused was committing an assault, and so the officer's arrest was lawful. The accused was therefore guilty of the assault charge.

---

175 *Ibid.* at paras. 17–18.
176 The test for the creation of common law police powers is based on the statutory duty of the police to investigate crime. See Chapter 2, Section B(4), and the text accompanying note 246.
177 *R. v. Castor*, 2006 ABPC 64.

On the other hand, in the specific context of section 10 rights, it is important to note that in R. v. *Harrer*[178] the Supreme Court of Canada said that when a statement given to a foreign police officer is obtained in breach of the right to counsel, it might be excluded if its admission in evidence would result in an unfair trial. This is so even though that foreign officer is not bound by the *Charter*. The right to a fair trial is protected by section 11(d) of the *Charter* and is a principle of fundamental justice under section 7. The majority was clear that such exclusion would not be the result of section 24 of the *Charter* but,

> Rather, I would reject the evidence on the basis of the trial judge's duty, now constitutionalized by the enshrinement of a fair trial in the *Charter*, to exercise properly his or her judicial discretion to exclude evidence that would result in an unfair trial.[179]

Of course, it had long been the Supreme Court's view that the breach of the right to counsel which leads to statements by the accused results in evidence which is "conscripted" from the accused. When such evidence is admitted in the trial, the trial may become unfair.

In its 2009 decision in *Grant*, the majority, in changing the factors to be considered in excluding evidence under section 24(2), said about conscripted evidence:

> This general rule of inadmissibility of all non-discoverable conscriptive evidence, whether intended by *Stillman* or not, seems to go against the requirement of s. 24(2) that the court determining admissibility must consider "all the circumstances." The underlying assumption that the use of conscriptive evidence always, or almost always, renders the trial unfair is also open to challenge. In other contexts, this Court has recognized that a fair trial "is one which satisfies the public interest in getting at the truth, while preserving basic procedural fairness to the accused": R. v. *Harrer*, [1995] 3 S.C.R. 562, at para. 45. It is difficult to reconcile trial fairness as a multifaceted and contextual concept with a near-automatic presumption that admission of a broad class of evidence will render a trial unfair, regardless of the circumstances in which it was obtained. In our view, trial fairness is better conceived as an overarching systemic goal than as a distinct stage of the s. 24(2) analysis.[180]

---

178 R. v. *Harrer*, [1995] 3 S.C.R. 562.
179 *Ibid.* at para. 21.
180 *Grant*, above note 2 at para. 65.

Further, when the majority addresses particular types of evidence in *Grant*, it is clear that they see statements from the accused as remaining in a category which will often result in exclusion where the right to counsel has been breached.[181] It seems, therefore, that while the issue of the right to counsel as it might be applied to private security officers is unlikely to apply in the same detailed way as with police officers, there may be times when the failure to provide rights similar to those enshrined in section 10(a) and (b) might result in an unfair trial. Indeed, in *R. v. Buhay*, the leading authority on "state agents," the Supreme Court did expressly refer to *Harrer* and other cases when it said:

> Before turning to s. 24(2), I wish to address briefly the approach taken by the Court of Appeal in this case. I will make two observations. First, we do not have to decide whether there would have been a "search" by the police had the security guards not replaced the contents inside the locker but had held it in a corner cupboard. This is not what they did here. Had they done so, we might have had to adapt the test in *Broyles*, *supra*, to determine if and when the security guards would have become state agents or, alternatively, if the "mere transfer of control" in that case could have been characterized as a "seizure" by the police within the meaning of s. 8.
>
> Second, and more importantly, I wish to stress that even if the reasoning of the Court of Appeal were sound and that there had been no search and seizure triggering s. 8 of the *Charter*, remedies other than under the *Charter* might be available in such a case to an accused seeking exclusion of the impugned evidence. Indeed, even in the absence of a *Charter* breach, judges have a discretion at common law to exclude evidence obtained in circumstances such that it would result in unfairness if the evidence was admitted at trial, or if the prejudicial effect of admitting the evidence outweighs its probative value (see, in the context of confessions: *Rothman v. The Queen*, [1981] 1 S.C.R. 640, at p. 696, *per* Lamer J., as he then was; *R. v. Oickle*, [2000] 2 S.C.R. 3, 2000 SCC 38, at para. 69, *per* Iacobucci J.; see also J. Sopinka, S. N. Lederman and A. W. Bryant, *The Law of Evidence in Canada* (2nd ed. 1999), at pp. 339-40); see also, in other contexts, *R. v. Harrer*, [1995] 3 S.C.R. 562, *per* La Forest J.; *Caucci*, *supra*, at paras. 13 and 17; Sopinka, Lederman and Bryant, *supra*, at pp. 30-33). Such an argument was not advanced in this case as the appellant maintained throughout that he was entitled to a *Charter* remedy for a s. 8 violation. In light of my conclusion on the s. 8 issue, it is not necessary to explore further whether this common law discretion could have

---

181 *Ibid.* at paras. 89–98.

extended to the exclusion of real evidence in circumstances such as here. Rather, we must turn to whether the marijuana illegally seized by the police should be excluded under s. 24(2) because its admission "would bring the administration of justice into disrepute."[182]

Therefore, it has been suggested that cases such as *Shafie* which allow evidence to be admitted even though no right to counsel was given might be seen to be wrongly decided on this basis.[183]

---

182 *R. v. Buhay*, 2003 SCC 30 at paras. 39–40.
183 See Glen Luther, 'Of Excision, Amplification and Standing: Making Sense of the Law of Evidence in the Context of Challenges to Warranted Searches" (2006) 11 Can. Crim. L. Rev. 1.

REASONABLE BELIEF

Reasonable Grounds for Arrest Made Out

R. v. Debot, [1989] 2 S.C.R. 1140: The police received confidential information from an informant concerning a future drug deal. The informant had previously provided useful information to the police (Cst. G) and was considered by the police to be reliable. The informant provided details said to have been received directly from one of the parties to the drug transaction indicating date, time, location, type of drug, and names of the parties to the offence. The police established visual surveillance of the anticipated site of the drug deal; a vehicle known to the police was observed along with persons entering/exiting the premises; Cst. G, by radio to an off-site officer (Sgt. B), confirmed that the accused was the registered owner of the vehicle. Sgt. B then instructed other officers to intercept and search the vehicle. On these facts Cst. B had reasonable and probable grounds to believe that the accused had drugs in his possession, despite reliance on hearsay from other officers. An officer instructed to carry out a search by another officer is entitled to assume that the officer ordering the search has reasonable grounds.

The tip provided by the informant was compelling and detailed: it went beyond mere rumour; the informant was reliable and not paid nor facing charges; and the police surveillance corroborated the information received.

R. v. Wong, [1990] 3 S.C.R. 36 (*obiter* conclusion on reasonable grounds for arrest for unlawful gaming): The police entered a recently vacated room which revealed that the furniture had been rearranged to be "suitable for gambling"; located many slips of paper in a garbage bin written in Chinese characters; the slips were similar to other notices known to be distributed elsewhere in the city; hotel records showed that the accused had rented the same room on two other occasions that month.

R. v. Storrey, [1990] 1 S.C.R. 241: Reasonable grounds to arrest for aggravated assault made out by accused's possession and ownership of a relatively unusual and uncommon car of the type used during the crime; (b) the accused had been stopped by the police on several occasions driving that car; (c) the accused had a past record of violence; and (d) the accused closely resembled the picture of another person picked out by the victims as their assailant.

R. v. Stillman, [1997] 1 S.C.R. 607: Reasonable grounds to arrest for murder made out where

(a) he was the last person seen with the deceased on the evening of her disappearance;

(b) he could not, or at least did not, account for his whereabouts between 9:00 p.m. and 11:30 p.m. on that evening when he returned to his residence; (c) when the appellant returned home he was wet and cold, his clothes were muddy and he had a scratch over his eye and blood on his face consistent with having been in a scuffle. When the deceased's body was found she appeared to have been physically beaten; (d) the appellant claimed to have been in a fight with some "Indians" but this story changed over time; (e) the appellant's worried and disturbed reaction to the police helicopter which was searching the river close to where the deceased was found; (f) immediately following the appellant's observation of the helicopter he left a suicide note and fled; (g) the appellant made a statement to Constable Cole saying, "I tried to stop her from killing herself. I left her there"; and (h) the RCMP received a report from two motorists that they had seen the deceased on the bridge crossing the Oromocto River and that she was with a male who met the description of the appellant (para. 31).

R. v. Latimer, [1997] 1 S.C.R. 217: Reasonable grounds to arrest for murder made out.

Objectively, the reasonable person in the position of the arresting officer would have concluded there were reasonable grounds for arrest. Those grounds included:

the carbon monoxide in Tracy's blood, strongly suggesting that she had been poisoned; the fact that it was extremely unlikely that Tracy's death had been accidental; the fact that, because of Tracy's physical condition, her death could not have been suicide; and finally, the fact that the accused had both opportunity and motive (para. 27).

R. v. Warford, 2001 NFCA 64: The police received a "tip" that the accused would be driving to a local nightclub, at a particular time, to sell cocaine. The informant had provided reliable information to the police on approximately six occasions over a period of about eighteen months. The tip identified the date on which the accused had received cocaine and identified the vehicle in which he would be driving to the nightclub. The police observed the accused leave his residence in that vehicle at the indicated time and date, and he began to drive on a route consistent with going to the named nightclub. The police had reasonable grounds to arrest when they stopped the vehicle a short distance from the nightclub. (See in contrast *R. v. Zammit*, (1993), 13 O.R. (3d) 76, 81 C.C.C. (3d) 112, below.)

R. v. M.A.L. (2003), 173 C.C.C. (3d) 439 (Ont.C.A.): The police had reasonable grounds to arrest the accused for seven carjackings from Asian victims in plazas in Scarborough where they had following evidence: the accused had previously been convicted of a very similar carjacking involving an Asian victim, which had occurred at a plaza where one of these seven carjackings had occurred; three of the four cars recovered by the police were found a short distance from the residence of the respondent's girlfriend, which was in the same general area where the various plazas were located; the accused and two companions were seen in the plaza where one of the robberies occurred about an hour and a half before the robbery, and his behaviour had been described by a witness as "suspicious"; in May, a police surveillance unit observed the accused in the plaza where one of the robberies had taken place the previous February; in late May and early June, the accused was seen in another one of the plazas where one of the robberies had occurred. That robbery took place in April. The accused approached a vehicle in a manner that caused the driver (who was Asian) to call 911. That witness had seen the accused approach his car in a similar manner on an earlier occasion, and he also saw him a third time; the accused's race, age, and height were consistent with the very general descriptions given by most of the victims of the carjackings.

Potential weaknesses in eyewitness identification evidence which would be relevant at trial were not relevant to determining whether the police had reasonable grounds to arrest.

R. v. Sinclair, 2005 MBCA 41: Reasonable grounds to arrest for possession of narcotics for the purpose of trafficking were made out on the following facts: a car drove into a doughnut shop parking lot at 1:00, a person approached and leaned into the vehicle for some type of interaction, the person and the vehicle both left. When the police stopped the vehicle, they heard a cellphone ringing and saw balls of tinfoil on the seat, which they testified was a typical way of packaging raw cocaine.

R. v. Bracchi, 2005 BCCA 461: There were reasonable grounds to arrest an accused where the police had received information from several sources that the accused was involved in cocaine trafficking. They observed him leave his house at night and drive some distance without his lights on, taking a circuitous route and sometimes speeding, from which they concluded that he was trying to avoid being noticed. The accused was heading towards an address known as "the compound": the police had in the past stopped about twenty vehicles leaving that address and all but one had been found to have cocaine. In addition, the police had in the past stopped a vehicle leaving the accused's address and had found cocaine, which the driver indicated he had bought from the accused. When the accused turned onto the street where the compound was located, police had reasonable grounds to believe that he was delivering cocaine.

R. v. Rajaratnam, 2006 ABCA 333: The police had reasonable grounds to arrest for possession of a narcotic on the basis that the accused, encountered at a bus station: a) purchased his ticket in a false name, at the last minute, with cash; b) could not provide a credible explanation regarding the timing and duration of his trip; c) became nervous when the police noticed that the name on his identification and ticket did not match; d) had checked a bag that smelled of Bounce fabric softener, which was known by the police to be an agent used to camouflage the smell of drugs; and e) tagged that bag with a false name.

(Note the comment of Justice Binnie in *R. v. Kang-Brown* at para. 88, with regard to last-minute ticket purchases in cash: "This is a factor developed in the original Jetway program at airports where ordinary travellers usually book air transportation in advance and do not pay for an expensive ticket in cash [see, e.g., *Monney*]. I think we can take judicial notice of the fact that people travelling by bus frequently buy their tickets not long before boarding. There is no evidence that cash payments are unusual.")

R. v. Johnson (2006), 213 O.A.C. 395, 69 W.C.B. (2d) 733 (Ont. C.A): Reasonable grounds to arrest for possession of a narcotic for purposes of trafficking were made out when the police, in a location frequently used for drug trafficking, saw a person they knew to be a crack-cocaine user approach the accused, saw the two acknowledge one another in a guarded fashion, saw the accused show a small item in his cupped hands, and then saw both men walking off together.

Hill v. Hamilton-Wentworth Regional Police Services Board, [2007] 3 S.C.R. 129: Reasonable grounds for arrest on robbery charges were made out where the police had: a Crime Stoppers tip; identification of the accused by a police officer based on a surveillance photo; several eyewitness identifications (some tentative, others more solid); a potential sighting of the accused near the site of a robbery by a police officer; eyewitness evidence that the robber appeared to be Aboriginal (which the accused was); and the belief of the police that a single person committed all ten robberies. The reasonable grounds were made out though the police also had received an anonymous Crime Stoppers tip implicating two other people for the robbery. The accused in fact had not committed the robberies and unsuccessfully sued for negligent investigation.

R. v. MacEachern, 2007 NSCA 69: There were reasonable grounds to arrest an accused for possession of narcotics when he walked in a large arc around a drug-sniffer dog and that dog twice gave a positive indication for the presence of drugs on the accused.

R. v. Juan, 2007 BCCA 351: The police arranged to buy cocaine from a dealer in an undercover operation. The vehicle arrived at the location and the driver showed the cocaine to the undercover officer. The accused was in the passenger seat of the drug dealer's car during this time. This constituted reasonable grounds to arrest him, on the basis of police testimony that no one uninvolved in the offence would be in the car for a pre-arranged drug deal.

R. v. Webster, 2008 BCCA 458: The smell of burned marijuana combined with seeing what appears to be a marijuana cigarette behind the accused's ear gives reasonable grounds to arrest for possession of marijuana. (See *R. v. Janvier,* 2007 SKCA 147, below, holding that the smell of burned marijuana alone does not give reasonable grounds with regard to current possession.)

R. v. Baddock, 2008 BCCA 48: Police received information from an informant about a dial-a-dope operation; the officer believed the informant to be reliable on the basis of past information received which had resulted in arrests when the officer had been able to purchase drugs by calling the phone numbers provided by the informant. The police called the number and arranged a meeting to buy drugs and were told that a small white car would arrive at a McDonald's parking lot fifteen minutes after the call. Within the stated timeline, a white Honda Civic arrived and parked in front of the McDonald's, and the driver and his passenger waited for two minutes without ever exiting the vehicle before driving away. The police officer followed the accused's car and stopped him. As he approached the vehicle, the officer redialed the dial-a-dope number, and upon reaching the vehicle observed that the accused's phone was ringing in his hand. On these facts the officer had reasonable suspicion justifying stopping the car before he redialled the dial-a-dope number, and had reasonable grounds to arrest after that.

R. v. Nolet, 2010 SCC 24: The police had reasonable grounds to arrest for possession of proceeds of crime. They found a tractor trailer driving with an empty load, without appropriate registration, operating outside of its jurisdiction, and with expired decals and a deficient log book. There was a passenger along for the ride and the cargo hold appeared to have been altered. When the officer then found a duffel bag with $115,000 in cash, he had reasonable grounds to believe it was the proceeds of crime. (See *R. v. Perello*, 2005 SKCA 8, 193 C.C.C. (3d) 151, below, where the discovery of $55,000 in cash was not sufficient to create reasonable grounds.)

Reasonable Grounds for Arrest Not Made Out

R. v. Greffe, [1990] 1 S.C.R. 755 (reasonable grounds for a search): RCMP received a tip that the accused was importing an unknown quantity of heroin to Calgary from Amsterdam; RCMP instructed customs officers to question/detain the accused. Accused was arrested and subjected to a body-cavity search. The informer provided details of accused's name; nature of the offence; flight information; a physical description of the accused's; the accused's clothing.

> With respect, a conclusion that the police had reliable information about the Appellant's attempt to import heroin must be based on more than the fact of a subsequent recovery of the drugs. There must be an independent inquiry into the source and reliability of the confidential information in order to determine whether, in the

totality of the circumstances, there existed reasonable and probable grounds to believe the appellant was carrying the heroin or whether there was mere suspicion. Relevant to this inquiry is whether the information received contains sufficient detail to ensure that it is based on more than mere rumour or gossip, whether the source or means of knowledge is revealed and whether there is any indicia of the reliability of the source of the information, such as the supplying of reliable information in the past (para. 24).

[T]he record reveals no evidence to support the existence of the grounds beyond a conclusory statement by the police (para. 47).

R. v. Zammit (1993), 13 O.R. (3d) 76, 81 C.C.C. (3d) 112: No reasonable grounds to arrest an accused for possession of narcotics based on a tip from a confidential informer that the accused would come into possession on a particular date. The informer's "tip" contained no details, such as the source of the drugs or the location and time of delivery, to ensure that it was based on more than mere rumour, and there was no evidence that the informer disclosed his or her source or means of knowledge. The accused had no reputation for involvement in drugs and no previous convictions for drug-related offences. The officer had never dealt with the informer before, and the only corroboration went to innocuous matters such as the address of the accused, a description of him and of his motor vehicle, and the name and address of his workplace. These were matters that would probably have been known by anyone familiar with the accused. (See in contrast *R. v. Warford*, 2001 NFCA 64, above.)

R. v. Feeney, [1997] 2 S.C.R. 13: Reasonable grounds to arrest for murder not made out.

The salient facts known to the police prior to their entry of the trailer are as follows:

(a) it appeared that Boyle's truck had been stolen before being in an accident, and Cindy Potter claimed to have seen "Michael" walking near the site of the accident; (b) Kelly Spurn told police that he assumed the appellant had crashed Boyle's truck since the appellant had crashed earlier that morning in about the same place with a different truck; and (c) Dale Russell told police that the appellant came home around 7:00 a.m. after drinking all night and that the appellant had earlier crashed a vehicle at the spot where Boyle's truck was found. In my view, these facts did not constitute reasonable and probable grounds to arrest the appellant for the murder of Boyle. Whether or not the appellant had been involved in two similar truck accidents, or might have stolen Boyle's truck, does not raise reasonable and probable grounds to believe that he had murdered Boyle. This evidence may have pointed to the appellant as a suspect, but these facts without more do not justify an arrest. When the police entered the trailer, objectively reasonable and probable grounds for an arrest, as opposed to grounds for prima facie suspicion, did not exist (para. 36).

R. v. Perello, 2005 SKCA 8, 193 C.C.C. (3d) 151: The discovery of $55,000 in cash in a vehicle registered in another province than the one it was being driven in does not give reasonable grounds to believe that the accused is committing the offence of possession of proceeds of crime.

R. v. Janvier, 2007 SKCA 147: The smell of burned marijuana in a vehicle does not give reasonable grounds to believe that the driver is currently in possession of further unburned marijuana. The smell of raw marijuana would be a direct sensory impression which would give reasonable grounds to believe a person possesses raw marijuana. The smell of burned marijuana might indicate that the person had possessed marijuana in the past, but to prove current possession two further inferences would be necessary: that the driver was the person who burned the earlier marijuana, and that a person who has recently smoked marijuana probably has more. Neither inference can automatically be drawn. (See in contrast *R. v. Webster*, 2008 BCCA 458, discussed above, holding that the smell of burned marijuana emanating from a vehicle *does* meet the reasonable-suspicion standard in relation to either the offence of possession of marijuana or impaired driving, and so authorizes an investigative detention.)

REASONABLE
SUSPICION[1]

Reasonable Suspicion Standard Met

R. v. Mann, [2004] 3 S.C.R. 59: Shortly before midnight the police received a dispatch call describing a break and enter in progress in down-
town Winnipeg. The suspect was described as a twenty-one-year-old
Aboriginal male, approximately 5'6", weighing 165 lbs., wearing a black
jacket with white sleeves, and believed to be "Zachary Parisienne." A
short while later the police observed the accused walking away from
the site of the offence. The Court found that the reasonable-suspicion
standard was met because the accused closely matched the description
and was only two or three blocks from the crime scene a short time
after the offence. It also stated that the high-crime nature of a neighbourhood is not itself a basis to detain someone, and is relevant only if
it shows the connection of an accused to a particular crime.

R. v. Greaves, 2004 BCCA 484, 189 C.C.C. (3d) 305, 24 C.R. (6th) 15: An
officer on duty received a report of an assault at a liquor store, perpe-
trated by a black male and several white males who had fled eastbound.
The dispatch record indicated one black male and five white males, the
black male being described as eighteen years of age, six feet tall, skinny
build, short black hair, light T-shirt, and black pants. The officer arrived
at the store within five minutes and found no one. He went east, where

---

1   This appendix deals only with reasonable suspicion in the context of investiga-
     tive detentions. There is also caselaw using the reasonable suspicion standard in
     other contexts, such as customs stops or approved-screening-device demands.

two blocks away he encountered a black male (the accused) with two white males. The accused did not closely fit the description of the black male described on the dispatch record, but the officer testified that he considered the grouping of a black male with two white males unique for that part of the city. The three men were drinking beer bottles and discarded bottles upon seeing the officer; when he made eye contact with him, they proceeded to jaywalk, apparently to avoid the officer. These facts were found to objectively justify a detention.

R. v. Scott, 2004 NSCA 141, 191 C.C.C. (3d) 183, 26 C.R. (6th) 145: Early in the morning, a woman robbed a convenience store wearing a ski mask and then fled the scene. RCMP arrived and traced footprints in the fresh snow from the store to an apartment building. As the officers approached the parking lot of the apartment building, they saw what they described as a red- or wine-coloured Grand Prix or Grand Am car, moving at an unusually high speed, leaving the parking lot. The officers radioed for assistance to locate and stop the car. Shortly afterward other officers spotted a wine-coloured Grand Prix enter a gas station. The police had reasonable suspicion and were entitled to detain the vehicle and it occupants.

R. v. Byfield, [2005] O.J. No. 228, 74 O.R. (3d) 206: Police officers observed a suspected female prostitute in an area of Toronto about which "police receive many complaints from the public about prostitution, drug dealing and theft" (para. 3). They observed the woman and her interactions on the street. She disappeared into a van, returning ten minutes later, then made a telephone call and five minutes later entered a car. Police followed the car, ran the plates, and learned that the registered owner was facing criminal charges and that he did not live anywhere near the area in which he was then driving. Police suspected that the woman was buying drugs from the man based on their unconfirmed suspicion that the woman was a drug-addicted prostitute. On these facts the police had reasonable grounds to suspect that the accused was a drug dealer and engaged in trafficking at the time. The Court of Appeal held:

> [20] On the trial judge's findings, the police did not stop the appellant based merely upon a hunch or intuition based on experience, nor merely because he was in a high-crime area. The officers were able to articulate the basis for their suspicion and provide a demonstrable rationale that the driver of the vehicle had engaged in a particular crime, namely drug trafficking . . . . The officers offered objective grounds for their suspicions that cannot be dismissed simply as neu-

tral facts. Their conclusion that the woman was a prostitute is consistent with the facts. The subsequent interpretation of her behaviour as indicating that the driver of the Honda was likely a drug dealer is somewhat more problematic. The behaviour was, however, unusual and the officers' interpretation seems neither unreasonable nor based solely on hunches, speculation and guesses . . . . That said, I would characterize this as a close case since the reasonableness of the officers' suspicion rests so heavily on their experience and the basis of that experience was not well demonstrated at trial. [Citations omitted.]

R. v. Cooper, 2005 NSCA 47, 195 C.C.C. (3d) 162, 28 C.R. (6th) 338: The accused was a passenger in a motor vehicle at 2:00 a.m. The police signalled the car to stop to check for compliance with a provincial statute regulating motor-vehicle usage and in particular restrictions in force that apply to new (young) drivers, at which point the car sped away and made evasive turns. Both the driver and the accused jumped from the still-moving vehicle and fled on foot. The police pursued the accused and upon catching up with him had reasonable suspicion that he was connected or implicated in an offence of resisting a signalled traffic stop. Had the accused merely been a passenger and had not run away, there would have been no grounds to detain him.

R. v. Bui, 2005 BCCA 482: Two accused were detained at Vancouver International Airport. The officer who detained Bui had twice previously investigated arrests of him (both of the prior two arrests occurring on the same day as one another), both at the Vancouver International Airport. In one the accused had been smuggling cigarettes and in the other he had been in possession of six pounds of marijuana. On that previous occasion, Bui had not exited the terminal through the arrivals level but had gone up the departures level where he was stopped, which was the route he was taking on this occasion. He had flown from Toronto on the previous occasion and on this date. On the previous occasion, Bui had given a Toronto address of and claimed to be related to a woman (the co-accused, Vu) whom the constable had arrested once in Vancouver Airport for possession of illegal cigarettes. He had seen Vu in the Vancouver Airport, acting suspiciously and failing to board her flight to Toronto, the day before he had previously arrested Bui, and he had later been informed that she had attempted to claim baggage that was subsequently found to contain fifty pounds of marihuana. On this occasion Vu was on the same flight from Toronto as Bui and exited the plane directly behind him, but it appeared to the constable that they were pretending not to know one another, though Bui's travel itinerary showed the two of them to be travelling on the same itinerary. In addition, they appeared to be nervous and maintained prolonged eye contact with the constable. Finally, the officer knew that the Vancouver-Toronto route was commonly used to smuggle cigarettes and money in one direction and marijuana in the other.

With regard to Vu, in addition to having arrested her previously for possession of illegal cigarettes, the officer had on an earlier occasion observed her behave suspiciously at the Vancouver Airport, culminating with her and another woman failing to board their flight to Toronto; their abandoned baggage was found to contain about fifty pounds of marijuana. He had also been informed by another police officer that someone named Muoi Thi Vu had tried to claim that baggage in Toronto. Bui had given Vu's name as his next of kin. The itinerary and tickets that both were travelling on had been issued by a travel agency in Toronto that was implicated in nearly half of the smuggling investigations the constable had worked on. Finally neither Bui nor Vu had any checked baggage. On these facts, the constable had reasonable suspicion with regard to each accused.

R. v. Duong, 2006 BCCA 325: A police officer saw the accused seated in a parked car in an area with a high incidence of property crime; twenty minutes later, the same officer saw that the accused and the vehicle remained in the same location. The accused was said to be looking out the window and possibly waiting for someone. The officer approached the accused to inquire what he was doing and then asked him to produce his driver's licence, which he did. The officer observed in plain view a car stereo that appeared to have its wires cut situated behind the passenger's seat. The officer asked about the ownership of the stereo and the car, to which the accused indicated that both belonged to his friend; the officer testified that it took longer to provide answers to these questions than it did to answer the least pointed questions. The officer also testified that the accused appeared slow and nervous and that there was a change in his demeanour, facial expression, and pattern of speech. The Court of Appeal found the officer did objectively have reasonable suspicion about the car stereo.

R. v. Schell, 2006 SKCA 128, 214 C.C.C. (3d) 62, 44 C.R. (6th) 330: In the early morning hours, an RCMP officer positioned his vehicle one-half block from the entrance to a bar in a small Saskatchewan town with his parking lights on to deter drunk driving. The officer observed two men leave the bar and walk around a corner; shortly thereafter, a white truck (which had been parked near the bar when the officer arrived) drove past. The officer followed the truck for three or four blocks, observing nothing abnormal about how the truck was being driven before stopping it. Given that it was around the time the bar was to close and the patrons were leaving, that the officer saw the accused leave the bar and shortly thereafter saw a vehicle he had previously identified leave the immediate vicinity of the bar and proceed down the street, there were reasonable grounds to detain.

R. v. Ingle, 2007 BCCA 445, 230 C.C.C. (3d) 77: The RCMP received a call at 12:14 a.m. reporting an attempted theft of a toolbox from a backyard in a mostly rural area. The suspects were described as two white males, sixteen to seventeen years of age, with one wearing a white T-shirt. The police set up a "containment area" at the intersection of the highway and the main artery leading to the caller's neighbourhood. The first vehicle to approach the highway from the containment area arrived at 1:00 a.m., approximately forty-five minutes after the call was received. The officer saw two occupants who he thought were males, and then followed the vehicle for 1.5 km before stopping it. At this time the officer smelled a strong odour of fresh marijuana and observed several large orange garbage bags in the accused's van. The accused driver was eventually arrested. He was thirty-one years old and did not match the description provided, nor did either man have on a white T-shirt; however, the officer testified that he would have stopped every vehicle exiting from the containment area at that time. Given the area, time of night, the location in comparison to the site of the theft complaint, and the fact that two males were allegedly involved, the officer had reasonable suspicion justifying the initial stop.

R. v. Baddock, 2008 BCCA 48: A police officer received information about a dial-a-dope operation, which he believed to be reliable on the basis of past tips from the same informant. The officer called the number and arranged to buy drugs from a small white car which would arrive at a McDonald's parking lot fifteen minutes later. Within the stated timeline, a white Honda Civic arrived and parked in front of the McDonald's, waited for two minutes, and then drove away. The police followed the car and stopped it. As he approached the vehicle, the officer redialed the dial-a-dope number, and upon reaching the vehicle he observed that the accused the driver) had a phone in his hand which was ringing. On these facts the officer had reasonable suspicion justifying stopping the car before he redialled the dial-a-dope number, and had reasonable grounds to arrest after that.

R. v. Nesbeth, 2008 ONCA 579, 238 C.C.C. (3d) 567: At 11:00 p.m., six police officers entered an apartment complex described by the officers as "plagued by drug use, drug sales, robberies, guns and gang violence." Two officers in a stairwell detected a strong odour of freshly smoked marijuana, and when the officers reached the 9th floor landing, the landing door opened and the respondent entered. The respondent seemed surprised when he saw the officers and immediately and very tightly clenched the knapsack that he was carrying. One of the officers asked the respondent, "Hey buddy, what are you doing?" The respondent replied, "Oh shit," turned around, opened the door, and began to run. The officers ran after him across the 9th floor. On the way, the respondent grabbed a shopping cart and attempted to knock it over in front of one of the pursuing officers. The pursuing officers were repeatedly yelling, "Stop, police." During the chase the accused threw away the knapsack. He was not detained until he was actually apprehended by the police. By that time, the facts known to the police included that the accused had immediately bolted when he saw the uniformed officers, had used some force in an attempt to impede the officers' progress by throwing a shopping cart in their way, had thrown away a knapsack that he had been tightly holding up until then, that it was late at night, and that the respondent was in the stairwell of a building known to be located in a high-crime area. (Note the observation in *Mann*, above, at para. 47, that "the presence of an individual in a so-called high crime area is relevant only so far as it reflects his or her proximity to a particular crime. The high crime nature of a neighbourhood is not by itself a basis for detaining individuals.")

R. v. Bramley, 2009 SKCA 49: The police stopped the accused's vehicle for speeding. The officers then spoke to the driver and made a number of observations from the circumstances and the answers. These facts were:

(a) The respondents lived in Surrey, British Columbia and were coming from that city. Constable Donison knew Surrey to be a known point of origin for illegal drugs.

(b) The respondents were travelling to Regina, a known destination point in the movement of illegal drugs.

(c) The respondents were driving a car which had been rented by a third party. Constable Donison understood this to be a practice used by drug traffickers.

(d) Mr. Bramley said he did not have enough money to rent a car, a $260.00 charge, but was nonetheless on a trip to Regina to visit friends.

(e) Mr. Bramley lived in Surrey but the renter of the vehicle, whom he identified as his wife, was noted on the rental agreement as being from Markinch, Saskatchewan. This is not the usual husband and wife arrangement.

(f) The rental agreement appeared to be improperly completed in that, on the endorsement concerning additional drivers, Mr. Bramley's name was in the place where the renter was to sign.

(g) Both Mr. Bramley and Mr. Schiller were described as being nervous when they were stopped. While acknowledging that people pulled over in traffic stops are often nervous at first, Constable Donison said such nervousness typically subsides as the stop progresses. In contrast, Mr. Bramley became more nervous over time.

(h) Between the time the respondents had sped past Constable Donison's parked cruiser and the time they were pulled over, Mr. Schiller had put his long hair up under his baseball cap. This was unusual and appeared to be an attempt by Mr. Schiller to make himself look more conservative.

(i) Both respondents had criminal records involving drug offence convictions. This included convictions, dated in Mr. Bramley's case, for possession for the purposes of trafficking in both Saskatchewan and British Columbia. (As noted earlier, counsel did not question or put in issue the propriety of Constable Donison asking Mr. Schiller, a passenger in the rental vehicle, for his driver's licence. The legality of that request is not an issue in this appeal.)

The Saskatchewan Court of Appeal held that these facts did give rise to reasonable suspicion. However, since it was reasonable suspicion with regard to a suspected offence rather than a known offence, the *Mann* test for investigative detention was not made out. (Note: the Saskatchewan Court of Appeal subsequently reversed its view on this issue, in *R. v. Yeh*, 2009 SKCA 112, holding that investigative detentions could be made out in the case of suspected offences.)

Reasonable Suspicion Standard Not Met

R. v. Cormier (1995), 166 N.B.R. (2d) 5 at para. 6 (C.A.): No reasonable suspicion where a police officer pulled over a large older model car on suspicion of smuggling.

> 6. In our opinion, Constable James did not have reasonable grounds to detain Mr. Cormier initially. He was acting on a hunch that be-

cause Mr. Cormier was driving a large older model car within the speed limit which was weighed down at the rear, he may have been smuggling. Constable James was not acting as a result of a reliable tip or, indeed, on any prior information. The vehicle was not known to him. The apprehension occurred far from the United States border. There was no suspected driving infraction. It was not a check stop. In our view, Constable James did not have reasonable grounds to stop Mr. Cormier. Indeed, it is the very legality or ordinariness of the situation that partly gave rise to Mr. Cormier's apprehension.

R. v. Cox (1999), 210 N.B.R. (2d) 90 at para. 12, 132 C.C.C. (3d) 256 (C.A.). A police officer stopped the accused who was driving an older vehicle with a large trunk, had clothes hanging from a clothes hook in the car, and was travelling within the speed limit. The New Brunswick Court of Appeal held:

> 12 The elements of the smuggler's profile here are no more than hunches, speculation and guesses that do not qualify as "objectively discernible facts." As such, they do not support a reasonable belief that Mr. Cox was implicated in unlawful activity that justified stopping his motor vehicle.

R. v. Calderon (2004), 188 C.C.C. (3d) 481, 23 C.R. (6th) 1 (Ont.C.A.): The police stopped a vehicle at 3:00 a.m. on the Trans-Canada Highway. A Canadian Police Information Centre check showed the vehicle to be a rental car, and it had a large trunk. The officers observed two cellular telephones, a pager on the belt of the passenger, road maps, fast-food wrappers on the floor of the car, and a large amount of luggage in the back seat instead of the trunk. The officers testified that they had taken a drug-interdiction course which caused them to rely on these factors as indicators that the occupants of the car might be drug traffickers. The evidence was that they had stopped between 160 and 180 cars based on these indicators in the past and had never before found drug traffickers. The Court of Appeal held that there was no reasonable suspicion. Most of the purported indicators were neutral and might be found in anyone's car. The Court of Appeal held that, given the neutrality and apparent unreliability of the indicators, their presence could not amount to reasonable grounds for detention.

R. v. Chaisson, 2006 SCC 11: A police officer noticed the accused and a passenger sitting in a darkened automobile behind a closed service station. The service station was adjacent to a restaurant that had just closed and to another that was open. The officer approached the parked automobile in his unlit cruiser. Based on the fact that the occupants were so absorbed in what they were doing that they did not notice him arrive and on their shocked reaction when they noticed his presence, the officer decided to search the vehicle. On these facts the officer did not have reasonable suspicion justifying a detention.

R. v. Houben, 2006 SKCA 129, 214 C.C.C. (3d) 519, 44 C.R. (6th) 338: The police were patrolling a residential neighbourhood in Saskatoon at 2:30 a.m. and observed a vehicle on four occasions travelling in different directions; they stopped the accused on the fourth occasion. The officers testified that the accused was doing nothing untoward at the time of the stop. The trial judge found that the officer stopped the driver to satisfy his curiosity; that there was nothing amiss with the accused's driving; that, in the officer's view and from experience, "undesirables" were active between 2:00 a.m. and 5:00 a.m.; that the area where the accused was stopped was not a high-crime area nor was it known to be frequented by prostitutes; and that the police were not engaged in a specific investigation of any crime at the time of the stop.

R. v. Nguyen, 2008 SKCA 160, 63 C.R. (6th) 24, 240 C.C.C. (3d) 39: The three accused were stopped for travelling too fast for road conditions. The officer detected nervousness, noted that the vehicle was rented and there was a smell of cologne in it, and decided to detain the accused for a drug investigation. The Court of Appeal held that these facts were not sufficient to give reasonable suspicion:

> 14. Before a police officer can detain a person for investigative purposes, there must be some aspect of the circumstances, relied upon by the officer, to permit a future judicial assessment as to whether a crime has been or is being committed or is about to be committed, as a first step in the *Mann* analysis. (See the judgment of Binnie J. in *Kang-Brown*.) An ongoing police investigation, a reported crime, or an odour of contraband of sufficient strength, as examples, might lead a judge to conclude in assessing police conduct after the fact that, at the point of detention, a crime has been or is being committed or is about to be committed. None of these indicia of a recent or ongoing criminal offence are present in this case.

> 20. When the Nguyen vehicle was stopped in this case, the only activity under investigation was that of travelling too fast for road conditions. When Duy Nguyen was subsequently placed under investigative detention for some other crime in relation to drugs, the only indicia of criminal activity beyond the speeding infraction was excessive nervousness, a strong odour of cologne and a rented car. Such nebulous and ambiguous factors — even when taken together

— cannot meet the criteria of *Mann* and *Simpson* so as to establish the existence of a recent or ongoing criminal offence.

R. v. N.O., 2009 ABCA 75: Shortly after midnight, an officer saw the accused exit his car and enter an apartment building that had two glass doors. Another male, who had been sitting on the stairs inside the second door, reached his hand through that door to the respondent's hand. A brief hand-to-hand exchange occurred. The male disappeared into the building and the respondent returned to his car. The officer then detained the accused for a drug investigation. The Alberta Court of Appeal held that these facts did not make out reasonable suspicion. The time was not so late that it could form part of the necessary constellation of circumstances objectively justifying detention. The officer could not see what had been handed off, and neither the fact that it was small or that no words were exchanged gave rise to reasonable suspicion. The officer did not know the individual he detained or the building he entered. He had testified that apartment blocks in the area were plagued with drug transactions in their lobbies, but his evidence about the location and type of building where such events occurred was too vague to contribute to reasonable grounds to detain. The court noted that the officer had not specified the size of the area or the types or numbers of apartment blocks in it, and held:

> With such specificity, there may be other facts when a detention could be justified. But on these facts, such a general approach gives rise to a grave risk of police interference with lawful activities. As Iacobucci J. stated in *Mann*, the high crime nature of a neighbourhood, alone, is not enough. Even though some apartment buildings in a neighbourhood may be known to the police as havens of drug activity, that does not mean that anyone who enters any apartment building in an ill-defined area or neighbourhood can objectively be suspected of criminal activity. (para. 40)

TABLE OF CASES

INDEX

ABOUT THE AUTHORS

Steve Coughlan is a professor at the Schulich School of Law, Dalhousie University. He is the author of *Criminal Procedure* (Irwin Law, 2008), as well as a co-author of the *Annual Review of Criminal Law*. He is one of the editors of the *Criminal Reports* and is a co-author of the National Judicial Institute Criminal Law Essentials e-letter. He is the recipient of a number of teaching awards, including the 2005 Association of Atlantic Universities Distinguished Teacher Award.

Glen Luther, Q.C. is an associate professor at the College of Law, University of Saskatchewan. He has previously taught at several law schools, including Osgoode Hall Law School, the University of Calgary, and Victoria University in New Zealand. He has extensive criminal litigation experience in Alberta and Saskatchewan, and has argued cases at all levels of courts. Professor Luther has received several awards for teaching excellence, and in 2009 was appointed Queen's Counsel by the Government of Saskatchewan.